The Nicene-Constantinopolitan Creed

πιστεύομεν εἰς ἕνα Θεὸν πατέρα, παντοκράτορα, ποιητὴν οὐρανοῦ καὶ γῆς, ὁρατῶν τε πάντων καὶ ἀοράτων.	Credo in unum Deum Patrem omnipotentem; factorem coeli et terrae, visibilium omnium et invisibilium.	We believe in one God, the Father, the Almighty, maker of heaven and earth, of all that is, seen and unseen.
καὶ εἰς ἕνα κύριον Ἰησοῦν Χριστόν, τὸν υἱὸν τοῦ Θεοῦ τὸν μονογενῆ, τὸν ἐκ τοῦ πατρὸς γεννηθέντα πρὸ πάντων τῶν αἰώνων, φῶς ἐκ φωτός, Θεὸν ἀληθινὸν ἐκ θεοῦ ἀληθινοῦ, γεννηθέντα, οὐ ποιηθέντα, ὁμοούσιον τῷ πατρὶ· δι᾿ οὗ τὰ πάντα ἐγένετο· τὸν δι᾿ ἡμᾶς τοὺς ἀνθρώπους καὶ διὰ τὴν ἡμετέραν σωτηρίαν κατελθόντα ἐκ τῶν οὐρανῶν καὶ σαρκωθέντα ἐκ πνεύματος ἁγίου καὶ Μαρίας τῆς παρθένου καὶ ἐνανθρωπήσαντα,	Et in unum Dominum Jesum Christum, Filium Dei unigenitum, et ex Patre natum ante omnia saecula Deum de Deo, Lumen de Lumine, Deum verum de Deo vero, genitum, non factum, consubstantialem Patri; per quem omnia facta sunt; qui propter nos homines et propter nostram salutem descendit de coelis, et incarnatus est de Spiritu Sancto ex Maria virgine, et homo factus est;	We believe in one Lord, Jesus Christ, the only Son of God, eternally begotten of the Father, God from God, Light from Light, true God from true God, begotten, not made, of one Being with the Father. Through him all things were made. For us and for our salvation he came down from heaven: by the power of the Holy Spirit he became incarnate from the Virgin Mary, and was made man.
σταυρωθέντα τε ὑπὲρ ἡμῶν ἐπὶ Ποντίου Πιλάτου, καὶ παθόντα καὶ ταφέντα, καὶ ἀναστάντα τῇ τρίτῃ ἡμέρᾳ κατὰ τὰς γραφάς, καὶ ἀνελθόντα εἰς τοὺς οὐρανούς, καὶ καθεζόμενον ἐκ δεξιῶν τοῦ πατρός, καὶ πάλιν ἐρχόμενον μετὰ δόξης κρῖναι ζῶντας καὶ νεκρούς· οὗ τῆς βασιλείας οὐκ ἔσται τέλος.	crucifixus etiam pro nobis sub Pontio Pilato, passus et sepultus est; et resurrexit tertia die, secundum Scripturas; et ascendit in coelum, sedet ad dexteram Patris; et iterum venturus est, cum gloria, judicare vivos et mortuos; cujus regni non erit finis.	For our sake he was crucified under Pontius Pilate; he suffered death and was buried. On the third day he rose again in accordance with the Scriptures; he ascended into heaven and is seated at the right hand of the Father. He will come again in glory to judge the living and the dead, and his kingdom will have no end.
καὶ εἰς τὸ πνεῦμα τὸ ἅγιον, τὸ κύριον, καὶ τὸ ζωοποιόν, τὸ ἐκ τοῦ πατρὸς ἐκπορευόμενον, τὸ σὺν πατρὶ καὶ υἱῷ συμπροσκυνούμενον καὶ συνδοξαζόμενον, τὸ λαλῆσαν διὰ τῶν προφητῶν·	Et in Spiritum Sanctum, Dominum et vivificantem, qui ex Patre Filioque procedit; qui cum Patre et Filio simul adoratur et conglorificatur; qui locutus est per Prophetas.	We believe in the Holy Spirit, the Lord, the giver of life, who proceeds from the Father and the Son. With the Father and the Son he is worshiped and glorified. He has spoken through the Prophets.
εἰς μίαν, ἁγίαν, καθολικὴν καὶ ἀποστολικὴν ἐκκλησίαν· ὁμολογοῦμεν ἓν βάπτισμα εἰς ἄφεσιν ἁμαρτιῶν· προσδοκῶμεν ἀνάστασιν νεκρῶν, καὶ ζωὴν τοῦ μέλλοντος αἰῶνος. Ἀμήν.	Et unam, sanctam, catholicam et apostolicam ecclesiam. Confiteor unum baptisma in remissionem peccatorum; et expecto resurrectionem mortuorum, et vitam venturi saeculi. Amen.	We believe in one holy catholic and apostolic Church. We acknowledge one baptism for the forgiveness of sins. We look for the resurrection of the dead, and the life of the world to come. Amen.

ANCIENT CHRISTIAN DOCTRINE

2

We Believe in One Lord Jesus Christ

EDITED BY

JOHN ANTHONY McGUCKIN

SERIES EDITOR

THOMAS C. ODEN

IVP Academic

An imprint of InterVarsity Press
Downers Grove, Illinois

BT
198
.W375
2009

InterVarsity Press
P.O. Box 1400, Downers Grove, IL 60515-1426
Internet: www.ivpress.com
E-mail: email@ivpress.com

InterVarsity Press* is the book-publishing division of InterVarsity Christian Fellowship/USA*, a student movement active on campus at hundreds of universities, colleges and schools of nursing in the United States of America, and a member movement of the International Fellowship of Evangelical Students. For information about local and regional activities, write Public Relations Dept., InterVarsity Christian Fellowship/USA, 6400 Schroeder Rd., P.O. Box 7895, Madison, WI 53707-7895, or visit the IVCF website at <www.intervarsity.org>.

Scripture quotations, unless otherwise noted, are from the Revised Standard Version of the Bible, copyright 1946, 1952, 1971 by the Division of Christian Education of the National Council of the Churches of Christ in the U.S.A., and are used by permission.

Selected excerpts from The Didache, The Epistle of Barnabas, The Epistles and Martyrdom of St. Polycarp, The Fragments of Papias, The Epistle to Diognetus, translated by James A. Kleist, S.J., Ancient Christian Writers 6, ©1948; Ephrem the Syrian, Hymns, translated and introduced by Kathleen McVey, preface by John Meyendorff, Classics of Western Spirituality, ©1989. Reprinted by permission of Paulist Press, Inc. <www.paulistpress.com>.

Selected excerpts from Henry Bettenson, ed., The Early Christian Fathers: A Selection from the Writings of the Fathers from St. Clement of Rome to St. Athanasius, ©1963; Henry Bettenson, ed., The Later Christian Fathers: A Selection from the Writings of the Fathers from St. Cyril of Jerusalem to St. Leo the Great, ©1970; St. Gregory of Nazianzus: Poemata Arcana, edited with a textual introduction by C. Moreschini, introduction, translation and commentary by D. A. Sykes, Oxford Theological Monographs, ©1997. Used by permission of Oxford University Press.

Selected excerpts from John A. McGuckin, St. Cyril of Alexandria and the Christological Controversy, ©2004. Used by permission of St. Vladimir's Seminary Press, Crestwood, N.Y.

Selected excerpts from J. Stevenson, ed., Creeds, Councils and Controversies: Documents Illustrative of the History of the Church A.D. 337-461, ©1966; Dionysius the Areopagite: On the Divine Names and the Mystical Theology, translated by Clarence Edwin Rolt, ©1920. Used by permission of SPCK, London.

Selected excerpts from Christology of the Later Fathers, edited by Edward Rochie Hardy in collaboration with Cyril C. Richardson, Library of Christian Classics 3, ©1954. Used by permission of Westminster Press.

Every effort has been made to trace and contact copyright holders for materials quoted in this book. The editors will be pleased to rectify any omissions in future editions if notified by copyright holders.

Design Credit: Cindy Kiple

Art Credit: The Adoration of the Trinity by Albrecht Dürer, at Kunsthistorisches Museum, Vienna, Austria. Erich Lessing/Art Resource, NY

ISBN 978-0-8308-2532-5

Printed in the United States of America ∞

 InterVarsity Press is committed to protecting the environment and to the responsible use of natural resources. As a member of Green Press Initiative we use recycled paper whenever possible. To learn more about the Green Press Initiative, visit <www.greenpressinitiative.org>.

Library of Congress Cataloging-in-Publication Data

We believe in one Lord Jesus Christ/edited by John Anthony McGuckin.
    p. cm.—(Ancient Christian doctrine; 2)
  Includes bibliographical references and index.
  ISBN 978-0-8308-2532-5 (cloth: alk. paper)
  1. Jesus Christ—History of doctrines—Early church, ca. 30-600. 2.
Nicene Creed. I. McGuckin, John Anthony.
  BT198.W375 2009
  232'.8—dc22
                    2009000460

P 32 31 30 29 28 27 26 25 24 23 22 21 20 19 18 17 16 15 14 13 12 11 10 9 8 7 6 5 4 3 2 1

Y 36 35 34 33 32 31 30 29 28 27 26 25 24 23 22 21 20 19 18 17 16 15 14 13 12 11 10 09

For Helmar Nielsen,
an extraordinary patron of
Early Christian thought
in the New World

Contents

A Guide to Using the Commentaries in the Ancient Christian Doctrine Series

Several features have been incorporated into the design of this commentary series. The following comments are intended to assist readers in making full use of each of the volumes.

Sections of the Creed

The five commentaries are first and foremost a phrase-by-phrase commentary on the Nicene-Constantinopolitan Creed. The portion of the Creed for each individual volume has been set in three languages—Greek, Latin and English—with the appropriate phrase under consideration highlighted in bold font in each language. Numerous English translations have been developed in recent years; we have used the ICET version of 1975 because of its current wide use.

Historical Contexts and Overviews

Following each section of the Creed is a short section labeled Historical Context. Where wording of the Creed reflects the culmination of discussions of highly controverted issues, readers are offered a brief summary of the controversy and the issues at stake in order for them to make more sense of the selections set forth. Where doctrine developed harmoniously without much controversy, that fact is noted and a brief description of the development of the doctrine is supplied. Following the historical context is a section labeled Overview, designed to provide a brief précis of the ensuing section's excerpts. It tracks a reasonably cohesive thread of argument among patristic comments, even though they are derived from diverse sources and generations.

Topical Headings

An abundance of varied patristic comment is available for each phrase of the Creed. At the same time the Creed itself forms a skeleton for supporting the larger doctrinal convictions of the church. Thus the commentary on the Creed can show the full range of the church's systematic theological concerns. For this reason we have broken the sections of the Creed into two levels. First are subsections that group common themes within the patristic comments. Then each individual patristic comment is tagged by a key phrase, metaphor or idea that suggests the essence of the excerpt.

Identifying the Patristic Texts

Following the topical heading of each excerpt, the name of the patristic commentator is given. An English translation of the patristic comment is then provided. This is immediately followed by the title of the patristic work in English and the appropriate textual reference—usually book, section and subsection. If the notation differs significantly between the English-language source footnoted and other sources, alternate references appear in the notes.

The Footnotes

Readers who wish to pursue a deeper investigation of the patristic works cited in this commentary will find the footnotes especially valuable. A footnote number directs the reader to the notes at the bottom of the right-hand column, where in addition to other notations (clarifications or biblical cross references) is found information on English translations (where available) or standard original language editions of the work cited. An abbreviated citation (normally citing the book, volume and page number) of the work is provided. A key to the abbreviations is provided in the front matter. Where there is any serious ambiguity or textual problem in the selection, we have tried to reflect the best available textual tradition. Where original language texts have remained untranslated into English, we provide new translations. Wherever current English translations are already well rendered, they are utilized, but where necessary they are stylistically updated. A single asterisk (*) indicates that a previous English translation has been updated to modern English or amended for easier reading. A double asterisk (**) indicates either that a new translation has been provided or that some extant translation has been significantly amended.

Outline of Contents, List of Ancient Authors and Texts Cited, and Index

In lieu of a subject index, a full outline of the sections and subsections has been included in the back matter of each volume. This should aid readers in finding specific theological content and make the volumes all the more useful for the study of historical and systematic theology. Each volume contains a list of ancient authors and texts cited, as well as a full Scripture index.

Biographical Sketches and Timeline

Many readers will find helpful brief biographical sketches of the patristic writers as well as a timeline placing them within the proper century and geographical location. Rather than repeating the sketches and timeline in each volume, we have decided to gather them at the conclusion of volume five. Similarly, we have supplied the general introduction to the series only in volume one. For any readers who have not purchased the whole set, the general introduction, sketches and timeline may be found online at www.ivpress.com by searching for the series information and following the appropriate links.

ABBREVIATIONS

ACW   Ancient Christian Writers: The Works of the Fathers in Translation. Mahwah, N.J.: Paulist Press, 1946-.

AF   J. B. Lightfoot and J. R. Harmer, trans. *The Apostolic Fathers*. Edited by M. W. Holmes. 2nd ed. Grand Rapids, Mich.: Baker, 1990.

AHSIS   D. Miller, trans. *The Ascetical Homilies of St. Isaac the Syrian*. Boston: Holy Transfiguration. Monastery, 1984.

ANCL   The Ante-Nicene Christian Library: Translations of the Writings of the Fathers Down to A.D. 325. Alexander Roberts and James Donaldson, eds. Edinburgh: T & T Clark, 1867-1897.

CACC   John A. McGuckin. *St. Cyril of Alexandria and the Christological Controversy*. Crestwood, N.Y.: St. Vladimir's Seminary Press, 2004.

CCC   J. Stevenson, ed. *Creeds, Councils and Controversies: Documents Illustrative of the History of the Church* A.D. 337-461. London: SPCK, 1966.

CCL   Corpus Christianorum. Series Latina. Turnhout, Belgium: Brepols, 1953-.

Cetedoc   Library of Christian Latin Texts on CD Rom. Turnhout, Belgium: Brepols, 2000.

CGSL   R. Payne-Smith, trans. *St. Cyril of Alexandria: Commentary on the Gospel of St. Luke*. Long Island, N.Y.: Studion Publishers, 1983.

CS   Cistercian Studies. Kalamazoo, Mich.: Cistercian Publications, 1973-.

ECF   Henry Bettenson. *The Early Christian Fathers: A Selection from the Writings of the Fathers from St. Clement of Rome to St. Athanasius*. London: Oxford University Press, 1963.

ESH   Ephrem the Syrian: *Hymns*. Translated and introduced by Kathleen McVey. Preface by John Meyendorff. Classics of Western Spirituality Series. New York: Paulist Press, 1989.

LCC   J. Baillie et al., eds. The Library of Christian Classics. 26 vols. Philadelphia: Westminster Press, 1953-1966.

LCF   Henry Bettenson. *The Later Christian Fathers: A Selection from the Writings of the Fathers from St. Cyril of Jerusalem to St. Leo the Great*. London: Oxford University Press, 1970.

MFC   Message of the Fathers of the Church. Edited by Thomas Halton. Collegeville, Minn.: Liturgical Press, 1983-.

NPNF   P. Schaff et al., eds. A Select Library of the Nicene and Post-Nicene Fathers of the Christian Church. 2 series (14 vols. each). Buffalo, N.Y.: Christian Literature,

	1887-1894; Reprint, Grand Rapids, Mich.: Eerdmans, 1952-1956; Reprint, Peabody, Mass.: Hendrickson, 1994.
ODN	*Dionysius the Areopagite: On the Divine Names and the Mystical Theology*. Translated by Clarence Edwin Rolt. London: SPCK, 1920.
PA	*St. Gregory of Nazianzus: Poemata Arcana*. Edited with a textual introduction by C. Moreschini. Introduction, translation and commentary by D. A. Sykes. Oxford Theological Monographs. New York: Oxford University Press, 1997.
PG	J.-P. Migne, ed. Patrologiae cursus completus. Series Graeca. 166 vols. Paris: Migne, 1857-1866.
PMS	Patristic Monograph Series. Cambridge, Mass.: Philadelphia Patristic Foundation: [Sole distributors, Greeno, Hadden], 1975-.
SLS	*St. Romanos: On the Life of Christ. Kontakia*. Translated by Ephrem Lash. Sacred Literature Series. London: Harper Collins, 1997.
TCT	J. F. Clarkson, J. Edwards, W. J. Kelly, and J. J. Welch, eds. *The Church Teaches*. St. Louis, Mo.: Herder Book Co., 1955.
WS	*Woodbrooke Studies: Christian Documents in Syriac, Arabic and Garshüni*. Edited and translated with a critical apparatus by Alphonse Mingana with introduction by James Rendel Harris. John Rylands Library. Cambridge, England: W. Heffer & Sons, 1927-.

INTRODUCTION

The Church Expressing Its Belief

The expression of the beliefs of the early church[1] was always a question of dynamic confession ("praise" is how we moderns should translate that word) rather than academic systematization. This is not to say that the faith articulations of the ancient Christians were not intellectually demanding; one has only to read the following selections from the theological writers of the early centuries to see that the opposite is true. Indeed, this was always the case from the beginning, since even the homespun parabolic teachings of Jesus are only deceptively simple. It means, rather, that the way the early Christians told and celebrated the story of their faith was invested in a veritable complex of different forms of affirmation, among which the writings of the intelligentsia (those who, after the fourth century, would come to be called the Fathers[2]) were only a small part.

The faith formulas of the Christians, and more than that dry term can possibly convey—their sheer delight and joy in Jesus (their "cheerful light"[3] and liberation, their savior, their anchor, and the other innumerable titles they loved to bestow on him in worship)—flowed out like an irrepressible spring in the liturgy long before they arrived at the stage of literary doctrinal formulations. This is why, for example, the creeds were first and foremost baptismal prayers long before they became conciliar tests of faith to stand against and remedy schools of thought that had been rejected as either peripheral or obnoxious by the common body of believers. It is this common

---

[1] Its kerygma: insofar as its belief, its preaching or sharing of the Good News and its cause for rejoicing and confessing that Good News were substantially the same "mystery of religion" (see 1 Tim 3:16, where this phrase introduces one of the first of all Christian creeds).

[2] And, thus, patristic literature. The Fathers were, generally speaking, bishops and leaders of Christian communities of worship, but the theory of "patristic literature" signifies far more than the title of honor (*Pateres*, or Fathers) given to them as clerical leaders. By the late fourth century, the term was being used to signify those leaders whose theology was seen to be of such purity and strength that they had a right to be regarded as worthy successors of the apostles. In this way a hierarchy of texts of value was produced: first and foremost the sacred Scriptures, then the creeds and liturgical confessions, then the writings of the notable Fathers. One of the last elements to be added into that developing canon after the canon was the creedal extension comprised by the great councils of the church. All these elements, from the writings of individual theologians to the statements of the bishops gathered at the ecumenical councils, can be found in this present collection.

[3] The title (*Phos Hilaron*) given to the Lord in one of the earliest instances of hymnal praise that constituted the church's "prayer at the fading of the light"—a poem of perhaps the second century that is still used in the liturgical vesperal services in churches of the East and the West.

mind of the ancient church that is often called the *sensus fidelium* ("the instinct of believers"). That sifting, preserving and defending of evangelical tradition we might call other names too, such as the great church, a notion scholars often use in historical contexts, or a term more often used by theologians, the apostolic tradition, the evocation of the authentic spirit of faithfulness to Jesus' teaching and spirit, which the church preserves across its journey through time. Innumerable controversies in the history of the church over what was or was not authentically evangelical should not blind us to the relatively simple fact that in antiquity the great church used a test of common sense to establish that criterion. Did a particular view harmonize with the Scriptures or not? Was a certain belief central, thus needing defense, or peripheral, something that could be left as a matter of divergent opinions (what would later be called *theologoumena*)? The real issue was, what did the sense of the faithful say, in contradistinction to the spirit of the age, which later was not always to be trusted?

But however much the first confessions were rooted in Scripture or liturgy and nurtured by traditions and common sense, it was inevitable that once theological literature had arrived at a form that had been refined and tested by controversies and challenges over several generations (some of which seemed to many to strike at the foundations of the Christian faith itself[4]) they should assume something of a classical status. The authenticity of this later, more controversial, literature as fitting commentaries on the Scriptures was generally admitted, and its effectiveness in combating highly speculative and often ahistorical exegeses of the structures of the Christian faith, particularly those of the Gnostics, made them assume a quasi-canonical status alongside the Scriptures, something that was eventually formally acknowledged, after the fourth century, by affording them patristic standing. By this stage (and it was a concept that was coming to be more and more clearly focused after the third century) it was much easier to chart the main lines of the orthodoxy of the great church, compared, for example, with the various forms of speculative theology that had come to be classed, by contrast, as heresy.[5] Some careless historians have implied that heresy and orthodoxy are anachronistic concepts that arose only after the second-century Gnostic crisis. A cursory perusal of the Johannine letters or the Pauline pastorals will

---

[4]Gnosticism and Arianism have often been called the proto-heresies of early Christianity, and they certainly form two poles around which many of the confessions in this book will revolve in explicit opposition. In christological terms (against Gnosticism) this meant an unerring stress first of all on Jesus' authentic humanity, that is, his flesh-liness and real embodiment in time and space, and (against Arianism) his spiritual glory as of the eternal Word of the everlasting Father, God from God and the selfsame now made flesh within time. To an extent the fourth-century and fifth-century fathers were logically correct when they tended to see all later christological heresy as variations on Gnosticism's and Arianism's foundational premises.

[5]The word *hairesis* in classical Greek tradition simply meant a "different opinion." From apostolic times, however (see 1 Jn 2:18-25), it was invested with a new sense by the early church, to convey the sense that fidelity was a key element in the transmission of the true gospel tradition and that speculative innovation by theologians was a lapse from truth rather than a refinement of it. In this sense the apostolic age invented the concept of heresy as a polar opposite to orthodoxy. The patristic era refined this further, but it did not invent the macro-structure. Irenaeus had discovered it already in the apostolic period and used it effectively against the Gnostics, regarded by most in antiquity as the primal heresy.

show any reader that the clear distinction of orthodoxy and heresy was already seen, by the end of the first century, to be a critical matter if faith in Jesus was to be preserved and handed on. The author of 2 Peter, as well as the writer of the Johannine letters,[6] suggest that heresy is not simply a set of intellectual mistakes about the tradition of the gospel but part of an eschatological decline from grace, something that will always affect the church as it transitions time and space and that always has to be guarded against.

What was at stake in all of this struggle to preserve the authentic tradition, however (even before these intelligent and reflected structures of orthodoxy were eventually set in place in this formal manner in the course of the development of church history[7]) was the fight from the beginning to retain, preserve and faithfully observe the tradition of Jesus as handed to the newly founded churches in and through the apostolic preaching. In short, what was seen to be of the essence was fidelity to apostolic tradition. That largely meant, for the church of the first three centuries, the new understanding of the Old Testament in the light of the great saving mysteries of Jesus and the reading of the events of the Lord's ministry in the light of the apostolic preaching and letters that took shape in the form of the New Testament. The first great fight for apostolic tradition is no less than what we have come to know as the defense of the canon of the New Testament.

Seen in this aspect, the closing of the canon was not a reactionary movement of censorship but rather one concerned with the deepest aspects of quality control. After the elevation of the canon as the first level of apostolic witness, there soon came the traditional prayers and praises and confessions that grew out of the Christian Scriptures, which were finally to grow into creeds, formal theological treatises, books of commentary, eucharistic and sacramental liturgies and many other documentary expressions of a lively and an organically harmonious development of the apostolic spirit through different generational contexts. The third and fourth centuries were often marked by bitter controversies over the fundamentals of the faith, not because, as many postmodern writers have recently tried to suggest, those fundamentals were not there or were so embryonic that no one could agree on them, but on the contrary because the divergences that had appeared among the congregations were widely felt to be so extraordinarily deviant[8] that the more generally accepted tradition of the apostolic literature was felt to be endangered. Indeed, anyone who was happy to accept the so-called Gospel of Philip as satisfactorily apostolic

---

[6]2 Pet 1:16–3:18; 1 Jn 4:1-6.

[7]The system of checks and balances for determining what an orthodox conception was: scriptural attestation of doctrine, liturgical support in the tradition of prayer or worship, creedal definition, episcopal consensus and conciliar adjudication—and we may also add the lamentable last stage of imperial proscription that followed after the last of these, after the fourth century, although theologically speaking this is not an integral part of the true discernment of tradition that the church receives as the gift of the Spirit. For an elaboration about the stages of this historical development, see John A. McGuckin, "Eschaton and Kerygma: The Future of the Past in the Present Kairos. The Concept of Living Tradition in Orthodox Theology," *St. Vladimir's Theological Quarterly* 42 no. 3-4 (winter 1998): 225-71.

[8]Photinianism, Marcionism and Gnosticism gave the proof of this long before the great Arian crisis.

inevitably had to diminish the real significance of the historicity of the passion accounts and the genuine significance of the fleshly incarnation of the Lord.

The Defense of the Apostolic Tradition

This book is a collation of those classical Christian responses of the great church that with elegance, conciseness and apostolic spirit were generally determined to set a bulwark around the foundations of the Christian kerygma, in refutation of all theories and speculations that might undermine its transmission across the generations. The task of sifting orthodoxy and heresy in our own beliefs and confessions (and in those we hear from others, for our age is certainly no less productive of new theologies and insights and confessions than any other preceding us) has especial relevance and continuing importance in our day, at least for all those Christians who have a continuing commitment to the concept of the transmission of the apostolic tradition.

There are many who would regard the very notion as anachronistic, historically unprovable or irrelevant. One of the cottage industries of the present moment among historical theologians is the rehabilitation of the ancient heresies, and often their invention when sufficient evidence no longer remains. We seem to live in a fever of conspiracy theory where orthodox oppressors heavy-handed poor heretics aside, and modern scholars feel obliged to side with the tragic losing side, who are even sometimes elevated as symbols of "God's own poor." The reality was far from that kind of romantic nonsense. If we had to put our finger on who was elitist and who was inclusivist in antiquity, it would have to involve a denunciation of the Gnostics, for example, as the most elitist of all. All credit to the great church who denounced them for it, in the name of a greater inclusivity based on common sense and common education. It was, after all, the Gnostics who derided the larger Christian congregations as the unwashed proletariat. To elevate many of these heretical movements, as often happens today, as harbingers of the common person's freedom is patently fallacious. The battle with these obnoxiously elitist sectarian movements was conducted generations before Christian bishops could ever call on the dubious assistance of secular power to enforce their views. Anti-Gnostic bishops, such as Irenaeus, won the day not least because they talked common sense but because the Gnostics could never win the hearts and minds of the large Christian congregations. The people believed their bishops, because they too felt the self-evident force of the argument that such elitist speculations did not match with the beauty and clarity of the gospel message of Jesus.

The great church labeled movements as heretical or deviant precisely because they were at a considerable variance from the standard tradition of the confession of Jesus as Lord, which had been adopted by the churches in that commonwealth of communities they knew around themselves. This growing sense of commonweal of churches (koinōnia, or fellowship) was built up from trade or personal relations at an early date, and eventually by the increasingly effective common nexus of episcopal leaders who were ever more literate after the second century and looked after the literature of their churches with a careful eye, sharing texts and letters and good practices with one another. Even from the first this commonwealth of churches was an international one. It can be witnessed already in what we now call the canon of the New Testament, from the fifties of the first century. By the third century it was an intercommunicating commonweal of churches spread around the Mediterranean and penetrating more deeply into the land mass of Asia Minor; and by the fourth century it was an intellectual heritage that was being increasingly codified and commented on by the leading intellectuals of the age, as well as enshrined in a form of liturgical prayers that were becoming increasingly standardized around the worship practices of great Christian city cultures such as Antioch, Rome, Caesarea-Jerusalem, Alexandria, Carthage and eventually Constantinople. Christian thinkers of the earliest centuries knew exactly what was meant by the great tradition of the gospel and were not slow to defend it. This book, therefore, is a collation of exactly those texts that were raised up in defense of the central pillars of belief; and nothing was regarded as so synoptic of the main foundations of belief as the baptismal creed, of which genre the creed of Nicaea, after the fourth century, was elevated as the supreme international example.

The importance of these texts, the very reason why they were designated patristic in the first place, is that they have been commonly regarded across centuries of the life of the church as authentic exegeses of the evangelical and apostolic tradition. As such they are the heart's blood of the one, holy, catholic and apostolic church of Christ that is called to make its journey across time and space confessing one and the same gospel in fidelity to its risen Lord, and with sufficient wit to know how to preach the ancient kerygma faithfully, allowing its renovating power to shine out in ever new historic conditions and philosophical environments.

When one looks at the creedal clauses in slow motion (something this book will allow the reader to do preeminently), it is startlingly obvious how almost all of them take their life as meditations on a foundational biblical phrase, most of which, in turn and in their own original contexts, were exclamations of praise. The technical term for this movement to praise in the face of the mighty works of the Lord was "doxology." It is a word derived from the Greek *doxa*, the "glory" of the Lord, which in and of itself evoked the glorification of the wonders of God from the heart of the church. In short, we might well say, the faith of the early church was doxological in essence. We would, indeed, not be going too far astray to infer that all true theology, ever since, has been doxological in essence; and when it has not been so, it has surely lapsed from the highest quality of theological statement, since it has forgotten its *telos* (its end, its goal and its purpose).

The Centrality of Jesus, Lord and Savior

The essence of the Good News that is the Christian gospel is that freedom brought to the world in the community of Christ, by the Lord's life-giving incarnation, ministry, death and resurrection, and the capacity this saving mystery (for it is a unified whole) confers on the redeemed for the true knowledge of God that illuminates, transfigures and vivifies the believer. The Greek patristic writers summed up this whole related nexus of the salvation wrought by Christ as the economy of salvation.[9] It is the perennial celebration of this economy that marks the christo-logical sections of the creed and that is the recurring leitmotif of all the sections of this present collection of texts. This celebration of the fundamental insight occurs in two main forms: first the insistence, in the teeth of Arianism, that the Lord who came to earth was one and the same as the eternal Word of God who had been with the Father from all ages and who himself had set within the creation the pattern of its inmost order and beauty;[10] and second, the bold af-firmation of Paul's apostolic dictum (Gal 6:14) that we ought to make our boast in the cross of the Lord Jesus. The insistence that Christ's sufferings and death were his redemptive triumph was lovingly explored throughout the early church, to such an extent that the theology of the cross (that *theologia crucis* that is so prevalent in the early Christian writers) becomes a veritable theology of glory and triumph.

The suffering Lord is the victor and hero. It is a far cry from the lugubrious theology of the passion of the later Middle Ages. This second aspect, however, is the predominant theme of the following volume in this series, one that is specifically dedicated to the creedal clauses governing the redemptive work of Christ, beginning from the phrase "he was crucified under Pontius Pi-late." It is the concern of this present volume to focus more exclusively on the creedal clauses be-ginning with "we believe in one Lord, Jesus Christ," and concluding with "and was made man."

The dominant note and character of all these extensive patristic comments on the primary christological clauses is their christocentric character. That may go without saying, but it may be significant to observe that their christocentricity is powerfully dynamic in substance and style. Christ is celebrated as Savior by recounting the force of his victory. Without understanding the nature of the conflict and the achievement of salvation he established in the new world order, the early church implies that one cannot properly understand the true significance of Jesus. The achievement of the Christ is of such cosmological importance, and of such importance in the life of God and the regard God has for his entire world, that the real status of Jesus' person is thereby revealed.

Much has been made in the latter part of the twentieth century of the so-called Christology from below or Christology from above. The terms are not ancient; in fact, they first appear in the mid-twentieth century. Moreover, they are not particularly good as tools for exegeting the mind of the ancient Fathers. They largely do not work, and if they presume, as often they do, that the Scriptures (except the Fourth Gospel) tend to be Christology from below, while the Fathers represent Christology from above, then they are simply wrong. Nothing could be further from the truth. Such crude categories have, for too long now, been overlaid on the great sophisti-cation of patristic Christology. It is long overdue for scholars and students to leave the anachro-nistic categories of the twentieth century to the side and begin to read, directly from the primary

---

[9]*Oikonomia tēs sōtērias.*

[10]Thereby establishing the grounds of the human capacity for the knowledge of the unapproachable Godhead of the Father, through the revelatory medium of the divine Word who patterned the order (*taxis*) of the creation, and most intimately the human spirit within that created order, as a veritable icon of the Word.

source once more, and with open ears and unblinkered eyes that will be open to the profound weight and immense maturity of early Christian theological reflection. The first thing that will strike the reader is that the early church, in all its christological thought, as can be abundantly seen from more or less any page of this book, has always approached the humble life of its Lord as a manifestation of the divine and transcendent mercy. Yet it understood his glory as part and parcel of his humiliation on the cross. For them, as was certainly true for the apostles Paul and John, the Lord of glory was the man of sorrows, and any separation of the Teacher of Nazareth from the incarnate Word who was, in and of himself, the perfect sacrament of God, was immediately recognized as a deviation from the central Christian tradition, whether one called that lapse Gnosticism, Docetism, Nestorianism, Photinianism or Arianism was of little moment.

The ability to access patristic Christology directly will, I hope, be what the present volume can best offer to the reader who wishes to gain a personal and more or less unmediated sense of the early theologians giving some of their most pithy and direct comment on the mystery of Jesus. Here is a collection of some of the best and liveliest of the patristic understanding of Christ's person and work, gathered around a celebration of the creed as the foundational element of the authentic apostolic tradition. This is not just a historic monument for the delectation of curiosity seekers or aficionados of ancient history. It is, more than that, a wellspring of apostolic witness.

It is one of the great tragedies of the current state of divided Christianity that this patristic literature is so little known by so many, or, worse, regarded as not a real heritage of the Protestant world, even though it might be of the Orthodox and Catholics. This treasure of the early church shines with the grace of the Spirit, and because of this it is the true catholic (that is, universal) heritage of all the churches of God. It is a lamp to light their way to a deeper understanding of the Scriptures. Such a regained sense of apostolicity is, I suggest, the great agenda of the present moment: the true vision of what real ecumenism ought to be aiming for, in a time when the splintered confessions of Christianity need urgently to renew their hope that they can still come together in a single, even though richly stranded, harmony of the confession of the one Christ, the selfsame Lord who still reigns actively over his redeemed church. For those of us who profess "one Lord, one faith, one baptism," it is not beyond our wit (at least if it is within our will) to confess also "one apostolic confession" rooted and founded in the great tradition such as is so clearly represented in these volumes.

The short introductions to the various sections of the creed that follow attempt to give a synopsis of the immediate context to what the various Fathers had to say about different aspects of the person of Christ (his eternal sonship, his incarnation, whether he had a soul, and so forth). These immediate remarks, then, will take a wider perspective and look at the generic christological attitude of the Fathers. There was relatively little speculative spirit in the church of the first ages. But once problems had been noted, answers were always sought after. Whenever there was widespread uneasiness with something that was felt to be a deviant innovation (a heresy), the crisis was usually the stimulus for a flurry of subsequent reflection and writing about what "ought to be" seen as the correct view. The literary efforts of the Fathers, therefore, and this is true until about the sixth century anyway, tend to be reactive rather than proactive. There are centuries, and clusters of controversies within centuries, that tend to produce flurries of work, and then there are periods of relative quiet, where the poets and liturgists could stand back from the heat of controversy and write more lyrically.

The christological writings of an Athanasius or a Basil, for example (men who spent more or less the whole of their active lives in white-hot controversy), and the literature of apologetics sound a different tone from the beautiful poetry of such as Ephrem the Syrian or Romanos the Melodist. What can also be seen is that the poets and liturgists are faithfully in harmony with these great controversialists. The Liturgy of St. Basil the Great, used in the Eastern churches throughout Lent, is so-called precisely because so much of the magnificent Christology of Basil has been incorporated into it in the form of the great eucharistic prayer. The Liturgy of St. John Chrysostom, the standard liturgy of the Orthodox church, is a vast and sustained hymn of praise using the patristic Christology of the fourth century as its base material. Far from being dry-as-dust dogmatics, the church shows the authenticity of its tradition by converting it back into the gold of doxology. Anyone who reads the Roman canon can see immediately what a sustained biblical chant it all is. Like one of the psalmists recounting the glorious deeds of the Lord and how he saved Israel through them, so the ancient Latin canon of the mass recounts the whole history of salvation from the righteous Abel, through Melchisidek, to the sacrifice of Jesus.

The following short introductions that open each major section will try to contextualize the different sections more discretely. When a particular argument sprang up (for example, whether the divine Logos was eternal or time-bounded), a large body of literature issued to meet it and work the question out from Scripture, where possible, or deduction from scriptural principles. Often that first question produced others, equally urgent. If the divine Logos was not eternal, for example, to what extent was the adjective "divine" appropriate? If the Logos was time-bound, surely that was the equivalent of confessing the Logos as a creature under God? Such was the logic of Arius, and some of the greatest of the fourth-century Fathers rose to the challenge of refuting him with sophisticated arguments about the nature of procession and order within the timeless Godhead, being themselves timeless things. To attempt to explain why a timeless order-ing of the divinity (what we now so blithely, and often without much thought, call the Trinity) can allow for the Father to originate the Son, while the Son is not thereby rendered secondary or inferior by nature to the Father, is certainly of an order of difficulty far more advanced than Arius's sea chanties that he taught his parish in Alexandria, reducing the whole gospel to the axiom that "There was [a time] when he [the Logos] was not."

The wit of the followers of the great tradition inserted a "not" at the front of his slogan and it now became even more condensed: "There was not when he was not." But Athanasius, while knowing that he had to answer such logical puzzles for the sake of quieting the scandal among the faithful, if not for the sake of honing the expression of authentic Christianity for the intel-ligentsia, was not ever led astray that this level of apologetic was the best way of interpreting the apostolic tradition. His wider writing, therefore, has a far greater range. The patristic Christology is seized with a more universally cosmic spirit, and it lifts its head from abstruse metaphysic, however important that may still be, and often enters the domain of magnificently elevating mystical discourse. This is often the case with the greatest of the orthodox theologians—they merge with high poetry. This is because the Logos of God is not merely the ultimate Truth but also the perfect beauty of God.

Not everything the Fathers have to say is equally convincing to the ears of moderns. It could hardly be expected to be so. Much of the argument is set within the conventions of a form of rhetoric and logic that may appear strange and archaic to most readers today. Their use of scriptural proof texts may also come across as odd to generations who have been accustomed to reading the Bible with the unimaginable luxury of a Bible of their own, and thus to reading with an eye to the wider context than the ancient church, which heard the Scriptures read to them in the course of public worship, generally had. We need to make allowances for them, just as we often need to make allowances for novels from other times and ages. But it is that making of allowances that so often educates us by making us stand a little apart from our own time and condition and, perhaps, our own limiting prejudices.

I hope that this entrance into the world of some of the great Christian spirits of the past will provide exactly this alienating education. They believed that the enlightenment provided by authentic theology was a divine gift, an enlightenment gifted by the Spirit of God. Many Christians are accustomed to such thoughts when reading the holy Scriptures, though even here perhaps that sense of the holy is being diminished in recent times by the prevalence of radically secularized styles of exegesis. Few, I suspect, would be accustomed to regarding the collection of patristic literature as akin to this, but many of the wisest Christians of times past saw the work of the Fathers in exactly that light: the writings of the saints of God who had come to share the mind of Christ[11] and were thus in a vantage position to explain the nature of Christ to others. Perhaps one can explain that patristic spirit more clearly by ending with the words of Athanasius of Alexandria, when he was commenting on how to read the Scriptures. His argument is that it is not enough to make a record of the words; what really matters is the conforming of the mind and heart to the spirit of what is signified. This, I think, is the essence of what is meant by the apostolic tradition in Christianity, and more simply, the essence of what is meant by passing from Christian dogmatics to Christian discipleship. It is also the root, therefore, of how theology can rise from being merely tedious dogmatizing to ascend even into the presence of God; being transfigured, by the grace of God, so as to pass from mere comprehension into godly illumination:

> Above all, you should live in such a way that you may have the right to eat of the tree of knowledge and of life, and thus come to eternal joys. . . . But for the searching of the Scriptures and for true knowledge of them, an honorable life is needed, and a pure soul and that

---

[11]See Phil 2:5.

virtue which is in accord with Christ. Only then, with an intellect that is guided on its path by this virtue, will the mind be able to reach its desired goal and comprehend the Scripture, at least as far as it is accessible to human nature to learn about the Word of God. For without a pure mind and the modeling of one's life after the pattern of the saints, no one could possibly comprehend the words of the saints. If someone wished to see the light of the sun, for example, they would at least wash and clarify their eyes, purifying themselves in some sort to be in harmony with the desired goal (so the eye, becoming lightened, might see the light of the sun); or, for example, if a person wanted to see a particular city or country, they should journey to the place to see it; well, so it is with anyone who wants to understand the inner mind of those who have spoken about God.[12]

---

[12]Athanasius *On the Incarnation* 57.1-3.

WE BELIEVE IN ONE LORD JESUS CHRIST

WE BELIEVE IN ONE LORD

καὶ εἰς ἕνα κύριον Ἰησοῦν Χριστὸν,	*Et in unum Dominum* Jesum Christum,	**We believe in one Lord,** Jesus Christ,
τὸν υἱὸν τοῦ Θεοῦ τὸν μονογενῆ,	*Filium Dei unigenitum,*	the only Son of God,
τὸν ἐκ τοῦ πατρὸς γεννηθέντα	*et ex Patre natum*	eternally
πρὸ πάντων τῶν αἰώνων,	*ante omnia saecula*	begotten of the Father,
φῶς ἐκ φωτός,	*[Deum de Deo], Lumen de Lumine,*	[God from God], Light from Light,
Θεὸν ἀληθινὸν ἐκ θεοῦ ἀληθινοῦ,	*Deum verum de Deo vero,*	true God from true God,
γεννηθέντα, οὐ ποιηθέντα,	*genitum, non factum,*	begotten, not made,
ὁμοούσιον τῷ πατρί·	*consubstantialem Patri;*	of one Being with the Father.
δι᾿ οὗ τὰ πάντα εγένετο·	*per quem omnia facta sunt;*	Through him all things were made.
τὸν δι᾿ ἡμᾶς τοὺς ἀνθρώπους	*qui propter nos homines*	For us
καὶ διὰ τὴν ἡμετέραν σωτηρίαν	*et propter nostram salutem*	and for our salvation
κατελθόντα ἐκ τῶν οὐρανῶν	*descendit de coelis,*	he came down from heaven:
καὶ σαρκωθέντα ἐκ πνεύματος ἁγίου	*et incarnatus est de Spiritu Sancto*	by the power of the Holy Spirit
καὶ Μαρίας τῆς παρθένου	*ex Maria virgine,*	he became incarnate from the Virgin Mary,
καὶ ἐνανθρωπήσαντα,	*et homo factus est;*	and was made man.

HISTORICAL CONTEXT: The root of the idea behind this first of the creed's christological clauses lies in the apostolic utterance of Paul, we know that "'there is no God but one.' For although there may be so-called gods in heaven and earth—as indeed there are many 'gods' and many 'lords'—yet for us there is one God, the Father, from whom are all things and for whom we exist, and one Lord, Jesus Christ, through whom are all things and through whom we exist. However, not all possess this knowledge."[1] Those who have the knowledge, he implies, confess it as the foundation of their faith, and so the Pauline text became, for later generations, the fundamental element of the confession of the lordship of Jesus. The lordship of Jesus, the risen Mediator who stands as the way to the Father ("through whom are all things") is articulated by the apostle as entirely a dynamic of salvation.

It is this character of the power (*dynamis*) of salvation that marks all the christological thought of the early church in later ages. In all the patristic commentaries, we see the relentless turning around of the concept of the *dynamis*, the power of salvation that Jesus has conferred on his church, and the manner in which the acceptance of that power allows the believers to understand who the person of Jesus is. It can never be the other way around. The church does not progress from its understanding of who Jesus is to a sense of his char-

[1] 1 Cor 8:5-7.

ismatic gift to the world but always the other way—from the experience of salvation (soteriology) to the understanding of the significance of the person.

The idea of the Son of God's mediation is significant in the following texts. It is a threefold understanding: first, how he shares the life of the eternal Father; second, how he mediates the power of God to the material creation that he orders as Logos; and third, how he stands as the mediator between the Father and humanity, which he redeems.

OVERVIEW: Jesus is the divine agent of God, whose divinity is wholly to be understood in relation to that of the Father (CLEMENT OF ALEXANDRIA, CYRIL OF ALEXANDRIA, COUNCIL OF CONSTANTINOPLE). Presumptions that the Lord must have an inferior divinity cannot be tolerated, as they retreat backwards to Hellenistic mythology. The Lord Jesus is God in all that the word means in its fullness (CLEMENT OF ALEXANDRIA, EUSEBIUS, PSEUDO-DIONYSIUS). This is no alternative God or rival to God. The church is given the revelation of the true God in and through the obedience of the Son, his humility and harmony with the Father (GREGORY OF NAZIANZUS, GREGORY OF NYSSA). These lowly characteristics are the proof positive of what is truly meant by his divine status as true Son of the merciful and life-giving Father (CYRIL OF ALEXANDRIA). The divinity of the Son is witnessed in the world by means of the saving power witnessed in Jesus (CLEMENT OF ALEXANDRIA, SYNOD OF ALEXANDRIA, CYRIL OF ALEXANDRIA). The incarnate Lord is the preexistent pattern of the created order, the providential power whereby the supreme Deity made and ordered the material universe (EUSEBIUS). The mysterious harmony of the Logos and the Father is fully understood only when one confesses the coequality of Father and Son. That means not simply sharing a similar status of being, or even sharing a same level of power in being, but more precisely the Son sharing the self-same being of the Father (GREGORY OF NYSSA, AMBROSE, GREGORY OF NAZIANZUS). This, in turn, means that the christological faith of the church is a trinitarian one, involving the need for a clear confession of how the incarnate Lord acts on earth as one of the holy Trinity (CYRIL OF ALEXANDRIA, PSEUDO-DIONYSIUS, CYRIL OF JERUSALEM, HILARY).

Jesus Christ Is Lord

THE HARMONY OF FATHER AND SON. GREGORY OF NAZIANZUS: For us the monarchy is formed by equality of nature, harmony of will, identity of activity and the concurrence with the One[2] of those beings who derive from the One,[3] a unity impossible among creaturely beings, so that while they are numerically distinct there is no severance in substance.[4] The original unity comes into action as a duality and reaches its final form as a trinity, and thus we have the Father, the Son and the Holy Spirit. The Father is the begetter and the emitter, but this does not mean that he undergoes a change and that there is any temporal succession or any physical relation. The Son and the Spirit are respectively offspring and emission, for I know no other terms that could be applied, such as to avoid completely any material suggestions.[5] ON THE SON, THEOLOGICAL ORATION 3(29).2.[6]

THE SINGLE GODHEAD. GREGORY OF NYSSA: But if a person keeps steadfast to the sound doctrine and believes that the Son is of the nature that is divine without admixture, he

---

[2]Gregory is referring to the Father here as the single Cause and source of unity of the Godhead. [3]The hypostases of the Son and the Spirit. [4]*Ousia*, nature or being. [5]Gregory believes the church should use these terms, which have been validated by the tradition (Scripture and Christian custom respectively) to refer to the "begetting" of the Son and the "procession"/"emission" of the Spirit, but he is anxious to divest them of any material or sexual connotation comparable to the ancient myths of the Olympian gods. [6]*LCF* 116-17*.

will find everything in harmony with the other truths of religion, namely, that our Lord is the maker of all things, that he is King of the universe, set above it not by an arbitrary act of capricious power but ruling by virtue of a superior nature; and besides this, he will find that the one first Cause, as taught by us, is not divided by any unlikeness of substance into separate first causes,[7] but one Godhead, one Cause, one Power over all things is believed in, that Godhead being discoverable by the harmony existing between these like beings and leading the mind on through one like to another like,[8] so that the Cause of all things, which is our Lord,[9] shines in our hearts by means of the Holy Spirit. AGAINST EUNOMIUS 1.36.[10]

THE INCARNATE IS ONE OF THE TRINITY. SECOND COUNCIL OF CONSTANTINOPLE (553): If anyone does not profess that our Lord Jesus Christ, who was crucified in his humanity, is truly God and Lord of glory and one of the holy Trinity, let such a one be anathema. ANATHEMA 10.[11]

God in Person

THE DEITY OF THE SON. CLEMENT OF ALEXANDRIA: God is indemonstrable and therefore is not an object of knowledge. But the Son is Wisdom and Knowledge and Truth and all that is akin to these, and he admits of demonstration and explanation. All the powers of the Spirit[12] gathered together into unity complete the notion of the Son, but he is not completely expressed by our conception of each of his powers. He is not merely one, as unity, or many, as having parts, but One as All. Hence he is All. For he is the circle of all powers, which in him are rounded and united. STROMATEIS 4.25 (156.1).[13]

THE LORD IS MAN AND GOD. CLEMENT OF ALEXANDRIA: Believe, O mortal, in him who is man and God: believe in him who suffered and is worshiped as the living God. Servants, believe in him who was dead; all people, believe in him who is the only God of all humankind. Believe and receive salvation for your reward. EXHORTATION TO THE GREEKS 10.(106).[14]

FAITH IN THE DIVINE SON. ACTS OF THE COUNCIL OF ALEXANDRIA (362): But since also certain people seemed to be contending together concerning the economy of the Savior in the flesh, we inquired of both parties. And what the one confessed, the others also agreed to, that the Word did not, as he came to the prophets, so dwell in a holy man at the consummation of the ages, but that the Word himself became flesh, and "being in the form of God," "took the form of a servant."[15] From Mary after the flesh he became man for us, and thus in him the human race is perfectly and wholly delivered from sin and quickened from the dead and is brought to the kingdom of the heavens. For they confessed also that the Savior did not have a body without a soul or without sense or intelligence; for it was not possible, when the Lord had become man for us, that his body should be without intelligence; nor was the salvation effected in the Word himself a salvation of body only, but of soul also. And being Son of God in truth, he became also Son of man, and being God's only-begotten Son, he became also at the same time "firstborn among many brethren."[16] So there was not one Son of God "before Abraham"[17] and another after Abraham. There was not one

---

[7] The proprium of being the uncaused Cause is the unique attribute of the Father. [8] It was a Platonic and widely accepted philosophical principle in antiquity that "only like could know like." [9] The Word of God is the "Cause of the created order," just as the Father is the "Cause of all," being the cause of the Trinity. Patristic thought generally ascribed transcendent being and causality to God the Father, while ascribing the energy of creation as an act of the divine Logos and the energy of sanctification and revelation to the Holy Spirit. [10] NPNF 2 5:84*. [11] TCT 178. [12] He means the divine nature. [13] ECF 234. [14] ECF 237. [15] Phil 2:7. [16] Rom 8:29. [17] Jn 8:58.

who raised up Lazarus and another who asked concerning him, but the same one said as man, "Where does Lazarus lie?"[18] and as God raised him up. He who was man in the body spat, but divinely, as Son of God, he opened the eyes of the man blind from his birth.[19] As Peter says,[20] in the flesh he suffered, as God opened the tombs and raised the dead. For these reasons, understanding all that is said in the gospel in this way, they assured us that they held the same truth about the Word's incarnation and becoming man. ATHANASIUS, ON THE SYNODS 7.[21]

THE WORD, GOD INCARNATE. CYRIL OF ALEXANDRIA: The Son, therefore, certainly is God by nature; and how then did the Father give him that "name that is above every name"?[22] To this we say that when he was flesh, that is, human like us, he took the name of a servant and assumed our poverty and low estate. But when he had finished the mystery of the dispensation in the flesh, he was raised to the glory that belonged to him by nature, not as to something unaccustomed or strange or that accrued to him externally and was given him from another, but rather as to that which was his own. For he spoke to God the Father in heaven, "Father, glorify me with the glory I had with you before the world was."[23] For, existing before the ages and before the worlds, as one that was of God and was God, he was clothed with the glory that belongs to the Godhead; and when he became a man, as I said, he endured neither mutation nor change but continued rather in that state in which he had constantly existed and such as the Father was who begot him, that is to say, like him in everything. HOMILIES ON THE GOSPEL OF LUKE 128.[24]

CHRIST IS WORD MADE FLESH. SECOND COUNCIL OF CONSTANTINOPLE (553): If anyone says that the Word of God who worked miracles was someone other than the Christ who suffered,[25] or that the divine Word was joined with the Christ who had been born of woman or that he was in him as one person within another;[26] and does not rather say that he who was made flesh and became man is the one, selfsame Jesus Christ our Lord, the Word of God; and that both the miracles and the sufferings that he voluntarily endured in his humanity are his: let such a one be anathema.[27] ANATHEMA 3.[28]

Only True God

THE SON UPHOLDS CREATION. EUSEBIUS OF CAESAREA: In the same manner, or rather in a manner that far surpasses all likeness or comparison, the perfect Word of the supreme God, as the only-begotten Son of the Father—not consisting in the power of utterance, or comprehended in syllables and parts of speech or conveyed by a voice that vibrates on the air, but being himself the living and effectual Word of the most High and subsisting personally as the power and wisdom of God—proceeds from his Father's deity and kingdom. Thus, being the perfect offspring of a perfect Father and the common preserver of all things, he diffuses himself with living power throughout creation and pours from his own fullness abundant supplies of reason, wisdom, light and every other blessing, not only on objects nearest to himself but also on those most remote, whether in earth or sea or any other sphere of

---

[18]Jn 11:34. [19]Mk 8:22. [20]1 Pet 4:1. [21]CCC 55-56*. [22]Phil 2:9. [23]Jn 17:5. [24]CGSL 509*. [25]The council was censuring the Nestorian view that a distinction ought to be made between the historical, suffering Jesus and the divine Lord and Word and argued, to the contrary, that the incarnation is a mystery of the union of the two natures in one selfsame divine person. [26]Some of the Syrian theologians had spoken of two Sons: the Son of God and the Son of man. They had initially intended to convey the two natures (human and divine). The council is determined to remove any suggestion that there could be two persons in the single Christ. [27]That is, be ecclesiastically censured. The main censure in the ancient church was that lay people were deprived of communion and clergy were deposed from ecclesiastical office if they did not maintain the common (i.e., catholic) faith. [28]TCT 175.

being. To all these, he appoints with perfect equity their limits, places, laws and inheritance, allotting to each their suited portion according to his sovereign will. ORATION ON CONSTANTINE 12.4-5.[29]

THE WORD REIGNS ETERNALLY. EUSEBIUS OF CAESAREA: This only-begotten Word of God reigns, from ages that had no beginning to infinite and endless ages, the partner of his Father's kingdom. ORATION ON CONSTANTINE 2.1.[30]

IMAGE OF THE FATHER. GREGORY OF NAZIANZUS: The one God is without beginning, without cause, not circumscribed by anything existing before or in time to come. He encompasses eternity; he is infinite, the great Father of the great and excellent Son, his Only-Begotten, the Father who experiences through the Son nothing corporeal, since he is Mind.[31] There is one other who is God, though not other in point of Godhead,[32] the Word of God. He, the living image of his Father, is alone Son of the one who is without beginning, unique Son of the only God, equal in excellence, so that the one should remain entirely Father, while the Son should be the founder of the universe who steers its course, at once the strength and understanding of the Father. PERSONAL POEMS 1.25-34, ON FIRST PRINCIPLES.[33]

THE TIMELESS LIVES IN TIME. PSEUDO-DIONYSIUS: And the Godhead is called the Trinity because its supernatural fecundity is revealed in a threefold personality (*hypostasis*) wherefrom all fatherhood in heaven and on earth exists and draws its name. And it is called the universal Cause since all things came into being through its bounty, from which all being springs. It is called Wise and Fair because all things that keep their own nature uncorrupted are full of all divine harmony and holy beauty. Especially it is called Benevolent

because, in one of its persons, it truly and wholly shared in our human lot, calling to itself and uplifting the low estate of humankind, from which, in an ineffable manner, the simple being of Jesus assumed a compound state[34] and the Eternal took on a temporal existence, and he who supernaturally transcends all the order of all the natural world was born in our human nature without any change or confusion of his ultimate properties. And in all the other divine enlightenments that the occult tradition of our inspired teachers[35] (by mystic interpretation in accordance with the Scriptures) has bestowed on us we also have been initiated. We apprehend these things in the present life (according to our powers) through the sacred veils of that loving kindness that in the Scriptures and the hierarchical traditions enwraps spiritual truths in terms drawn from the world of sense and superessential truths in terms drawn from being,[36] clothing with shapes and form things that are shapeless and formless.[37] THE DIVINE NAMES 1.4.[38]

THE FATHER SHARES ALL WITH THE SON. PSEUDO-DIONYSIUS: And as to the dominion over the whole world belonging to the whole

---

[29]NPNF 2 1:598. [30]NPNF 2 1:583. [31]The Fathers often described the Father as Mind, producing the thought of the Logos (divine Word). The word *Logos* could mean either "word" or "thought." [32]That is, the Word is personally (hypostatically) distinct from the Father but not distinct from the Father in any way that pertains to the divine nature (i.e., substantially distinct), since the Word has the selfsame nature of the Father. [33]PA 3-5. [34]That is, the Word who was ontologically simple as preexistent divine Wisdom assumed a human nature in the time of the incarnation and thus became compounded (bearing two natures) for the sake of the world's salvation. [35]That is, the sacred tradition of the apostles and church fathers. [36]Dionysius, a sixth-century Christian philosopher and mystic, is making the point that there are levels of understanding when it comes to divine mysteries. At one level, we draw comparisons about God from the natural order, but when we gain higher understanding of divine things we intuit more transcendent ideas about God that are more in the nature of metaphysical abstractions ("superessential") that do not depend on simple material comparisons. [37]That is, even at the highest stages our ideas of God fall short, for the divine mystery is beyond all our limited ideas and experiences of being. [38]ODN 56-57*.

Godhead, it is impossible, I believe, to say (as far as concerns the paternal and the filial Godhead[39]) how often in the Scriptures the name of Lord is repeated as belonging both to the Father and to the Son. Moreover, the Spirit, too, is Lord, and the names Fair and Wise are given to the whole Godhead. All the names that belong to the whole Godhead (e.g., Deifying Virtue and Cause) Scripture introduces into all its praises of the supreme Godhead comprehensively, as when it says that "all things are from God,"[40] and more in detail, as when it says that "through him are, and to him are all things created";[41] that "all things subsist in him"[42] and that "you send out your Spirit and they shall be created."[43] And, to sum it all in brief, the divine Word declared, "I and the Father are one."[44] And, "All things that the Father has are mine,"[45] and "All that are mine are yours, and yours are mine."[46] And again, all that belongs to the Father and to himself he also ascribes, in the common unity, to the divine Spirit; namely, the divine operations, the worship, the originating and inexhaustible creativeness and the ministration of the bountiful gifts. The Divine Names 2.1.[47]

The Triune God in the Work of the Incarnate Son

The Unity of the Divine Trinity. Clement of Alexandria: O wonderful mystery! The Father of all things is one; the Word of all things is one; the Holy Spirit is one and the same everywhere. Christ the Educator 1.6 (42).[48]

The Work of the Son in the Trinity. Cyril of Jerusalem: The Father gives to the Son, and the Son communicates to the Holy Spirit.[49] The Father through the Son, with the Holy Spirit, confers all his gifts. The gifts of the Father are none other than those of the Son and those of the Holy Spirit. For there is

one salvation, one power, one faith; one God, the Father; one Lord, his only-begotten Son; one Holy Spirit, the Paraclete. It is enough for us to know these things. Do not be curious about the Spirit's nature or hypostasis. If it had been explained in Scripture, I should have spoken of it: let me not venture on what has not been revealed. It is enough for salvation to know that there is a Father, a Son and a Holy Spirit. Catechetical Lectures 16.24.[50]

The Divine Names Signify Realities. Second Creed of the Council of Antioch (341): Our Lord Jesus Christ enjoined his disciples, "Go and make disciples of all the nations, baptizing them in the name of the Father and the Son and the Holy Spirit,"[51] namely, of a Father who is truly Father, and a Son who is truly Son and of the Holy Spirit who is truly Holy Spirit, the names not being given without meaning or effect but denoting accurately the peculiar subsistence (hypostasis), rank and glory of each that is named, so that they are three in subsistence and in agreement one. Holding then this faith and holding it from beginning to end in the sight of God and Christ, we anathematize every heretical heterodoxy. And if any teaches contrary to the sound and right faith of the Scriptures, that time or season or age either is or has been before the generation of the Son, let him be anathema. Or, if anyone says that the Son is a creature as one of the creatures, or an offspring as one of the offsprings or a work as one of the works, and not the aforesaid articles one after another, as the divine Scriptures have delivered, or if someone teaches or preaches beside what we received, let such a person be anathema. For all that has been delivered in the divine Scriptures, whether by prophets or apostles, do we

---

[39]That is, insofar as relates to the deity of the Father and the Son. [40]1 Cor 11:12. [41]Rom 11:36. [42]Col 1:17. [43]Ps 104:30. [44]Jn 10:30. [45]Jn 6:15. [46]Jn 17:10. [47]*ODN* 66-67*. [48]*ECF* 237. [49]Jn 16:13-14. [50]*LCF* 38. [51]Mt 28:19.

truly and reverentially both believe and follow. ATHANASIUS, ON THE SYNODS 23.[52]

THE CHARACTERISTICS OF EACH PERSON. GREGORY OF NAZIANZUS: We do not speak of the Son as unbegotten, for there is only one Father; nor do we speak of the Spirit as a son, for there is only one Only-Begotten, so that the persons have their singularity in a divine manner, the one in respect of sonship, the other in respect of procession, not sonship. . . . The Father, the Son and the Holy Spirit have this in common: that they are uncreated, and they are divine. The Son and the Holy Spirit have this in common: that they are derived from the Father. Peculiar to the Father is his ingeneracy; peculiar to the Son, his generation; and to the Holy Spirit, his being sent. . . . Be content to know this, that the Monad is adored in the Triad, the Triad in the Monad. ORATION 25.17.[53]

THE SON HAS THE DEITY OF THE FATHER. AMBROSE OF MILAN: There is fullness of divinity in the Father, fullness of divinity in the Son: this is not a diverse divinity but one and the same. There is no confusion, for it is one thing: no multiplicity, for there is no difference. For, as Scripture says, there was "one soul and one heart in all believers";[54] everyone "who cleaves to the Lord is one Spirit,"[55] the apostle said; a man and wife are "in one flesh";[56] all we people are of one substance, as far as regards our nature: Scripture says this of human beings, that they, though many, form a unity.[57] Now there can be no comparison between human and divine persons; so if there can be such unity in human beings, how much more are the Father and Son a unity in divinity, where there is no difference either of substance or will. ON THE CHRISTIAN FAITH 1.17-19.[58]

THE PERFECT UNION OF TRINITY. HILARY OF POITIERS: There is one Author of all

things. For God the Father is one, from whom are all things; and our Lord Jesus Christ is one, through whom are all things; and the Spirit is one, who is God's gift in all things. All things therefore are set in order with their own powers and excellences. There is one power, from whom are all things; one offspring, through whom are all things; one gift of perfect hope. Nothing can be found lacking to that unity of perfection, which comprises, in Father, Son and Holy Spirit, infinity in the Eternal, his likeness in his Image, his availability in the Gift. ON THE TRINITY 2.1.[59]

THE WORD AS INTERMEDIARY. EUSEBIUS OF CAESAREA: For since it was impossible that perishable bodies, or the rational spirits that he had created, should approach the supreme God, by reason of their immeasurable distance from his perfections, for he is unbegotten, above and beyond all creation, ineffable, inaccessible, unapproachable, dwelling, as his holy Word assures us, in the light that none can enter; but they were created from nothing and are infinitely far removed from his unbegotten Essence; well has the all-gracious and almighty God interposed, as it were, an intermediate power between himself and them, even the divine omnipotence of his only-begotten Word. And this power, which is in perfect nearness and intimacy of union with the Father, which abides in him and shares his secret counsels has yet condescended, in fullness of grace, as it were to conform itself to those who are so far removed from the supreme majesty of God. How else, consistently with his own holiness, could he who is far above and beyond all things unite himself to corruptible and corporeal matter? Accordingly, the divine Word, thus connecting himself with this universe and receiving into his hands the reins, as it were, of the world, turns and directs it as a skillful

---

[52]CCC 13*. Cf. Socrates *Scholasticus Ecclesiastical History* 2.10.14-18. [53]*LCF* 116*. [54]Acts 4:32. [55]1 Cor 6:17. [56]Mt 19:5-6. [57]Rom 12:5. [58]*LCF* 182. [59]*LCF* 56-57.

charioteer according to his own will and pleasure. ORATION ON CONSTANTINE 11.12.[60]

THE WORD REGULATES CREATION. EUSEBIUS OF CAESAREA: It is this Word of God who has stooped to the earth on which we live and created the manifold species of animals and the fair varieties of the vegetable world. It is this same Word who has penetrated the recesses of the deep, has given their being to the finny race and produced the countless forms of life that there exist. It is he who fashions the burden of the womb and informs it in nature's laboratory with the principle of life. By him the fluid and heavy moisture is raised on high, and then, sweetened by a purifying change, descends in measured quantities to the earth and at stated seasons in more profuse supply. Like a skillful husbandman, he fully irrigates the land, tempers the moist and dry in just proportion, diversifying the whole with brilliant flowers, with aspects of varied beauty, with pleasant fragrance, with alternating varieties of fruits and countless gratifications for the taste of people. But why do I dare essay a hopeless task, to recount the mighty works of the Word of God and describe an energy that surpasses mortal thought? By some, indeed, he has been termed the nature of the universe, by others, the world soul, by others, fate. Others again have declared him to be the most high God, strangely confounding things most widely different,[61] bringing down to this earth, uniting to a corruptible and material body and assigning to that supreme and unbegotten power, who is Lord of all, an intermediate place between. ORATION ON CONSTANTINE 11.15-16.[62]

THE FATHER WORKS BY THE SON AND SPIRIT. GREGORY OF NYSSA: But in the case of the divine Nature we do not similarly learn that the Father does anything by himself in which the Son does not work conjointly, or again that the Son has any special operation apart from the Holy Spirit; but every operation that extends from God to the Creation and is named according to our variable conceptions of it has its origin from the Father, proceeds through the Son and is perfected in the Holy Spirit. ON NOT THREE GODS.[63]

THE SON IS DIVINE AS THE FATHER IS. GREGORY OF NYSSA: The Father is God; the Son is God; and yet by the same proclamation God is one, because no difference either of nature or of operation is contemplated in the Godhead. For if, according to the idea of those who have been led astray, the nature of the holy Trinity were diverse, the number would by consequence be extended to a plurality of gods, being divided according to the diversity of essence in the subjects. But since the divine, single and unchanging nature, that it may be one, rejects all diversity in essence, it does not admit in its own case the significance of multitude; but as it is called one nature, so it is called in the singular by all its other names, God, Good, Holy, Savior, Just, Judge, and every other conceivable name that fits God; whether one says that the names refer to nature or to operation we shall not dispute the point. If, however, anyone cavils at our argument, on the ground that by not admitting the difference of nature it leads to a mixture and interchange of the persons, we shall make to such a charge this answer—that

---

[60]NPNF 2 1:596-97. [61]Eusebius belonged to the school of Origen and is insisting here, in terms drawn from Origen's more antique way of expression, on the radical difference between the supreme Godhead and the divine Word who is God's agent of creation. The later fourth-century fathers reexpressed the distinction between the most high God and God the Word in terms of the difference between Father and Son. For many Nicenes, such as Athanasius, for example, Eusebius's antique language smacked of Arianism (an attempt to deny the full and coequal divinity of the Word). Eusebius was not an Arian but was hostile to Athanasius because he felt that the Nicene language of "full and coequal deity of Father and Son" had blurred the necessary sense of distinct "offices" in the Trinity. It would not be until the end of the fourth century, with the trinitarian work of the Cappadocian fathers, that this semantic problem could be resolved. [62]NPNF 2 1:597. [63]NPNF 2 5:334.

while we confess the invariable character of the nature, we do not deny the difference in respect of cause *(to aition)* and that which is caused *(aitiaton)*, by which alone we apprehend that one person is distinguished from another—by our belief, that is, that one is the Cause and another is of the Cause; and again in that which is of the Cause we recognize another distinction. For one is directly from the first Cause, and another through that which is directly from the first Cause, so that the attribute of being only-begotten abides without doubt in the Son. ON NOT THREE GODS.[64]

THE SON GLORIFIES AND IS GLORIFIED. GREGORY OF NYSSA: The phrase "I have glorified you"[65] is said by our Lord to the Father; and again he says, "Glorify me with the glory I had with you before the world was."[66] The divine voice answers, "I have glorified and will glorify again."[67] You see the revolving circle of the glory moving from Like to Like? The Son is glorified by the Spirit; the Father is glorified by the Son; again the Son has his glory from the Father; and the Only-Begotten in this way becomes the glory of the Spirit. For with what shall the Father be glorified, except with the true glory of the Son? And again with what shall the Son be glorified, but with the majesty of the Spirit? In like manner, again, faith

completes the circle and glorifies the Son by means of the Spirit and the Father by means of the Son. ON THE HOLY SPIRIT (AGAINST MACEDONIUS).[68]

THE WORD MEDIATES BETWEEN GOD AND CREATION. EUSEBIUS OF CAESAREA: And so, the agency of the Word of God is universal: everywhere present and pervading all things by the power of his intelligence. He looks upward to his Father and governs this lower creation (which is inferior to and consequent on himself) in accordance with his will, as the common preserver of all things. Intermediate, as it were, and attracting the created to the uncreated Essence, this Word of God exists as an unbroken bond between the two, uniting things most widely different by an inseparable tie. He is the providence that rules the universe; the guardian and director of the whole; he is the power and wisdom of God, the only-begotten God, the Word begotten of God. For "in the beginning was the Word, and the Word was with God, and the Word was God. All things were made by him, and without him was not anything made that has been made,"[69] as we learn from the words of the sacred writer. ORATION ON CONSTANTINE 12.6-7.[70]

---

[64]NPNF 2 5:336. [65]Jn 17:4. [66]Jn 17:5. [67]Jn 12:28. [68]NPNF 2 5:324*. [69]Jn 1:1-3. [70]NPNF 2 1:598-99*.

JESUS CHRIST

καὶ εἰς ἕνα κύριον **Ἰησοῦν Χριστόν,**	Et in unum Dominum **Jesum Christum,**	We believe in one Lord, **Jesus Christ,**
τὸν υἱὸν τοῦ Θεοῦ τὸν μονογενῆ,	Filium Dei unigenitum,	the only Son of God,
τὸν ἐκ τοῦ πατρὸς γεννηθέντα	et ex Patre natum	eternally
πρὸ πάντων τῶν αἰώνων,	ante omnia saecula	begotten of the Father,
φῶς ἐκ φωτός,	[Deum de Deo], Lumen de Lumine,	[God from God], Light from Light,
Θεὸν ἀληθινὸν ἐκ θεοῦ ἀληθινοῦ,	Deum verum de Deo vero,	true God from true God,
γεννηθέντα, οὐ ποιηθέντα,	genitum, non factum,	begotten, not made,
ὁμοούσιον τῷ πατρί·	consubstantialem Patri;	of one Being with the Father.
δι' οὗ τὰ πάντα εγένετο·	per quem omnia facta sunt;	Through him all things were made.
τὸν δι' ἡμᾶς τοὺς ἀνθρώπους	qui propter nos homines	For us
καὶ διὰ τὴν ἡμετέραν σωτηρίαν	et propter nostram salutem	and for our salvation
κατελθόντα ἐκ τῶν οὐρανῶν	descendit de coelis,	he came down from heaven:
καὶ σαρκωθέντα ἐκ πνεύματος ἁγίου	et incarnatus est de Spiritu Sancto	by the power of the Holy Spirit
καὶ Μαρίας τῆς παρθένου	ex Maria virgine,	he became incarnate from the Virgin Mary,
καὶ ἐνανθρωπήσαντα,	et homo factus est;	and was made man.

HISTORICAL CONTEXT: As did Paul, the patristic age regarded the Lord's name and the ancient messianic title as predominantly one thing—the personal designation of the incarnate Lord. "Christ" generally signifies the status of the Word of God in the historical condition of the incarnation. The Fathers resonate with the title, aware of its Davidic and messianic resonances, though they were not particularly interested in developing the christological title messianically; it was overshadowed by the power of the Logos title to all effects. They were, however, ready to see in it a way of connecting all the historical vicissitudes of the incarnate economy (the Lord's human fragility, his ministry and passion) with the church's larger sense of the eternal providence of God, who planned the mission of Christ within the vast and foreseen cosmic scheme of creation and redemption. "Christ" becomes a cipher by which the Fathers consider the corpus of Scripture as a proleptic description of the incarnation. The earliest writers, such

as Ignatius and Clement of Rome, show how the first nonbiblical kerygmatic confessions of Jesus as Savior were rooted in the sense that he was the fulfillment of scriptural promise.

These listings of the biblical promises and their fulfillment in Jesus can often be seen to be the seed from which the earliest baptismal creeds would grow. The second-century Gnostic movement, more particularly the Pontic theologian Marcion, had cried for the abandonment of the Old Testament as unworthy of the freshness of the evangelical message. Theologians such as Irenaeus and Origen labored hard to insist that a true understanding of Jesus' mission had to be rooted in the context of the whole biblical story of salvation. "Christ" was thus a patristic symbol for the continuity of Jesus in the prophetic tradition of Israel's religion, while at the same time the incarnation was always received by the church as a radical new beginning. The delicate balancing act of accepting the Old Testament while reinterpreting it strictly through the

New was a notable achievement of patristic theology. Cyril of Alexandria's work in this respect became something of a highwater mark of patristic exegesis.

Overview: The unshakable faith of the church is secured by the faithful being "nailed to the cross of Christ" in the certainty of his historical mission to save humankind and the security of their confession of the authentic kerygma of the gospel (Ignatius). This faith is established through the apostles and their successors, the bishops who teach the evangelical faith (Clement of Rome). In later days the revelation of the Word continues to unfold in his church, where Gospels are established and apostolic tradition is observed and grace consequently exults (Letter to Diognetus). Jesus is the Messiah and is clothed in the vesture of Scripture (Ephrem). In the Spirit, Christ explains all the mysteries of salvation to his faithful by means of Scripture (Cyril of Alexandria). Like a musician he plays the two harps of the Old and New Testament, which are seated on his knee (Ephrem). The common theme of the Scriptures is that the Lord is the expected One (Epistle of Barnabas). He is in himself the fulfillment of the Scriptures (Ignatius), their heart and their goal (Ephrem). The motive for the Word's advent to his people, as recounted in Scripture, is his saving concern and compassion (Clement of Alexandria). He comes among us as the fulfillment of the long-expressed hope of the cosmos (Clement of Rome, Eusebius, Cyril of Jerusalem). This great Word, coming in his extensive mission of salvation, is therefore many-faceted and bears many different titles (Gregory of Nazianzus, Ephrem, Cyril of Jerusalem). These reflect his varied offices as priest, healer, mediator and Savior (Clement of Rome, Pseudo-Clement of Rome, Ignatius, Polycarp, Gregory of Nazianzus, Ephrem).

The Kerygma of the Gospel

The Fundamentals of Belief. Ignatius of Antioch: I glorify Jesus Christ, the God who made you so wise, for I observed that you are established in an unshakable faith, having been nailed, as it were, to the cross of the Lord Jesus Christ in both body and spirit and firmly established in love by the blood of Christ, totally convinced with regard to our Lord that he is truly of the family of David with respect to human descent, Son of God with respect to the divine will and power, truly born of a virgin, baptized by John "in order that all righteousness might be fulfilled by him,"[1] truly nailed in the flesh for us under Pontius Pilate and Herod the tetrarch (from its fruit we derive our existence, that is, from his divinely blessed suffering) in order that he might raise a banner for the ages through his resurrection for his saints and faithful people, whether among Jews or among Gentiles, in the one body of his church. To the Smyrneans 1.1-2.[2]

The Faith Established Through the Apostles. Clement of Rome: The apostles received the gospel for us from the Lord Jesus Christ. Jesus the Christ was sent forth from God. So, then, Christ is from God; the apostles are from Christ. Both, therefore, came of the will of God in good order. Having, therefore, received their orders and being fully assured by the resurrection of our Lord Jesus Christ and full of faith in the Word of God, they went forth with the firm assurance that the Holy Spirit gives, preaching the good news that the kingdom of God was about to come. So, preaching both in the country and in the towns, they appointed their first fruits, when they had tested them by the Spirit, to be bishops and deacons for the future believers. 1 Clement 42.1-4.[3]

---

[1]Mt 3:15. [2]*AF* 185. [3]*AF* 75.

THE WORD UNFOLDS GRACE IN THE CHURCH. LETTER TO DIOGNETUS: There is nothing strange in my discourse, nor is my argument contrary to reason. No, after becoming a disciple of apostles, I am now becoming a teacher of the Gentiles. What has been handed down I deliver exactly to such as become disciples of the Truth. Really, can anyone who has been correctly taught and has fallen in love with the Logos fail to strive to learn exactly what has been plainly shown by the Logos to disciples to whom the Logos appeared in person and made revelations in plain language? He was not understood by unbelievers but gave a detailed explanation to disciples, and these, reckoned by him as trustworthy, came to know the mysteries of the Father. For this reason he sent the Logos to appear in the world, who, discredited by his people, was preached by apostles and believed by Gentile nations. He was in the beginning, appeared new and was found to be old, and is ever born anew in the hearts of the saints. He is the eternal One, who today is accounted a Son. By him the church is enriched, and grace, ever unfolding in the saints, is multiplied. Grace grants understanding, reveals mysteries, announces seasons, glories in believers, gives freely to seekers such as do not break their promised word or transgress the bounds fixed by the fathers. And then the fear of the Lord becomes a theme of song, prophetic inspiration is recognized, the trustworthiness of the Gospels is firmly established, apostolic tradition is observed and the grace of the church is exultant. LETTER TO DIOGNETUS 11.1-6.[4]

SCRIPTURE IS CHRIST'S VESTURE. EPHREM THE SYRIAN: With the scribes our Lord debated. Clothed in their Scripture, he cast them down in controversy. With the breastplate of truth, the psalms, he was girded. He questioned them and was questioned, and victorious was he whose shield was the Torah, and Isaiah his sword and spear and the prophets

the arrows for his bow. His names silently renounce the Stranger,[5] for Jesus is Messiah, and our Lord and our God. HYMNS ON VIRGINITY 37.7-8.[6]

SALVATION IS EXPLAINED THROUGH SCRIPTURE. CYRIL OF ALEXANDRIA: When he had quieted their reasonings by what he said, by the touch of their hands and by eating the food, he then opened their mind to understand that it was necessary for him to suffer, even on the wood of the cross. The Lord, therefore, recalls the minds of the disciples to what he had said beforehand, for he had forewarned them of his sufferings on the cross, according to what the prophets had spoken long before, and he opens also the eyes of their heart, for them to understand the ancient prophecies. The Savior promises the disciples the descent of the Holy Spirit that God had announced of old by Joel,[7] and power from above, that they might be strong and invincible and preach to all, everywhere, without any fear, the divine mystery. He says to them, now that they had received the Spirit after the resurrection,[8] "Receive the Holy Spirit," and adds, "But stay a while in Jerusalem, and wait for the promise of the Father, of which you have heard from me. For John indeed baptized with water, but you shall be baptized with Holy Spirit";[9] in water no longer, for they had received this already, but with the Holy Spirit; he does not add water to water but completes that which was deficient by adding what was wanting to it. Having blessed them and gone a little in advance, he was carried even to heaven, that he might share the Father's throne even with the flesh that was united to him. And this new pathway the Word made for us when he appeared in human form. Hereafter in due time he will come again in the glory of his Father with the angels and

---

[4]ACW 6:145-46*. [5]His names contain a mystical power that renounces and casts out Satan. [6]ESH 426. [7]Joel 2:28. [8]Jn 20:22. [9]Acts 1:5.

will take us up to be with him. Therefore, let us glorify him who, being God the Word, became man for our sakes; who suffered willingly in the flesh, and rose from the dead and abolished corruption; who was taken up, and hereafter shall come with great glory to judge the living and the dead and will give to each according to their deeds; by whom and with whom to God the Father be glory and power with the Spirit, to ages of ages. Amen. Homilies on the Gospel of Luke 24.45.[10]

The Expected One

Scripture Foretells the Lord's Economy. Epistle of Barnabas: It is indeed with this purpose in view that the Lord endured to surrender his body to destruction: we are to be sanctified by the remission of sins, that is, through the sprinkling of his blood. For this is what the Scripture says in speaking of him partly to Israel and partly to us. It says as follows: "He was wounded because of our iniquities and languishes because of our sins; by his bruises we were healed; as a sheep he was led to the slaughter, like a lamb that is dumb before its shearer."[11] Surely, we ought to be exceedingly grateful to the Lord for making clear the past to us, enabling us to act wisely in the present and not leaving us without discernment in regard to the future. Epistle of Barnabas 5.1-3.[12]

The Scriptures Foretold Christ. Epistle of Barnabas: The fact is, the Master has made known to us through the prophets, the past and present, and given us a foretaste of the future. And so, when we see these things one by one becoming actual fact, just as he said, we ought to be all the more generous and inspired in our effort to advance in the fear of him. Epistle of Barnabas 1.7.[13]

Christ Fulfilling All Scripture. Ignatius of Antioch: Moreover, I urge you to do nothing in a spirit of contentiousness but in accordance with the teaching of Christ. For I heard some people say, "If I do not find it in the Archives,[14] I do not believe it in the gospel." And when I said to them, "It is written," they answered me, "That is precisely the question." But for me the Archives are Jesus Christ. The inviolable Archives are his cross and death, and his resurrection and the faith that comes through him; by these things I want, through your prayers, to be justified. To the Philadelphians 8.2.[15]

Christ Is the Goal of All Scripture. Ephrem the Syrian: This stream of symbols[16] was unable to cleave the sea into which it fell and to flow toward another since the Sea of truth received it. Since it is a wondrous gulf, all creatures cannot fill it. It confines all of them but is not confined by them. The prophets poured into it their glorious symbols. Priests and kings poured into it their wondrous types. All of them poured into all of it. Christ was victorious and rose up. By his explanations for symbols, by his interpretations for similes, he, like the sea, will receive into himself all the streams. Consider that if all the kings willed to turn aside all the rivers so that they would not come to the sea, the rivers would still come to it by force. Therefore, the sea is Christ, who is able to receive the sources and springs and rivers and streams that flow forth from within Scripture. No other sea could ever contain such depths from all the rivers that poured into it. And no one else to whom you referred the Scriptures would ever be able to fulfill its histories in himself. For it is Christ who perfects its symbols by his cross, its types by his body, its adornments by his beauty and all of it by all of him! Hymns on Virginity 9.7-15.[17]

---

[10]*CGSL* 620*. [11]Is 53:7. [12]ACW 6:42*. [13]ACW 6:38. [14]The Old Testament Scriptures. [15]*AF* 181-83. [16]The Old Testament. [17]ESH 302-3**.

MYSTICAL AWARENESS OF CHRIST. EPHREM THE SYRIAN: Give me by grace, O blessed Sea, one droplet of compassion that I may invest it and come by means of your flow[18] to you. The symbols were silent in love, for they saw that Truth was coming. Blessed is he whose parables have fulfilled all Scripture that had drawn his pictures. HYMNS ON VIRGINITY 10.17-18.[19]

THE SONG OF ALL SCRIPTURE. EPHREM THE SYRIAN: Great is the symbol of the Lamb who is quiet in his life and sings in his death. His loins are for festivities and the strings of his lyre for melodies and songs. So old is the teaching that its time is not known. It dwells in youth, although it is scorned along with it. It becomes small and makes it great to honor it very much. All these things teach by their symbols: they open by their sufferings the treasure of their riches, and the suffering of the Son of the gracious One is the key of his treasures. HYMNS ON VIRGINITY 11.18-20.[20]

The Living Word

THE WORD GUIDES OUR SALVATION. CLEMENT OF ALEXANDRIA: This Word, the Christ, the cause of our being, for he was in God, as also of our well-being, has now himself appeared to humankind. He alone is both God and man; he is for us the source of all good. From him we learn the good life and are brought to the life eternal.[21] . . . This is the New Song, the Epiphany, which has now shone out among us, of that Word who was in the beginning[22] and who was before the beginning. And now, quite recently, he has been manifested—the Savior who was before. He has been manifested who was in Him-Who-Is, because the Word, who was with God,[23] has appeared as our teacher, he by whom the universe was created. The Word who in the beginning gave us life when he fashioned us, as Creator, has taught us the good life, as

our teacher, that he may afterwards, as God, provide us with life eternal. Not that he now has for the first time pitied us for our wandering; he pitied us from of old, from the beginning. But now, when we were perishing, he has appeared and has saved us. EXHORTATION TO THE GREEKS 1.7.[24]

CHRIST IS THE MANY-NAMED GIFT OF GOD. EUSEBIUS OF CAESAREA: Hence there is one God, and not two, or three or more, for to assert a plurality of gods is plainly to deny the being of God at all. There is one Sovereign. His Word and royal law is one: a law not expressed in syllables and words, not written or engraved on tablets and therefore subject to the ravages of time but the living and self-subsisting Word, who himself is God and who administers his Father's kingdom on behalf of all who are after him and subject to his power. His attendants are the heavenly hosts, the myriads of God's angelic ministers, the superterrestrial armies of unnumbered multitude and those unseen spirits within heaven itself whose agency is employed in regulating the order of this world. Ruler and chief of all these is the royal Word, acting as regent of the supreme Sovereign. To him the names of captain, and great high priest, prophet of the Father, angel of mighty counsel, brightness of the Father's light, only-begotten Son, with a thousand other titles, are ascribed in the oracles of the sacred writers. And the Father, having constituted him the living Word, and law, and wisdom, the fullness of all blessing, has presented this best and greatest gift to all who are the subjects of his sovereignty. ORATION ON CONSTANTINE 3.6-7.[25]

THE ETERNAL SON OF GOD. GREGORY OF

---

[18]That is, that I may come to God through the mystical ocean of the Word of God, which is at once both the Scripture and the divine Logos. [19]ESH 306. [20]ESH 309. [21]Tit 2:11-13. [22]Jn 1:1. [23]Jn 1:1. [24]ECF 236-237. [25]NPNF 2 1:584.

NAZIANZUS: Nothing ever existed before the great Father. For he who contains the universe and is dependent on the Father knows this, the one who is sprung from the great Father, the Word of God, the timeless Son, the image of the original, a nature equal to his who begot him. For the Father's glory is his great Son, and he was manifested in a way known only to the Father and to the Son made known by him. For there was nothing that came close to Godhead. PERSONAL POEMS 2.5-12, ON THE SON.[26]

CHRIST PLAYS THE SCRIPTURES LIKE A HARPIST.

EPHREM THE SYRIAN: The Word of the most High came down and put on a weak body with hands, and he took two harps[27] in his right and left hands. The third he set up before himself to be a witness to the other two, for the middle harp taught that their Lord is playing them. Glory to your wise decrees! HYMNS ON VIRGINITY 29.1.[28]

THE CREATIVE WORD OF GOD.

CYRIL OF JERUSALEM: Christ, then, is the only-begotten Son of God and Maker of the world. For "he was in the world, and the world was made by him, and he came to his own,"[29] as the Gospel teaches us. By the Father's will, Christ is the maker not only of the things that are seen but also of the things that cannot be seen. For, as the apostle says, in him all things were created that are in heaven and on the earth, things visible and invisible, "whether thrones, or dominions, or principalities or powers; all things have been created by him and for him, and he is before all, and in him all things consist."[30] Even if you speak of the worlds, of these also Jesus Christ is the maker by the Father's will. "For in these last days God spoke to us by his Son, whom he appointed heir of all things, by whom also he made the worlds."[31] To him be the glory, honor, might, now and ever, and to the ages of ages. Amen. CATECHETICAL LECTURES 11.24.[32]

The Name Jesus Christ

A NAME OF MYSTERIES AND SYMBOLS.

EPHREM THE SYRIAN: The letter yodh of Jesus, our King,[33] is the queen of all numbers. On her perfection depends all reckoning, as in Jesus all meanings are mixed. The Greatest of all descended utterly to unspeakable humiliation. He returned from that humiliation to seize the unlimited height on the right hand.[34] It is a great wonder that from that height he did not proceed little by little to descend and come to smallness. He flew from the womb of divinity to humanity. For the sun (that sun of yours) announces your mystery as if by mouth. In the winter, as your type,[35] it descends to a low level; in summer, like you, it ascends to the height and rules over all. HYMNS ON THE NATIVITY 27.13-16.[36]

THE NAME SIGNIFIES PRIEST AND SAVIOR.

CYRIL OF JERUSALEM: And he is called by two names, Jesus Christ; Jesus, because he saves,[37] and Christ,[38] because he is a priest. And knowing this, the inspired prophet Moses conferred

---

[26]*PA* 5. [27]The first two harps Ephrem speaks of are the Old Testament and the New; the third harp is the book of nature in whose harmonies God has also revealed himself. · [28]ESH 390-91. [29]Jn 1:10-11. [30]Col 1:16-17. [31]Heb 1:2. [32]NPNF 2 7:70-71**. [33]The letter yodh is the first letter of Jesus' name in Syriac, and it has a numerical value. Much ancient scriptural reflection, Jewish as well as Christian, turned around the mystical associations of literal and numerical symbolism. [34]Ephrem is thinking of Phil 2:5-11. [35]Types were figures contained in the biblical text or the natural world that symbolically synopsized a mystery of faith. Here the winter sun, low in the sky, is like the Lord's incarnation into humility. The summer sun, glorious in its power, is a symbol (type) of the resurrection glory of Christ. For Ephrem, the perfect and great numerical value of the 100 (yodh) is a mystery revealed in the name Jesus, a name whose own biblical symbolism was connected with the figure of the "high priest Jesus" (LXX) who wore filthy robes; in patristic thought this was a constant type of the sufferings of the Lord in his incarnation. So, in a complex mix of biblical symbols, Ephrem is here reflecting on how the name and life of Jesus are biblically presented in a mystical set of hidden symbols needing to be penetrated by the Spirit's insight. [36]ESH 212. [37]Joshua (Hebrew; the Greek equivalent is Jesus) signifies "Savior." [38]The Hebrew term *Messiah* (the Greek equivalent is *Christ*) signifies "anointed one." As the messiahs (kings) and priests of Israel were both anointed, the word *Christ* is being used associatively to designate Jesus' priesthood in this instance.

these two titles on two men distinguished above all: his own successor in the government, Auses, he renamed Jesus;[39] and his own brother Aaron he surnamed Christ,[40] that by two well-approved men he might represent at once both the high priesthood and the kingship of the one Jesus Christ who was to come. For Christ is a high priest like Aaron; he did not glorify himself to be made a high priest, but rather the one that spoke to him: "You are a priest forever according to the order of Melchizedek."[41] CATECHETICAL LECTURES 10.11.[42]

JESUS, HEALER OF SOUL AND BODY. CYRIL OF JERUSALEM: Jesus, then, means according to the Hebrew "Savior," but in the Greek tongue "the Healer," since he is physician of souls and bodies, curer of spirits, curing the blind in body and leading minds into light, healing the visibly lame and guiding sinners' steps to repentance, saying to the palsied, "Sin no more," and, "Take up your bed and walk."[43] For since the body was paralyzed for the sin of the soul, he ministered first to the soul, that he might extend the healing to the body. If, therefore, any of us are suffering in soul from sins, there is the Physician for us, and if anyone here is of little faith, let us say to him, "Help my unbelief."[44] If anyone is hemmed in with bodily ailments, do not be faithless but draw near, for to such diseases also Jesus ministers, and then we shall learn that Jesus is the Christ. CATECHETICAL LECTURES 10.13.[45]

CHRIST IS KNOWN AND UNKNOWN. CYRIL OF JERUSALEM: The Jews denied this Christ when he had come, but the devils confessed him. His ancestor David had him in mind when he said, "I have prepared a lamp for my anointed."[46] Some have interpreted this lamp to be the brightness of prophecy, others the flesh that he took on him from the Virgin, according to the apostle's word, "But we have this treasure in earthen vessels."[47] The

prophet also had him in mind when he said, "He announces his Christ to humankind."[48] Moses also knew him, Isaiah knew him, and Jeremiah; not one of the prophets was ignorant of him. Even devils recognized him, for he rebuked them, as the Scripture says, "Because they knew that he was Christ."[49] The chief priests did not know him, but the devils confessed him; the chief priests did not know him, yet a woman of Samaria proclaimed him, saying, "Come, see a man who told me everything I ever did. Surely this is the Christ?"[50] CATECHETICAL LECTURES 10.15.[51]

THE ANOINTED HEAVENLY PRIEST. CYRIL OF JERUSALEM: That we have hope in Jesus Christ has been sufficiently shown, according to our ability, in what we delivered to you yesterday.[52] But we must not simply believe in Christ Jesus or receive him as one of the many who are improperly called Christs. For they were figurative Christs, but he is the true Christ; not having risen by advancement from among people to the priesthood but ever having the dignity of the priesthood from the Father. CATECHETICAL LECTURES 11.1.[53]

CHRIST THE ONLY-BEGOTTEN SON. CYRIL OF JERUSALEM: And for this cause the faith, guarding us beforehand lest we should suppose him to be one of the ordinary Christs, adds to the profession of the faith[54] that we believe "in one Lord, Jesus Christ, the only-begotten Son of God." And again on hearing of a Son, do not think of an adopted son but a son by nature, an only-begotten son, having no brother. For this is the reason why he is called Only-Begotten,

---

[39]Num 13:16. [40]As in Ex 30:30, where Aaron is "anointed" (Christ-ed). [41]Ps 110:4; Heb 5:6, 10; Heb 6:20. [42]NPNF 2 7:60*. [43]Jn 5:8, 14. [44]Mk 9:24. [45]NPNF 2 7:61*. [46]Ps 132:17. [47]2 Cor 4:7. [48]Amos 4:13 (LXX). [49]Lk 4:41. [50]Jn 4:29. [51]NPNF 2 7:61**. [52]Cyril was delivering a Lenten series of baptismal preparation lectures to his catechumens in Jerusalem. [53]NPNF 2 7:64. [54]That is, the creed, which Cyril is here expounding phrase by phrase.

because in the dignity of the Godhead and his generation from the Father, he has no brother. But we call him the Son of God, not from ourselves but because the Father himself named Christ his Son,[55] and a true name is that which is set by fathers on their children. CATECHETICAL LECTURES 11.1-2.[56]

CONFESSING CHRIST AS SON OF GOD. CYRIL OF JERUSALEM: Our Lord Jesus Christ became man but was unknown to the crowds. Wishing to teach that which was not known, he called together his disciples and asked them, "Who do men say that I, the Son of man, am?"[57] He asked not from vanity but because he wanted to show them the truth, so that they might not think lightly of him as if he were a mere man, while all the while they were living alongside the divine, only-begotten Son of God. And when they answered him that some said he was Elijah, and others Jeremiah, he said to them, "They may be excused for not knowing, but you, my apostles, who in my name cleanse lepers, and cast out devils and raise the dead, should not to be ignorant of the nature of him through whom you do these wonderful works." And then they all became silent, for the matter was too high for human comprehension. Then Peter, who was leader of the apostles and the chief herald of the church, was enlightened in his mind from the Father. He did not say these things by his own cunning invention or from his own human deductions, but he said to him, "You are the Christ," adding, "the Son of the living God." After that his words received Christ's blessing (for indeed they were above human ability), and the Savior set a seal on what he had said, showing to all that it was the Father who had revealed this to him. For the Savior then said, "Blessed are you, Simon BarJona, for flesh and blood has not revealed this to you, but my Father who is in heaven." This is why whoever acknowledges our Lord Jesus Christ to be the Son of God partakes of this blessedness; but

whoever denies the Son of God is a poor and miserable creature. CATECHETICAL LECTURES 11.3.[58]

SON OF GOD AND SON OF DAVID. CYRIL OF JERUSALEM: If you hear the Gospel saying, "The book of the generation of Jesus Christ, the Son of David, the Son of Abraham,"[59] you should understand "according to the flesh." For he is the Son of David at the end of the ages, but the Son of God before all ages, without beginning. The one, which he formerly did not have,[60] he received; but the other, which he already has, he has eternally as begotten of the Father. He has two fathers: one, David, according to the flesh, and one, God, his Father in a divine manner. As the Son of David, he is subject to time, and to handling and to genealogical descent, but as Son according to the Godhead, he is subject neither to time nor to place nor to genealogical descent: "For who shall declare his generation?"[61] God is a Spirit;[62] and he who is a Spirit has spiritually begotten (since he is incorporeal) an inscrutable and incomprehensible generation. The Son says of the Father, "The Lord said to me: You are my son, today I have begotten you." Now this "today" is not recent but eternal: a timeless today, before all ages. "From the womb, before the morning star, I have begotten you."[63] CATECHETICAL LECTURES 11.5.[64]

The Various Offices of the Redeemer

THE SAVING OFFICES OF CHRIST. CLEMENT OF ROME: "The sacrifice of praise will glorify me, and that is the way by which I will show him the salvation of God."[65] This is the way, dear friends, in which we found our salvation,

---

[55]Lk 9:35. [56]NPNF 2 7:64*. [57]Mt 16:13. [58]NPNF 2 7:64*. [59]Mt 1:1. [60]Referring to the two births of the Lord: one in time, and one in eternity; one from Mary, the other from the Father. [61]Is 53:8; Acts 8:33. [62]Jn 4:24. [63]Ps 2:7; Ps 110:3 (LXX). [64]NPNF 2 7:65*. [65]Ps 50:23.

namely, Jesus Christ, the high priest of our offerings, the guardian and helper of our weakness. Through him let us look steadily into the heights of heaven. Through him we see, as in a mirror, his faultless and transcendent face. Through him the eyes of our hearts have been opened. Through him our foolish and darkened mind springs up into the light. Through him the Master[66] has willed that we should taste immortal knowledge, for "he who is the radiance of his majesty is as much superior to angels as the name he has inherited is more excellent than theirs."[67] 1 CLEMENT 35.12–36.2.[68]

CHRIST AS MEDIATOR AND PRIEST. CLEMENT OF ROME: Finally, may the all-seeing God and Master of spirits and Lord of all flesh, who chose the Lord Jesus Christ, and us through him to be his own special people, grant to every soul that has called on his magnificent and holy name, faith, fear, peace, patience, steadfastness, self-control, purity and sobriety, that they may be pleasing to his name through our high priest and guardian, Jesus Christ, through whom be glory and majesty, might and honor to him, both now and forever and ever. Amen. 1 CLEMENT 64.1.[69]

CHRIST AS JUDGE. PSEUDO-CLEMENT OF ROME: Brothers, we ought to think of Jesus Christ as we do of God, as "Judge of the living and dead."[70] And we ought not to belittle our salvation, for when we belittle him, we also hope to receive but little. And those who listen as though these are small matters do wrong; and we also do wrong, when we fail to acknowledge from where, and by whom and to what place we were called, and how much suffering Jesus Christ endured for our sake. 2 CLEMENT 1.1-2.[71]

THE LORD AND TEACHER OF LIFE. PSEUDO-CLEMENT OF ROME: Let us, therefore, not just call him Lord, for this will not save us. For he says, "Not everyone who says to me 'Lord,'

Lord' will be saved, but only the one who does what is right."[72] So then, brothers, let us acknowledge him in our actions by loving one another, by not committing adultery or slandering one another or being jealous, but by being self-controlled, compassionate and kind. And we ought to have sympathy for one another, and not be avaricious. By these actions let us acknowledge him, and not by their opposites. 2 CLEMENT 4.1-3.[73]

STONES OF A TEMPLE. IGNATIUS OF ANTIOCH: You are stones of a temple, prepared beforehand for the building of God the Father, hoisted up to the heights by the crane of Jesus Christ, which is the cross, using as a rope the Holy Spirit; your faith is what lifts you up, and love is the way that leads up to God. So you are all fellow pilgrims, carrying your God and your shrine, your Christ and your holy things, adorned in every respect with the commandments of Jesus Christ. TO THE EPHESIANS 9.1-2.[74]

HIGH PRIEST AND DOOR TO SALVATION. IGNATIUS OF ANTIOCH: The priests, too, were good, but the high priest, entrusted with the Holy of Holies, is better; he alone has been entrusted with the hidden things of God, for he himself is the door of the Father, through which Abraham and Isaac and Jacob and the prophets and the apostles and the church enter in. All these come together in the unity of God. But the gospel possesses something distinctive, namely, the coming of the Savior, our Lord Jesus Christ, his suffering and the resurrection. For the beloved prophets preached in anticipation of him, but the gospel is the imperishable finished work. All these things together are good, if you believe with love. TO THE PHILADELPHIANS 9.1-2.[75]

---

[66]God the Father. [67]Heb 1:4. [68]AF 69. [69]AF 101. [70]Acts 10:42. [71]AF 107. [72]Mt 7:21. [73]AF 109-11. [74]AF 143. [75]AF 183.

HIGH PRIEST AND SON OF GOD. POLYCARP OF SMYRNA: Now may the God and Father of our Lord Jesus Christ, and the eternal high priest, the Son of God, Jesus Christ, build you up in faith and truth, and in all gentleness, and in all freedom from anger, and forbearance and steadfastness and patient endurance and purity, and may he give you a share and place among his saints, and to us with you, and to all those under heaven who will yet believe in our Lord and God Jesus Christ and in his Father who raised him from the dead. TO THE PHILIPPIANS 12.2.[76]

JESUS, OVERSEER OF OUR HEARTS. CLEMENT OF ALEXANDRIA: The Spirit of the Lord is a lamp that searches out the inner chambers of the heart.[77] And as a person, by acting righteously, becomes more enlightened, so the shining spirit comes closer, and in this way the Lord draws near to the righteous, and nothing escapes him of our thoughts and of the reasonings we entertain. I mean the Lord Jesus, who by the will of the Almighty, "is the overseer of our heart,"[78] whose blood was consecrated for us. STROMATEIS 4.17.(107.5).[79]

THE SON OF MAN AND SHEPHERD. GREGORY OF NAZIANZUS: He is Son of man, on account of Adam and on account of the Virgin from whom he came. He is from Adam as his forefather and from the Virgin as his mother. He is from them in accordance with the law of generation, and quite apart from it.[80] He is Christ because of his Godhead, for this is the anointing of his manhood.[81] In his case, this anointing did not sanctify by its action (something which is true of all others who are anointed) but rather by the presence in his fullness of the anointing one.[82] And the effect of this anointing is that the one who anoints is called man and thereby makes that which is anointed God. He is the way, because he leads us through himself. He is the door, since he lets us in. He is the shepherd, for he makes us dwell in a place of green pastures, and brings us up by restful waters and leads us there, protecting us from wild beasts, converting the erring, bringing back that which was lost, binding up that which was broken, guarding the strong and bringing them together in the fold beyond with words of pastoral knowledge. ORATION 30.21.[83]

CHRIST OF MANY TITLES. GREGORY OF NAZIANZUS: These are the titles of the Son. Walk through them. Peruse those that are lofty in a godlike spirit and those that are corporeal in a corresponding fashion. Or rather, treat all of them in a godlike fashion so that you yourself may become a god.[84] For you will ascend from lowly things for his sake who came down from on high for our sake. In all, and above all, keep to this and you shall never err, either in regard to the loftier or the lowlier titles; "Jesus Christ is the same yesterday and today"[85] in the incarnation, and in the Spirit, forever and ever. Amen. ORATION 30.21.[86]

MANY NAMES OF THE ONLY SON. SECOND CREED OF THE COUNCIL OF ANTIOCH (341): We believe, in conformity with the evangelical and apostolical tradition, in one God, the Father almighty, the framer and maker and administrator of the universe, "from whom are all things."[87] And in one Lord Jesus Christ, his Son, only-begotten God, "by whom are all

---

[76]AF 219. [77]Prov 20:2. [78]Citing 1 Clem 1.21. [79]ECF 234-35*. [80]He descended from Adam in accordance with the laws of nature and was born of Mary in transcendence of the laws of nature, since she was a virgin. [81]Gregory reverses the expectation of his audience by associating the Christ anointment with the deity rather than the humanity of Jesus, for the latter had been a traditional exegesis of the Antiochene theologians, several of whom were in his audience for this oration. [82]The holiness is not conferred by the anointing of God, as is the case with prophets, but is conferred by the direct indwelling presence of the divine Logos, which is the case only for Jesus, the incarnate deity. [83]LCC 3:192-93**. [84]Alluding to Jn 10:34-35. The patristic notion of deification by grace connoted the state of the enlightened disciple whose ever deepening approach to God rendered him or her "godlike." [85]Heb 13:8. [86]LCC 3:193**. [87]1 Cor 8:6. [88]1 Cor 8:6.

things,"[88] who was begotten before the ages from the Father, God from God, whole from whole, sole from sole, perfect from perfect, King from King, Lord from Lord, living Word, living Wisdom, true Light, Way, Truth, Resurrection, Shepherd, Door, both unalterable and unchangeable; "exact image of the Godhead,"[89] substance, will, power and glory of the Father: "the firstborn of all creation,"[90] who was "in the beginning with God," God the Word, as it is written in the Gospel, "And the Word was God,"[91] by whom all things were made and "in whom all things consist";[92] who in the last days descended from above and was born of a virgin, according to the Scriptures, and became man, mediator between God and humankind, and apostle of our faith, and Prince of life, as he says: "I came down from heaven, not to do my own will but the will of him who sent me."[93] ATHANASIUS, ON THE SYNODS 23.[94]

LORD OF VIRGINS AND HARP OF PROPHETS. EPHREM THE SYRIAN: The lyre of the prophets who proclaimed him, singing before him, and the hyssop of the priests who loved him, eagerly desiring his presence, and the diadem of kings who handed it down in succession, belong to this Lord of virgins, for even his mother is a virgin. He who is king gives the kingdom to all. He who is priest gives pardon to all. He who is the Lamb gives nourishment to all. HYMNS ON THE NATIVITY 2.2.[95]

The Nature of Divine Sonship

THE SIGNIFICANCE OF JESUS' TITLES. CYRIL OF JERUSALEM: Believe in one Lord Jesus Christ, the only-begotten Son of God. For we say, "one Lord Jesus Christ," that his sonship may be "only-begotten." We say "one," so that you do not imagine any other. We say "one," that you do not profanely scatter the many names of his action[96] among many sons.[97] For he is called a door,[98] but do not take the name literally, as if it were a thing of wood, but as a

spiritual, living door, one that discriminates those who enter in. He is called a way,[99] not one trodden by feet, but leading to the Father in heaven; he is called a sheep,[100] not an irrational one, but one which through its precious blood cleanses the world from its sins, which is led before the shearers and knows when to be silent. This sheep again is called a shepherd, who says, "I am the good Shepherd";[101] a sheep because of his humanity, a shepherd because of the loving kindness of his Godhead. And with regard to rational sheep, note how the Savior says to the apostles, "Behold, I send you as sheep in the midst of wolves."[102] Again, he is called a lion,[103] not as a devourer of people but indicating, as it were, by the title, his kingly and steadfast and confident nature. He is also called a lion in antithesis to that lion who is "our adversary, who roars and devours" those who have been deceived.[104] For the Savior came as the strong "Lion of the tribe of Judah,"[105] not as having changed the gentleness of his own nature but as Savior for those who believe and as treading down the adversary. He is called a stone, not a lifeless stone, cut out by human hands, but a chief cornerstone,[106] and "whoever believes in him shall not be put to shame."[107] He is called Christ, not as having been anointed by human hands but because he is eternally anointed by the Father to his high priesthood on behalf of humankind. He is called dead, not as having his abode among the dead, as all who are in hades, but as being

---

[89]Heb 1:3. [90]Col 1:15. [91]Jn 1:1-2. [92]Col 1:17. [93]Jn 6:38. [94]CCC 12*. Cf. Socrates Scholasticus *Ecclesiastical History* 2.10.10-12. [95]ESH 76. [96]The titles of Christ, both divine and human, connote varied aspects of his one saving work (his economy) and cannot be divided out into separate "human" and "divine" categories, as Nestorius was trying to do. On the contrary, all are attributable to one Son and one Lord Jesus. [97]Cyril of Alexandria would later argue at the Council of Ephesus (431) that the Syrian tradition of Diodore of Tarsus, Theodore of Mopsuestia and Nestorius was wrong to refer to two Sons (the Son of God and the Son of man) "as if" they were separate persons. [98]Jn 10:7, 9. [99]Jn 14:6. [100]Jn 1:29; Is 53:7. [101]Jn 10:11. [102]Mt 10:10, 16. [103]Gen 49:9; Rev 5:5. [104]1 Pet 5:8. [105]Rev 5:5. [106]Is 28:16. [107]Rom 9:33.

alone "free among the dead."[108] He is called Son of man, not as having had his generation from earth, as each of us, but as "coming on the clouds to judge both living and dead."[109] He is called Lord, not improperly as those who are called lords among people, but rather as having a natural and eternal lordship. CATECHETICAL LECTURES 10.3-4.[110]

THE SON IS GOD FROM GOD. CYRIL OF JERUSALEM: When you hear that he is a Son, do not understand this improperly. You should know that he is truly the Son; a Son by nature and without beginning. He did not come out of bondage into a higher state of adoption but was a Son eternally begotten by an inscrutable and incomprehensible generation. Likewise, when you hear the name of Firstborn, do not think of this in a human manner. A human firstborn may have other siblings also. It is written somewhere, "Israel is my son, my firstborn."[111] But Israel is, as Reuben was, a firstborn son who was rejected. Reuben went up to his father's couch,[112] and Israel cast his Father's son out of the vineyard and crucified him.[113] The Scripture also says to other people, "You are the sons of the Lord your God,"[114] and, "I have said you are gods, and you are all sons of the most High."[115] Note how Scripture reads, "I have said," not, "I have begotten." When God so said, these people received a sonship that they did not possess before. But Christ was not begotten to be other than he was before. He was begotten from the beginning, Son of the Father, being above all beginning and all ages. He is the Son of the Father, "in all things like to him"[116] who begot him, eternal of an eternal Father, life of Life begotten, and light of Light, and truth of Truth, and wisdom of the Wise, and king of King, and God of God and power of Power. CATECHETICAL LECTURES 11.4.[117]

THE SON OF GOD ETERNALLY BEGOTTEN. CYRIL OF JERUSALEM: He is the Son of God by nature and not by adoption and is begotten of the Father. Whoever loves the one who begot should also love the one who is begotten of him. Whoever despises the one that is begotten casts back an insult on the one who begets.[118] Whenever you hear of God begetting, do not let your minds sink down to bodily things. Do not think it means a corruptible generation, or else you will be guilty of impiety. God is a Spirit.[119] His generation is spiritual. Bodies can only beget bodies, and for the generation of bodies time must intervene, but time does not intervene in the generation of the Son from the Father. In relation to humans, what is begotten is made imperfect. The Son of God, however, was begotten perfect. What he is now, so he is from the beginning, for he was begotten without beginning. CATECHETICAL LECTURES 11.7.[120]

CHRIST IS A TRUE SON. CYRIL OF JERUSALEM: The Father, who is very God, begot the Son like himself, that is, very God. It was not as teachers beget disciples, and not as Paul says to his readers, "For in Christ Jesus I begot you through the Gospels."[121] In this case, he who was not a natural son became a son by discipleship. In the case of Christ, however, he was a son by nature, a true son. This is not the same with you who are about to be illuminated[122] and are now in the process of becoming children of God. You also will become sons, but this is by the adoption of grace, as it is written, "But as many as received him, to them he gave the power to become children of God, those who believed in his name, and who were begotten not of blood, or from the will of the flesh

---

[108]Ps 88:5; Jn 5:27. [109]Mt 24:30; 2 Tim 4:1. [110]NPNF 2 7:57-58**. [111]Ex 4:22. [112]Gen 49:3-4. [113]Mt 21:38. [114]Deut 14:1. [115]Ps 82:6. [116]"Like to God in all things" is based on 2 Cor 4:4. [117]NPNF 2 7:64-65*. [118]Faith in the divinity of the Son is not extraneous to faith in the one God but integral to it, and indeed its chief expression, insofar as the revelation of the deity of the Son is the Father's way of saving the world (Christ as the economy of salvation). [119]Jn 4:24. [120]NPNF 2 7:66*. [121]1 Cor 4:15. [122]The baptismal candidates gathered to hear his sermon.

or the will of a person, but from God."[123] We have truly been begotten of water and of the Spirit, but Christ was not begotten from the Father in this way. At the time of his baptism, when the Father spoke to him, saying, "This is my son,"[124] note how God did not say, "This has now become my son," rather, "This is my son." This was so that he might reveal that even before the operation of baptism he was a son. CATECHETICAL LECTURES 11.9.[125]

THE WORD HYPOSTATICALLY EXISTENT. CYRIL OF JERUSALEM: The Father begot the Son, but it was not in the way that a human mind is said to beget a word. The mind is substantially existent in us,[126] but when a word is spoken, it disperses into the air and comes to an end. But we know Christ to have been begotten not as a mere spoken word, rather as a Word substantially existing[127] and living. This Word is not spoken by the lips and dispersed but is begotten of the Father eternally and ineffably, and substantially so.[128] For "In the beginning was the Word, and the Word was with God, and the Word was God."[129] Sitting at God's right hand, the Word understands the Father's will and creates all things at his bidding. The Word descended and ascended,[130] whereas a mere word of utterance does neither of these things when spoken. He is the Word who speaks and says, "The things I speak of are those which I have seen with my Father."[131] The Word possesses power and reigns over all things, for the Father "has committed all things to the Son."[132] CATECHETICAL LECTURES 11.10.[133]

THE SON BORN AS GOD FROM GOD. CYRIL OF JERUSALEM: Do not be ashamed to confess your ignorance, since you share ignorance with the angels. Only he who begot knows the one who was begotten; and he who is begotten of him knows the one who begot. He who begot knows what he begot: and the Scriptures also testify that he who was

begotten is God. For "as the Father has life in himself, so he has given to the Son to have life in himself."[134] It is also said that "all people should honor the Son, even as they honor the Father."[135] Again Scripture says, "as the Father gives life" to whoever he will, "even so the Son gives life to whom he will."[136] The one who begot suffered no loss, and just so there is nothing lacking in him who was begotten. Yes, I know that I have said these things many times, but it is for your safety that they are said so often. The one who begot does not have any father. And he who was begotten has no brother. He who begot was certainly not changed into the Son,[137] and he who was begotten did not become the Father. Of one "only Father" there is one "only-begotten Son," not two unbegottens[138] or two only-begottens; but only one Father, the unbegotten

---

[123]Jn 1:13. [124]Mt 3:17. [125]NPNF 2 7:66**. [126]The human mind is hypostatic (a personal existence in ancient terms), but human words are not hypostatic. [127]Existing as a personal subject or hypostasis; the living Word of the Father. [128]The Word, who is the second hypostasis of the Trinity, has no other substance (being) than that of God and is thus divine (God of God). [129]Jn 1:1. [130]Descended to earth in the incarnation and was exalted in the glorification (alluding to the *katabasis* and *anabasis* mentioned so many times in the Fourth Gospel. [131]Jn 8:38. [132]Jn 5:22. [133]NPNF 2 7:66-67**. [134]Jn 5:26. [135]Jn 5:23. [136]Jn 5:21. [137]Cyril is alluding to the opinion of some second-century monarchians (ridiculed by Tertullian as Patripassians) that the Son was really the Father in the guise of a historical revelation (the Trinity, that is, as merely three different aspects of the same person). It was a position known as modalism. [138]The Father is unbegotten, the Son begotten. These are their hypostatic unique characters (*idiomata*). Cyril is here representing a form of early Nicene theology that even in his time was becoming problematized by the neo-Arian theologians of the late fourth century who argued that "unbegottenness" was a fundamental definition of deity. So, if the Son was not "unbegotten," he could not be divine. It would belong to Cyril's younger contemporaries, the Cappadocian fathers, to make the necessary reply that an eternal begetting from the substance of God, such as the only-begotten Son had from the unbegotten Father, was the same as being "nonoriginated" (that is, divine), insofar as it touched on the status of creaturehood or noncreaturehood. It was a complex and important set of arguments that troubled all the later fourth-century church, and which, because of the successful clarifications of the Cappadocians, meant that the Nicene faith could be emphatically reaffirmed at the First Council of Constantinople in 381, in a more clearly trinitarian format.

(for only he is unbegotten who has no father); and one Son, eternally begotten of the Father. He is not begotten in time but before all ages, and he is not increased by advancement but begotten as that which he now is.[139] CAT-ECHETICAL LECTURES 11.13.[140]

THE SON IS INSEPARABLE FROM THE FA-THER. CYRIL OF JERUSALEM: And to be brief, let us neither separate them[141] nor make a confusion of them. Never say that the Son is foreign to the Father,[142] and never admit those who say that the Father is at one time Father and at another time Son,[143] for these are strange and impious statements and not the doctrines of the church. But the Father, having begotten the Son, remained the Father and is not changed. He gave birth to Wisdom but never lost wisdom himself. He gave birth to Power but never became weak. He gave birth to God but did not lose his own Godhead and never lost anything himself by diminution or change. In the same way he who was begotten has nothing deficient in him. The one who gave birth is perfect, and the one who was begotten is perfect too. It was God who gave birth and God who was begotten, being himself God of all, yet calling the Father his own God. For he is not ashamed to say, "I ascend to my Father and your Father, to my God and to your God."[144] CATECHETICAL LECTURES 11.18.[145]

---

[139]Cyril means begotten eternally as "God from God," as the Son derives substantial existence from the Father. It is the Father's substance that the Son has as his own, and thus the Son is God as the Father is, and eternal as the Father is. This was a critical and central affirmation of the Nicene faith in Cyril's day, as in our own. [140]NPNF 2 7:67-68*. [141]The persons (*hypostases*) of the Father and Son. [142]A confession of the Arian party (the hetero-ousiasts). [143]The monarchian modalists (nontrinitarians). [144]Jn 20:17. [145]NPNF 2 7:69*.

THE ONLY SON OF GOD

καὶ εἰς ἕνα κύριον 'Ιησοῦν Χριστόν,	Et in unum Dominum Jesum Christum,	We believe in one Lord, Jesus Christ,
τὸν υἱὸν τοῦ Θεοῦ τὸν μονογενῆ,	**Filium Dei unigenitum,**	**the only Son of God,**
τὸν ἐκ τοῦ πατρὸς γεννηθέντα	et ex Patre natum	eternally
πρὸ πάντων τῶν αἰώνων,	ante omnia saecula	begotten of the Father,
φῶς ἐκ φωτός,	[Deum de Deo], Lumen de Lumine,	[God from God], Light from Light,
Θεὸν ἀληθινὸν ἐκ θεοῦ ἀληθινοῦ,	Deum verum de Deo vero,	true God from true God,
γεννηθέντα, οὐ ποιηθέντα,	genitum, non factum,	begotten, not made,
ὁμοούσιον τῷ πατρί·	consubstantialem Patri;	of one Being with the Father.
δι' οὗ τὰ πάντα ἐγένετο·	per quem omnia facta sunt;	Through him all things were made.
τὸν δι' ἡμᾶς τοὺς ἀνθρώπους	qui propter nos homines	For us
καὶ διὰ τὴν ἡμετέραν σωτηρίαν	et propter nostram salutem	and for our salvation
κατελθόντα ἐκ τῶν οὐρανῶν	descendit de coelis,	he came down from heaven:
καὶ σαρκωθέντα ἐκ πνεύματος ἁγίου	et incarnatus est de Spiritu Sancto	by the power of the Holy Spirit
καὶ Μαρίας τῆς παρθένου	ex Maria virgine,	he became incarnate from the Virgin Mary,
καὶ ἐνανθρωπήσαντα,	et homo factus est;	and was made man.

HISTORICAL CONTEXT: The fourth century was roiled in turmoil over an apparently simple question: Was Jesus divine or not? This turmoil has come to be known retrospectively as the Arian crisis. The elevation of the Nicene-Constantinopolitan Creed as an international standard of orthodox faith in the deity of Jesus was one of the major results of a century of conflict in which christological speculation proceeded at a hitherto unknown pace. The question of the divinity of Jesus was not asked for its own sake, as an idle speculation, but rather as a way of asking what was the purpose of the mission of the Son of God. It was a question that the Gnostic era had instigated at the end of the first century and that the second-century Monarchian crisis launched into the wider Christian world. The later third century would soon be dominated by the christological work of Origen of Alexandria, whose extensive development of Logos theology in relation to Christology set the agenda for most of the work of the patristic theologians of centuries to follow, whether they were his disciples or his foes. After Origen, the question of Christ's sonship and status became posed more and more explicitly as a question about the divine preexistence of the Lord Jesus, and the argument embroiled almost every theologian of the fourth century and afterwards. The Nicene fathers were to insist, as they sought for a calm center in the storm of controversy, that the church's confession of Jesus as the only Son of God expressed clearly enough that the Lord was not one of many saints or angelic powers who could be designated by such a name. He was what the church had sensed from the beginning: Son of God in a unique and divine sense.

OVERVIEW: The Son, as truly divine, can be called "our God" (IGNATIUS). He does not belong to the created order (ATHANASIUS, GREGORY OF NAZIANZUS, CYRIL OF JERUSALEM) but is of the very eternal essence of God

(GREGORY OF NAZIANZUS) and is one of the divine and timeless members of the Trinity (BASIL). First and foremost as Son before the ages, the Son of God also came to his creation within history, a movement toward humanity motivated by the compassion of his desire to save (EPHREM). In this hidden economy of humility he was not recognized by most, but the angels and true-hearted believers saw through the veil of his fragility to discern the power of the divinity within (EPHREM, CYRIL OF JERUSALEM). The Son of God rallies the faithful around him, creating a community of saints (HERMAS). His teachings advance along with his all-mastering role as guide and orderer of the earthly cosmos (EUSEBIUS, CYRIL OF JERUSALEM). He was the tabernacle of the presence of God on earth during his earthly ministry (ISAAC). All that he said about loving God with the whole heart and whole mind is brought to fulfillment in the manner in which his church gives its whole devotion to him (GREGORY OF NYSSA).

The Deity of Christ

JESUS, OUR GOD, BORN OF MARY. IGNATIUS OF ANTIOCH: Our God, Jesus the Christ, was conceived by Mary according to God's plan, both from the seed of David and of the Holy Spirit. He was born and was baptized, in order that by his suffering he might cleanse the water. TO THE EPHESIANS 18.2.[1]

THE SON IS NOT IN THE RANKS OF CREATURES. ATHANASIUS: He would not have been worshiped or spoken of in this way[2] if he belonged merely to the rank of creatures. But as it is, since he is not a creature but the offspring of the God who is worshiped, an offspring proper to his substance and a Son by nature, this is why he is worshiped and is believed to be God, and is Lord of hosts, and has author-

[1] AF 149. [2] Referring to Heb 1:6; Is 45:14; Jn 13:13; 20:28.

ity, and is All-sovereign, just as the Father is; for he himself says, "All things that belong to the Father are mine."[3] For it is proper to the Son to have all that the Father has and to be such that the Father is beheld in him, and that through him all things were made and that in him the salvation of all is brought about and is established. AGAINST THE ARIANS 2.24.[4]

THE SON IS OF GOD'S OWN NATURE. BASIL OF CAESAREA: The distinction between *ousia* and *hypostasis* is the same as that between the general and the particular; as, for instance, between the animal[5] and the particular man. And so, in the case of the Godhead, we confess one essence[6] so as not to give a variant definition of existence, but we confess a particular hypostasis, in order that our conception of Father, Son and Holy Spirit may be without confusion and clear. If we have no distinct perception of the separate characteristics, namely, fatherhood, sonship and sanctification, but form our conception of God from the general idea of existence, we cannot possibly give a sound account of our faith. We must, therefore, confess the faith by adding the particular to the common. The Godhead is common; the fatherhood particular. We must therefore combine the two and say, "I believe in God the Father." The same course must be pursued in confessing the Son; we must combine the particular with the common and say, "I believe in God the Son." So in the case of the Holy Spirit we must make our utterance conform to the appellation and say, "I believe also in the divine Holy Spirit." Hence it results that there is a satisfactory preservation of the unity by the confession of the one Godhead, while in the distinction of the individual properties regarded in each there is the confession of the peculiar properties[7] of the persons.[8] . . . Those who identify essence, or substance, and *hypostasis*[9] are compelled to confess only three persons[10] and, in their hesitation to speak of three *hypostases*,[11] are convicted of failure to avoid the error of Sabellius,[12] for even Sabellius himself, who in many places confuses the conception, yet, by asserting that the same hypostasis changed its form to meet the needs of the moment, does endeavor to distinguish persons. LETTER 236.6.[13]

THE SON IS UNIQUELY BORN OF GOD. GREGORY OF NAZIANZUS: In my opinion he is called Son because he is identical with the Father in essence, and because he is from the Father. And he is called Only-Begotten, because he is the only son of the only Father, and only a son, and also because the manner of his sonship is peculiar to himself and not shared by corporeal realities. He is called the Word, because he is related to the Father as Word to Mind. This follows from his passionless generation and from the union, and is part of his revelatory function. The relation can be

---

[3]Jn 16:15. [4]ECF 388-89*. [5]That is, the species humankind. [6]Or substance (*ousia*). [7]Or characteristics (*idiomata*). [8]The three divine *hypostases*. [9]This had been a complicated semantic problem in earlier Christian generations, especially the third century, when the words *ousia* and *hypostasis* had been used by some writers as synonyms for essence (both having the sense of *ousia*). By the time Basil is writing, in the late fourth century, the distinction between the words is more generally observed: that *ousia*/essence/being should be the generic notion and *hypostasis*/person/subsistent should mean the particular "existent." This was the semantic foundation on which the Cappadocian fathers were able to lay out the explanation of orthodox trinitarian doctrine: three distinct and inseparably united persons (distinctly subsistent *hypostases*), all of whom shared the selfsame divine nature or essence (the one divine *ousia* of the Father). [10]Here Basil uses the word *prosopa*, another synonym for *hypostasis*. The variety of different Greek christological and trinitarian terms that were being used in the fourth century but had not been standardized in their usage, as yet, caused much confusion in that period. [11]Some theologians, not least Latin-speaking ones, thought that if one confessed three *hypostases* in the Godhead, it was tantamount to admitting three divine essences and thus to confessing three gods. Basil is at pains to point out that their mistake is one of language, since three hypostases who share the selfsame essence means there can be only one God. [12]Sabellius was a second-century teacher who was a modalist, teaching that God was only one single person who changed his mode of revelation (now as a Father, now as a Son, now as a Spirit) to effect different forms of revelation. Here Basil is ironically describing his critics as "worse than" Sabellius, who was generally regarded as an ignoramus in the fourth century. [13]CCC 115.

compared with that between a definition and the thing defined, since this is also called a *logos*. As Scripture says, whoever has the mental perception of the Son (for this is the meaning of the phrase "has seen") has also seen the Father.[14] Thus, the Son is a concise demonstration, an easy exposition, of the Father's nature. ORATION 30.20.[15]

HE WHO MADE US BECAME FLESH TO SAVE US. EPHREM THE SYRIAN: God had seen that we worshiped creatures, so he put on a created body so as to use our bad habit to catch us. Behold, by this fashioned one[16] our Fashioner healed us, and by this creature our Creator revived us. His force did not govern us.[17] Blessed is he who came in what is ours and mingled us[18] into what is his. O you who are greater than measure, who became immeasurably small, from glorious splendor you humbled yourself to ignominy. Your indwelling mercy inclined you to this. Let your compassion incline me to become praiseworthy in my evil.[19] Blessed is the one who became a source of melodies and entirely gave thanks to all of you.[20] He became a servant on earth; he was Lord on high; inheritor of the height and depth, who became a stranger. But the One who was judged wrongly will judge in truth, and he in whose face they spat, breathed the spirit into the face.[21] He who held a weak reed was the scepter for a world that grows old and leans on him. He who stood and served his servants, sitting,[22] will be worshiped. He whom the scribes scorned, the seraphim sang "holy" before him. HYMNS ON THE NATIVITY 21.12-15.[23]

THE ANGELS KNOW CHRIST IS NO CREATURE. EPHREM THE SYRIAN: Every thing has quantity and weight and measurements. Mute and quiet and silent is their nature.[24] As if endowed with speech, they extend persuasion by their silence to us who have weighed and measured and quantified. You, our Lord,

Mind and Intellect, have never been measured, weighed and quantified. Rational measures cry out in the creation that your generation cannot be weighed or your depth quantified or your height measured! HYMNS ON VIRGINITY 52.10.[25]

HE REVEALED HIS DIVINITY TO MOSES. CYRIL OF JERUSALEM: Moses says to him, "Show me yourself."[26] You see that the prophets in those times too saw the Christ, that is, as far as each was able. "Show me yourself," that I may see you with understanding. But God said, "No mortal shall see my face and live."[27] For this reason then (because no one could see the face of the Godhead and live), he[28] took on himself the face of human nature,

---

[14]Jn 14:9. [15]LCC 3:190-91. [16]That is, Christ, who came in the form of a creature (a thing fashioned like the false gods people were worshiping), that is, in a body that was created. [17]That is, the economy of salvation through the humble mystery of incarnation was not a forcible bending of the human race back to the service of God but a gracious invitation to return. [18]Many of the Fathers use the image of the blending and mingling of deity and humanity in the person of Christ (at once God and man) as a generic analogy of how the Godhead worked for the dynamic transfiguration of the assumed flesh (in Jesus) and the powerful salvation (deification) of the human race in general. Ephrem uses the idea generically in that way here. By the fifth century the concept of mingling had become the subject of intense speculation and was ruled out as impermissibly loose for the understanding of a true Christology. The term was censured in the way Apollinaris used it and was the subject of much further discussion at the councils of Ephesus (431), Chalcedon (451) and Constantinople II (553). Ephrem is innocent of all that complex of ideas. [19]That is, a double sense: that Ephrem might turn from evil and be a worthy disciple and that he might see how the ignominious race (humankind) has been immensely exalted by the fact that God assumed the creaturely condition to save it. [20]The Word's incarnation Ephrem describes as a "playing of a harp" to the glory of God (hymns such as these were also once sung to the harp in ancient Syria), and his meaning here is that this music of thanks or eucharistic song, which was the incarnate economy, gave God the Father and all the heavenly ranks a fitting praise that had hitherto been lacking from the earth. [21]Pairing in contrast Mk 15:19 (the spitting at the passion) and Jn 20:22 (the out-breathing of the Spirit). [22]The washing of the feet at the Last Supper. [23]ESH 176. [24]The nature of angels cannot be assessed by the same quantities as apply to material creatures. [25]ESH 468. [26]Ex 33:13. [27]Ex 33:20. [28]The patristic writers generally assume that it was the Word of God, the Son, rather than the Father, who appeared in epiphanies to the ancient prophets.

that we might see this and live. And yet when he wished to show even that with just a little majesty, when "his face shone like the sun,"[29] the disciples fell down overcome with fear. If his bodily countenance, then, not even shining in the full power of the one who performed this sign, but merely according to the capacity of the disciples, gave them such fear that even so they could not bear it, how could any person gaze on the majesty of the Godhead? Cat-echetical Lectures 10.7.[30]

The Son Is True God. Cyril of Jerusa-lem: The Son is truly God and has the Father in himself. He is not changed into the Father, for it was not the Father who was made man, but the Son. Let the truth be freely spoken. The Father did not suffer for us, but the Father sent the one who suffered. We must not say, "There was a time when the Son was not."[31] And we must not confess a Son who is the Father.[32] On the contrary, let us walk on the king's highway[33] and deviate neither to the left or the right. Do not call the Son Father in the mistaken belief you are giving him honor. And do not imagine the Son is one of the creatures in the belief that this will honor the Father. But let one Father be worshiped through one Son, and never let their worship be separated. Let one Son be proclaimed, who sits at the right hand of the Father before all ages and shares his throne not by any temporal advancement after his passion but rather by eternal possession. Catechetical Lectures 11.17.[34]

Faith Attached Personally to Jesus Christ

The Lord Sustains Those Who Bear His Name. Hermas: The name of the Son of God is great and incomprehensible and sustains the whole world. If, therefore, all creation is sustained by the Son of God, what do you think of those who are called by him and bear the name of the Son of God and walk

in his commandments? Do you see, then, what kind of people he sustains? Those who bear his name with their whole heart. So he himself has become their foundation and gladly sustains them because they are not ashamed to bear his name. Shepherd, Similitude 9.14 (91).[35]

The Word Is Our Life and Our Light. Eusebius of Caesarea: Through his vivify-ing power all nature grows and flourishes, re-freshed by his continual showers and invested with a vigor and beauty ever new. Guiding the reins of the universe, he holds its onward course in conformity to the Father's will. He moves, as it were, the helm of this mighty ship. This glorious agent, the only-begotten Son of the supreme God, begotten by the Father as his perfect offspring, the Father has given to this world as the highest of all goods. He infuses his word, as spirit into a lifeless body, into unconscious nature. Through the divine power he imparts light and energy to that which in itself was a rude, inanimate and formless mass. Therefore it is fitting on our part to acknowledge and see him as everywhere present and as giving life to matter and the ele-ments of nature. In him we see light, even the spiritual offspring of inexpressible Light. He is truly one in essence, as being the Son of the single Father, though he possesses in himself many and varied powers. Oration on Con-stantine 12.7-8.[36]

The Lord of the World. Cyril of Je-rusalem: We believe then in one Lord Jesus Christ, the only-begotten Son of God, begot-ten of his Father, truly God before all worlds, "by whom all things were made."[37] For whether

---

[29]Mt 17:2. [30]NPNF 2 7:59*. [31]The catchphrase of the Arian party, which denied the eternity and thus the deity of the Son. [32]The opposite error of denying the Arians' radical separation of Father and Son, by affirming their synonymity. [33]An ancient rhetorical phrase for "taking the balanced median position." [34]NPNF 2 7:68-69*. [35]AF 495. [36]NPNF 2 1:599**. [37]1 Cor 8:6.

they are thrones, or dominions, or principalities or powers,[38] "all things were made through him,"[39] and of all created things none is exempted from his authority. Let every heresy be silenced that brings in different creators and makers of the world; and let the tongue that blasphemes the Christ the Son of God be silenced too. Catechetical Lectures 11.21.[40]

The Son Gives Life and Peace. Cyril of Jerusalem: Believe, therefore, in Jesus Christ, Son of the living God, and a Son only-begotten, according to the Gospel, which says, "For God so loved the world, that he gave his only-begotten Son, that whoever believes in him should not perish but have everlasting life."[41] And again, "Whoever believes in the Son is not judged, but has passed out of death into life."[42] But whoever does not believe in the Son shall not see life, since "the wrath of God abides on him."[43] And John testified concerning him, saying, "And we beheld his glory, glory as of the only begotten from the Father, full of grace and truth";[44] at whom the devils trembled and said, "Ah, what have we to do with you, Jesus, Son of the living God?"[45] Catechetical Lectures 11.6.[46]

With All Your Heart and Strength. Gregory of Nyssa: No one can say that we ought to love the Son with all our heart and strength but should honor him only with half. If the Son is to be honored with the whole heart, as we render to him all our love, then how can one find anything superior to his honor, when such a degree of honor is paid to him in the coin of love, as much as our whole

heart is capable of? In this case of beings who are essentially honorable,[47] therefore, it is foolish to talk about a superior honor and by inference suggest an inferior honor.[48] Against Eunomius 1.24.[49]

The Word Is the Tabernacle of God. Isaac of Nineveh: I give praise to your holy nature, Lord,[50] for you have made my nature a sanctuary for your hiddenness and a tabernacle for your mysteries, a place where you can dwell and a holy temple for your divinity, namely, for him who holds the scepter of your kingdom, who governs all you have brought into being, the glorious tabernacle of your eternal being, the source of renewal for the ranks of fire that minister to you,[51] the way to knowledge of you, the door to the vision of you, the summation of your power and great wisdom, Jesus Christ, the only-begotten from your bosom and the remnant gathered in from your creation, both visible and spiritual. The Second Part 2.5.6.[52]

---

[38]Rom 8:38-39. That is, the Word is not merely the fashioner of the material world order but also the maker of the angelic ranks in the time before the world was made: thus the eternal Son of the everlasting Father, not a superior angelic being, as Arius had suggested. [39]Jn 1:3. [40]NPNF 2 7:70*. [41]Jn 3:16. [42]Jn 5:24. [43]Jn 3:36. [44]Jn 1:14. [45]Mk 5:7. [46]NPNF 2 7:65-66*. [47]The honor due to the Father and Son proceeds from their innate being (as sharing the selfsame divine nature) and is thus coequal (no degrees of glory within the same infinite being). [48]The neo-Arian theologian Eunomius, whom Gregory is attacking here, had argued that the Son was essentially "inferior to the absolute Father, having a created nature 'other to God.'" [49]NPNF 2 5:67**. [50]Isaac is addressing this hymn to God the Father, offering praise for the wonderful economy of salvation manifested in the incarnate Word. [51]The angels. [52]CS 175: 57. This recently discovered manuscript of Isaac's works has been temporarily designated under the generic title of "The Second Part."

ETERNALLY BEGOTTEN OF THE FATHER

καὶ εἰς ἕνα κύριον Ἰησοῦν Χριστὸν,	*Et in unum Dominum Jesum Christum,*	*We believe in one Lord, Jesus Christ,*
τὸν υἱὸν τοῦ Θεοῦ τὸν μονογενῆ,	*Filium Dei unigenitum,*	*the only Son of God,*
τὸν ἐκ τοῦ πατρὸς γεννηθέντα	**et ex Patre natum**	**eternally**
πρὸ πάντων τῶν αἰώνων,	**ante omnia saecula**	**begotten of the Father,**
φῶς ἐκ φωτός,	*[Deum de Deo], Lumen de Lumine,*	*[God from God], Light from Light,*
Θεὸν ἀληθινὸν ἐκ θεοῦ ἀληθινοῦ,	*Deum verum de Deo vero,*	*true God from true God,*
γεννηθέντα, οὐ ποιηθέντα,	*genitum, non factum,*	*begotten, not made,*
ὁμοούσιον τῷ πατρὶ·	*consubstantialem Patri;*	*of one Being with the Father.*
δι᾽ οὗ τὰ πάντα εγένετο·	*per quem omnia facta sunt;*	*Through him all things were made.*
τὸν δι᾽ ἡμᾶς τοὺς ἀνθρώπους	*qui propter nos homines*	*For us*
καὶ διὰ τὴν ἡμετέραν σωτηρίαν	*et propter nostram salutem*	*and for our salvation*
κατελθόντα ἐκ τῶν οὐρανῶν	*descendit de coelis,*	*he came down from heaven:*
καὶ σαρκωθέντα ἐκ πνεύματος ἁγίου	*et incarnatus est de Spiritu Sancto*	*by the power of the Holy Spirit*
καὶ Μαρίας τῆς παρθένου	*ex Maria virgine,*	*he became incarnate from the Virgin Mary,*
καὶ ἐνανθρωπήσαντα,	*et homo factus est;*	*and was made man.*

HISTORICAL CONTEXT: The question of the divine status of the Son of God was couched, from the mid-third century onwards, in the question of the eternity of the Son-Logos. Origen had expressed the view that the Son-Logos shared in the eternity of God the Father, even if the Logos proceeded from the Father's own being in a logical relation of priority and succession (Father and Son). In the early decades of the fourth century, this theological problem had become acute in the school of Lucian, an early Christian sophist and martyr, who was the teacher of Arius. How could the Logos be eternal if he came as a second from God the Father?

Arius was to press the logic of this strongly in the first quarter of the fourth century, so as to insist on the single absolute transcendence of the Father, with the Logos of God envisaged as emanating from him as a quasi-divine being, not a divinity in the same sense as God; more, as it were, an honorary deity, an angelic and lofty being held in intimate closeness to God because of the unswerving probity of his devotion. For the ease of teaching this complex view to his parishioners, Arius coined the phrase "There was when he [the Logos] was not." This was the birth of the Arian crisis—the affirmation that the Son was not an eternal being.

The Nicene party, led by Alexander and Athanasius, countered with the position that there can be no such thing as an honorary deity. And if the Son of God was not eternal, then he was clearly part of the ranks of creatures. But if he was divine, then it followed of necessity that the Son was eternal and born from the Father "before all ages." The latter phrase in particular meant born "before the creation, and that passage of time that marks the unfolding of the creation." It was theological shorthand for an affirmation that the Son-Logos was the agent of the creation itself. Athanasius deftly altered the Arian slogans he found on the walls of his city, adding a critical amendment of "never," so as to make them read: "There was never a time when he [the Logos] was not." The Fathers at the Council of Nicaea lay great stress on this creedal clause "begotten before the ages." It graphically sums up the Pauline and Johannine[1] doctrine that the eternal Son of God was the Father's agent of creation; not part of the ranks of creatures but the Lord who created the ranks of creatures in the predetermined plan[2] of his Father's mercy.

OVERVIEW: God the Father can never be without his own Logos (ORIGEN). This would be as foolish as to imagine God could ever be devoid of his truth or his own mind (TERTULLIAN), or that Light could ever be distinct and separate from its own radiance (ATHANASIUS, GREGORY OF NYSSA, CHRYSOSTOM). The Logos-Son issues from the Father, indeed, but not in a sequence that can be imagined as time-bound or involving sequential priority, which are purely material conceptions inappropriate to the deity (GREGORY OF NAZIANZUS, GREGORY OF NYSSA). The Logos-Son is the divine comaker of humanity alongside his Father (ORIGEN). The character of eternity is necessary to the Creator and is discernible in the Logos-Son (GREGORY OF NYSSA). It would be inconceivable for the creator Lord and Logos not to have existed at some stage (GREGORY OF NYSSA). In fact, the author of time transcends time (GREGORY OF NAZIANZUS). When one considers the Son's eternal birth from God, however, it is a notion that exceeds our time-bound imaginations and the capacity of our created minds (ORIGEN, CYRIL OF JERUSALEM). The Son is born from God's own being and shares the selfsame being of God, which is why the Son is eternal, just as the Father is (ATHANASIUS). The Father and Son have distinction in the sense that they have different modes of being, but they nonetheless have the same being (GREGORY OF NAZIANZUS, GREGORY OF NYSSA) and thus are both from everlasting. The concept of the eternal Father carries in the power of the name and idea the sense of

the eternal Son (ATHANASIUS, GREGORY OF NYSSA, LEO).

God and Time

THE SON IS LIGHT FROM LIGHT. ORIGEN: John tells us that "God is light,"[3] and Paul calls the Son "the radiance" of eternal light.[4] Therefore, as light can never be without radiance, how can it be said that there was a time when the Son was not?[5] For that is as much as to say that there was a time when Truth was not, when Wisdom was not, when Life was not, and so on. . . . But we have to apologize for using such phrases as "there was never a time when he was not,"[6] for these words have a temporal significance; but when they are used of the Father and the Son and Holy Spirit, they are to be understood as denoting something supratemporal. ON FIRST PRINCIPLES 4.4.28.[7]

THE SON IS OLDER THAN ALL CREATION. ORIGEN: [Unlike the newly-minted Egyptian god Serapis,] the Son of God, the "firstborn of all creation,"[8] though he seemed to become man but recently, is not for that reason a new God. For the sacred Scriptures know that he is older than all created things and that it was to him that God said, concerning the creation of humankind, "Let us make people after our image and likeness."[9] AGAINST CELSUS 5.37.[10]

THE SON IS NOT AFTER THE FATHER IN TIME. GREGORY OF NAZIANZUS: "When

[1]Col 1:16; Phil 2:6; 1 Cor 8:6; Jn 1:1-4, 9-10. [2]Eph 1:1-12. [3]1 Jn 1:5. [4]Heb 1:3. [5]This would later become the slogan of the Arian party, which denied the eternity and thus the deity of the Son. [6]This, likewise, would be adopted later as the slogan Athanasius arranged for his party to spread abroad at Alexandria in an attempt to refute the Arian propaganda. Both parties in the early Arian crisis were calling on the authority of the great Origen. From this passage, it is clear that it is Athanasius, however, who has correctly interpreted him. [7]ECF 320. [8]Col 1:15. [9]Gen 1:26. [10]ECF 334.

did this happen?"[11] Those acts are above and beyond time. But, if one must speak childishly, they are simultaneous with the being of the Father. "When did the Father come to be?" There was not when he was not. The same applies to the Son and the Holy Spirit. Ask me again, and I shall answer you. "When was the Son begotten?"[12] When the Father was not begotten.[13] "When did the Spirit proceed?" When the Son did not proceed but was begotten timelessly, in a way we cannot understand. When we try to avoid the suggestion of temporality in illustrating timelessness, we are frustrated, for "when," and "before" and "originally" cannot be divested of temporal implication, however hard we try. The only thing we can do is to take eternity as denoting a period commensurate with supratemporal realities, a period not divided and measured by the course of the sun or any kind of motion, as time is measured. If those beings[14] are coeternal, must they not be equally without beginning? They derive from the first being,[15] though they are not after him. "Without beginning" implies "eternal." Yes; but "eternal" does not necessarily imply "without beginning," seeing that these beings are referred to the Father as their origin. Thus they are not without beginning in respect of cause. But it is clear that a cause is not necessarily prior in time to its effects, for the sun is not prior to the sunlight. Yet they are in a sense without beginning, in respect of time (even though you may use this notion as a bogey to scare simple minds), for they are not subject to time since time originates from them. ORATION 29.2.[16]

THE SON IS ONE WITH THE FATHER.

GREGORY OF NAZIANZUS: The Father is the principle of unity, for from him the other two derive their being, and in him they are drawn together: not so as to be fused together but so as to cohere. There is no separation in the Trinity, in terms of time or will or power. These factors make human beings a plurality, each individual at odds with one another and even with themselves. But unity properly belongs to those who have a single nature and whose essential being is the same.[17] ORATION 42.15.[18]

THE SON IS GENERATED TIMELESSLY.

GREGORY OF NYSSA: There will be no danger in pronouncing him[19] eternal and yet not ungenerate. On the one hand, because the existence of the Son is not marked by any intervals of time and the infinitude of his life flows back before the ages and onward beyond them in an all-pervading tide, he is properly addressed with the title of eternal. Again, on the other hand, because the thought of him as Son in fact and title gives us the thought of the Father as inalienably joined to it, he thereby stands clear of an ungenerate existence being imputed to him, while he is always with a Father who always is, as those inspired words of our Master[20] expressed it: "Bound by way of generation

---

[11] That is, when was the Son begotten of God—within time or outside of time? [12] The imaginary interlocutor asks him the question again. [13] And Gregory gives the paradoxical answer to show that the question is illegitimate. This is part of his overall theological strategy in his Orations, to argue that all of Arian theological logic is deeply questionable. [14] The persons of the Trinity. [15] The Father as cause (*aition*) of the Triunity. Gregory argues that the causal priority of an eternal reality does not imply precedence either in time or in status if that cause, as being in essence one and timeless, confers both eternity and coequality on what it causes from its own essence. The neo-Arians had argued that the causality of the Father logically necessitated that the Son and Spirit who came from him could be neither eternal nor fully divine. Gregory answers that it is their logic that is flawed, not the trinitarian faith of the church. God's essential causality, he implies, should not be confused with the divine causality (making) of creatures, since this does not proceed from the essence of God but from God's dynamic will and power. [16] *LCF* 117. [17] The Son and Spirit have no other being (or nature or essence) than that of the Father and so are essentially one with the Father, while still being personally (hypostatically) distinct. This is Gregory's classic account of why Christians, who confess the threefold divine hypostases of Father, Son and Spirit, are nevertheless confessing only one Godhead. [18] *LCF* 119-20*. [19] The divine Word, second person of the Trinity. [20] Gregory is referring to his brother, Basil of Caesarea.

to his Father's ungeneracy."[21] AGAINST EUNO-MIUS 1.42.[22]

THE SON IS ETERNAL SINCE HE IS GOD.
GREGORY OF NYSSA: For when the Evangelist, in his discourse concerning the nature of God, separates at all points nonexistence from him who is, and, by his constant repetition of the word was[23] carefully destroys the suspicion of nonexistence, and calls him the only-begotten God, the Word of God, the Son of God, equal with God, and all such names, we have this judgment fixed and settled in us, that if the only-begotten Son is God, we must believe that he who is believed to be God is eternal. And indeed he is truly God, and assuredly is eternal and is never at any time found to be nonexistent. For God, as we have often said, if he now is, also assuredly always was, and if he once was not, neither does he now exist at all. AGAINST EUNOMIUS 8.1.[24]

THERE WAS NO TIME WHEN HE DID NOT EXIST. GREGORY OF NYSSA: There are no intervals in the sphere of existence "before the ages," nor are there any differences of being. . . . The generation of the Son is not within time, any more than the creation was before time. It is utterly wrong to introduce division into an order of existence that admits no separation and to interpolate an interval of time into the creative cause of the universe by asserting that there was a time when the author of all existence did not exist. AGAINST EUNOMIUS 1.26.[25]

THE SON IS RADIANCE ALWAYS WITH THE SUN. JOHN CHRYSOSTOM: Someone may ask, "How can Christ be a Son, without being younger than the Father, for anything which derives its being must be later than its source?" We answer that such arguments suppose a human context, . . . though we are discussing the nature of God. . . . Come now, does the sun's radiance proceed from the sun's own sub-

stance, or from elsewhere? Any sensible person is bound to acknowledge that it proceeds from the sun's own substance. But although the radiance proceeds from the sun, we cannot assert that it is later in time than the substance of that body, for the sun has never appeared without its rays. . . . Why then do you not believe this to be so in the case of the invisible and ineffable nature? . . . That is why Paul calls him the "brightness,"[26] thus showing his derived existence and his coeternity. Moreover, were not all the ages and every measure of time created by him? . . . Therefore there is no interval of time between Son and the Father. If so, then the Son cannot be after but coeternal; since "before" and "after" are ideas that imply time. HOMILY 4 ON THE GOSPEL OF JOHN 1.[27]

THE SON IS ALWAYS WITH THE FATHER IN THE KINGDOM. COUNCIL OF SARDICA (343): But we believe and maintain and think that those holy words "I and the Father are one"[28] point out the oneness of the hypostasis,[29]

---

[21] The later Nicene generation, especially the Cappadocian fathers, had to wrestle with the problem posed by the late Arian party, led by Aetius and Eunomius, that "ingenerate" was a quintessential character of God. If the Son, by the admission of the Nicenes, was "generate of God the Father," then how could they claim that he was God, since he could not be ingenerate and generate at the same time? Gregory of Nazianzus answered the problem by pointing out that being ingenerate was not a statement of essence, divine or otherwise, but a statement of relationship, and so the Arians had their logic wrong. Gregory of Nyssa, however, here tries another line of argument, following the earlier thinker, Origen, and suggests that the Word has the character of generate and ingenerate. As he is from the Father, he is generate; but as he is from an eternal Father, there was never a time when he was not the begotten Son, and thus is, in effect, ingenerate insofar as he is eternal, just as the ingenerate Father is who has none other before him. [22]NPNF 2 5:100. [23]In the first verses of the Gospel of John. [24]NPNF 2 5:201. Scholars today often refer to this work as *Against Eunomius* book 3. [25]*LCF* 158. [26]Heb 1:3. [27]*LCF* 170. [28]Jn 10:30 [29]Here Theodoret is using the word *hypostasis* archaically (against the flow of the fifth century) to signify the divine nature (*ousia*). The later fifth-century church finally decided to adopt the advice of Gregory of Nazianzus, given at the end of the fourth century, that *ousia* should be reserved as word for "nature" and *hypostasis* should designate "persons" in the Trinity, but here and there, as in this case, one still met with examples of archaic language. Theodoret means

which is one both of the Father and of the Son. We also believe that the Son reigns with the Father, that his reign has neither beginning nor end and that it is not bounded by time or subject to any contingencies, for what has always existed can never have commenced and can never terminate. THEODORET ECCLESIAS-TICAL HISTORY 2.8.47.[30]

THE SON HAD NO BEGINNING. COUNCIL OF CHALCEDON (451):[31] Those who say,[32] "There was when the Son of God was not," and "Before he was begotten he was not," and "He came into being from things that are not," or "He is of another substance or essence," or "He is mutable or alterable," the catholic and apostolic church anathematizes. CONCILIAR ANATHEMAS.[33]

THE TWO BIRTHS OF THE SON OF GOD. SECOND COUNCIL OF CONSTANTINOPLE (553): If any do not confess that there are two generations of God the Word, one before the ages of the Father, nontemporal and bodiless, the other at the last days when the same came down from heaven and was incarnate of the holy, glorious, *Theotokos*[34] and ever-virgin Mary, and born of her, let them be anathema. ANATHEMA 2.[35]

The Eternal Father of the Son

THE SON IS SO BY NATURE, NOT ADOPTION. ORIGEN: We are forbidden the impiety of supposing that the way in which God the Father begets and sustains his only-begotten Son is equivalent to the begetting of human by human or animal by animal. There is here a great difference, so it is fitting that this should be so, since nothing can be found in existence or conceived or imagined that can compare with God. Human thought cannot apprehend how the unbegotten God becomes the Father of the only-begotten Son. For it is an eternal and ceaseless generation, as radiance is gener-

ated from light. For he does not become the Son externally, by the adoption of the Spirit, but he is by nature the Son. He is the radiance of the eternal light, the unblemished mirror of the activity of God and the image of his goodness.[36] As we said before, we refer to Wisdom as deriving its existence only from him who is the beginning of all things, and from him all wisdom has its origin, for he alone is Son by nature; and this is why he is called Only-Begotten. ON FIRST PRINCIPLES 1.2.4-5.[37]

THE SON IS ETERNALLY BEGOTTEN. ORIGEN: The existence of the Son is generated by the Father. This must be accepted by those who profess that nothing is ungenerate, that is with underived existence, except only God the Father. For caution is needed lest anyone should fall into those absurd fables invented by those who picture for themselves some kind of prolations,[38] so as to assign parts to the divine nature and to divide the essential being of God the Father. . . . Rather as an act of will proceeds from the mind without cutting a part off the mind, or being separated or divided from it, in some such way the Father is to be thought of as begetting the Son. ON FIRST PRINCIPLES 1.2.6.[39]

GOD'S REASON WAS ETERNALLY WITHIN HIM. TERTULLIAN: Before all things existed, God was alone. He was himself his own universe, his own place, everything. He was alone in the sense that there was nothing external to him, nothing outside his own being. Yet even then he was not alone, for he had with him something that was part of his own being,

---

that the Father and Son have the same nature, not that they are the same person. [30]CCC 18. [31]Citing the Creed of Nicaea (325). [32]The Arian party. [33]CCC 335. [34]The God-birther, or mother of God, the title of the Virgin defined at the Council of Ephesus (431) to signify the divinity of the Christ. [35]LCC 3:379. [36]See Col 1:15; Heb 1:3; Wis 7:25. [37]ECF 318-319**. [38]Origen is referring to the second-century Gnostics who envisaged a series of divine emanations mediating between the supreme Godhead and the lower worlds. [39]ECF 319.

namely, his Reason.[40] For God is rational, and Reason existed first with him, and from him extended to all things. That Reason is his own consciousness of himself. The Greeks call it *Logos*, which is the term we use for discourse,[41] and thus our people usually translate it literally as, "Discourse was in the beginning with God,"[42] although it would be more correct to regard Reason as anterior to Discourse, because there was not Discourse with God from the beginning, but there was Reason, even before the beginning, and because Discourse takes its origin from Reason and thus shows Reason to be prior to it, as the ground of its being. Yet even so there is no real difference. Although God had not yet uttered his Discourse, he had it in his own being, with and in his Reason, and he silently pondered and arranged in his thought those things that he was soon to say by his Discourse.[43] AGAINST PRAXEAS 5.[44]

THE WORD IS EVERLASTING BRIGHTNESS. ATHANASIUS: Was God "who is," ever without reason?[45] Was he, "who is light," without radiance? Or was he always the Father of the Word? . . . Who can endure to hear them say that God was ever without reason . . . or that God was not always Father? . . . God is, eternally. Thus, since the Father always is, his brightness exists eternally, and that is his Word. Again, God "who is" has, derived from himself, the Word who also "is."[46] The Word has not supervened from previous nonexistence, nor was the Father once without reason [Word]. . . . If a person looked at the sun and asked, concerning its radiance, "Did that which is make something that did not exist before, or something that already existed?" he would not be regarded as reasoning sensibly; he would in fact be crazy in supposing that what comes from the light is something external to it and asking when and where and whether it was made. Such reasoning and such questions about the Son and the Father would display a greater degree of insanity, for this is to make the Word an external addition to the

Father and to speak erroneously of a natural offspring as created thing by saying, "He did not exist before he was begotten."[47] AGAINST THE ARIANS 1.24-25.[48]

BEGOTTEN BEFORE ALL CREATION. COUNCIL OF SARDICA (343): It is most absurd to affirm that the Father ever existed without the Son, for that this could never be the case has been testified by the Son, who said, "I am in the Father, and the Father in me,"[49] and, "I and the Father are one."[50] We cannot deny that he was begotten, but we say that he was begotten before all things, which are called visible and invisible, and that he is the creator and artificer of archangels and angels, and of the world and of the human species. It is written, "Wisdom which made all things has taught me,"[51] and again, "All things were made by him."[52] THEODORET ECCLESIASTICAL HISTORY 2.8.41-42.[53]

THE AUTHOR OF TIME. GREGORY OF NAZIANZUS: The apostle writes, "From him, and through him and for him are all things: to him be the glory forever, Amen."[54] The Father is Father and without beginning, for he is underived. The Son is Son, and not without beginning, in the sense that he derives from the Father. But if one is thinking of a temporal beginning, then the Son is indeed without

---

[40]His Logos, or Word. [41]That is, *Logos* was also the common word in Greek for a rhetorical oration or speech. [42]The common translation of "Word" (Jn 1:1) has endured to this day, but Tertullian argues that "Mind" would have been a better version of the Greek. [43]Tertullian is here reflecting on the tradition of the earlier theologians who had preceded him (the Apologists), who had generally envisaged the dynamic utterance of the divine Word from God the Father as an act of the creation of the material world. Thus, the Logos was God's primary agent of creation. They had also made the distinction Tertullian is alluding to between God's immanent wisdom (*Logos endiathetos*) and his expressed or spoken Reason/Word (*Logos prophorikos*). [44]ECF 162-63. [45]Or, Word. [46]Divine existence is self-existence and is to be referred to only in the continuous present, resisting the past or future tenses as inappropriate. "He who is" is the quintessential divine name as revealed to Moses at the epiphany of the burning bush. [47]A central tenet of the Arian school. [48]ECF 382. [49]Jn 14:10-11. [50]Jn 10:30. [51]Wis 7:22. [52]Jn 1:3. [53]CCC 17. [54]Rom 11:36.

beginning, for the author of time is not subject to time. ORATION 39.12.[55]

THE SON ORIGINATES ETERNALLY FROM GOD.

GREGORY OF NAZIANZUS: That which is without beginning, and the beginning, and that which is with the beginning,[56] these are one God. Neither lack of beginning or lack of generation constitutes the nature of that which has no beginning: for an entity's nature is never constituted by what it is not but by what it is; it is defined by positing what it is, not by removing what it is not.[57] The Beginning[58] is not separated, by virtue of its being a beginning, from that which has no beginning,[59] for beginning is not the nature of the former, nor is lack of beginning the nature of the latter. These are attributes of the nature, not the nature itself.[60] And that which is with the Unoriginate and with the Originate[61] is not something other than what they are. But the Unoriginate has the name of Father; the Originate has the name of Son; that which is "with the Originate" is called the Holy Spirit. But these three have the same nature, namely, Godhead.[62] ORATION 42.15.[63]

DIFFERENT IN PERSON BUT THE SAME IN GODHEAD.

GREGORY OF NYSSA: The idea of cause differentiates the persons of the holy Trinity, declaring that one exists without a Cause and another is of the Cause.[64] Moreover the divine nature is understood by all to be unchangeable and undivided. For these reasons we rightly declare the Godhead to be one, and God to be one, and employ in the singular all other names that express divine attributes.[65] ON NOT THREE GODS.[66]

DIFFERENT MODES OF THE SELFSAME BEING.

GREGORY OF NYSSA: But in speaking of cause and of the cause, we do not by these words denote nature (for no one would give the same definition of "cause" and of "nature"), but we indicate the difference in manner of existence.[67] For when we say that one is caused and that the other is without cause, we do not divide the nature by the word *cause* but only indicate the fact that the Son does not exist without generation, nor the Father by generation. ON NOT THREE GODS.[68]

---

[55]*LCF* 119. [56]Gregory is referring to the Father in a dense set of allusions here as the one without beginning (*anarchos*: as deriving existence from no one) and to the Son as the one who has beginning (*archē*: insofar as he is referred to in this way in Jn 1:1, has the Father as his principle and is himself the *archē* or principle of the created order) and to the Spirit as the "one with the Arche" or the "one with the Son" (the *synarchos*, or coprinciple). [57]Gregory is attacking the neo-Arian claim that ingenerateness was the quintessential description of deity, and since the Son was generate of the Father, he could not be divine. Elsewhere he usually argues that ingeneracy describes only relationship, not nature (thus one can make a statement about the Son's person/*hypostasis*, but not one about the status of his divine nature/*ousia*); but in this instance he also argues that a term of negation (ingeneracy) cannot logically define the concept of God in any sense, since God is an all-positive being and negative semantic terms cannot approach the idea. The neo-Arians had made much of their skill in logic and used it to attack the concept of the divine eternity of the Son, which is why Gregory spends time deconstructing their logical pretensions. [58]The Son. [59]The Father. [60]That is, the priority seemingly invoked by the concept of the Father originating the Son is not an issue of the divine nature at all, despite what the Arians had implied. If the divine nature is essentially timeless, the priority of the Father must be equally timeless, and the Son's "origination" no less timeless since it derives from the timeless one in eternity. Thus in no way can a timeless origination be said to affect the status of the Son's divinity, as the Arians had implied. [61]The Holy Spirit. [62]In other words, the specific names designate the distinct *hypostases* or persons of the Trinity, but the common nature (*ousia*) of all three is the selfsame divine being of the Father. If the Son and Spirit differ from the Father in terms of their manner of origination (differing in *hypostasis*, that is), they do not differ at all from the Father in terms of nature (*ousia*). [63]*LCF* 119. [64]The Father is uncaused; the Son is caused. [65]Everything that can be referred to God denotes the divine nature, as such, and is common to all three divine persons in the Trinity. However, being uncaused and being caused clearly differentiate the Father and the Son, and so these particular characteristics do not refer to the divine nature as such (which is common in all respects and in all ways) but must refer rather to the divine *hypostases* (the characteristics of the distinct persons who all share the selfsame single nature). [66]*CCC* 114 (PG 45:133-36). [67]The causality of the Father and the origination of the Son are not attributable as characters of being (differences that are in the natures of Father and Son, which would make the Son different from God), since both Father and Son have the selfsame nature. The causality and origination are, on the contrary, modes of being (*tropoi hyparxeos*), not attributes of being; that is, they are different ways of personalizing the same reality. [68]*CCC* 114 (PG 45:133).

The Son Is Uncreated but Generated.
Gregory of Nyssa: We regard the Trinity as
consummately perfect and incomprehensibly
excellent, yet as containing clear distinctions
within itself that reside in the peculiarities[69] of
each of the persons: as possessing invariableness
by virtue of its common attribute of uncreatedness[70] but differentiated by the unique character
of each person. This peculiarity contemplated
in each sharply and clearly divides one from the
other. The Father, for instance, is uncreated and
ungenerated as well. He was never generated any
more than he was created. While this uncreatedness is common to him and the Son and the
Spirit, he is ungenerate as well as Father. This is
peculiar and uncommunicable, being not seen in
the other persons. The Son in his uncreatedness
touches the Father and the Spirit, but as the Son
and the Only-Begotten he has a character that is
not that of the Almighty or of the Holy Spirit.
Against Eunomius 1.22.[71]

**The Concept of Father Indicates That
of Son.** Gregory of Nyssa: In regard to essence he is one, and so the Lord ordained that
we should look to one name.[72] But in regard
to the attributes indicative of the persons, our
belief in him is distinguished into belief in
the Father, the Son and the Holy Spirit. He is
divided without separation and united without confusion.[73] For when we hear the title
"Father," we apprehend the meaning to be this,
that the name is not understood with reference
to itself alone but also by its special significa-
tion indicates the relation to the Son. For the
term "Father" would have no meaning apart by
itself, if "Son" were not connoted by the utterance of the word *Father*. When we learned the
name "Father," we were taught at the same time,
and by that selfsame title, faith also in the Son.
Against Eunomius 2.2.[74]

The Eternal Son of the Father

The Eternal Son Appears at Time's

End. Ignatius of Antioch: Since, therefore,
in the persons mentioned above I have by faith
seen and loved the whole congregation, I have
this advice: Be eager to do everything in godly
harmony; the bishop presiding in the place
of God and the presbyters in the place of the
council of the apostles, and the deacons, who
are most dear to me, having been entrusted with
the service of Jesus Christ, who before the ages
was with the Father and appeared at the end of
time. Let all, therefore, accept the same attitude
as God and respect one another, and let no one
regard his neighbor in merely human terms, but
in Jesus Christ love one another always. To the
Magnesians 6.1-2.[75]

**The Son Teaches That the Father Is
Above All.** Irenaeus: If anyone asks why it is
that the Lord has made it plain that "the Father
alone knows the hour and the day,"[76] although
he has communion with the Son in all things,
he could not at present find an answer more
suitable or more proper or less perilous than
this: that we may learn from our Lord himself
(our one true teacher) that the Father is above
all. As he says, "The Father is greater than I."[77]
Our Lord has proclaimed that the Father is superior in respect of knowledge to the intent that
we should leave to God complete knowledge and

---

[69]*Idiomata*: individual characteristics that define each of the three
hypostases (persons). For the Father, it is ingeneracy; for the Son,
it is begottenness; for the Spirit, it is procession from the Father.
The patristic writers regarded these *idiomata* as great mysteries
of the complex unity of the inner being of God, not just semantic
niceties, but were not willing to elaborate much on their meanings,
as they generally believed such things ought not to be spoken about
in public theological discourse—indeed, that such things could not
be spoken about by limited human intelligences. [70]Each person,
that is, is uncreated, as this is a common character of the divine
nature (*ousia*) common to all three. [71]NPNF 2 5:61. [72]The Godhead must be confessed as one, as in the standard invocation of
liturgical prayer: "In the name of the Father, and of the Son and of
the Holy Spirit." There is only one name for all, not three names.
[73]A generation later the fathers of the Council of Chalcedon (451)
will reapply this phrase of Gregory's to describe the union of the
two natures in Christ. [74]NPNF 2 5:102**. By modern scholars
this is often known as the "Refutation of Eunomius's Apology."
[75]*AF* 153-55. [76]Mt 24:36. [77]Jn 14:28.

questions such as this,[78] so long as we are subject to the conditions of this world. AGAINST HERESIES 2.28.8.[79]

THE SON MAKES THE FATHER KNOWN.
IRENAEUS: The Son always coexists with the Father and has revealed the Father from of old, from the beginning. AGAINST HERESIES 2.30.9.[80]

THE SON IS THE WISDOM OF GOD. ORIGEN: We must first recognize that there is a distinction between the nature of the deity in Christ, as the only-begotten Son of the Father, and his human nature, which he took in these last times in fulfillment of God's purpose. And first we must examine the nature of the only-begotten Son. . . . The only-begotten Son of God is his Wisdom existing substantially. . . . How could anyone believe that God the Father could have existed at any time without begetting Wisdom? . . . For that would be to say either that God could not beget Wisdom before he did beget it . . . or that he could have done so but did not wish to . . . and either supposition is patently absurd and impious. We must believe that Wisdom is without any beginning. . . . He is called the Word because he is, as it were, the interpreter of the secrets of the mind of God. ON FIRST PRINCIPLES 1.2.1-3.[81]

THE SON BORN TIMELESSLY. ORIGEN: No one can be a father without the existence of a son. . . . The title of Omnipotent cannot be older than that of Father, for it is through the Son that the Father is omnipotent.[82] . . . All things were subjected by means of wisdom, that is, word and reason. . . . This is the fairest and clearest glory of omnipotence, when all things are subjected by reason and wisdom, not by force and constraint. . . . The existence of the Son derives from the Father, but not in time, nor does it have any beginning, except in the sense that it starts from God. ON FIRST PRINCIPLES 1.2.10.[83]

THE SON DOES NOT DIMINISH THE DIVINE UNITY. TERTULLIAN: But I derive the Son from no other source but from the substance of the Father. I describe him as doing nothing without the Father's will, as receiving all power from the Father. How then can I be abolishing the monarchy from the faith when I safeguard it in the Son, as handed down to the Son by the Father? Let this assertion be taken as applying also to the third degree of the Godhead, since I regard the Spirit as having come from no other source but from the Father, through the Son. Have a care then that it is not rather you who abolish the monarchy in overthrowing its order and mode of working that is arranged in as many persons as God wished. But so surely does the monarchy remain unimpaired, despite the introduction of a trinity, that it has to be restored by the Son to the Father.[84] . . . We see, then, that the Son is no detriment to the monarchy, although it is now vested in the Son, because it remains unimpaired while thus vested, and the Son will restore it unimpaired to the Father. . . . He who has delivered the kingdom, and he to whom he has delivered it, must necessarily be two. AGAINST PRAXEAS 4.[85]

THE SON REIGNS WITH HIS FATHER. MARCELLUS OF ANCYRA: But following the holy Scriptures I believe that there is one God and his only-begotten Son or Word, who ever exists with the Father and has never in any sense had a beginning of existence, truly having his being from God, not created, not made, but ever being

---

[78] Thus, the confession of ignorance by Christ was an economic one. It was not meant to show the innate separation of human and divine consciousness in the Lord; rather, it was meant to discourage the apostles from speculations about the end time, which would not be profitable to them. [79]ECF 106. [80]ECF 104. [81]ECF 318. [82]Origen's argument here is that the Father is revealed to the world as the omnipotent One because the Son, as his wisdom, was the agent of creation. It is because all things are subjected to the Father through Christ the Logos that the Father enjoys the "glory" of omnipotence in the confession of the creation. [83]ECF 320-21. [84]Tertullian refers to such biblical texts as Ps 110:1; 1 Cor 15:24, 27-28. [85]ECF 161-62.

with, ever reigning with God and the Father, "of whose kingdom," according to the testimony of the apostle, "there shall be no end."[86] He is Son, he is Power, he is Wisdom. He is the peculiar and true Word of God, our Lord Jesus Christ, inseparable from God, "through whom all things were made that were made."[87] The Gospel testifies to him, saying, "In the beginning was the Word, and the Word was with God, and the Word was God. All things were made by him, and without him was not anything made." This is the Word about whom Luke the Evangelist also bears witness, saying, "Even as they delivered to us who from the beginning were eyewitnesses and ministers of the Word."[88] About him David also spoke: "My heart has uttered a good Word."[89] So also does our Lord Jesus Christ teach us through the Gospel, saying, "I came forth from the Father and am come."[90] He in the last days came down for our salvation, and, born from the Virgin Mary, assumed manhood. LETTER TO POPE JULIUS.[91]

THE FATHER ALWAYS HAS HIS SON BESIDE HIM. ATHANASIUS: The Son is implied with the Father, for one cannot use the title "father" unless a son exists; whereas in calling God "maker" we do not necessarily signify the things that come into being; for a maker is before his works. But in calling God "Father" we at once intimate the Son's existence. Therefore whoever believes in the Son believes in the Father, for he believes in what belongs to the Father's substance; and thus there is one faith in one God. And whoever worships and honors the Son worships and honors the Father, for the Godhead is one; and therefore there is one honor and one worship that is given to the Father in and through the Son. And one who worships thus worships one God. AGAINST THE ARIANS 3.6.[92]

THE SON DOES NOT ORIGINATE WITHIN HISTORY. CYRIL OF JERUSALEM: For godliness it is enough for you to know, as we have said, that God has one only Son, one naturally

begotten, who did not begin his being when he was born in Bethlehem but was before all ages. Hear the prophet Micah saying, "And you, Bethlehem, house of Ephrata, are small to be among the thousands of Judah. But from you shall come forth a Ruler, who shall feed my people Israel. His proceeding is from the beginning, from the days of eternity.[93] So, do not think of him who is now come forth from Bethlehem, but worship him who was eternally begotten of the Father. Do not allow anyone to speak of a beginning of the Son in time, but as a timeless beginning acknowledge the Father.[94] For the Father is the beginning of the Son, timeless, incomprehensible, without beginning. The fountain of the river of righteousness, even of the Only-Begotten, is the Father, who begot him as he alone knows how.[95] Know this too, that our Lord Jesus Christ is King eternal. CATECHETICAL LECTURES 11.20.[96]

THE SON IS ALWAYS WITH THE FATHER. COUNCIL OF SARDICA (343): If he had had a beginning, he could not have always existed, for the ever-existent Word does not have a beginning. God will never have an end. We do not say that the Father is the Son or that the Son is the Father, but that the Father is the Father and that the Son is the Son of the Father. We confess that the Son is the Word of God the Father and that beside him there is no other. We believe the Word to be true God, wisdom and power. We affirm that he is truly Son, yet not in the way in which people are said to be children, for they are said to be the

---

[86]Lk 1:33. Marcellus had been accused of teaching the Son would hand over the kingdom to the Father at the final end and be reabsorbed back into a divine monad. Here he distances himself from that position. [87]Jn 1:1-3. [88]Lk 1:2. [89]Ps 44:2 (LXX). [90]Jn 16:28. [91]CCC 9-10, found in Epiphanius *Panarion* 72.2.6-9. [92]ECF 395-96. [93]Mic 5:2; Mt 2:6. [94]The phrase works as a word play in Greek: the Father is a timeless *archē* (principle, origin), and so the Son who comes from him must be timelessly originated. [95]All patristic thought reserves the knowledge of the manner of the trinitarian origins of the hypostases as something only God can comprehend. [96]NPNF 2 7:69*.

sons of God on account of their regeneration or of their merit, and not on account of their being of one *hypostasis*[97] with the Father, as is the Son. Theodoret Ecclesiastical History 2.8.42-43.[98]

The Son Is Always Light from Light.

Gregory of Nyssa: And if the Son, always appearing with the thought of the Father, is always found in the category of existence, what danger is there in owning the eternity of the Only-Begotten, who "has neither beginning of days nor end of life."[99] For as he is Light from Light, Life from Life, Good from Good, and Wise, Just, Strong, and all else in the same way, so most certainly is he Eternal from Eternal. Against Eunomius 1.42.[100]

The Son Is in the Eternity of the Father.

Gregory of Nyssa: As, then, being in the incorruptibility of the Father, he is incorruptible, good in his goodness, powerful in his might, and, as being in each of these attributes of special excellence that are conceived of the Father, he is that particular thing, so, also, being in his eternity, he is assuredly eternal. Now the eternity of the Father is marked by his never having taken his being from nonexistence and never terminating his being in nonexistence. He, therefore, "who has all things that are the Father's"[101] and is contemplated in all the glory of the Father, even as, being in the endlessness of the Father, he has no end, so, being in the unoriginateness of the Father, he has, as the apostle says, "no beginning of days"[102] but at once is "of the Father" and is regarded "in the eternity of the Father." Against Eunomius 8.1.[103]

Difference and Sameness with the Father.

Gregory of Nyssa: The characteristic of the Father's person (hypostasis) cannot be transferred to the Son or the Spirit, nor, on the other hand, can that of the Son be accommodated to one of the others, or the property

(*idiōma*) of the Spirit be attributed to the Father and the Son. But the incommunicable distinction of the properties is considered in the common nature.[104] It is the characteristic of the Father to exist without cause. This does not apply to the Son and the Spirit, for the Son "went out from the Father,"[105] as says the Scripture, and the "Spirit proceeds from God"[106] and from the Father, but as the being without cause, which belongs only to the Father, cannot be adapted to the Son and the Spirit, so again the being caused, which is the property of the Son and of the Spirit, cannot, by its very nature, be considered in the Father. On the other hand, the state of being "not ungenerated" is common to the Son and the Spirit;[107] hence, in order to avoid confusion in the subject, one must again search for the pure difference in the properties, so that what is common be safeguarded, yet what is proper be not mixed. On the Lord's Prayer 3.[108]

The Son Is Almighty and Eternal.

Leo the Great: And not knowing what to believe about the incarnation, Eutyches should have at

---

[97] The fourth-century council is using the word *hypostasis* in the archaic sense here (signifying "nature"). Already by the fifth century it had become traditional to use *ousia* to connote nature and *hypostasis* to denote persons in the context of trinitarian language. Theodoret is trying to justify his antipathy to being forced to consistent semantics (in the context of the fifth-century christological controversy) by appealing to older texts, though eventually he did conform to the new semantic rules. [98] CCC 17. [99] Heb 7:3. [100] NPNF 2 5:99-100. [101] Jn 16:15. [102] Heb 7:3. [103] NPNF 2 5:201*. This text is sometimes called *Against Eunomius* book 3. [104] That is, what is distinctive to each of the three persons of the Trinity has to be considered in the overarching light that all three have the selfsame divine nature. [105] Jn 16:27. [106] Jn 15:26. [107] That is, the Son and the Holy Spirit share the distinct character (peculiar to their divinity) of being generated of the Father: the Son by the generation of filiation, the Spirit by the generation of procession. The Cappadocian fathers are emphatic that the Father is the single, common Cause of both the other two *hypostases* and that this unique causal dynamism is the root of the divine unity within the holy Trinity—being itself none other than the monarchy of the Father. This is why the Greek tradition always tended to resist the later Latin development of the *Filioque* (the attribution of the Son's pretemporal role in the procession of the divine Spirit). [108] ACW 18:54-55*.

least received with patient hearing that general and uniform confession in which the whole body of the faithful profess to believe: In God the Father almighty, and in Jesus Christ his only Son, our Lord, who was born of the Holy Spirit and the Virgin Mary, by which three statements the devices of well-nigh all heretics are overthrown. For when God is believed to be both almighty and Father, it follows that the Son is shown to be coeternal with him, differing in nothing from the Father,[109] because he was born "God of God," Almighty of Almighty, Coeternal of Eternal; not later in time or inferior in power or dissimilar in glory or divided in essence; but the same only-begotten, eternal Son of the eternal Father was born of the Holy Spirit and the Virgin Mary. LETTER 28.2 (THE TOME OF LEO).[110]

The Son's Unique Filiation and Sonship

THE FATHER UTTERS A GOOD WORD. TERTULLIAN: This mode of operation of the divine consciousness is revealed in the Scripture also under the title of Wisdom. . . . Notice that Wisdom speaks, as created[111] as a second person: "The Lord created me as the beginning of his ways, for his works."[112] . . . That is, he created and begot his own consciousness.[113] . . . When God first willed to create,[114] . . . he first produced the Word, which had within it its own inseparable reason and wisdom, so that all things might come to be through that by which they had been pondered and arranged, yes, and already made, in God's consciousness; all they lacked was to be openly apprehended and grasped in their own forms and concrete existences.[115] This then is the time when the Word takes on itself its outward manifestation and dress, that is, sound and utterance, when God said, "Let there be light."[116] This was the entire nativity of the Word, when it proceeded from God, who created it for thinking with the title of Wisdom . . . and begot it to put the thought into effect. . . . Then the Word makes God his

Father, since by proceeding from him he became the first-begotten Son: first begotten, as begotten before all things; Only-Begotten, as begotten uniquely from the womb of his heart, as the Father bears witness: "My heart has uttered a good Word."[117] AGAINST PRAXEAS 6-7.[118]

THE SON IS CHANGELESS. ATHANASIUS: It is superfluous to examine their question: "Is the Word capable of change?"[119] It is enough merely to write down the kind of things they say, to show their reckless impiety. They ask such nonsensical questions as "Has he free will, or not?" "Is he good from choice, of free will, and can he change, if he so will, being by nature capable of change?" . . . It is blasphemy even to utter such things. For if the Word were capable of change and alteration, where will he come to a stop, and what will be the end of his development? And how will the changeable possibly be like the changeless? In which of his states will we be able to see the Father in him? . . . And how can he be wholly "in the Father," if his moral decision is undetermined? Perhaps he is not yet

---

[109]As Gregory has pointed out above, this does not apply to the *hypostases*, for the Son and the Spirit are not uncaused, but does apply to the single divine *ousia* (nature) because this is not merely the same (as generically understood) for all three hypostases; rather, it is concretely the same, that is, it is the selfsame nature of the Father that the Son and the Spirit possess. They have none other than the Father's nature, which is why the three are one. [110]CCC 315-16. [111]That is "made." In Tertullian's day, before the great Arian crisis of the fourth century, theologians were not troubled by using this term to denote the making of the Son by the Father (that is, to connote the Son's birth from God). After the Arian crisis, however, the term and this proof text from Scripture became an instance of the question whether the Logos was created (that is, was a creature among creatures), and no orthodox theologian ever again would be as free and easy with these terms. [112]Prov 8:22. [113]It is clear from this that Tertullian does not mean to impute creaturely status to the Logos. [114]Here he means when the Father first willed the creation of the cosmos. [115]The doctrine of the Apologists, that the wisdom of God was the primary agent of the creation of the material world. To effect what God's mind had immanently conceived, the Logos was uttered (that is, the immanent Logos, *endiathetos*, becomes the externally active Logos *prophorikos*). [116]Gen 1:3. [117]Ps 44:2 (LXX). [118]ECF 163-64. [119]The Arians had argued that the Word, because he was not eternal as the Father was, was therefore *treptos*, or changeable, like all other creatures.

perfect, since he is changeable and is developing day by day! . . . But he must be perfect, if he is equal with God. Against the Arians 1.35.[120]

The Maker of All Rational Life. Cyril of Jerusalem: Do not separate the Son from the Father, and never make a confusion by believing in a Son-Fatherhood.[121] Instead, believe that there is one only-begotten Son, from one God, who is before all ages God the Word. He is not a spoken word that is diffused into the air and cannot be compared with such impersonal words. He is the Word, the Son, the Maker of all who partake of reason, the Word who hears the Father and himself speaks. Catechetical Lectures 4.8.[122]

The Father Gives Dominion to the Son. Cyril of Jerusalem: This is the first proof:[123] receive now a second plain one. "The Lord said to my Lord, sit on my right hand."[124] The Lord says this to the Lord, not to a servant, but to the Lord of all, and to his own Son, to whom he put all things in subjection.[125] "But when he said that all things are put under him, it is clear that he is excepted, which did put all things under him,"[126] and what follows; that God may be all in all. The only-begotten Son is Lord of all things and is still the obedient Son of the Father, because "he did not grasp after dominion"[127] but received it by nature of the Father's own will. The Son did not grasp it, and neither did the Father grudge to give him it. Catechetical Lectures 10.9.[128]

The Son's Birth, an Awesome Mystery. Cyril of Jerusalem: For my part I have always been amazed by the curiosity of these bold people who fall into impiety imagining it to be reverence. Though they know nothing of thrones, and dominions, and principalities and powers, which are the workmanship of Christ, still they attempt to scrutinize their Creator. Tell me first, O most daring person, how does throne differ from dominion, and

then scrutinize what pertains to Christ. Tell me what is a principality, what is a power and what is a virtue, or what is an angel? After that you can search out their Creator, for "all things were made by him."[129] But you will not, indeed cannot, ask thrones or dominions. What else is there that "knows the deep things of God,"[130] except the Holy Spirit, who spoke the divine Scriptures? But not even the Holy Spirit has spoken in the Scriptures concerning the generation of the Son from the Father. So why are you busying yourself about things that not even the Holy Spirit has written in the Scriptures? Catechetical Lectures 11.12.[131]

The Son, Always in the Bosom of the Father. Gregory of Nyssa: But in fact the Deity is incapable of change and alteration. So, everything that is excellent and good is always contemplated in the fountain of excellence. But "the only-begotten God, who is in the bosom of the Father,"[132] is excellent, and beyond all excellence. Mark you, he always says, "who is in the bosom of the Father," not "who came to be" there. Against Eunomius 2.2.[133]

The Majestic Son Born Among Us. Ephrem the Syrian: Above and below there were two harbingers for the Son: the star of light shouted out joyfully from above,[134] and John proclaimed from below.[135] Two harbingers: both

---

[120]ECF 383*. [121]The hyphenated Son-Fatherism (*huiopator*) was an ironical way in which the patristic period referred to the second-century modalist Adoptionist who did not admit any distinctness of person between the Father and the Son but saw them as simply different modes of operation of the one and same divine person. [122]NPNF 2 7:21**. [123]Cyril has been giving scriptural demonstrations of the divine equality of the Son. [124]Acts 2:34. [125]Heb 2:8. [126]1 Cor 15:27. [127]Phil 2:6. [128]NPNF 2 7:59**. [129]Jn 1:3. [130]Job 11:7; 1 Cor 2:10. [131]NPNF 2 7:67**. [132]Jn 1:18. [133]NPNF 2 5:102. Modern scholars sometimes refer to this text as "The Refutation of Eunomius's Apology." [134]At the nativity in Bethlehem: his first epiphany among humankind. [135]At the baptism, his second epiphany. The ancient Eastern church celebrated the two events, Christmas and baptism, at the liturgical feast of Epiphany on January 6. Only in the early fifth century did the East start to add the Latin custom of observing December 25 as a nativity festival.

an earthly one and a heavenly one. That heavenly one showed his nature that is from God's majesty. And the earthly one also showed his nature that is from humanity. O great wonder! that his divinity and his humanity were announced by them. Whoever considered him earthly the star of light would convince that he was heavenly. And whoever considered him spiritual,[136] John would convince that he was also bodily.[137] HYMNS ON THE NATIVITY 6.9-11.[138]

A BABY MORE ANCIENT THAN HIS

MOTHER. EPHREM THE SYRIAN: Who indeed has seen the baby who is more ancient than his bearer? The ancient One entered and became young in her. He emerged an infant and grew by her milk. He entered and became small in her. He emerged and grew through her— a great wonder! HYMNS ON THE NATIVITY 12.1.[139]

---

[136]That is, only having a semblance of material flesh (Docetism). [137]By virtue of baptizing Jesus physically in the waters. [138]ESH 112. [139]ESH 133*.

GOD FROM GOD

καὶ εἰς ἕνα κύριον Ἰησοῦν Χριστὸν,	Et in unum Dominum Jesum Christum,	We believe in one Lord, Jesus Christ,
τὸν υἱὸν τοῦ Θεοῦ τὸν μονογενῆ,	Filium Dei unigenitum,	the only Son of God,
τὸν ἐκ τοῦ πατρὸς γεννηθέντα	et ex Patre natum	eternally
πρὸ πάντων τῶν αἰώνων,	ante omnia saecula	begotten of the Father,
φῶς ἐκ φωτός,	[Deum de Deo], Lumen de Lumine,	[God from God], Light from Light,
Θεὸν ἀληθινὸν ἐκ θεοῦ ἀληθινοῦ,	Deum verum de Deo vero,	true God from true God,
γεννηθέντα, οὐ ποιηθέντα,	genitum, non factum,	begotten, not made,
ὁμοούσιον τῷ πατρὶ·	consubstantialem Patri;	of one Being with the Father.
δι' οὗ τὰ πάντα ἐγένετο·	per quem omnia facta sunt;	Through him all things were made.
τὸν δι' ἡμᾶς τοὺς ἀνθρώπους	qui propter nos homines	For us
καὶ διὰ τὴν ἡμετέραν σωτηρίαν	et propter nostram salutem	and for our salvation
κατελθόντα ἐκ τῶν οὐρανῶν	descendit de coelis,	he came down from heaven:
καὶ σαρκωθέντα ἐκ πνεύματος ἁγίου	et incarnatus est de Spiritu Sancto	by the power of the Holy Spirit
καὶ Μαρίας τῆς παρθένου	ex Maria virgine,	he became incarnate from the Virgin Mary,
καὶ ἐνανθρωπήσαντα,	et homo factus est;	and was made man.

HISTORICAL CONTEXT: The creedal affirmation of the belief that the Son was "God from God" is an element that predates the Nicene controversy and once more stands as a synopsis of the church's generic New Testament confession of the divine status of the Son, as the Word of God sent from the Father's side. It reflects the scriptural sense of the divinity of Jesus as marked in such passages as John 1:1-2, John 1:18,[1] John 8:42, John 20:28, 1 Timothy 3:16,[2]

---

[1]"The only-begotten God," the reading of the earliest New Testament manuscripts. [2]Several of the ancient New Testament manuscripts read "God manifested in the flesh."

Colossians 2:9, and elsewhere. This notion of the deity of the Son is not spelled out in great detail. In the New Testament passages where it occurs, the sense is primarily related to the notion of the divine power and honor that the Son enjoys as the heavenly apostle *(shaliach)* of the divine Father. But the church was deeply rooted in the prophetic Scriptures, and the Christian communities shared the sensitivity of the synagogue in late antiquity, that Godhead was not a title to be loosely bandied about in the manner of the Gentiles, with their many lords and gods.[3]

Although the first biblical affirmations of the deity of Jesus were meant to emphasize the oneness of the divine power transmitted from the Father to the Son, it was inevitable, as the Christians moved through the second century and more and more into a world of Greek idioms and experience, that the distinct issue of Jesus' divinity, considered as something parallel to the divinity of the Father, should have to be considered. It was the Gnostic Christians who first broached that approach, with a vision of degrees of Godhead declining down in a cascade of emanations from the First Principle and declining in the quality of Godhead as each divine declension or *Aeon* came closer to the material world and away from the supreme Transcendent. By the end of the second century, together with the church's decisive rejection of the Gnostic system of divine emanations as something inimical to biblical tradition, Christian theologians were faced with the problem of articulating a new solution to the pressing question: How could Jesus' divine status be expressed within the framework of a fundamental monotheistic faithfulness to the biblical truth that there was only one God, and none other? The first attempts at solving this christological dilemma can be witnessed in the Monarchian theologians of the second century, who tried to reduce the concepts of Father and Son to synonyms for the same person in different modes of action. Theologians such as Irenaeus, Tertullian and Origen offered strong refutations of that movement as reductionist and obscurantist and elevated Logos theology in the second and third centuries to depict the Word as truly divine, in such a unity of divinity as would apply between the Father and his own Mind (Logos-Sophia), though sent out distinctly from the Father for the task of creation and salvation. The divinity of the Word was thus the divinity of the Father, while the individual identity of the Word (the Person) was recognizably discrete. There was in pre-Nicene thought of this type, however, an underlying current of subordinationism in many authors.

The Word, though God, is not God in the same way as the Father is God. That affirmation sometimes led to the confusion of some theologians who deduced that the Word was not God "at the same level" as God is God. It would take the Arian crisis of the fourth century to bring out a phalanx of theologians of high caliber such as Athanasius and the Cappadocian fathers, Gregory of Nazianzus, Basil of Caesarea and Gregory of Nyssa, who would turn their minds to the clarification of this issue. Highly conscious that the notion of divinity is an absolute one (if one is a monotheist) and that deity admits no degree, they set out to clarify the issue of the Son's divinity with a newfound precision and force.

OVERVIEW: The Word derives from God without ever being separate from God, just as the radiance is never separate from the light that emits it (TERTULLIAN). The Word and Son is not just like God but is equal to God (HILARY). The whole tenor of New Testament teaching proclaims that the Son is inseparable from the Father (MARCELLUS). The divine throne is shared from all eternity, as the Word sits on it next to the Father (CYRIL OF JERUSALEM). All Christian sentiment thus recognizes that it is an aberration to separate the Son from the Father by ranking him among

---

[3]1 Cor 8:5.

the creatures (ATHANASIUS). All that characterizes what we mean by the divinity of the Father is witnessed in the character of the Son of God also (ATHANASIUS). While the Word can be recognized as a distinct person (hypostasis) within the deity, the divine nature and status that he possesses is none other than the Father's own Godhead, for there is only one Godhead (GREGORY OF NAZIANZUS, GREGORY OF NYSSA). This profound union and coincidence of being between the two is shown in the constant and perfect harmony of action and will between the Father and the Son in all things (AUGUSTINE).

The Son Is of the Very Nature of God

THE IMMEASURABLE FATHER IS MEASURED IN THE SON. IRENAEUS: God makes all things in measure and order, and with him nothing is without proportion. He was right who said that the immeasurable Father is measured in the Son; for the Son is the measure of the Father, since he contains the Father.[4] AGAINST HERESIES 4.4.2.[5]

THE SON IS THE TRUE OFFSPRING OF GOD. TERTULLIAN: For God produced the Word, as the Paraclete also teaches, as a root produces the shoot, a spring the river, the sun a ray: for these manifestations are projections of those substances from which they proceed. I would not hesitate to call a shoot "the son of a root," a river "the son of a spring," a ray "a son of the sun." For every original source is a parent, and what is produced is its offspring. Much more is this true of the Word of God, who has received the name of Son as his proper designation, but the shoot is not detached from the root . . . nor is the Word detached from God. Thus in accordance with those analogies I confess that I speak of two, God and his Word, the Father and his Son. For root and shoot are two but conjoined. . . . Everything that proceeds from anything must necessarily be another thing, but it is not

therefore separate. When there is one other, there are two; where there is a third, there are three. The Spirit makes the third from God and the Son, as the fruit from the shoot is the third from the tree, the canal from the river the third from the source, the point of focus of a ray third from the sun. But none of those is divorced from the origin from which it derives its own qualities. Thus the Trinity derives from the Father by continuous and connected steps, and it in no way impugns the monarchy while it preserves the reality of the economy. AGAINST PRAXEAS 8.[6]

THE SON SHARES THE FATHER'S GOODNESS. HILARY OF POITIERS: I know, dearest brothers, that some acknowledge the likeness while denying the equality of the Son with the Father.[7] . . . If they say that there is a difference between likeness and equality, I ask what is the basis of equality? For if the Son is like the Father in essence and goodness and glory and time, I ask in what way does he appear not to be equal? . . . If the Father has given to the Son, whom he has generated impassibly, a nature that was not other than his own or different from his own, it must have been his own nature that he gave. Thus "like" means his "own," and that entails equality, the absence of difference. Things that show no difference are one, not by unity of person but by equality of nature. ON THE COUNCILS 74.[8]

---

[4]Irenaeus is throughout making a word play on *logos*, which apart from signifying "Word" also connoted "order," and this is why he describes the Son as the "ordering" or "measure" of the Father. There is a twofold implication in his argument: first, that if the Logos "measures up to" God, he must be fully divine of the divine; and second, that the Logos is a measure of God, who is able to give finite creatures a scaled-down understanding of God. The Logos, as divine, reveals the infinite and unnapproachable God to finite minds. [5]ECF 104. [6]ECF 165-66. [7]Hilary is referring to the party known as the Homoiousians, who believed the Son was of a "like essence" to the Father but not of the "same essence" as the Father (*homoousios*). This influential fourth-century ecclesiastical party were being wooed by the Nicene camp in Hilary's time, and in 362 Athanasius eventually achieved a reconciliation with them at the synod of Alexandria. The Nicenes regarded them as "not too far" from the Nicene faith. In older textbooks they are sometimes described as the semi-Arians. [8]LCF 48-49.

THE SON IS INDIVISIBLE FROM GOD.

MARCELLUS OF ANCYRA: We have learned from the holy Scriptures that the Godhead of the Father and the Son is indivisible. For if anyone separates the Son (the Word) from almighty God, he must either think that there are two Gods (and this has been judged to be foreign to the divine teaching) or confess that the Word is not God (and this also is manifestly alien to the correct faith, since the Evangelist says, "And the Word was God"[9]). But I have accurately learned that the power of the Father, that is, the Son, is indivisible and inseparable. For the Savior himself, the Lord Jesus Christ, says, "The Father is in me, and I am in the Father,"[10] and, "I and the Father are one,"[11] and, "Whoever has seen me has seen the Father."[12] I have received this faith from the holy Scriptures and was taught it by our fathers in God, and I preach it in the church of God, and I have now written it to you. LETTER TO POPE JULIUS.[13]

BELIEVE IN THE SON OF GOD.

CYRIL OF JERUSALEM: Believe also in the Son of God, that one and only Son, our Lord Jesus Christ, God begotten of God, Life begotten of Life, Light begotten of Light, like to his Begetter in all respects.[14] He did not begin his existence in time but has been before all ages eternally and incomprehensibly begotten of the Father. He is the Wisdom and Power of God and his Righteousness in personal subsistence. He sits at the right hand of the Father before all ages. CATECHETICAL LECTURES 4.7.[15]

THE WORD CANNOT BE A CREATURE.

ATHANASIUS: Let us look at the replies that the Arians gave to Alexander of Alexandria, who is now in peace, at the beginning, when their heresy was being formed. They wrote, "He is a creature, but not as one of the creatures; a work, but not as one of the works; an offspring, but not as one of the offsprings." . . . What is the use of this disingenuous talk, say-ing that he is "a creature and not a creature"? . . . Let the Word be excepted from the works and be restored to the Father, as being the Creator, and be acknowledged to be Son by nature; or, if he is merely a creature, let him be acknowledged to have the same status as the other creatures have in relation to each other; and let each of them, as well as he, be said to be "a creature, but not as one of the creatures," and so on. For you Arians have said that "offspring" is the same as "work" in writing "generated or made." For though the Son may excel the rest by comparison, yet he remains a creature like them, for among those who are by nature creatures one may find some excelling others. "Star excels star in glory."[16] But if the whole earth sings the praises of the Creator and the truth, and blesses him and trembles before him, and if its Creator is the Word and he himself says, "I am the truth,"[17] then it follows that the Word is not a creature but is the sole true Word of the Father. In him all things are set in order, and he himself has his praises sung by all, as Creator. For he himself says, "I was by his side, ordering,"[18] and also, "My Father works until now, and I work."[19] AGAINST THE ARIANS 2.19-20.[20]

THE SON IS ETERNAL SINCE HIS FATHER IS SUCH.

ATHANASIUS: The Arians say, "How can the Son exist eternally with the Father? For human beings are born as children of men in

---

[9]Jn 1:1. [10]Jn 10:38. [11]Jn 10:30. [12]Jn 14:9. [13]Cited in Epiphanius *Panarion* 72.3.2-4 (CCC 10*). [14]Cyril here skirts a troublesome issue that was dividing the bishops of his day: should the church's faith confess the "same substance" between Father and Son (Nicene Homoousians) or like substance (Homoiousians) or simple likeness (Homoians) between Father and Son (moderate Arianism)? By teaching his catechumens they ought to confess the eternal existence of the Son as Light from Light, he shows himself to be on the Nicene side, but by avoiding the term *homoousios* he tries to leave a door open to the Homoiousian position. Although he avoids all mention of substance or essence, his addendum, "like to the Father in all respects," shows his leaning to the Homoousian party, though it made many Nicenes suspect him as a dubious ally. [15]LCF 35*. [16]1 Cor 15:41. [17]Jn 14:6. [18]Prov 8:30. [19]Jn 5:17. [20]ECF 387-88*.

course of time. The father is, say, thirty years old, and the child is begotten then and starts his existence. In fact, every human child "did not exist before he was begotten." And again they whisper, "How can the Son be the Word, or the Word be the image of God? For human speech is a combination of syllables that merely signifies the speaker's meaning and immediately ceases and disappears." Now if they are discussing a human individual, then they may argue about his word and his child on the human level. But if they are talking of God, the Creator, they must not think of him on the human level. The character of the parent determines the character of the offspring. People are begotten in time and beget in time; they come into being from nonexistence, and therefore their word ceases and does not remain. But "God is not like humankind,"[21] as the Scripture has said; but rather, he is "he who exists"[22] and exists forever. Therefore his Word is "that which exists" and exists eternally with the Father, as radiance from a light. AGAINST THE ARIANS 2.34-35.[23]

THE SON IS RADIANCE FROM LIGHT. ATHANASIUS: The whole being of the Son belongs to the Father's substance, as radiance from light and stream from source. He who sees the Son sees what belongs to the Father and knows that the Son's being is in the Father just as it is from the Father. For the Father is in the Son as the sun is in its radiance, the thought in the word, the source in the stream. Having said, "I and the Father are one thing,"[24] he adds, "I am in the Father and the Father in me"[25] to show the identity of the Godhead and the unity of the substance. For they are "one thing," not in the sense of a thing divided into two parts, these being nothing but one thing; nor in the sense of one thing with two names, so that the Son is at one time Father, at another time his own Son. Sabellius held this opinion and was condemned as a heretic. But they are two, in that the Father is father and not also son;

the Son is son and not also father; but the nature is one (for the offspring is not unlike the parent, being his image), and all that is the Father's is the Son's. The Son is not another God, for he was not devised from outside the Father. If this had been so, and if we assume a Godhead beside that of the Father, there might surely have been many gods. Even if the Son is distinct from the Father, as his offspring, even so as God he is identical with him. He and the Father are one by a specific and proper nature and by the identity of the one Godhead. For the radiance also is light, not a second light besides the sun, or a different light or a light by participation in the sun, but a whole proper offspring of it. No one would say that there are two lights, even though the sun and its radiance are two. Evidently the light from the sun, which illuminates things everywhere, is one. In the same way the Godhead of the Son is the Father's. This is why it is undivided and why "God is one, and there is none other besides him."[26] Accordingly, since they are one, and the Godhead itself is one, the same things are predicated of the Son as of the Father, except the title of "Father." So, for instance: "God"—"the Word was God";[27] "All-sovereign"—"Thus says he who was and is and is coming, the all-sovereign";[28] "Lord"—"one Lord, Jesus Christ";[29] and "Light"—"I am the light."[30] AGAINST THE ARIANS 3.3-4.[31]

THE SON'S DISTINCT HYPOSTASIS. GREGORY OF NAZIANZUS: "For us there is one God the Father, from whom are all things; and one God the Son, through whom are all things";[32] and one Holy Spirit, "in whom are all things." The phrases "from whom," "through whom" and "in whom" do not make a severance in the natures (if they did, there would never be an interchange of the prepositions or of the order of

---

[21]Jdt 8:16. [22]Ex 3:14. [23]*ECF* 390-91*. [24]Jn 10:30. [25]Jn 14:10. [26]Is 45:5. [27]Jn 1:1. [28]Rev 1:8. [29]1 Cor 8:6. [30]Jn 8:12. [31]*ECF* 394-95**. [32]1 Cor 8:6.

the names), but they mark the personal distinctions within the unconfused nature. ORATION 39.12.[33]

THE WORD IS GOD'S MIND. GREGORY OF NYSSA: In a human context we say that a word comes from the mind, being neither completely identical with the mind nor utterly different from it: for it is distinct, as being from it, yet it cannot be conceived as different, since it reveals the mind itself; it is in nature identical with the mind but distinct, as being a separate subject. Similarly the Word of God is distinct from God by reason of its self-subsistence, while by displaying in itself the qualities that are regarded as belonging to God, it is identical in nature with him who is recognized by the possession of the same qualities. ADDRESS ON RELIGIOUS INSTRUCTION 1.2.[34]

THE FATHER'S NATURE IS THAT OF THE SON. GREGORY OF NYSSA: Our previous contention, therefore, is true, that the everlast-ingness of the Son is included, along with the idea of his birth, in the Father's ingeneracy; and that, if any interval were to be imagined dividing the two, that same interval would fix a beginning for the life of the Almighty, which is a monstrous supposition. AGAINST EUNOMIUS 1.26.[35]

THE SON IS ONE WITH GOD IN ALL ACTIONS. AUGUSTINE: There is one will of Father and Son, and one inseparable activity. Thus, therefore, one may understand that the incarnation and the birth from a virgin, by which the Son is understood to have been "sent," was effected by one and the same activity of Father and Son, working inseparably and, of course, with the Holy Spirit not separated from the work, as is plainly said: "She was found pregnant by the Holy Spirit."[36] THE TRINITY 2.9.[37]

---

[33]*LCF* 119. [34]*LCF* 151. [35]NPNF 2 5:70-71. [36]Mt 1:18.
[37]*LCF* 215.

LIGHT FROM LIGHT

καὶ εἰς ἕνα κύριον Ἰησοῦν Χριστόν,	Et in unum Dominum Jesum Christum,	We believe in one Lord, Jesus Christ,
τὸν υἱὸν τοῦ Θεοῦ τὸν μονογενῆ,	Filium Dei unigenitum,	the only Son of God,
τὸν ἐκ τοῦ πατρὸς γεννηθέντα	et ex Patre natum	eternally
πρὸ πάντων τῶν αἰώνων,	ante omnia saecula	begotten of the Father,
φῶς ἐκ φωτός,	[Deum de Deo], **Lumen de Lumine,**	[God from God], **Light from Light,**
Θεὸν ἀληθινὸν ἐκ θεοῦ ἀληθινοῦ,	Deum verum de Deo vero,	true God from true God,
γεννηθέντα, οὐ ποιηθέντα,	genitum, non factum,	begotten, not made,
ὁμοούσιον τῷ πατρί·	consubstantialem Patri;	of one Being with the Father.
δι᾽ οὗ τὰ πάντα ἐγένετο·	per quem omnia facta sunt;	Through him all things were made.
τὸν δι᾽ ἡμᾶς τοὺς ἀνθρώπους	qui propter nos homines	For us
καὶ διὰ τὴν ἡμετέραν σωτηρίαν	et propter nostram salutem	and for our salvation
κατελθόντα ἐκ τῶν οὐρανῶν	descendit de coelis,	he came down from heaven:
καὶ σαρκωθέντα ἐκ πνεύματος ἁγίου	et incarnatus est de Spiritu Sancto	by the power of the Holy Spirit
καὶ Μαρίας τῆς παρθένου	ex Maria virgine,	he became incarnate from the Virgin Mary,
καὶ ἐνανθρωπήσαντα,	et homo factus est;	and was made man.

HISTORICAL CONTEXT: The Scripture, throughout, favors the analogy of God's being as light and its energy in the world being experienced as an active and life-giving radiance. The first spoken "word" of God in the Genesis creation account was "Let there be light." Christian theologians noted this, as they reflected on God's ultimate "Word," and ever afterwards they connected with the image of light as the finest biblical type for conceiving the character of God's Logos-Sophia as illuminator and creative force.

The psalmist spoke of the "light of God's face" falling as a blessing on Israel[1] and of God as being "wrapped in light as in a robe,"[2] a text that entered the fabric of Christian prayer as the main psalm of evening worship. The notion of light was also prevalent in Scripture as a symbol of the observance of the Law[3] and of moral fidelity. When Isaiah spoke of the renewal God had promised his people, a text that the early Christians from the beginning saw fulfilled in the advent of the incarnate Lord, he spoke of Israel seeing a "great light" that "had dawned on them."[4] The epiphany of God to Moses at Sinai is described in terms that suggest it is a light so intense that a mere human cannot look on it and live.[5] Moses has to veil his face to speak to the Israelites, a text that was before the minds of the Evangelists who narrated the story of the transfiguration of Jesus,[6] who emitted the light of the Glory-Shekinah of the Father in an important and central Gospel episode. The symbol of light was therefore a ready symbol of the glory of God to the earliest Christian theologians, and from the outset the Lord was described as a "light for the Gentiles,"[7] the divine light that was to come into the world[8] for its salvation and illumination. When the creed refers to the Son of God as "Light from Light," therefore, it is specifically annotating the relationship of

---

[1]Ps 4:6. [2]Ps 104:2. [3]Ps 119:105. [4]Is 9:2. [5]Ex 33:18-23; 34:6-9; 34:29-35. [6]Mk 9:1-8; Mt 17:1-8; Lk 9:28-36. [7]Lk 2:32. [8]Jn 1:4, 9; 8:12; 12:35-36, 46.

Son to Father and describing it in biblical terms as the single Glory of God shining in the person and the saving work of the Son. The image of light from light inspired whole generations of patristic theologians across many centuries, who saw it as a vivid cipher of the divine unity and harmony of action, as well as a powerful message to underline that all the incarnate economy was motivated by God's desire to illuminate his creation and elect a transfigured people.

OVERVIEW: God calls humanity to the light through Jesus the Savior, who is the enlightener of the world. His gift of salvation is our enlightenment (CLEMENT OF ROME, PSEUDO-CLEMENT OF ROME). Like a great sun peering into all things, the Word of God illuminates and scrutinizes every aspect of a person's life (CLEMENT OF ALEXANDRIA). The light of God the Father is so vast and brilliant that earthly conceptions cannot bear to look on it directly, and so the Son and Logos stands as a mediator of the divine brightness to the cosmos. The Word adapts the infinite brightness to suit our capacity and in order to teach us, and to this extent our salvation is in essence a divine illumination and reformation (TERTULLIAN, ORIGEN). Because the Son mediates the true light of God to the world, it is not possible that we can distinguish the Son's light from that of the Father. The Son offers the world the same radiance of the Father, not a dimmed version of it (ATHANASIUS). When the church recognizes that the Son of God is the Light of the Father, it confesses that this is the same as acknowledging the Homoousion. Whoever sees the light of the Son has seen the Father.

How God Illumines Fallen Creatures

THROUGH CHRIST, WE ARE CALLED INTO LIGHT. CLEMENT OF ROME: We will ask with earnest prayer and supplication that the Creator of the universe may keep intact the specified number of his elect throughout the whole world, through his beloved servant[9] Jesus Christ, through whom he called us from darkness to light, from ignorance to the knowledge of the glory of his name. Grant us, Lord, to hope on your name, which is the primal source of all creation, and open the eyes of our hearts, that we may know you, who alone is highest among the high and remains holy among the holy. 1 CLEMENT 59.2-3.[10]

GOD CALLED US OUT OF DARKNESS. PSEUDO-CLEMENT OF ROME: What repayment, then, shall we give to him, or what fruit worthy of what he has given to us? And how many blessings do we owe him? For he has given us the light; as a father he has called us sons; he saved us when we were perishing. What praise, then, shall we give him, or what repayment in return for what we received? Our minds were blinded, and we worshiped stones and wood and gold and silver and brass, the works of mortals; indeed, our whole life was nothing else but death. So while we were thus wrapped in darkness and our vision was filled with this thick mist, we recovered our sight, by his will laying aside the cloud wrapped around us. For he had mercy on us, and in his compassion he saved us when we had no hope of salvation except that which comes from him, and even though he had seen in us much deception and destruction. For he called us when we did not exist, and out of nothing he willed us into being. 2 CLEMENT 1.3-8.[11]

GRACIOUSLY GOD SAVES US. LETTER TO DIOGNETUS: O the surpassing kindness and love of God for humankind! No, he did not hate us, or discard us or remember our wrongs. He exercised forbearance and long-suffering. In

---

[9] The ancient Christian Greek title of Christ, *pais theou*, was a double-entendre evoking several biblical titles at once: it means at one and the same time the "Child of God" (the "Son of God" of the Gospel accounts) and also "Servant of God" (the Suffering Servant of Isaiah, whose wounds would cleanse the people). Clement knowingly plays on this association here by describing the servant as "the Beloved" (as in Mt 3:17). [10] *AF* 95. [11] *AF* 107.

mercy, of his own accord, he lifted the burden of our sins. Of his own accord he gave up his own Son as a ransom for us; the saint for sinners, the guiltless for the guilty, the innocent for the wicked, the incorruptible for the corruptible, the immortal for the mortal. Indeed, what else could have covered our sins but his holiness? In whom could we, the lawless and impious, be sanctified but in the Son of God alone? O sweetest exchange; O unfathomable accomplishment; O unexpected blessings; the sinfulness of many is buried in One who is holy, the holiness of One sanctifies the many who are sinners. LETTER TO DIOGNETUS 9.2-5.[12]

THE WORD LOOKS ON OUR DEEDS. CLEMENT OF ALEXANDRIA: As the sun illumines not only the heaven and the whole world, shining on both land and sea, but also sends his rays through windows and small chinks into the furthest recesses of a house, so the Word, poured out everywhere, beholds the smallest actions of our life. STROMATEIS 7.3.21.[13]

THE SON ILLUMINATES ALL CREATION. ORIGEN: Let us see how we are to understand the saying of Paul concerning Christ, that he is the "radiance of God's splendor and the representation of his being."[14] "God is light," says John.[15] The radiance of this light is the only-begotten Son, who proceeds from the Father without separation, as radiance from the light, and gives light to the whole creation. . . . Through radiance we understand and experience what the light itself is. This radiance presents itself gently to the feeble eyes of mortals and gradually trains and accustoms them, as it were, to endure the full blaze of the light. It removes from them all that clogs and impedes their vision, in accord with the word of the Lord, "Cast out the beam from your eye."[16] Thus it makes them able to receive the splendor of the light; and in this also it becomes a kind of mediator between us and the light. ON FIRST PRINCIPLES 1.2.7.[17]

THE WORD IS THE RADIANCE OF THE FATHER. ATHANASIUS: We see that the radiance from the sun is integral to it and that the substance of the sun is not divided or diminished, but its substance is entire, and its radiance perfect and entire, and the radiance does not diminish the substance of the light but is as it were a genuine offspring from it. Thus we see that the Son is begotten not from without but from the Father and that Father remains entire, while the "stamp of his substance"[18] exists always and preserves the likeness and image without alteration. AGAINST THE ARIANS 2.33.[19]

THE SON IS GOD'S OWN LIGHT. BASIL OF CAESAREA: The preceding words prove that this was the meaning of the Fathers.[20] For after the assertions, "light from light," "begotten of the Father's substance, not made," they added the phrase "of the same substance."[21] In this they showed that the meaning attached to "light," when applied to the Father, holds good when applied to the Son. The very notion of light makes impossible any difference between one true light and another. Then, since the Father is unoriginated light and the Son is begotten light, but each is light, the Fathers were right to use the term "of the same substance," in order to establish the equal dignity of their nature. "Of the same substance" does not, as some have supposed, describe entities connected by a fraternal relation.[22] The term is used when the source and that which derives its being from the

---

[12]ACW 6:143. [13]ECF 235. [14]Heb 1:3. [15]1 Jn 1:5. [16]Lk 6:42. [17]ECF 295*. [18]Heb 1:3. [19]ECF 390. [20]Basil is referring to the conciliar fathers gathered at Nicaea in 325, and he goes on to make an exegesis of the creed according to their intent. This is the origin of the concept of patristic theology—the mind of the Fathers who taught the orthodox faith. [21]Homoousios (consubstantial) with the Father. [22]Basil is acknowledging that some in his generation thought that the admission of the Son's coequal consubstantiality with the Father destroyed any notion in the Godhead of the Father's unoriginate and unique status and was thus not authentic theology and not faithful to the ancient monotheistic tradition. He is holding out an olive branch to them here, arguing that they have misunderstood the meaning of the word *consubstantial* as the Nicenes have taught it.

5

source are identical in nature. LETTER 52.2.[23]

SEE GOD IN THE LIGHT OF HIS SON. GREGORY OF NYSSA: But then, after passing that summit of theology, I mean the God over all, we turn as it were back again in the racecourse of the mind and speed through conjoint and kindred ideas from the Father, through the Son, to the Holy Spirit. For once having taken our stand on the comprehension of the ungenerate Light, we perceive that moment from that vantage ground of the Light that streams from him, like the ray coexistent with the sun, whose cause indeed is in the sun but whose existence is synchronous with the sun, not being a later addition but appearing at the first sight of the sun itself. . . . Indeed, it will not be a ray of the sun that we shall perceive but another sun blazing forth, as an offspring out of the ungenerate sun and simultaneously with our conception of the first, and in every way like him, in beauty, in power, in luster, in size, in brilliance, in all things at once that we observe in the sun. AGAINST EUNOMIUS 1.36.[24]

BRIGHTNESS OF THE FATHER'S GLORY. GREGORY OF NYSSA: The body of the sun is expressly imaged by the whole disk that surrounds it, and he who looks on the sun argues, by means of what he sees, the existence of the whole solid substratum. Just so . . . the majesty of the Father is expressly imaged in the greatness of the power of the Son, so that the one may be believed to be as great as the other is known to be. Just as the radiance of light sheds its brilliancy from the whole of the sun's disk (for in the disk one part is not radiant and the rest dim), so all that glory that the Father is sheds its brilliancy from its whole extent by means of the brightness that comes from it, that is, by the true Light. And just as the ray is of the sun (for there would be no ray if the sun were not), yet the sun is never conceived as existing by itself without the ray of brightness that is shed from it. This is why the apostle,

delivering to us the continuity and eternity of that existence that the Only-Begotten has of the Father, calls the Son "the brightness of his glory."[25] AGAINST EUNOMIUS 8.1.[26]

The Son Reveals the Light of the Father

JESUS REVEALS THE KNOWLEDGE OF GOD. DIDACHE: After you have taken your fill of food,[27] give thanks as follows: We give you thanks, O holy Father, for your holy name that you have enshrined in our hearts, and for the knowledge and faith and immortality that you have made known to us through Jesus, your Servant. To you be the glory for evermore. DIDACHE 10.1-2.[28]

THE SON IS OUR TEACHER ABOUT THE FATHER. CLEMENT OF ALEXANDRIA: We must believe truly[29] in the Son; that he is the Son, that he came, and how he came, and why; and about his suffering. But we must also have knowledge of the person of the Son. But, to begin with, there is no faith without knowledge or knowledge without faith. Nor does the Father exist without the Son, for "Father" immediately implies "Father of a Son," and the Son is the true teacher about the Father. And in order that a person may believe in the Son, he must know the Father in relation to whom the Son exists. Again, in order that we may come to know the Father, we must believe in the Son, because the Son of God is our teacher; for the Father brings us from faith to knowledge by means of the Son, and to knowledge of the Son and the Father that follows the Gnostic Rule;[30] for the

---

[23]*LCF* 64. [24]NPNF 2 5:84-85. [25]2 Cor 4:6. [26]Some scholars call this treatise *Against Eunomius* book 3 (NPNF 2 5:202*). [27]This is one of the earliest Christian accounts of the eucharistic ritual. [28]ACW 6:20-21*. [29]The context of Clement's argument was that some had asserted that while we have actual knowledge of Spirit (that is, Deity), we can only have faith in the Son. [30]Writing in Alexandria, a city that was then a center for many Gnostic teachers, Clement attempts to claim back the title of "gnostic" to describe the truly illuminated Christian. He argues here that theology is properly conceived when it follows the real

rule of the genuine Gnostic is an intuition and apprehension of truth through the Truth.[31] STROMATEIS 5.1.(1).[32]

THE LIGHT OF THE SON IS THE MEDIUM OF CREATION. TERTULLIAN: At first, when the Son was not yet manifest, God said, "Let there be light,"[33] and light came into being. And the Word himself was straightway, "the true light that enlightens everyone coming into this world,"[34] and through him the light of the world came to be.[35] Thenceforward God willed to create, and created, through the Word, with Christ as his assistant and minister. AGAINST PRAXEAS 12.[36]

THE WORD COMES AS LIGHT. ORIGEN: God, then, is utterly one and uncompounded, but our Savior, when God sent him forth to be a propitiation and the firstfruits of all creation, became many[37] because of the many; or rather perhaps, he became all things, inasmuch as all creation has need of him; all creation, namely, which is capable of receiving freedom.[38] And therefore he becomes the light of humankind, when people who had been plunged in darkness by wickedness need "the light that shines in the darkness and is not overcome by the darkness."[39] He could not have become the light of humankind if people had not been in darkness. Similarly we must suppose in regard to his being the "first begotten of the dead."[40] For if we suppose that the woman had not been deceived and Adam had not fallen, but man who was "created for incorruption"[41] had kept hold of incorruption, the Savior would not have gone down "to the dust of death," nor would he have died, had there been no sin, nor would he have had to die because of his love of humankind. . . . If humankind had not sinned, we may suppose that he would have remained Wisdom and Word and Life, and certainly Truth. But he would not have all the other attributes that he took on himself for our sake.[42]

COMMENTARY ON THE GOSPEL OF JOHN 1.20. (22).[43]

THE WORD DIMS HIS RADIANCE FOR US. ORIGEN: Celsus[44] thinks that the assumption by the immortal divine Word of a mortal body and a human soul entails a change and alteration in time. Let him learn that the Word remains the Word in his essential being and does not suffer what the body or soul suffers. The Word comes down at a certain time to be with us who cannot behold the splendor and brightness of his Godhead and, as it were, becomes flesh, uttered in bodily terms,[45] until such time as the one who has received him in this shape, being gradually raised to a higher level by the Word, may be able to gaze on what I may call his primary form. AGAINST CELSUS 4.15.[46]

gnostic rule, that is, unlike the other kinds of Gnostics who claim self-revelatory powers. Clement argues that the real illumined one is subject to scriptural truth and to the revelations that make him truly "knowing" (gnostic), since such a believer is then taught by God, Truth personified. [31]Jn 14:6. [32]ECF 235-36. [33]Gen 1:3. [34]Jn 1:9. [35]Jn 1:10. [36]ECF 166. [37]Following the ancient philosophical distinction between the sublime deity, which was One and uncompounded and free of all material vicissitudes, and the incarnate Logos, which Origen speaks of as having entered into relation with time and materiality in the incarnation, as the agent of the Father. For Origen, therefore, there is a distinction between the absolute One (the Father), and the Son (Word) who proceeds from "the One" as the "Second." He sketches out a trinitarian vocabulary two generations before such a vocabulary is constituted at the Second Ecumenical Council, at Constantinople in 381. [38]He refers to ensouled (noetic) creation; the restorative purpose of the earthly mission of the Logos. [39]Jn 1:5. [40]Rev 1:5. [41]Wis 2:23. [42]Origen refers to the pastoral and salvific titles: Savior, Shepherd, Light of the World, and so forth. These he calls the *epinoiai* (aspects) of the Logos who, through them, becomes all things to all people in a dazzling variety of manifestations of his presence in the material cosmos. [43]ECF 292. [44]A pagan hostile critic of Christianity who, a generation before Origen, had argued that the doctrine of the incarnation was merely another myth of the unlearned that anthropomorphized God. [45]It is true, that is, that the word "becomes flesh" for the sake of the human race; but that phrase, Origen argues, ought not to be taken in a crassly mythical sense as Celsus seems to be doing. The Word does not become flesh but rather remains divine spirit and descends into materiality only to serve a pedagogic function, to raise human minds out of their obsession with material forms. [46]ECF 299-300.

TRUE GOD FROM TRUE GOD

καὶ εἰς ἕνα κύριον Ἰησοῦν Χριστόν,	Et in unum Dominum Jesum Christum,	We believe in one Lord, Jesus Christ,
τὸν υἱὸν τοῦ Θεοῦ τὸν μονογενῆ,	Filium Dei unigenitum,	the only Son of God,
τὸν ἐκ τοῦ πατρὸς γεννηθέντα	et ex Patre natum	eternally
πρὸ πάντων τῶν αἰώνων,	ante omnia saecula	begotten of the Father,
φῶς ἐκ φωτός,	[Deum de Deo], Lumen de Lumine,	[God from God], Light from Light,
Θεὸν ἀληθινὸν ἐκ θεοῦ ἀληθινοῦ,	**Deum verum de Deo vero,**	**true God from true God,**
γεννηθέντα, οὐ ποιηθέντα,	genitum, non factum,	begotten, not made,
ὁμοούσιον τῷ πατρὶ·	consubstantialem Patri;	of one Being with the Father.
δι᾽ οὗ τὰ πάντα ἐγένετο·	per quem omnia facta sunt;	Through him all things were made.
τὸν δι᾽ ἡμᾶς τοὺς ἀνθρώπους	qui propter nos homines	For us
καὶ διὰ τὴν ἡμετέραν σωτηρίαν	et propter nostram salutem	and for our salvation
κατελθόντα ἐκ τῶν οὐρανῶν	descendit de coelis,	he came down from heaven:
καὶ σαρκωθέντα ἐκ πνεύματος ἁγίου	et incarnatus est de Spiritu Sancto	by the power of the Holy Spirit
καὶ Μαρίας τῆς παρθένου	ex Maria virgine,	he became incarnate from the Virgin Mary,
καὶ ἐνανθρωπήσαντα,	et homo factus est;	and was made man.

HISTORICAL CONTEXT: This creedal clause is evidently a repetition of the previous one "God from God." Dittography in the ancient confessional clauses usually suggests that a clarification has been called for, at some particular moment, as something in the earlier creedal confession has come into controversy at some stage in the church's life. And indeed this is the case here. From the third century onwards Origen of Alexandria's theology had become widespread. This great Christian thinker had many insights in his large-scale Logos theology that were traditional and favored a view of the eternal and divine status of the Son, but he was also concerned to mark a strong distinction between the being of God the Father and that of God the Son. It is a distinction that he tended to make with formulas of his own, speculative reflections that in the next generation after him caused much controversy among the interpreters who continued to read him. One of Origen's distinctions was to call the Father *autotheos* (very God) and the Word simply God. It would be something comparable to an attempt to distinguish between "God" and "god." Another of his distinctions was to call the Logos *deuteros theos*, or second god, as distinct from the first Cause, which was the Father alone. Some of this reflection is based on the Savior's words in John 17:3, "And this is life, to know you the only true God" (*alēthinos theos*), which Origen took to be a reference to the specific title of the Father (true God or very God). He was always more than sensitive to such hidden mysteries in the minute details of the scriptural verses, especially those that contained the direct words of the Logos. Several of the surviving Origenian scholars of the early fourth century were still using such terminology, which many had found defective even in the third century, and the problem flared up in the early years of the Arian crisis, when both sides of the Nicene fence (Arius as well as Athanasius) declared straightforwardly that divinity, being an absolute category, was not capable of such distinctions as superior and inferior, of "God" and "god." One of the real causes of the Nicene crisis was, in fact, the collapse of some parts of the antique Origenian system of theological categorizations.

OVERVIEW: The Word is the very Wisdom of God, and his very Truth (ORIGEN). He is the "visible" of the Father, and the Father is the "invisible" of the Son (IRENAEUS). He is not the Father, being a discrete person, but he is nevertheless divine of the same being (GREGORY OF NAZIANZUS), equal to the Father in Godhead (ATHANASIUS, AUGUSTINE) and lacks nothing of the divine dignity (CYRIL OF JERUSALEM). The heretics have wrongly supposed that the Father must also be the "God of the Son and the Spirit" (GREGORY OF NYSSA), but the Word is the only true revelation of the being of God (ORIGEN). The divine "I am" includes all three members of the divine Triad (CLEMENT OF ALEXANDRIA). All that the Father is, he gives to the Son (GREGORY OF NYSSA), and the Son reveals the almighty power of God in his role as cocreator of humanity (CYRIL OF JERUSALEM). If the Son was anything less than the Father or deficient in respect to deity in any sense, he could not reveal the true God in any substantial way, as the Christian faith claims. The Son, nevertheless, is coeternal and consubstantial with the Father (AUGUSTINE). In the end of times the Father sends his Son to earth in a humble economy of salvation (ATHANASIUS, SYNOD OF ANTIOCH), but even in this hidden ministry he is the kingly emissary of the high King and is truly divine (LETTER TO DIOGNETUS).

The Son Is Truly God, Just as the Father Is

GOD'S WORD IS SOVEREIGN. ORIGEN: He himself is wisdom itself and righteousness itself and truth itself; is he not also sovereignty itself? COMMENTARY ON THE GOSPEL OF MATTHEW 14.7.[1]

THE WORD STANDS AS GOD TO ALL THE CREATION. ORIGEN: While in respect of the Father he is the image of goodness, in respect of all others he is as the Father's goodness is in respect of him. COMMENTARY ON THE GOSPEL OF MATTHEW 15.10.[2]

THE LORD JESUS, DIVINE AND HUMAN. GREGORY OF NAZIANZUS: The Father could be called the God, not of the Word but of him who was seen by humankind.[3] For how could he be the God of him who is himself genuinely God? In the same way he is the Father, not of him who was seen but of the Word. Thus in regard to the two natures in Christ one title for God is properly applied, another title improperly; in regard to us the same is true, but vice versa. For he is properly termed our God but improperly termed Father. This is what occasions the error of the heretics, namely, the combination of names, the names being interchanged because of the commingling of the two natures. This is shown by the fact that when the natures are considered separately, the distinction of nomenclature corresponds with the distinction of the conceptions. Notice how Paul says, "the God of our Lord Jesus Christ, the Father of glory."[4] God of Christ but Father of the glory. Though both compose a single whole,[5] it is not by unity of nature but by coalescence of those two natures. What could be more intelligible? ORATION 30.8.[6]

THE WORD SHARES THE THRONE OF GOD. CYRIL OF JERUSALEM: Believe also in the Son of God, one and only, our Lord Jesus Christ,

---

[1] *ECF* 321. [2] *ECF* 321. [3] Gregory is arguing, in the larger context, about the right interpretation of the Gospel words from Jn 14:28 (the Father is greater than I) and Jn 20:17 (I am ascending to my God and your God). He states here that the words of Jesus about God's superiority are economic, that is, they refer to the economy of incarnate salvation, in the sense of expressing the sensibility of the human nature, wherein Jesus, as befits his human stature, confesses the Father as his God. [4] Eph 1:17. [5] He means the two natures of Christ coalescing into the single unity of the incarnate Lord. [6] *LCF* 105.

who was begotten God of God, begotten Life of Life, begotten Light of Light; who is in all things like to him that begot,[7] who did not receive his being in time but was before all ages eternally and incomprehensibly begotten of the Father: the Wisdom and the Power of God and his Righteousness personally subsisting, who sits on the right hand of the Father before all ages. For he did not receive the throne at God's right hand, as some have thought, because of his patient endurance, being crowned as it were by God after his passion but had throughout his being, a being by eternal generation. He holds his royal dignity and shares the Father's seat, being God and Wisdom and Power, as has been said; reigning together with the Father and creating all things for the Father yet lacking nothing in the dignity of Godhead and knowing him that has begotten him, even as he is known by him that has begotten. To speak briefly, remember what is written in the Gospels, that "no one knows the Son except the Father, and no one knows the Father except the Son."[8] CATECHETICAL LECTURES 4.7.[9]

JESUS IS VERY GOD AND CREATOR. CYRIL OF JERUSALEM: Christ the Lord is he who was born in the city of David. And know this too, that Christ is Lord with the Father even before his incarnation, not only accepting the statement by faith but receiving proof from the Old Testament. Go to the first book [Genesis]: God says, "Let us make man," not in "my" image but in "our" image. And after Adam was made, the sacred writer says, "And God created man. In the image of God he created him."[10] For he did not limit the dignity of the Godhead to the Father alone but included the Son also, that it might be shown that humanity is not only the work of God but also of our Lord Jesus Christ, who is himself also very God. CATECHETICAL LECTURES 10.6.[11]

THE SON IS IN PERFECT CONCORD WITH

THE FATHER. CYRIL OF JERUSALEM: If you wish to receive yet a third testimony to Christ's Godhead, hear what Isaiah[12] says: "Egypt has labored, and the merchandise of Ethiopia," and soon after, "In you they shall make supplication, because God is in you, and there is no God save you. For you are God, and we did not know it, the God of Israel, the Savior."[13] You see that the Son is God, having in himself God the Father, saying almost the very same thing he said in the Gospels: "The Father is in me, and I am in the Father."[14] He does not say, "I am the Father," but "the Father is in me, and I am in the Father." And again he did not say, "I and the Father am one," but "I and the Father are one," that we should neither separate them or make a confusion of Son-Father.[15] They are one because of the dignity pertaining to the Godhead, since God begot God. They are one in respect of their kingdom, for the Father does not reign over these while the Son reigns over those, lifting himself up against his Father like Absalom, but the kingdom of the Father is likewise the kingdom of the Son. They are one, because there is no discord or division between them, for whatever the Father wills, the Son equally wills. CATECHETICAL LECTURES 11.16.[16]

THE SON IS THE TRUE REVELATION OF GOD. CYRIL OF JERUSALEM: One who has seen the Son has seen the Father, for the Son is in all things like him who begot him. He is begotten Life of Life, and Light of Light, Power of

---

[7]Cyril here confesses the total similitude of the Son to the Father. The Nicene party under Athanasius resisted this throughout the fourth century and demanded the confession of the consubstantiality *(homoousion)* of the Son, the position that was to be endorsed as Nicene orthodoxy at the second ecumenical council of 381, which Cyril lived to endorse. [8]Mt 11:27. [9]NPNF 2 7:20-21*. [10]Gen 1:27. [11]NPNF 2 7:58-59*. [12]Isaiah. The Fathers generally describe the biblical names through the Greek Septuagint versions. [13]Is 45:15. [14]Jn 14:10. [15]Cyril is referring to the second-century movement of Son-Fatherism *(huiopator)*, a monistic modalism that regarded Father and Son as separate names and manifestations of the selfsame spirit. [16]NPNF 2 7:68*.

Power, God of God; and the characteristics of the Godhead are unchangeable in the Son. Whoever is found worthy to behold the Son's Godhead attains the fullness of the Father. CATECHETICAL LECTURES 11.18.[17]

THE SON HAS ALL THAT THE FATHER HAS. GREGORY OF NYSSA: Does what has been said leave us any longer in ignorance of him who is "God over all,"[18] who is so entitled by Saint Paul, our Lord Jesus Christ; who, as he himself says, holding in his hand "all things that the Father has"[19] assuredly grasps all things in the all-containing hollow of his hand and is sovereign over what he has grasped; and no one takes from the hand of him who in his hand holds all things? If, then, he has all things and is sovereign over that which he has, why is he who is thus sovereign over all things something else[20] and not Almighty? If heresy replies that the Father is sovereign over both the Son and the Holy Spirit, let them first show that the Son and the Holy Spirit are of mutable nature. AGAINST EUNOMIUS 2.11.[21]

THE SON SHARES ALL THE CHARACTER OF THE FATHER. GREGORY OF NYSSA: But as he is Light of Light and Life of Life and Truth of Truth, so is he Lord of Lord, King of King, God of God, Supreme of Supreme; for having in himself the Father in his entirety, whatever the Father has in himself he also, assuredly, has. Since all that the Son has belongs to the Father, the enemies of God's glory are inevitably compelled, if the Son is a slave, to drag down to servitude the Father as well. For there is no attribute of the Son that is not absolutely the Father's. "For all that is mine is yours," he says, "and yours is mine."[22] AGAINST EUNOMIUS 10.4.[23]

THE SON IS EQUAL IN GLORY TO THE FATHER. AUGUSTINE: Now if the Son is said to be sent by the Father in respect that the one is Father, the other Son, this in no way

hinders our belief that the Son is equal to the Father, consubstantial and coeternal, and yet that the Son is sent by the Father. Not because one is greater than the other, but because one is Father, the other Son. One is begetter, the other begotten. The Son is from the Father, not the Father from the Son. . . . The Son is "a kind of clear effluence of the splendor of almighty God." And the effluence and its source are of one and the same substance. For it does not flow as water from a hole in the ground or in the rock but as light from light. "The brightness of the eternal light"[24] means the light of eternal light. For the brightness of light is light and is coeternal with the light from which it springs. If the brightness is less than the light, it is its obscurity, not its brightness. THE TRINITY 4.27.[25]

THE TRINITY'S UNITY AND DIFFERENTIATION. PSEUDO-DIONYSIUS: There is, on the other hand, a differentiation made in the Superessential[26] doctrine of God, not merely such as I have just mentioned[27] but also that the attributes of the Superessential divine generation[28] are not interchangeable. The Father alone is the source[29] of the Superessential Godhead, and the Father is not a Son, nor is the Son a Father; for the divine persons all preserve, each without alloy, their own particular attributes of praise.[30] Such, then, are the instances of undif-

---

[17]NPNF 2 7:69**. [18]Rom 9:5. [19]Jn 16:15. [20]Gregory alludes here to the Arian party of Heterousiasts (Different Being) who argued that the Son was a different thing to the Father, insofar as he was created while the Father was uncreated. [21]In modern editions this is known as Gregory's "Refutation of Eunomius's Apology" (NPNF 2 5:120*). [22]Jn 17:10. [23]Modern scholars sometimes refer to this treatise as *Against Eunomius* book 3 (NPNF 2 5:228). [24]Wis 7:26. [25]*LCF* 215-16. [26]A favorite phrase of Dionysius, signifying that all earthly thought and language fail to describe the God who is beyond all human thought and all essential reality as we conceive it in material terms. [27]Namely, that in the unity of the Trinity each person possesses its own distinct and personal existence without confusion. [28]Of the Son from the Father. [29]*Arche*. Dionysius is here restating the trinitarian theology of Gregory of Nazianzus. [30]Dionysius regards the theological distinctions as doxological: meant to be confessed by the church in prayerful praise.

ference and of differentiation in the ineffable unity and subsistence of God. THE DIVINE NAMES 2.5.[31]

THE ONLY-BEGOTTEN GOD DEIFIES THE WORLD. ISAAC OF NINEVEH: You have given your entire treasure to the world: if you gave the Only-Begotten from your bosom and from the throne of your being for the benefit of all, what further do you have that you have not given to your creation? The world has become mingled with God, and in him creation and the Creator have become one! THE SECOND PART 2.5.18.[32]

The Divine Mission of the Son Before the Ages

THE SON IS THE VISIBLE ASPECT OF THE FATHER. IRENAEUS: Through the creation the Word reveals God the Creator; through the world is revealed the Lord who made the world; through the handiwork is revealed the artificer; through the Son is revealed the Father who begot him. All alike confess this,[33] but all do not believe it. By the Law and Prophets the Word proclaimed himself and the Father; and the whole people alike heard, but all did not believe. And through this same Word, made visible and tangible, the Father was displayed, although all did not believe in him. Yet all saw the Father in the Son; for the Father is the invisible of the Son, the Son the visible of the Father. AGAINST HERESIES 4.6.5.[34]

THE WORD WAS AN INVITATION FROM GOD. LETTER TO DIOGNETUS: The wish to save, to persuade and not to coerce, inspired his mission. Coercion is incompatible with God. His mission was an invitation, not a vindictive measure; an act of love, not an act of justice. Some day, of course, God will send him as a judge, and who will then endure his coming? Do you not see how they are thrown before the wild beasts to make them disown the Lord, and still they refuse to be overcome? Do you not see that

the more of them are penalized, the more their numbers grow? LETTER TO DIOGNETUS 7.4-8.[35]

THE MISSION OF THE SON SENT BY THE KING. EPISTLE TO DIOGNETUS: It was not an earthly invention, as I have said, that was committed to their keeping;[36] it was not a product of a mortal brain that they consider worth safeguarding so anxiously, nor have they been entrusted with the dispensing of merely human mysteries. Quite the contrary! It was really the Lord of all, the Creator of all, the invisible God himself, who, of his own free will, from heaven, lodged among people as the truth and the holy incomprehensible Word and firmly established the same in their hearts. Nor did God do this, as one might conjecture, by sending to humankind some subordinate, whether angel or principality or one of those in charge of earthly things, or one entrusted with the administration of heavenly things. No, God sent the Designer and Architect of the universe in person, the very one by whom he created the heavens, by whom he enclosed the sea within its proper bounds, whose inscrutable counsels all the elements of nature faithfully carry out, the one from whom the sun has received the schedule of the daily courses it is to keep, the one whom the moon obeys as he bids it give light at night, whom the stars obey in following the course of the moon, from whom all things have received their order, their bounds and their due place in the universe: all things, both the heavens and the things in the heavens, the earth and the things in the earth, the sea and the things in the sea, the fire, the air, the underworld, the things in the heights above, the things in the deep below, the things in the intermediate space. Such was he whom God sent to them! And did he do so, as a human brain might conceive, to tyrannize, to frighten or to terror-

---

[31]*ODN* 71. [32]*CS* 175:58. [33]That is, all humanity, by virtue of its existence, attests to the truth of this fundamental ontological structure of revealed existences. [34]*ECF* 105. [35]*ACW* 6:141. [36]The author is referring to the tradition of the Gospel kerygma entrusted to the first disciples.

ize? Certainly not! On the contrary, his mission was an act of gracious clemency, as when a king sends his son who is himself a king! He sent him as God. He sent him as Man to men. LETTER TO DIOGNETUS 7.1-4.[37]

THE WORD IS THE JUSTICE OF GOD. CLEMENT OF ALEXANDRIA: God is one, and beyond one and above the Monad itself. Therefore the pronoun "you"[38] is emphatic and indicates the one really existing God who is, and was and will be. Those three divisions of time are included in the name "I am." . . . The goodness of God is apprehended from his character as Father. . . . His attribute of justice derives from the mutual relationship of the Father and the Son, his Word who is in the Father. CHRIST THE EDUCATOR 1.8.(71).[39]

THE WORD IS THE JUDGE OF ALL. CLEMENT OF ALEXANDRIA: Most perfect, most holy, most lordly, most commanding, royal and beneficent is the nature of the Son, most closely joined to the only Almighty. His is the greatest preeminence, which orders all things according to the Father's will and guides everything correctly, working all things by unwearying and unfailing power, beholding the hidden thoughts through its activities, for the Son of God never quits his watchtower. He is not divided or severed, nor does he pass from place to place. He is always everywhere and not circumscribed anywhere. He is wholly mind, wholly the Father's light, all eye, seeing all things, hearing all things, knowing all things, searching out the powers by his power. The whole army of angels and of gods[40] is subject to him, to the Word of the Father who has taken on himself the holy dispensation[41] because of him who made them subject. STROMATEIS 8.2.5.[42]

THE WORD ENLIGHTENS AND CONFERS LIFE. ORIGEN: If by participation in the Word we are raised from the dead and enlightened, and also, it may be, shepherded by him and

ruled over, it is clear that through him we are made rational by divine inspiration, since he does away with the irrationality and deadness in us, inasmuch as he is the Word [reason itself] and the resurrection. COMMENTARY ON THE GOSPEL OF JOHN 1.37.[43]

THE WORD IS THE REVEALER OF GOD. ORIGEN: The Word can also be a Son, in regard to his proclamation of the hidden things of his Father, as a person's word may be called the "child of his mind." For just as our word is the messenger of what is seen by the mind, so the Word of God knows the Father and reveals the Father whom he knows, since no created being can approach him without a guide. For "no one knows the Father except the Son, and he to whom the Son has revealed him,"[44] and in that he is Word he is the angel [messenger] of mighty Counsel "whose rule came on his shoulder."[45] For he ruled as King through his suffering of the cross. COMMENTARY ON THE GOSPEL OF JOHN 1.38.(42).[46]

THE DIVINE WORD COMES HUMBLY AMONG US. ATHANASIUS: The Word of God is not a creature, but creator, and says in the fashion of Proverbs, "he created me"[47] at the time when he put on created flesh.[48] There is something

---

[37]ACW 6:140-41*. [38]Referring to Jn 17:21, which he is commenting on. [39]ECF 234. [40]By which he means the lesser spiritual powers (Cthonic daimons) who have subverted pagan worship, seeking to have themselves worshiped by the pagan rites (a common Christian explanation of Greco-Roman religion). Clement is addressing Christ's lordship to believers and potential converts. [41]The economy of the revelation to the world and the incarnation. [42]ECF 235. [43]ECF 290. [44]Mt 11:27. [45]Is 9:6 (LXX). [46]ECF 291. [47]Prov 8:22. [48]The assertion in Prov 8:22 that wisdom (Logos) was created by God in the "beginning of his ways" was a major scriptural testimony used by the Arians in the fourth century to argue that the Logos was a part of the creation and not consubstantial with God. Athanasius here, as in many other parts of his theology, argues that the text has to be exegeted in proper context: namely, that it does not refer to the "beginning of God's ways" (that is, the eternal pretemporal being of God) but rather to the beginning of Wisdom's role in the creation; in other words, that the created aspect of the Logos signifies the material body the Logos decided to assume, in order to save that very material creation the Logos inaugurated pretemporally.

else that may be understood from the passage itself. . . . He calls the Father Lord, not because he was a servant but because he "took the form of a servant."[49] For it was right for him on the one hand to call God "Father," as being the Word from the Father; on the other hand to call the Father "Lord," since he came "to finish the work"[50] and took a servant's form. . . . If he says that he was "created for the works," it is clear that he means to signify not his substance but the "dispensation"[51] that happened for his works, and this dispensation is subordinate to being. AGAINST THE ARIANS 2.50-51.[52]

THE WORD ASSUMES FLESH IN THE LAST DAYS. FIRST CREED OF THE COUNCIL OF ANTI-OCH (341): We have learned from the beginning to believe in one God, the God of the universe, the creator and administrator of all things, both those intelligible and those perceived by the senses; and in one only-begotten Son of God before all ages, subsisting and coexisting with the Father who begat him, through whom also all things visible and invisible were made; who in the last days, according to the Father's good pleasure, descended, and assumed flesh from the holy Virgin, and having fully accomplished all his Father's will, suffered, and rose again, and ascended into the heavens and is sitting at the right hand of the Father; and is coming to judge the living and the dead, and continues King and God forever. ATHANASIUS, ON THE SYNODS 22.[53]

The Equality of the Son

THE SON OF GOD IS LIFE AND LIFE-GIVING. ATHANASIUS: The words "I am in the Father, and the Father is in me"[54] do not mean, as the Arians suppose, that they are decanted into each other, being each filled from the other, as in the case of empty vessels, so that the Son fills the Father's emptiness and the Father the Son's, each of them separately not being full and perfect . . . ; for the Father is full and perfect, and the Son is "the fullness of the Godhead."[55] Again, God is not in the Son in the same way as he comes into the saints and thus strengthens them. For the Son is himself the "power and wisdom"[56] of the Father. It is by partaking of him that created things are sanctified in the Spirit. But he himself is not Son by participation; on the contrary, he is the Father's proper offspring. The Son is not in the Father in the sense that "we live and move and exist in him."[57] For he is the life, as being from the fount of the Father, in which all things are brought to life and have substantial existence. Life itself does not live "in Life," for then it would not be Life; but rather he brings all things to life. AGAINST THE ARIANS 3.1.[58]

EQUAL TO THE FATHER AS GOD, BUT SUBJECT AS MAN. AUGUSTINE: Many statements in the Scriptures imply, or even openly assert, that the Father is greater than the Son. People have erred because they have not been careful enough to examine the whole tenor of the Scriptures and thus have sought to transfer what is said of Christ Jesus as man to his mode of being before his incarnation, which was and is eternal. And they allege that the Son is inferior to the Father because the Lord himself is quoted as saying, "The Father is greater than I."[59] But it is demonstrable that in this respect the Son is also inferior to himself. For if "he emptied himself, receiving the form of a servant,"[60] he must surely have become inferior to himself.[61] For this taking of the form of a servant did not entail his losing the form of God. . . . In both forms he was the same only-begotten Son of God the Father, in the form of God equal to the Father, in the form of a servant "the mediator between God and humankind, the man Christ Jesus."[62]

---

[49]Phil 2:7. [50]Jn 17:4. [51]The incarnation. [52]ECF 392-93. [53]CCC 12. Cf. Socrates Scholasticus *Ecclesiastical History* 2.10.6-7. [54]Jn 14:10. [55]Col 1:19. [56]1 Cor 1:24. [57]Acts 17:28. [58]ECF 393-94**. [59]Jn 14:28. [60]Phil 2:7. [61]An argument where Augustine is pressing the logic to its nonsensical end, to the point that scriptural texts cannot be forced in a literalistically simplistic way if one is to gain a proper comprehension of the meaning.

Then obviously in the form of a servant he is inferior to himself in the form of God. . . . He is equal to the Father in nature, inferior to him in conditions . . . In the form of God he made humankind; in the form of a servant he was made man. . . . Therefore, since the form of God received the form of a servant, he is both God and man; but God, because God took hu-manity, man, because of the taking of humanity. And by that taking neither is turned or changed into the other; Godhead is not changed into a creature, so as to cease to be Godhead, or crea-ture into Godhead, so as to cease to be creature. The Trinity 1.14.[63]

[62]1 Tim 2:5.   [63]LCF 214.

BEGOTTEN, NOT MADE

καὶ εἰς ἕνα κύριον Ἰησοῦν Χριστόν,	Et in unum Dominum Jesum Christum,	We believe in one Lord, Jesus Christ,
τὸν υἱὸν τοῦ Θεοῦ τὸν μονογενῆ,	Filium Dei unigenitum,	the only Son of God,
τὸν ἐκ τοῦ πατρὸς γεννηθέντα	et ex Patre natum	eternally
πρὸ πάντων τῶν αἰώνων,	ante omnia saecula	begotten of the Father,
φῶς ἐκ φωτός,	[Deum de Deo], Lumen de Lumine,	[God from God], Light from Light,
Θεὸν ἀληθινὸν ἐκ θεοῦ ἀληθινοῦ,	Deum verum de Deo vero,	true God from true God,
γεννηθέντα, οὐ ποιηθέντα,	**genitum, non factum,**	**begotten, not made,**
ὁμοούσιον τῷ πατρί·	consubstantialem Patri;	of one Being with the Father.
δι᾽ οὗ τὰ πάντα ἐγένετο·	per quem omnia facta sunt;	Through him all things were made.
τὸν δι᾽ ἡμᾶς τοὺς ἀνθρώπους	qui propter nos homines	For us
καὶ διὰ τὴν ἡμετέραν σωτηρίαν	et propter nostram salutem	and for our salvation
κατελθόντα ἐκ τῶν οὐρανῶν	descendit de coelis,	he came down from heaven:
καὶ σαρκωθέντα ἐκ πνεύματος ἁγίου	et incarnatus est de Spiritu Sancto	by the power of the Holy Spirit
καὶ Μαρίας τῆς παρθένου	ex Maria virgine,	he became incarnate from the Virgin Mary,
καὶ ἐνανθρωπήσαντα,	et homo factus est;	and was made man.

Historical Context: The insistence on the Son as "begotten, not made" is another par-ticular aspect of the fourth-century Arian con-troversy that breaks its way into the text of the creed at this point. Insofar as the larger bibli-cal analogy of the Son of God's birth from the Father could be used to designate a wide range of modes of emanation from God (angels and saints could be in a sense spoken of as born of God), the Nicene fathers were concerned with this additional clause to specify that the Son's process of being begotten from the Father is uniquely different from all others. Adding on the qualification "begotten before all ages" is specifically meant to attack the central Ar-ian premiss that the Son was a creature whom God the Father brought into being at a certain time in the plan of salvation. The creedal af-firmation elevates against such notion the twin insistence that the Son was born of God (not made or created or emitted in any less than personal sense) and that the birth of the Son takes place within eternity, that is, within the divine being, not as something extrinsic or alien to it. Both images, that of a natural birth (the Son is confessed by the church's faith as a son in the strongest sense of natural paternal closeness, or identity, that such an image conveys) and that the eternal birth describes and defines the full divine status of the being of the Son, were felt to be necessary additions to the ancient baptismal creed in order to meet the Arian problem head on.

Several Arian theologians had begun to argue in the fourth century that the divine sonship of Christ was an analogy for the sanctification of a creature and, therefore, the biblical references to the heavenly Son of God ought to be taken as references to God's creation of his angelic helpers. They argued that this applied especially to the great angel, the Logos, who though he was heavily involved in the salvation of the world, was still, nonetheless, the firstborn (that is, first-created) of the supreme Monad of the divinity and was a son of God on the same terms as the rest of creation, only perhaps more impressively so. To teach the doctrine that Jesus was the earthly Son of God, precisely because he was the incarnation of the eternal Son of God and that in his case alone birth means the antithesis of creation, this clause in the creed, "begotten, not made," was added.

OVERVIEW: The birth of the Son is something divine and mysterious that surpasses human capacity and imagination, which are space- and time-bound, as it is not (IRENAEUS). The divine begetting, being timeless, manifests all the characters of divine perfection in the timelessness of the Son (ATHANASIUS, CYRIL OF JERUSALEM, GREGORY OF NYSSA). This is why the Son is the timeless perfection of God his Father (AUGUSTINE). The Word is the natural offspring of the Father, not an adopted son (ATHANASIUS), and this is why he has the

selfsame being, not a share in the being of God (BASIL). The particular title "only-begotten Son" demonstrates this most succinctly and implicitly teaches the consubstantiality of the Father and Son. The eternal sonship, however, is also a mystery meant for the salvation of the world, for the Son is the Savior of the cosmos (CYRIL OF JERUSALEM, EUSEBIUS). The incarnation of the eternal Son invests the human race with glory (EPHREM), and the incarnation becomes the point of union between deity and humanity (HILARY). The fragility of the Son of God on earth does not detract from his glory as eternal Son. The Word effects the transfiguration of humanity itself in and through his own adoption of human nature (CYRIL OF ALEXANDRIA).

The Son Is Eternally Begotten

THE SON'S BIRTH FROM GOD. IRENAEUS: If anyone asks us how the Son was produced from the Father, we reply that no one understands that production, or generation, or calling or revelation, or whatever term anyone applies to his begetting, which in truth is indescribable. Valentinus[1] does not understand it, or Marcion, or Saturninus, or Basilides, or angels, or archangels, or principalities or powers. Only the Father knows, who begat him, and the Son who was begotten. Thus, since his generation cannot be described, no sensible person exerts himself to talk of begettings and productions or undertakes to explain what is indefinable. All people certainly know that a word is emitted from the mind, and so those who have thought out the term "emissions" have not hit on anything important, nor have they discovered some hidden mystery in applying to the only-begotten Word of God a meaning that is a matter of common

---

[1]A second-century Gnostic teacher. Here Irenaeus introduces a series of all the chief Christian Gnostics, whom he lumps together. All of them regarded the Son of God as an emanation of the divine, subordinate to the supreme divine principle and different from it.

knowledge. They call him indescribable and unnamable and then, as if they had assisted at his birth, they talk largely about "the production and generation of his first begetting" and liken him to a word emitted by human speech. But we shall not go astray if we say about him, as about matter, that God produced him. For we have learned from Scripture that God is the first source of all. But whence or how he emitted material substance the Scriptures have not revealed. And it is not our duty to indulge in conjecture and make guesses about infinite things that concern God. The knowledge of such matters is to be left to God. AGAINST HERESIES 2.28.6.[2]

THE SON, BEGOTTEN FROM PERFECTION.

ATHANASIUS: It is right to call the Son the eternal offspring of the Father, for the substance of the Father was never imperfect so that what belonged to it might be added later. To beget in time is characteristic of humankind. For humans nature is incomplete; God's offspring is eternal, for his nature is always perfect. AGAINST THE ARIANS 1.14.[3]

THE WORD IS THE AGENT OF CREATION.

ATHANASIUS: If God is maker and creator and creates his works through the Son, and we cannot but regard things that came to be as having existence through the Word, is it not blasphemous, since God is the maker, to say that his craftsman, his Word and Wisdom, "once was not"?[4] This is as much as to deny that God is the maker, if he has not, as his own, his craftsman, that is, his Word, derived from himself; for then the Word through whom he fashions his work is adventitious, alien, essentially unlike.... If the Word is not eternally with the Father, then the Trinity is not eternal; there was first a unity that later has become a trinity by addition.[5] ... And, what is worse, the Trinity is found to be disparate, consisting of alien and different natures and substances.... It may conceivably receive further addition,

ad infinitum. ... It may diminish, for clearly what is added may be subtracted. AGAINST THE ARIANS 1.17.[6]

THE SON DOES NOT COME INTO BEING.

ATHANASIUS: Created things have come into being by God's pleasure and by his will, but the Son is not a creation of his will, nor has he come into being subsequently, as the creation did. Rather, he is by nature the proper offspring of the Father's substance.[7] He is the proper Word of the Father, and we cannot, therefore, suppose any will existing before him, since he is the Father's living counsel and power, fashioning what the Father had decided on.... By the act of will by which the Son is willed by the Father, the Son himself loves and wills and honors the Father.[8] AGAINST THE ARIANS 3.63, 66.[9]

THE SON HAS THE SAME BEING AS THE FATHER.

BASIL OF CAESAREA: The difference between ingenerate and generate is not one of greater and less, like that between the greater and the lesser light. It is the difference that separates attributes that cannot possibly coexist in the same subject. It is inconceivable that a subject possessing one of these characters should change to the opposite character, the ingenerate becoming generate or vice versa.... There is here a diametrical opposition. Therefore those who suppose generacy and ingeneracy to be within the category of substance[10] find themselves in absurdities. For these will be a begetting of contrary from contrary; and instead of the natural affinity, an inevitable discord will appear between them in respect of substance

---

[2]ECF 101-2. [3]ECF 380-81. [4]A significant Arian axiom, that the Word came into existence and once was not, that is, there was a time when the Word did not exist, so as to distinguish the (divine) Word from the absolute Deity. [5]Athanasius offers this as a lamentable logical result of the Arian belief, knowing that change, addition or alteration in the being of God is not permissible under the logical terms of the ascription of deity itself, such things only occurring within created natures. [6]ECF 381-82. [7]And thus, consubstantial with God (*homoousios*). [8]That is, the Son and Father have the selfsame divine will. [9]ECF 389. [10]*Ousia.*

itself. This shows more folly than impiety to say, in respect of anything whatsoever, that its substance is self-contradictory. It has long been the accepted doctrine even among non-Christian philosophers (whose teachings our opponents treat as of no account when they do not find them supporting their blasphemies) that contradiction cannot conceivably exist within substance. But anyone who accepts the truth that generacy and ingeneracy are certain distinctive properties observed in the substance, which lead to the clear and unconfused conception of the Father and the Son, will escape the danger of this impiety, and, at the same time, will preserve consistency in his reasoning. For those special properties that are observed in the substance, like characters or forms, make a distinction within the common nature by these individualizing characters, while they do not split up the unity of nature. The Godhead is common. Fatherhood and sonship are, as it were, individual properties; as a result of the interweaving of the two, the common and the particular, the apprehension of the truth comes, arises in us. And so, when we hear of "ingenerate light," we think of the Father, while "generate light" conveys to us the notion of the Son. In respect that both are light there exists no contrariety in them. In respect that one is generate and the other ingenerate, a contrast is observed. It is the nature of special properties to display a difference within the identity of the substance, and it frequently happens that these special properties are mutually contrary and utterly distinct, without destroying the unity of the substance. Thus . . . in the case of animals we have the special properties of winged and pedestrian, aquatic and terrestrial, rational and irrational, yet there is one underlying substance, and these special properties do not alter that substance and do not produce disunity. AGAINST EUNOMIUS II.28.[11]

THE EXPRESS IMAGE OF GOD. GREGORY OF NYSSA: It is clear, then, that however great

the person of the Father is, so great also is the "express image"[12] of that person, for it is not possible that the express image should be less than the person contemplated in it. And this the great John also teaches when he says, "In the beginning was the Word, and the Word was with God."[13] For in saying that he was "in the beginning" and not "after the beginning," he showed that the beginning was never without the Word; and in declaring that the Word was with God, he signified the absence of defect in the Son in relation to the Father; for the Word is contemplated as a whole together with the whole being of God. ON THE FAITH.[14]

THE SON ALWAYS WAS. CYRIL OF JERUSALEM: We believe in the only-begotten Son of God, who was begotten of the Father, very God. For the true God does not beget a false god, as we have said, nor did he deliberate and afterwards beget. Rather, he begot eternally, and much more swiftly than our words or thoughts. We speak within time and expend time, but in the case of the divine Power, the generation is timeless. As I have often said, God did not bring the Son from nonexistence into being and did not take what was nonexistent into sonship. On the contrary, the Father, who is eternal, ineffably and eternally begot one unique Son who has no brother. There are not two first principles, however, since the Father is the head of the Son, and the beginning is one. The Father begot the Son, who is truly God, named Emmanuel, which being interpreted is "God with us." CATECHETICAL LECTURES 11.14.[15]

THE ONLY BEGOTTEN SON IS NOT A CREATURE. THEODORE OF MOPSUESTIA: If he is an only Son, it is clear that he alone is born of God, and he alone is a Son consubstantial with his Father. The expression "only Son" denotes

[11]*LCF* 66-67. [12]Heb 1:3. [13]Jn 1:1. [14]NPNF 2 5:338. [15]NPNF 2 7:68**.

all these things and even more, because those who are called children of God are numerous, while this one is alone the "only Son." It is, indeed, written: "I have said, you are gods; and, all of you children of the most High";[16] and again, "I have nourished and brought up children."[17] Since there are many who are called children, this one would not have been called an only Son if there was not a great difference between them. They were called "children by grace" because they became near to God and members of the household, and because of this membership of the household they deserved, by grace, to be called by this name. This one, however, was called an only Son because he alone is a Son consubstantial with his Father. He was not called a Son because he, like others, became by grace worthy of the adoption of sons, but because he was born of the very nature of the Father. He was called, and he is, a Son. Although these things are clear and evident in the Sacred Books, and although it is patent to everyone that no one can be called an only Son except the one who is truly of the same nature as his Father, the unholy and erroneous opinion of the heretics remained for some time without rectification. Of all those who had received the knowledge of Christ, Arius was the first to dare and to say impiously that the Son was a creature. ON THE NICENE CREED 3.[18]

GOD'S CHANGELESSNESS ALSO BELONGS TO THE SON. AUGUSTINE: Nothing is predicated of God *per accidens*[19] because nothing in him is subject to change, but that does not mean that everything is predicated of him in respect of substance. There are relative predicates, as Father in relation to Son, Son in relation to Father, but those are not accidental either, for the Father is always Father, the Son always Son. . . . Therefore, although being Son is different from being Father, there is no difference of substance; for those predicates are relative, yet not accidental, because they are not susceptible of change. THE TRINITY 5.6.[20]

THE FATHER ENGENDERS THE SON ETERNALLY. AUGUSTINE: When the Son says, "As the Father has life in himself, so has he granted to the Son to have life in himself,"[21] it is not meant that the Father has given life to a Son who hitherto was lifeless but that he has begotten him timelessly, in such a way that the life which the Father has given to the Son in begetting him is coeternal with the life of the Father who has given it. THE TRINITY 15.47.[22]

The Incarnation

THE INCARNATION INVESTS HUMANITY WITH GLORY. EPHREM THE SYRIAN: You are the Son of the Creator, who resembles his Father. As Maker, he made himself in the womb. He put on a pure body and emerged. He made our weakness put on glory, by the mercy that he brought from his Father's presence. From Melchizedek, the high priest, the hyssop came to you;[23] a throne and a crown from the house of David; a family and a people from Abraham. HYMNS ON THE NATIVITY 9.2-3.[24]

A WOVEN GARMENT OF THE FLESH. EPHREM THE SYRIAN: Nazareth thanks you that it was worthy of your birth. O Nazarene, it offers your childhood a crown, and it offers another crown to your hiddenness.[25] By your conception in the womb, it was first aware of your pure woven garment and your pleasing plaited crown: the name and the body that completed you.[26]

---

[16]Ps 82:6. [17]Is 1:2. [18]WS 5:40. [19]In ancient philosophical thought "accidental attributes" were those that were external to a thing (size, color, or so on) that did not affect its essential reality. A table, for example, would still be a table whether it was large or small, green or red. Augustine's point here is that all that is true of God is essentially true, as nothing in God is accidental, since this would be an inherent contradiction of divine status. However, the basic logic of this does not entail that all statements about God are directly referred to his divine substance as such, since references to the persons of the Trinity are not references to the divine substance but to the divine hypostases. [20]LCF 231-32. [21]Jn 5:26. [22]LCF 228. [23]That is, Christ. [24]ESH 125. [25]Ephrem refers to the public and mystical (hidden) aspects of the incarnation. [26]The woven garment is his manner of referring to the flesh of the invisi-

HYMNS ON VIRGINITY 32.1.[27]

GOD ADOPTS A BODY TO COME TO THE WORLD AS SAVIOR. CYRIL OF JERUSALEM: Learn also another cause of the incarnate economy. Christ came that he might be baptized and might sanctify baptism. He came that he might work wonders, walking on the waters of the sea. Since then, before his appearance in flesh, "the sea saw him and fled, and Jordan was turned back,"[28] the Lord took to himself his body that the sea might endure the sight and Jordan receive him without fear. This, then, is one cause; but there is also a second. Through Eve, yet a virgin, came death; through a virgin, or rather from a virgin, must the Life appear: that as the serpent beguiled the one, so Gabriel might bring good tidings to the other. People forsook God and made carved images of people. Since, therefore, an image of a person was falsely worshiped as God, God became truly Man, that the falsehood might be done away. CATECHETICAL LECTURES 12.15.[29]

CHRIST IS DAVID'S LORD AS WELL AS DAVID'S SON. CYRIL OF ALEXANDRIA: How, therefore, is the Son of David David's Lord[30] and seated also at the right hand of God the Father, and on the throne of Deity? Or is it not altogether according to the unerring word of the mystery, that the Word, being God, and sprung from the very substance of God the Father and being in his likeness and on an equality with him, became flesh, that is, man, perfectly so, and yet without departing from the incomparable excellence of the divine dignities, continuing rather in that estate in which he had ever been and still being God, though he had become flesh and "in form like to us"?[31] He is David's Lord, therefore, according to that which belongs to his divine glory and nature and sovereignty, but David's son according to the flesh. HOMILIES ON THE GOSPEL OF LUKE 137.[32]

THE INCARNATE LORD REFUTES ERROR.

CYRIL OF ALEXANDRIA: Do you care to see another virtue of the Child? Do you care to see that he is by nature God, who in the flesh was of woman? Then learn what the prophet Isaiah says of him: "And I drew near to the prophetess, and she conceived and bore a male; and the Lord said to me, Call his name 'Quick take captive, and spoil hastily.'"[33] For before the child shall know how to call out father or mother, he shall take the strength of Damascus."[34] For contemporaneously with the birth of Christ the power of the devil was spoiled. In Damascus he had been the object of religious service and had had there very many worshipers; but when the holy Virgin brought forth, the power of his tyranny was broken, for the heathen were won over to the knowledge of the truth. Their firstfruits and leaders were the magi, who came from the East to Jerusalem; whose teacher was the heaven, whose schoolmaster was a star. HOMILIES ON THE GOSPEL OF LUKE 2.[35]

The Godhead and the Incarnate Lord

INCARNATION FOR THE AID OF THE WORLD. EUSEBIUS OF CAESAREA: In short, he performed all his works through the medium of that body that he had assumed for the sake of those who were otherwise incapable of apprehending his divine nature. In all this he was the servant of his Father's will, himself remaining still the same as when he was with the Father; unchanged in essence, unimpaired in nature, unfettered by the trammels of mortal flesh nor hindered by his abode in a human body from

ble God; and the crown is not only an allusion to the crown of thorns (the public aspect of the economy of salvation) but also to Christ's crown of royal dignity—the messianic anointing the Logos gave to the incarnate assumed flesh. Most of Ephrem's poetry plays in this way on twofold polarities of revelations and hidden mysteries. [27]ESH 403. [28]Ps 114:3. [29]NPNF 2 7:75*. [30]Mt 22:43-45. [31]Phil 2:7-8. [32]CGSL 545-46. [33]Is 8:3. [34]Damascus in patristic biblical exegesis signifies the power of Satan over the world, especially as this was focused in idolatry (seen as the root of all error and wickedness among human society). Cyril is arguing that by his incarnation, Jesus destroyed idolatry and commenced the liberating enlightenment of all humanity. [35]CGSL 53*.

being elsewhere present. No, at the very time of his intercourse with people, he was pervading all things, was with and in the Father, and even then was caring for all things both in heaven and earth. Nor was he precluded, as we are, from being present everywhere or from the continued exercise of his divine power. He gave of his own to humankind but received nothing in return. He endowed mortality out of his divine power but was not changed himself by mortality. ORATION ON CONSTANTINE 14.6-8.[36]

THE LORD WAS NOT DIMINISHED BY THE INCARNATION. EUSEBIUS OF CAESAREA: Hence his human birth to him brought no defilement, nor could his impassible essence suffer at the dissolution of his mortal body. For let us suppose a lyre should receive an accidental injury or its chord be broken. It does not follow that the performer on the lyre suffers. Nor, if a wise person's body undergoes punishment, can we fairly assert that his wisdom, or the soul within him, are maimed or burned. Far less can we affirm that the inherent power of the Word sustained any detriment from his bodily passion, any more than, as in the instance we have already used, the solar rays that are shot from heaven to earth contract defilement, though in contact with mire and pollution of every kind. We may, indeed, assert that these things partake of the radiance of the light, but not that the light is contaminated or the sun defiled by this contact with other bodies. And indeed these things are themselves not contrary to nature. But the Savior, the incorporeal Word of God, being Life and spiritual Light itself, whatever he touches with divine and incorporeal power must of necessity become endued with the intelligence of light and life. Thus, if he should touch a body, it becomes enlightened and sanctified. It is at once delivered from all disease, infirmity and suffering, and that which before was lacking is supplied by a portion of his fullness. And such was the tenor of his life on earth; now proving the sympathies of his human nature with our

own, and now revealing himself as the Word of God. He is wondrous and mighty in his works as God. ORATION ON CONSTANTINE 14.9-12.[37]

THE INCARNATION UNITES GODHEAD TO HUMANITY. HILARY OF POITIERS: Jesus Christ is man and God: his existence as God does not begin with his birth as man, nor does he cease to be God when he becomes man; and after his human life there is the whole of manhood and the whole of Godhead in his divinity. . . . There is a distinction between the three states: God, before his human life; then God and man; and thereafter wholly God and wholly man. ON THE TRINITY 9.6.[38]

THE INCARNATE LORD IS WHOLLY GOOD. CYRIL OF ALEXANDRIA: And because he was God, ineffably made flesh, he knew only the good and was exempt from that depravity that belongs to humanity. And this too is an attribute of the supreme Substance, for that which is good by nature, firmly and unchangeably, belongs specially to it, and it only, for there is none good, but one God, as the Savior has himself said.[39] HOMILIES ON THE GOSPEL OF LUKE 2.[40]

THE GROWTH OF JESUS IS NOT AN ALTERATION IN GOD. CYRIL OF ALEXANDRIA: For the wise Evangelist did not introduce the Word in his abstract and incorporeal nature and so say of him that "he increased in stature and wisdom and grace,"[41] but after having shown that he was born in the flesh of a woman and took our likeness, he then assigns to him these human attributes, and calls him a child and says that he waxed in stature, as his body grew little by little, in obedience to corporeal laws. And so he is said also to have increased in wisdom, not as receiving fresh supplies of wisdom, for God is perceived by the understanding to be entirely perfect in all things and altogether incapable of

---

[36]NPNF 2 1:603-4**. [37]NPNF 2 1:604*. [38]*LCF* 50. [39]Lk 18:19. [40]*CGSL* 53*. [41]Lk 2:52.

---

being destitute of any attribute suitable to the Godhead, but because God the Word gradually manifested his wisdom proportionally to the age that the body had attained. The body then advances in stature and the soul in wisdom, for the divine nature is capable of increase in neither one nor the other, seeing that the Word of God is all perfect. And with good reason he connected the increase of wisdom with the growth of the bodily stature, because the divine nature revealed its own wisdom in proportion to the measure of the bodily growth. HOMILIES ON THE GOSPEL OF LUKE 5.[42]

THE LORD POSSESSES THE GLORY OF GOD EVEN AS MAN. CYRIL OF ALEXANDRIA: In every way, therefore, we may perceive that the Word of God, even when he was man, nevertheless continued to be one Son.[43] For he performs those works that belong to deity, possessing the majesty and glory of the Godhead inseparable from him. If so we believe, he will crown us with his grace: by whom and with whom to God the Father be glory and dominion with the Holy Spirit, to ages of ages. Amen. HOMILIES ON THE GOSPEL OF LUKE 10.[44]

THE INCARNATION DRAWS THE WORLD TO THE LORD. CYRIL OF ALEXANDRIA: Come therefore, and let us approach the Savior's words, opening wide the eye of the mind. And his words are, "Everything has been delivered to me by my Father."[45] For he was and still is Lord of heaven and earth, and sits with the Father on his throne and equally shares his government over all. But inasmuch as he became man by humbling himself to our estate, he further speaks in a manner fitting to the dispensation in the flesh and does not refuse those expressions that suit the measure of his state, when he had emptied himself, that he might be believed on as having become like to us and as having put on our poverty. He, therefore, who was Lord of heaven and earth, and, in a word, of all things, says that "everything was delivered" to him by the Father. For he has been

made ruler of all under heaven. Of old only Israel after the flesh bowed the neck to his laws. But God the Father willed to make all things new in him and by his means to reconcile the world to himself. For he became mediator between God and humanity and was made our peace, in that he united us by himself to God the Father; for he is the door and the way whereby this is done; for he has even plainly said, "No man comes to the Father but by me."[46] He, then, who of old delivered Israel by the hand of Moses from the tyranny of the Egyptians and appointed the law to be their schoolmaster has now called the whole world. He himself has spread the net of the gospel message for it, according to the good will of God the Father. And this is the reason why he says, "Every thing has been delivered to me by my Father." HOMILIES ON THE GOSPEL OF LUKE 66.[47]

THE INCARNATION BRINGS SALVATION IN THE FLESH. CYRIL OF ALEXANDRIA: For he is also the image of his person, who by right of his nature possesses everything that God is who begot him; by being of the selfsame substance, and of an equality admitting of no variation and of a similarity to him in everything. Being, therefore, by nature God, he is said to have received of the Father the "name that is above every name,"[48] when he had become man, that he might be believed in as God and the King of all, even in the flesh that was united to him. But when he had endured the passion on the cross for our sakes and had abolished death by the resurrection of his body from the dead, he ascended to the Father and became "as a man journeying to a far country."[49] For heaven is a different country from earth, and he ascended that he might receive for himself a kingdom. HOMILIES ON THE GOSPEL OF LUKE 128.[50]

---

[42]CGSL 64*. [43]Cyril, throughout his writings, insists on the personal, subjective unity of the Word of God enfleshed: that Jesus of Nazareth was one and the same as the word of God incarnate. [44]CGSL 77. [45]Mt 11:27. [46]Jn 14:6. [47]CGSL 281*. [48]Phil 2:9. [49]Lk 15:13. [50]CGSL 509*

OF ONE BEING WITH THE FATHER

καὶ εἰς ἕνα κύριον Ἰησοῦν Χριστόν,	Et in unum Dominum Jesum Christum,	We believe in one Lord, Jesus Christ,
τὸν υἱὸν τοῦ Θεοῦ τὸν μονογενῆ,	Filium Dei unigenitum,	the only Son of God,
τὸν ἐκ τοῦ πατρὸς γεννηθέντα	et ex Patre natum	eternally
πρὸ πάντων τῶν αἰώνων,	ante omnia saecula	begotten of the Father,
φῶς ἐκ φωτός,	[Deum de Deo], Lumen de Lumine,	[God from God], Light from Light,
Θεὸν ἀληθινὸν ἐκ θεοῦ ἀληθινοῦ,	Deum verum de Deo vero,	true God from true God,
γεννηθέντα, οὐ ποιηθέντα,	genitum, non factum,	begotten, not made,
ὁμοούσιον τῷ πατρὶ·	**consubstantialem Patri;**	**of one Being with the Father.**
δι᾽ οὗ τὰ πάντα ἐγένετο·	per quem omnia facta sunt;	Through him all things were made.
τὸν δι᾽ ἡμᾶς τοὺς ἀνθρώπους	qui propter nos homines	For us
καὶ διὰ τὴν ἡμετέραν σωτηρίαν	et propter nostram salutem	and for our salvation
κατελθόντα ἐκ τῶν οὐρανῶν	descendit de coelis,	he came down from heaven:
καὶ σαρκωθέντα ἐκ πνεύματος ἁγίου	et incarnatus est de Spiritu Sancto	by the power of the Holy Spirit
καὶ Μαρίας τῆς παρθένου	ex Maria virgine,	he became incarnate from the Virgin Mary,
καὶ ἐνανθρωπήσαντα,	et homo factus est;	and was made man.

HISTORICAL CONTEXT: By the time of the Council of Nicaea in 325, it had become apparent to many who had been debating the christological issues over the last few decades that the Arian party could use many biblical terms and concepts in a radically different sense from what they seemed to mean to the orthodox. The Son's birth from the Father, for example, was read by Arians as a synonym for "being made." The Word's issuing from "before the creation" was read as meaning "as the first act of creation." So, the Nicene fathers were determined, at the council of 325, to make a statement within the series of christological clauses that could not be interpreted in an ambiguous sense.

Into the series of descriptions of how the Son was born of God, as true God from true God, and as eternal from eternal and as Son from Father, they inserted this explanatory clause: "that is, born of the being of the Father." This affirmation of the Son's birth from the very being (ousia) of God was a highly abstract and shorthand way of summing up the generic biblical doctrine of the Son's birth from the Father. The use of the philosophical concept of "birth from out of the divine essence" was meant to emphasize and underscore the potency of other biblical metaphors about the divine sonship, rather than replace or supersede them. But in a real sense history had been made, for the affirmation that the Son was "consubstantial (homoousion) with the Father" marks the very first time that a major doctrinal statement had been credally expressed in anything other than purely biblical phrases. The Homoousion was not a term to be found in the scriptures, and this fact worried some of the bishops who were aware that credal utterances had traditionally been fashioned from biblical citations or biblical paraphrases in the main. However, consubstantiality was known across all the party lines to be the one thing that all Arians agreed was entirely unacceptable. This was partly why it was inserted here for a refutatory purpose. The doctrine of consubstantiality teaches that the Son is of the divine essence, in fact is God in the selfsame sense that the Father is God. Before Athanasius of Alexandria decided to use the term as a rallying point after the council, his preferred synonym had been "identity in essence" (*tautotēs tēs ousias*) between the Father and Son.

Not all the theologians of the fourth century who affirmed the *homoousion* understood it in this most elevated philosophical sense, that the consubstantiality meant identity of divine essence and thus involved one in the confession of the coequality of Father and Son in terms of the divine nature, and it would require much further work from Athanasius and the Cappadocian fathers to clarify this and demonstrate how it led inexorably into a full trinitarian theology. All who affirmed the *homoousion*, however, knew it to mean that Jesus was to be confessed as truly God, without equivocation and without mental reservation. To that extent it has often been regarded as the epitome of the Nicene confession of orthodoxy. In its time, it was meant to be a brief synopsis of what the biblical confessions meant in simple and condensed form, not a replacement of them.

Overview: The Son does not participate in the being of the Father. He is born of it and enjoys it as his own (Athanasius). The *homoousion* is not the be all and end all of Christian theology and is troublesome to many (Basil), but it correctly and effectively epitomizes orthodox faith (Hilary). The word ought not to be taken in a materialistic, or physical, sense of "common matter," since God is not of that kind of substance (Eusebius, Basil). When it is understood intelligently, it signifies that the Son is not a creature and does not come from nothing, as does the rest of creation, but rather is born of God (Basil). The highest and truest sense of the word *homoousion* is that the Father and the Son have the selfsame, the identical, being (Gregory of Nazianzus, Basil). The concept is in communion with the scriptural Christology, at least if the latter is properly understood (Gregory of Nazianzus, Gregory of Nyssa).

Being of One Substance with the Father

The Son Is of the Father's Being. Athanasius: Your assertion that "the Son is from nothing" and "did not exist before he was begotten" implies that the names of Son, God, Wisdom, are given him in virtue of participation.[1] . . . Participation in what? . . . In the Spirit? No, the Spirit "takes from the Son."[2] . . . Therefore it is of the Father that "he partakes," for this is the only remaining possibility. But of what does he partake, and from whence? If it is something external, provided by the Father, he no longer partakes of the Father, nor can he be called the Father's Son. . . . Therefore what he partakes must be "of the substance of the Father."[3] And if this is something other than the substance of the Father . . . there will be something intermediate between this that is from the Father and the substance (whatever that be) of the Son. . . . We are forced to say that the Son is entirely that which is "of the substance of the Father." Against the Arians 1.15-16.[4]

The Homoousion Is Our Guide. Hilary of Poitiers: The orthodox believer will assert "one substance of Father and Son," but he must not start from that, nor must he hold this as the chief truth, as if there could be no true faith without it. He will assert "one substance" without danger, when he has first said, "The Father is ingenerate; and the Son has his origin and existence from the Father and is like the Father in goodness, honor and nature." The Son is subject to his Father, as the origin of his being. . . . He does not come from nothing; he is generate. He is not unborn, but he shares in timelessness. He

---

[1]*Methexis*: by derivation from God in a relation such as creatures enjoy derived being from God. [2]Jn 16:14. [3]The Logos is consubstantial (*homoousios*) with the Father, that is, shares the same nature or being. [4]*ECF* 381.

is not the Father, but the Son derived from him. He is not a portion, he is a whole: not the Creator himself, but his image; the image of God, born of God, from God. He is not a creature; he is God. But he is not another God in underlying substance, but one God though essence of undiffering substance. God is one, not in person but in nature. ON THE COUNCILS 69.[5]

THE HOMOOUSION IS NOT A MATERIAL CONCEPTION. EUSEBIUS OF CAESAREA: So also the phrase "the Son is consubstantial with the Father"[6] stands up if properly examined, not in the manner of bodies or similarly to mortal animals,[7] or by division or cutting up of the essence or by any suffering or alteration or change of the essence and power of the Father; for the unbegotten nature of the Father is free from all these things. But the phrase "consubstantial with the Father" indicates that the Son of God bears no similarity with the creatures of God that came into being, but is in every way made like only to the Father who begot him and is not of any other hypostasis or essence, but of the Father. It seemed proper to assent to the term itself, expounded in this manner, since I knew of some learned and distinguished bishops and writers among the ancients who made use of the term homoousios in the doctrinal discussion about the Father and the Son. LETTER ON THE COUNCIL OF NICAEA.[8]

WE DO NOT MEAN CONSUBSTANTIALITY AS HERETICS USED IT. BASIL OF CAESAREA: For it is true that the members of a synod, dealing with Paul of Samosata, reprobated this word (homoousios)[9] as having the wrong kind of sound. For they said that "consubstantial" suggested the notion of a physical substance and the things made out of it; the parceling out of a substance into particular things giving the appellation "consubstantial" to the things into which it has been divided. Such a notion is appropriate in the case of bronze and the coins made from that substance, but in the case of

God the Father and God the Son there can be no thought of a substance prior or superior to the two particulars: it would be the extreme of impiety to entertain or to express such an idea. What could be prior to the Unbegotten? LETTER 52.1.[10]

TRUE BELIEVERS ACCEPT THE HOMOOUSION. BASIL OF CAESAREA: We are the heirs of those who at Nicaea issued the great proclamation of true religion. Their doctrine has been generally received without cavil, but the word consubstantial, reluctantly accepted by some, is still not universally admitted. One may be justified in blaming those who reject it, while at the same time acknowledging that they may have some excuse.[11] Their refusal to follow the Fathers and to regard their pronouncement of higher authority than their own opinion is deserving of censure for its excessive arrogance. LETTER 52.1.[12]

THE SON IS NOT "FROM NOTHING." BASIL OF CAESAREA: And such a blasphemous notion[13] would destroy our faith in the Father and the Son, for it is a fraternal relation that unites those things that derive their subsistence from one source. And because there were still some

---

[5]LCF 48.   [6]Eusebius, who had reluctantly assented to the Nicene homoousion at the council in 325, was subsequently called on by his local church in Palestine to explain what the Nicene Creed meant in its key phrases.   [7]Eusebius had been reluctant to assent to the homoousion because he felt it was too "material" a term to fittingly designate God's immaterial essence.   [8]LCC 3:339.   [9]The first appearance of the word consubstantial was in the synodical process against Paul of Samosata from the early third century, who had described the Logos as "consubstantial with God," but in the sense that it was not a distinct hypostasis, merely another of the several attributes of the Monad of divine power. The Arian party were delighted to seize on this inauspicious prehistory of the Nicene phrase (albeit the Nicenes used it in an entirely different sense) so as to embarrass them. Basil is here dusting off their objections. [10]LCF 63.   [11]Basil's ecclesiastical ministry of reconciliation was very much bent, in his latter years, on reconciling the objectors to the word homoousion, whom he felt held the essence of the Nicene faith nevertheless.   [12]LCF 63.   [13]That Father and Son were consubstantial as if they were two expressions of the same elemental constitution.

who asserted that the Son was produced from nothing, the Nicene fathers added the phrase "of the same substance" to rule out this irreverence. For the conjunction of the Son with the Father is timeless and continuous. LETTER 52.2.[14]

THE HOMOOUSION EXPRESSES DISTINCTNESS AND UNITY IN GOD.

BASIL OF CAESAREA: This expression (*homoousios*) also corrects the perversion of Sabellius,[15] for it removes the idea of identity of subsistences and introduces the full conception of persons. Thus the expression is sound and reverent, since it establishes the distinctive marks of the subsistences while asserting the absence of difference in nature. But when we are told that the Son is "of the substance of the Father, begotten, not made," we must beware of lapsing into ideas of some kind of physical process. There is no division of substance, as if it were taken from the Father and given to the Son; nor did the substance generate by a process of flux or by production, like a plant bearing fruit. The mode of divine generation is ineffable and inconceivable by human thought. LETTER 52.3.[16]

FALSE UNDERSTANDINGS TO BE REJECTED.

BASIL OF CAESAREA: Eunomius[17] says that we "cannot say that while both share the same substance, one has precedence in rank and by reason of temporal priority." Now if by community of *ousia* he understands a preexisting matter that is distributed and divided between those who derive from it, then we ourselves could not accept such a notion. Most emphatically not; and we declare that those who make this assertion, if there are such, are no less irreverent than those who allege dissimilarity. But if community of *ousia* is taken to mean that both are regarded as having an identical principle of being, then it is confessed that light is also the substance of the Only-Begotten, and whatever principle of being one ascribes to the Father is attributed also to the Son. If that is taken to be the meaning of community of substance, then we accept the doctrine. AGAINST EUNOMIUS 1.19.[18]

THE CORRECT UNDERSTANDING OF CONSUBSTANTIALITY.

BASIL OF CAESAREA: How ought one to call the Son *homoousios* with the Father, without involving oneself in any of these notions?[19] Will you please explain this more fully? Well, I have taken it that whatever we assume the Father's *ousia* to be, we are bound, *ex hypothesi* to assume the same of the ousia of the Son. So that if one speaks of the Father's *ousia* as intellectual light, eternal, ingenerate, one must speak of the Son's *ousia* as intellectual light, eternal, ingenerate. In view of this conception, it seems to me that the phrase "like without difference" is more appropriate than *homoousios*.[20] If a light shows no difference of degree from another light, I conceive that one would not be right in calling it "the same" as the other, since each light exists in the individuality of its *ousia*; but one would rightly describe it as "precisely similar in respect of *ousia*, without difference." LETTER 361, TO APOLLINARIS.[21]

SYNONYMS FOR THE HOMOOUSION.

BASIL OF CAESAREA: If I must express my own personal opinion, I am prepared to accept the phrase "like in substance," provided that "without any difference" is added. I accept it as conveying the same meaning as "consubstantial" accord-

---

[14]*LCF* 63-64. [15]An early third-century teacher (monarchian) who had held that the Father, Son and Spirit were but three names for the same reality. [16]*LCF* 64. [17]A leading Arian theologian, known for his rigorous method of logical argument. Here he is attacking Basil for affirming the *homoousion* and then still arguing that there is a sense of precedence in the Trinity. [18]*LCF* 81. [19]Unfitting materialist conceptions of the substantial unity of Father and Son. [20]Here Basil attempts to call back a group of Nicene critics, many of whom were hostile to Athanasius and his radical Nicene movement, by suggesting to them an alternative to the Nicene *homoousion* which was more or less the same in theological sense. Basil's efforts to call together a wider group of Nicene sympathizers who were not all enamored of the *homoousion* catchword made him an object of intense suspicion to Athanasius throughout his life. [21]*LCF* 65.

ing to the sound interpretation of that word. This was the opinion of the Fathers at Nicaea, when they gave to the Only-Begotten such appellations as "Light from Light," "True God from true God," and added "consubstantial" as a corollary. Thus no difference can possibly be conceived between light and light, truth and truth, or between the substance of the Only-Begotten and the substance of the Father. As I said, I admit the phrase "of like substance," if it is taken in this sense. But if the qualification "without any difference" is cut out, which is what happened at Constantinople,[22] then I suspect the phrase as diminishing the glory of the Only-Begotten. For we frequently employ the notion of similarity in cases of obscure resemblance, where the similitude is far inferior to the original. LETTER 9.3.[23]

FATHER AND SON DO NOT EMERGE FROM A COMMON SUBSTANCE. BASIL OF CAESAREA: When I speak of one *ousia*, beware of thinking of one divided into two. Think of the Son as having existence from the Father, as source, not of the Father and Son emerging from one preexistent *ousia*. We are not speaking of brothers; we are acknowledging Father and Son. There is identity of *ousia*, since the Son derives from the Father, not made by a command but begotten from his nature; not separated from the Father by division but shining forth entire, while the Father remains entire. And please do not say, "He is preaching two gods! He is teaching polytheism!" There are not two gods; there are not two fathers. It is the one who introduces two sources who is preaching two gods. HOMILY 24.4.[24]

THE SON IS BORN FROM THE FATHER'S OWN BEING. BASIL OF CAESAREA: There is one source, and one being derived from that source; one archetype and one image. Thus the principle of unity is preserved. The Son exists as begotten from the Father, and in himself naturally representing the Father. As the Father's image,

he shows a perfect likeness; as an offspring, he safeguards the *homoousion*. HOMILY 24.4.[25]

THE HOMOOUSION SAFEGUARDS THE DIVINE UNITY. BASIL OF CAESAREA: And anyone who speaks of the begotten as of a different *ousia* from the begetter also speaks of two gods. He thereby introduces polytheism because of the unlikeness of *ousia*. If you teach that there is one begotten Godhead and another unbegotten, or that ingeneracy is the *ousia* of the Father and generacy the *ousia* of the Son, then it is you who are preaching polytheism.[26] HOMILY 24.4.[27]

THE SON DEMONSTRATES THE FATHER'S NATURE. GREGORY OF NAZIANZUS: In my opinion he is called Son because he is identical with the Father in respect of substance: and, besides this, he derives from the Father. He is called Only-Begotten, not in the sense of being the only Son, of one Father only, and being nothing but a Son, but in the sense of being begotten in a unique way, as distinct from the birth of corporeal children. He is called Word because his relation to the Father is that of word to mind. . . . One might perhaps say also that of a definition to a thing that is defined, for the word (*logos*) also has this meaning. "He who has understood" (for that is what the word "seen" means) "the Son has understood the Father."[28] The Son is a compendious and intelligible demonstration of the Father's nature. . . . And one could be right in suggesting that another reason for this title is his immanence in things, for everything that exists has Logos as its constitutive principle. ORATION 30.20.[29]

---

[22]At a synod in the capital where *homoousion* was rejected and homoiousianism was advocated, with imperial pressure (the so-called semi-Arian heresy). [23]*LCF* 62-63. [24]*LCF* 81-82. [25]*LCF* 82. [26]Basil is here refuting the Eunomian heretical notion that generacy and ingeneracy represent different natures of Father and Son, and elsewhere he shows that they represent different modalities of the selfsame nature. [27]*LCF* 82. [28]Jn 6:46; 14:9. Gregory discusses the Johannine passage where Jesus makes this answer to Philip, who has just asked to "see" the Father. [29]*LCF* 110.

Why Scripture Rejects Heretical Opinions

HOW TO READ THE SCRIPTURES PROPERLY. ATHANASIUS: "They shall perish, but you remain."[30] From this passage even the Arians might realize, if they were willing, that the Maker is different from his works. He is God, while they come into being and are made out of nothing. For "they shall perish" does not mean that creation was destined for destruction; rather, it is designed to show the nature of created things by expressing their end. Things capable of destruction have come from nothing, and in themselves they testify that once they did not exist, even though because of the grace of their maker they do not in fact perish. Therefore . . . it is said of the Son, "you remain," to show his eternity, for he is incapable of destruction. . . . To say that "he did not exist before his generation" is a statement alien to him. It is proper to him to exist always and to "remain," together with the Father. . . . He is proper to the Father's substance and one in nature with it. For that reason the Son did not say, "My Father is better than I" (so that no one should suppose him to be foreign to the Father's nature) but "Greater than I"; greater, that is, not in size or in virtue of duration but because of his begetting from the Father. In fact, by saying "greater" he again shows that he is proper to the substance of the Father. AGAINST THE ARIANS 1.58.[31]

UNDERSTANDING SCRIPTURAL REFERENCES TO THE GOD-MAN. GREGORY OF NAZIANZUS: Here[32] you have the appellations of the Son. Read over them, understanding the exalted titles in a manner befitting the Godhead and those that refer to his bodily existence, with sympathy for his humanity. Or rather keep throughout the attitude that befits the Godhead, so that you may become divine by ascending from below because of him, who for your sake descended from above. In all, and before all, keep hold of this text, and you will not go astray in respect of the exalted or the humble titles: "Jesus Christ yesterday and today" in bodily form, but in his spiritual being "the same, even forever. Amen."[33] ORATION 30.20.[34]

THE DIFFERENT SCRIPTURAL REFERENCES TO THE SON. GREGORY OF NYSSA: But to those who quote from the Proverbs the passage, "The Lord created me"[35] and think that they hereby produce a strong argument that the creator and maker of all things was created, we must answer that the "only-begotten God"[36] was made, for us, many things. For He was the Word and was made flesh; and he was God and was made man; and he was without body and was made a body; and besides, he was "made sin," and "a curse," and "a stone," and "an axe," and "bread," and "a lamb," and "a way," and "a door," and "a rock," and many such things; not being by nature any of these but being made these things for our sakes, by way of dispensation. ON THE FAITH.[37]

---

[30]Heb 1:8, 10, 11. [31]*ECF* 386-87**. [32]Gregory has been enumerating the many varied titles of Christ in the Scriptures. [33]Heb 13:8. [34]*LCF* 110-11. [35]Prov 8:22. [36]Jn 1:18. [37]NPNF 2 5:337.

THROUGH HIM ALL THINGS WERE MADE

καὶ εἰς ἕνα κύριον Ἰησοῦν Χριστὸν,	Et in unum Dominum Jesum Christum,	We believe in one Lord, Jesus Christ,
τὸν υἱὸν τοῦ Θεοῦ τὸν μονογενῆ,	Filium Dei unigenitum,	the only Son of God,
τὸν ἐκ τοῦ πατρὸς γεννηθέντα	et ex Patre natum	eternally
πρὸ πάντων τῶν αἰώνων,	ante omnia saecula	begotten of the Father,
φῶς ἐκ φωτός,	[Deum de Deo], Lumen de Lumine,	[God from God], Light from Light,
Θεὸν ἀληθινὸν ἐκ θεοῦ ἀληθινοῦ,	Deum verum de Deo vero,	true God from true God,
γεννηθέντα, οὐ ποιηθέντα,	genitum, non factum,	begotten, not made,
ὁμοούσιον τῷ πατρὶ·	consubstantialem Patri;	of one Being with the Father.
δι' οὗ τὰ πάντα ἐγένετο·	**per quem omnia facta sunt;**	**Through him all things were made.**
τὸν δι' ἡμᾶς τοὺς ἀνθρώπους	qui propter nos homines	For us
καὶ διὰ τὴν ἡμετέραν σωτηρίαν	et propter nostram salutem	and for our salvation
κατελθόντα ἐκ τῶν οὐρανῶν	descendit de coelis,	he came down from heaven:
καὶ σαρκωθέντα ἐκ πνεύματος ἁγίου	et incarnatus est de Spiritu Sancto	by the power of the Holy Spirit
καὶ Μαρίας τῆς παρθένου	ex Maria virgine,	he became incarnate from the Virgin Mary,
καὶ ἐνανθρωπήσαντα,	et homo factus est;	and was made man.

HISTORICAL CONTEXT: This clause of the creed is predominantly concerned with reiterating the New Testament teaching that speaks of the Word as the divine agent of God's creation (Jn 1:3; Col 1:16). The vision of the cosmic Christ that it evokes is one that undergirds much of the early church's understanding. As it was fundamentally the Word who shaped the world as God's creative power, so it was appropriate that the Word was the only one who could reshape and rescue it from its distress. The maker was thus one and the same as the redeemer. Early Logos theologians of the late second and early third century delighted in seeing the Logos as the underlying pattern of being within the cosmos. All intellectual and spiritual understanding, especially, were the gift of the divine Logos, and indeed constituted the root of the "image of God" within humanity.

By the middle of the third century, Origen had greatly amplified the systematic nature of Logos thought, and in his extensive biblical commentaries he had shown how the whole plan of salvation and redemption was a great story of the Word's compassionate involvement with his cosmos. For most of the third-century Logos theologians, the Word was the divine force as it interacted with the world, whereas the Father was the divine being contemplated in its more transcendent glory. For these theologians, the Father's origination of the creation was entrusted to the Logos for its accomplishment. Accordingly, by the beginning of the fourth century, many Christian thinkers were asking questions about the relative status of Father and Logos in the order of creation. Arian theorists in particular began to argue that the Word was the "firstborn of all creation" (Col 1:15) in the sense that he was "first ranked among the created beings." Arian cosmology tended to see the Logos as the first of the angel creations of God, who was then used by the Father to bring into being the material world order. The Nicene fathers reacted strongly to this teaching, countering that the supreme agent of creation could not himself be a creature. If he was so defined, the ascription of creative power to the Word would be erroneous, and blasphemous. "Creation," in other words, was a wholly and strictly a divine attribute, and if "all things" (by which the Nicene fathers specifically meant all the spiritual orders of angels as well as all the material orders of human and animal creation) were made through the Word, it was a clear affirmation, as far as they were concerned, of the Word's divine status. The Nicenes knew, however, that even the Arians who affirmed the creative power of the Logos tended to understand it in a way that dissociated creative force from divine status. This was why, throughout the fourth century, much attention was given to the notion of the eternity of the Logos and his unique power in initiating the created orders of spiritual and material beings, from the vantage point of preexistent union with the Father. When they treated creative agency, they were aware that only by qualifying the term with "preexistent" or "eternal" was the anti-Arian argument secured.

OVERVIEW: The Son of God is active and powerful before time begins (THEODORE). He is the source of all blessing for the created order (EPHREM). His is a timeless origination, a being without beginning, from the eternity of the Father himself (GREGORY OF NAZIANZUS). As God's creative power, the Son of God makes and shapes all things (ATHANASIUS) in God's desired order (ORIGEN). The Logos-Son is the mediator of God's salvific power to all humanity (CLEMENT OF ALEXANDRIA). Having made the cosmos, the Word governs and sustains it in being in a harmoniously ordered way (EUSEBIUS). From eternity the Son of God ordained humanity's salvation as an act of loving compassion on his own handiwork (IRENAEUS).

There Is No "Before" with Him

THE SON OF GOD IS FAR ABOVE TIME.

THEODORE OF MOPSUESTIA: We were stating that in saying "born of his Father before all the worlds," they showed us that he is a Son truly not figuratively only, as the heretics pretend that he is a Son only in a borrowed name like those who were called "children by grace." He is alone the true Son of God the Father because he is the Only-Begotten and is alone born of God his Father. This is the reason they added[1] "born of his Father before all the worlds." This was due to the only-begotten Son of God, who is a true Son, not in name only. And he is from the nature of the Father and eternally from him and with him. It is not possible for us to imagine that there is anything between God the Father and God the Son, as God is high above everything. He who is above everything is also above time and from eternity. If, therefore, God the Father is eternal and if the Son is God, then he is also eternal, God from God and Eternal from Eternal. There is nothing between God and God. As it is not possible to imagine that either times or worlds precede God, so there is nothing before the Son as he also is God, because he is born of his Father before everything and is eternal, born of the One who is eternal. ON THE NICENE CREED 4.[2]

THE WORD IS BEFORE ALL THINGS. THEODORE OF MOPSUESTIA: He is from eternity and did not come into existence later, but he was in the beginning before everything. He who comes into existence later is called "the last," and the last is not the first; and he who is the first was not in the beginning.[3] If, therefore, he was in

---

[1] The Nicene fathers. [2] WS 5:43. [3] Theodore is not suggesting temporal succession in the Trinity but is meditating on the biblical titles specific to Father and Son. The Father is the "Beginning" (that is, the *archē* of Jn 1:1), and the Son is the "last Adam" (1 Cor 15:45) and the "First and Last" (Alpha and Omega, Rev 22:13) in the sense of the eschatological agent of the Father. His style, however, was often full of such double-entendres that could be read in disconcerting ways and were often obscurely expressed. Ultimately the Second Council of Constantinople (553) censured him posthumously for phrases like this one that read damagingly if taken out of context.

the beginning, he was also the first, as there is nothing that precedes the beginning. If he is the first, he is not the last, and if he is not the last, he did not come into existence later. "In the beginning he was,"[4] and he was in the beginning from God, that is to say, he was from eternity and before all the worlds with God. And to show that he was with God, and not from outside, as something foreign and not from the very nature of divinity, the blessed Evangelist called him the "Word." ON THE NICENE CREED 3.[5]

GOD'S WISDOM IS ETERNALLY PRESENT IN GOD. THEODORE OF MOPSUESTIA: He was from eternity from the one who is eternally from eternity. Indeed, the word of the soul, the rational character of which is accomplished in itself, is with it and in it by nature, and it is through it that this same soul is known to be rational. And it comes out of the soul, and is seen from it and in it, and is always with it and known through it. In this same way the Son is from the Father, like the word is from the soul. He is eternally from him, with him and in him, and he is known from eternity with him. "He was in the beginning,"[6] that is to say, he was from eternity, from the beginning and before everything; not that he came into existence later, but that he was in the beginning and always. He was eternally from him and eternally with him, like the word is with the soul, from which and with which it always is. ON THE NICENE CREED 3.[7]

THE SON BEGINS TIMELESSLY FROM THE FATHER. GREGORY OF NAZIANZUS: If time precedes my human existence, time is not prior to the Word whose begetter is timeless. When there existed the Father who is without beginning, the Father who left nothing beyond his Godhead, then there also existed the Son of the Father, having that Father as his timeless beginning, as light originates from that beautiful great circle of the sun (though all images fall short of the great God), lest interposing any-

thing between Father and Son, both everlasting beings, we should sever the royal Son from the royal Father. For what is prior to God, be it time or will, is to me a division of Godhead. As God, as progenitor, he is a mighty progenitor. But if it is a great thing for the Father to have no point of origin for his noble Godhead, it is no lesser glory for the revered offspring of the great Father to come from such a root. So do not sever God from God. You have not recognized the Son apart from the Father. The expressions "ingenerate" and "generation from the Father" do not constitute two different forms of Godhead (who invented that notion?), but both are externals around Godhead. But to my mind, the nature of Godhead is indivisible. PERSONAL POEMS 2.18-35, ON THE SON.[8]

The Coeternal Creator

ALL IS FROM THE FATHER THROUGH THE SON. ORIGEN: "All things came into being through him."[9] The agent "through whom" never has the first place but always the second. . . . Thus if all things were brought into being through the Word, it was not "by him" but "by" one greater and mightier than the Word.[10] And who would this be but the Father? COMMENTARY ON THE GOSPEL OF JOHN 2.10.(6).[11]

GOD'S WISDOM FASHIONS ALL THINGS. ORIGEN: A house or ship is built according to the principles of architecture or shipbuilding, and the house or ship has as its beginning the

---

[4]Jn 1:1. [5]WS 5:41. [6]Jn 1:1. [7]WS 5:42. [8]PA 7. [9]Jn 1:3. [10]After the fourth century, this bare expression of "greater" and "lesser" in the Trinity was no longer acceptable and was one of the things that led to Origen's posthumous condemnation. What Origen means by it here, however, is comparable to the later Fathers who only apparently seem to contradict him when they speak of the Word as "equal to the Father." The reason the Word is equal to the Father is that the Word has the selfsame being which is the Father's, and thus all its characteristics (omnipotence, eternity, and so on). The Nicene doctrine of the coequality of the divine *hypostases* does not contradict the equally fundamental axiom of the Father's being as the sole *archē*, or principle, of the divinity. [11]ECF 332.

principles and reasons that are in the artisans. Just so, I suppose, all things came into being in accordance with the reasons of things that were to be, which were revealed before by God. This is because "in wisdom he has made all things."[12] And we must say that having created, so to speak, an animate Wisdom, God gave to this Wisdom the task of imposing shape and form on existing things and on matter, from the principles inherent in Wisdom. . . . And if we carefully examine all the functions of the Word, he is the beginning only in respect of being Wisdom. It is not in respect of his being Word [that is, reason] that he is really the beginning, if, that is, the Word "was in the beginning." Thus, one may make bold to say that the most fundamental of all the functions designated by the title of the "firstborn of all creation"[13] is Wisdom. COMMENTARY ON THE GOSPEL OF JOHN 1.19.(22).[14]

THE WORD PRESERVES THE FATHER'S CREATION. EUSEBIUS OF CAESAREA: On the other hand, the sacred doctrine teaches that he who is the supreme Source of good, and Cause of all things, is beyond all comprehension and therefore inexpressible by word, or speech or name; surpassing the power, not of language only but of thought itself. Uncircumscribed by place or body; neither in heaven, nor in ethereal space nor in any other part of the universe; but entirely independent of all other things, he pervades the depths of unexplored and secret wisdom. The sacred oracles teach us to acknowledge him as the only true God, apart from all corporeal essence, distinct from all subordinate ministration. Hence it is said that all things are from him but not through him. And he himself, dwelling as Sovereign in secret and undiscovered regions of unapproachable light, ordains and disposes all things by the single power of his own will. At his will whatever is exists. Without that will, it cannot be. And his will is in every case for good, since he is essentially Goodness itself. But he through whom

are all things, even God the Word, proceeding in an ineffable manner from the Father above, as from an everlasting and exhaustless fountain, flows onward like a river with a full and abundant stream of power for the preservation of the universal whole. ORATION ON CONSTANTINE 12.1-2.[15]

GOD MADE ALL THINGS BY HIS WORD. ATHANASIUS: The Word of God was not made for us; rather, we were made for him, and "in him all things were created."[16] Nor is it true that because of our weakness he, the strong, was brought into being by the Father, who then existed alone,[17] in order that he might fashion us through him as by an instrument. Nothing could be further from the truth. For even if God had decided not to make created things, still the Word would have been "with God" nonetheless, and the Father in him, while created things could not have come into being without the Word. As the light enlightens all things with its radiance, and without that radiance nothing would be illuminated, so the Father wrought all things through the Word, as by a hand. For instance, God said, "Let there be light."[18] . . . And he did not speak in order that some subordinate might hear, understand what the speaker wanted and then go and perform the task. This is what happens in human affairs. But the Word of God is creator and maker, and he is the Father's very will. AGAINST THE ARIANS 2.31.[19]

The Preexistent Logos

THE TRUE SON FROM ALL ETERNITY. THEODORE OF MOPSUESTIA: They used words[20] suitable to belief in the Son. It was as if they had said, We call him a Son, not a mere man

---

[12]Ps 104:24. [13]Col 1:15. [14]*ECF* 333. [15]NPNF 2 1:598. [16]Col 1:16. [17]A view propounded by some of the early Apologists who argued that the Logos came into being only for the act of creation, and so his existence was commensurate with the origins of time. [18]Gen 1:3. [19]*ECF* 389-90. [20]The Nicene fathers.

and not like one who is figuratively called a son, such as those who are called children by grace because of their adoption in a household. No, for he alone is a true Son. He is a true Son because he is an only Son. He is truly born of his Father, is from him and from his nature and is eternally like him. There is no created thing that is before the worlds, as the one who is before the worlds is the one who is alone from eternity. As the Father is from eternity so also the Son who is from him is from eternity. He did not come into existence after a time, nor was he born later, but he was born eternally, before all the worlds, from the one who is from eternity, and he is with him from eternity, as the Evangelist said: "In the beginning was the Word."[21] ON THE NICENE CREED 3.[22]

THE WORD IS BORN BEFORE ALL TIME.

THEODORE OF MOPSUESTIA: "And the Word was God." After saying that he "was" and that he "was with God," he added, "And the Word was God," so that he should show clearly that he was not from a nature different from that of God or that he was different from him in the Godhead but rather that he was identical with the one from whom he was and that he was God with the One who was God. The Evangelist said wonderfully, "And the Word was God," in order to show that he is what God is and that he is what our blessed fathers rightly described: "born of him before all the worlds." In this they wished to convey that from eternity and before all the worlds, he was in the beginning from him and with him. ON THE NICENE CREED 3.[23]

THE ETERNAL ORIGIN OF BLESSINGS.

EPHREM THE SYRIAN: Blessed are you, Ephrata, mother of kings, from whom shone forth the Lord of diadems. It was Micah who announced to you, "He is from eternity, and the length of his times is incomprehensible."[24] Blessed are your eyes[25] that met him before all! You he found worthy to see him when he shone forth: the origin of blessing and beginning of joys. You

received him before the universe. HYMNS ON THE NATIVITY 25.11.[26]

The Pre-Incarnational Activity of the Eternal Son

THE SON ETERNALLY ORDAINED OUR SALVATION.

IRENAEUS: There is, therefore, one God, who by his Word and Wisdom created and arranged all things; but this is the Creator (Demiurge) who has granted this world to the human race and who, as regards his greatness, is indeed unknown to all who have been made by him (for no one has searched out his height, either among the ancients who have gone to their rest or any of those who are now alive). But as regards his Love, he is always known through him by whose means he ordained all things. Now this is his Word, our Lord Jesus Christ, who in the last times was made a man among humanity, that he might join the end to the beginning, that is, join humanity to God. Therefore, the prophets, receiving the prophetic gift from the same Word, announced his advent according to the flesh, by which the blending and communion of God and Man took place according to the good pleasure of the Father. The Word of God foretold from the beginning that God should be seen by people and hold converse with them on earth; should confer with them; and should be present with his own creation, saving it, and becoming capable of being perceived by it and freeing us from the hands of all that hate us, that is, from every spirit of wickedness. AGAINST HERESIES 4.20.4.[27]

THE WORD MEDIATES GOD'S PROVIDENCE.

CLEMENT OF ALEXANDRIA: The Son, being the Father's power, easily accomplished all his purposes. He does not leave even the smallest thing uncared for by his control. Otherwise

---

[21]Jn 1:1. [22]WS 5:41**. [23]WS 5:42. [24]Mic 5:2 (LXX). [25]God's Israel under the figure of Ephrata. [26]ESH 202. [27]ANCL 5:441

the whole would not have been well made by him. I suppose that from the supreme power comes that careful scrutiny that is applied to all the parts, down to the very smallest. It works on all the parts of creation, until we reach the supreme Controller of the whole universe who governs all things according to his Father's will. All beings, rank on rank in order, behold the universal salvation, until we arrive at the great high priest. For from one cause, the source of energy according to the Father's will, depend the first, second and third orders, and then at the edge of the world of sense[28] is the blessed hierarchy of angels. Below them, ordered in due subordination, are the ranks of beings, from one and through one receiving and conferring salvation, extending to human beings. Thus, just as even the smallest piece of iron is moved by the influence of a magnet, which extends through a series of iron rings, so virtuous beings are drawn by the Holy Spirit and are closely united to the first "mansion," and this influence passes down to the last in order. The wicked are neither controlling nor are controlled, and so they fall headlong downwards. The divine law is always that a person who is set on virtue is raised up. STROMATEIS 7.2.(9).[29]

---

[28]The world of sensible realities (rational existences). [29]ECF 240-41.

FOR US

καὶ εἰς ἕνα κύριον Ἰησοῦν Χριστόν,	Et in unum Dominum Jesum Christum,	We believe in one Lord, Jesus Christ,
τὸν υἱὸν τοῦ Θεοῦ τὸν μονογενῆ,	Filium Dei unigenitum,	the only Son of God,
τὸν ἐκ τοῦ πατρὸς γεννηθέντα	et ex Patre natum	eternally
πρὸ πάντων τῶν αἰώνων,	ante omnia saecula	begotten of the Father,
φῶς ἐκ φωτός,	[Deum de Deo], Lumen de Lumine,	[God from God], Light from Light,
Θεὸν ἀληθινὸν ἐκ θεοῦ ἀληθινοῦ,	Deum verum de Deo vero,	true God from true God,
γεννηθέντα, οὐ ποιηθέντα,	genitum, non factum,	begotten, not made,
ὁμοούσιον τῷ πατρί·	consubstantialem Patri;	of one Being with the Father.
δι' οὗ τὰ πάντα εγένετο·	per quem omnia facta sunt;	Through him all things were made.
τὸν δι' ἡμᾶς τοὺς ἀνθρώπους	**qui propter nos homines**	**For us**
καὶ διὰ τὴν ἡμετέραν σωτηρίαν	et propter nostram salutem	and for our salvation
κατελθόντα ἐκ τῶν οὐρανῶν	descendit de coelis,	he came down from heaven:
καὶ σαρκωθέντα ἐκ πνεύματος ἁγίου	et incarnatus est de Spiritu Sancto	by the power of the Holy Spirit
καὶ Μαρίας τῆς παρθένου	ex Maria virgine,	he became incarnate from the Virgin Mary,
καὶ ἐνανθρωπήσαντα,	et homo factus est;	and was made man.

HISTORICAL CONTEXT: The great theological controversies of the Gnostic era, lasting throughout the second century and into the third, had turned on an idea of the Godhead that was overwhelmingly important for the Hellenistic religious mentality, namely, that deity must not be sullied by material chaos. Thus, the Gnostics could not confess either that the sublime transcendent God could either make this material world or be interested, let alone involved, in its vicissitudes. Much of that attitude ran on into the Arian movement and influenced its Christology unconsciously.

In catholic Christianity, on the contrary, it fell to the witness of the Scriptures to assert with great power that the God of revelation was wholly and entirely the Creator God who, precisely because he was creator and fashioner, had a deep and faithful love for his creation and willed its unfolding into beatitude. It was this establishment of the catholic reading of theology over and against the Gnostics and Arians that can be seen in the later patristic theology, which instinctively explains all the mysteries of Christology and the incarnate economy by reverting to the fundamentals: that the mission of the Son of God on earth was for no other reason than the same compassion God the Father had for the cosmos. All the apparent strangeness of the Jesus story, both as a narrative of the descent of the heavenly Logos to earth and as a tale of the sufferings of the Messiah while on earth, can be explained, the Fathers consistently taught, by the fact that the sublime compassion of God motivated all that he did, and that the divine interest and love for creation was in him to such a degree that humility and mercy became the only trophies of glory that interested him. Such a Lord was transcendent in his stooping down and powerfully great in his smallness. The altruism involved in that creedal clause "for our sake, and for our salvation" is far from being easily comprehended. In fact, it is something more sublime and transcendent than could ever have been invoked by a Gnostic vision of a Godhead that was significant by remaining remote and sublimely indifferent.

Overview: The afflictions of Christ, far from being a cause of scandal, are the power that gives life to the world (Epistle of Barnabas). It is incomprehensible why heretics find the humil-

ity of the incarnate Word problematical and distasteful. Such an attitude is comparable to a sickly invalid laughing at a noble doctor just because he stooped down in compassion (Basil, Gregory of Nazianzus). Like a great doctor, the incarnate Word wished to assume humanity in order, thereby, to go straight to the root of our suffering and to administer healing in the flesh that he had assumed (Gregory of Nyssa). To prepare for this advent to humanity, the Word prepared the mind of believers over a long time through Scripture (Tertullian). He came to us in order to save (Hilary, Athanasius) and to reenergize the human race (Gregory of Nyssa). The humility of the divine Son of God is the perfect remedy for the root cause of all humanity's woes, its endemic arrogance (Augustine). His poverty pays humankind's debts (Ephrem). Lodged in the flesh, his divine power checks and breaks the force of the contagion of death that had spread through our race (Leo). His incarnation makes the human race into the elect children of God, called to respond in faith (Chrysostom). To see the economy of salvation in this way is to appreciate what a wonderfully gratuitous gift it is (Polycarp).

On Behalf of Us Humans

The Lord Suffers to Give Life to the World. Epistle of Barnabas: You notice, then, children of joy, that the good Lord has revealed everything to us in advance, that we may know to whom a full measure of thanks and praise is due from us. The Son of God, although he is Lord and Judge of the living and the dead, underwent suffering, so that his affliction might give us life. Let us, therefore, believe that the Son of God could not suffer except for our sake. Epistle of Barnabas 7.1-2.[1]

Incarnation Was Chosen for Our Benefit. Basil of Caesarea: Will the heretic also

---

[1]ACW 6:46.

taunt him with the manger,[2] though it was by means of this that he himself, when devoid of reason, was nourished by the Word? Will he reproach the poverty of the carpenter's son who was not furnished with a bed? That is why the Son is inferior to the Father;[3] because for your sake he became dead, to free you from mortality and make you partake of the heavenly life. It is just as if one should find fault with a physician for bending down to sickness and breathing its stench, in order that he may heal the sufferers. LETTER 8.5.[4]

THE PARADOXES OF THE INCARNATION.

GREGORY OF NAZIANZUS: For he whom you now treat with contempt was once above you. He who is now man was once the Uncompounded. What he was, he continued to be. What he was not, he took to himself. In the beginning he was, uncaused; for what is the cause of God? But afterward for a cause he was born. And that cause was that you might be saved, who now insult him and despise his Godhead, because of this, that he took on him your denser nature, having converse with flesh by means of mind, while his inferior nature, the humanity, became God[5] because it was united to God and became one person because the higher nature prevailed . . . in order that I too might be made God so far as he is made man.[6] He was born, but he had been begotten. He was born of a woman, but she was a virgin. The first is human; the second, divine. In his human nature he had no father, but also in his divine nature, no mother. ORATION 29.19.[7]

THE INCARNATION IS THE HEALING OF HUMANITY.

GREGORY OF NYSSA: Those who submit to surgery or cautery are angry with their doctors as they smart under the agony of the operation. But if restoration to health follows and the pain passes, then they are grateful to those who effected the cure. In the same way, when after tedious processes the evil is expelled that had been mixed with human nature and had grown up with it, and when there has taken

place the restoration to the original state of those who are now lying in wickedness, then will arise a unison of thanksgiving from all creatures, as well as from those who have suffered chastisement in the process of purification as from those who needed no purification at all. Such are the benefits conferred by the great mystery of the divine incarnation. By mingling with humanity, sharing all the distinctive features from nature (birth, nurture, growth) and going right on to the experience of death, he effected all those aforementioned results, freeing humankind from wickedness and healing even the inventor of wickedness himself.[8] For the purification of the disease, however painful, is the healing of infirmity. ADDRESS ON RELIGIOUS INSTRUCTION 26.[9]

THE WORD GUIDES HUMAN HISTORY.

TERTULLIAN: For it was the Son who descended from time to time to have converse with people,[10] from Adam to the patriarchs and prophets; in vision, in dream, "in a looking glass, in an enigma,"[11] always preparing from the beginning that course that he was to follow out to the end. Thus he was always learning, even as God, to have intercourse with people on earth, being none other than the "Word"[12] who was to be

---

[2]Arian apologists mocked the Nicene belief that Jesus was personally and directly the incarnate Word, on the grounds that the human fallibilities and passibilities demonstrated in the earthly life (the sufferings and death on the cross in particular) were wholly unfitting for the impassible Logos. [3]Basil's overall argument is that the earthly economy does indeed present a subordinate vision of the Son, but that the proper way to interpret this is not to conclude that the Logos is himself inferior to God; rather, that the incarnate Lord emptied himself out in service and in great humility for the sake of his world. [4]*LCF* 68. [5]Was deified, or transfigured, by the presence of the Logos in the flesh. [6]Gregory repeats the axiom of Irenaeus and Athanasius, that the incarnation of the divine effects the deification of the human: that the cause of the incarnation of God was the elevation of the human race back to union with God. [7]LCC 3:173-74. [8]Adam. [9]*LCF* 145. [10]Tertullian's context of argument here is that it was the divine Logos, not the Father, who descended to earth to have dealings with humanity in the course of the history of revelation. All theophanies and salvific acts of the Old Testament were thus the deeds of the Logos. [11]1 Cor 13:12. [12]The word *logos* also means "discursive intercourse."

made flesh. Now he was learning this in order that he might prepare the way of faith for us, to make it easier for us to believe that the Son of God has descended into the temporal world, seeing that we know that something of the kind had been done in times past. These things were written, as they were also done, on our behalf, on whom the ends of the ages have come. AGAINST PRAXEAS 16.[13]

THE SON'S HUMILITY HEALS HUMANITY. AUGUSTINE: The Son of God assumed human nature, and in it he endured all that belongs to the human condition. This is a remedy for humankind of a power beyond our imagining. Could any pride be cured, if the humility of God's Son does not cure it? Could any greed be cured, if the poverty of God's Son does not cure it? Or any anger, if the patience of God's Son does not cure it? Or any coldness, if the love of God's Son does not cure it? Lastly, what fearfulness can be cured, if it is not cured by the resurrection of the body of Christ the Lord? Let humankind raise its hopes and recognize its own nature. Let it observe how high a place it has in the works of God. Do not despise yourselves, you humans: the Son of God assumed humanity. Do not despise yourselves, you women: God's Son was born of a woman. But do not set your hearts on the satisfactions of the body, for in the Son of God we are "neither male nor female."[14] Do not set your heart on temporal rewards, for if it were good to do so, that human nature that God's Son assumed would have thus set its heart. Do not fear insults, crosses and death, for if they did humanity harm, then the humanity that God's Son assumed would not have endured them. ON THE AGONY OF CHRIST 12.[15]

INCARNATION SETS A TERM TO SIN AND DEATH. LEO THE GREAT: Now this birth in time has taken nothing from, and added nothing to, that divine and eternal birth but has bestowed itself wholly on the restoration of man who had been deceived; that he might conquer

death and by his own power destroy the devil who had the sovereignty of death. For we could not have overcome the author of sin and death unless he had taken on him our nature and made it his own, whom neither sin could defile nor death detain. LETTER 28.2 (THE TOME OF LEO).[16]

The Grace of God in the Incarnation

WE ARE SAVED BY HIS FREE GRACE. POLYCARP OF SMYRNA: I congratulate you on the fact that your firmly rooted faith, celebrated ever since the earliest days, persists till now and still brings forth fruit to the honor of our Lord Jesus Christ, who patiently went to meet his death for our sin; he whom God raised by ending the throes of death. You never saw him and yet believe in him with sublime and inexpressible joy, a joy that many desire to experience. You are assured that you have been saved by a gratuitous gift, not by our actions, indeed no, but by the will of God through Jesus Christ. TO THE PHILIPPIANS 1.2-3.[17]

THE LIGHT OF INCARNATION CLEANS OUR BLEMISHES. EPHREM THE SYRIAN:
Glory to the Son of the gracious One,
    rejected by the sons of the evil one.
Glory to the Son of the just One, crucified
    by the children of the wicked one.
Glory to the One who released us and was
    bound in place of us all.
Glory to that One who pledged himself to
    pay the debt.
Glory to the beautiful One who portrayed us
    in his similitudes.
Glory to that serene One who looked not at
    our blemishes.
Glory to that One who begot his Light in the
    darkness,
For the darkness was hidden by the vices

---

[13]ECF 167. [14]Gal 3:28. [15]LCF 218-19. [16]CCC 316. [17]ACW 6:76.

concealing its secrets,
But the Light stripped off and took away
from us the garment of blemishes.
Glory to the heavenly One who mingled his salt
with our mind, his milk with our souls.
His body became bread to revive our mortality.
Thanks be to the rich One who paid the debt
in place of us all,
He did not borrow, but he signed and became
indebted for us again.
By his yoke he brought away from us the
shackles that held us captive.
HYMNS ON THE NATIVITY 3.8-10.[18]

**THE LORD'S SUFFERINGS REMOVE OUR
WOES.** EPHREM THE SYRIAN:
Let us thank him who was beaten and who
saved us by his wound.
Let us thank him who took away the curse by
his thorns.
Let us thank him who killed death by his
dying.
Let us thank him who was silent and vindicated us.
Let us thank him who cried out in death that
had devoured us.
Blessed is he whose benefits have laid waste
the enemies of God.
Let us glorify him who watched and put to
sleep our captor.
Let us glorify the One who went to sleep and
awoke our slumber.
Glory to God the healer of human nature.
Glory to the One who plunged in and sank
our evil into the depth
And drowned our drowner.
Let us glorify with all our mouths the Lord
of all means of salvation.
Blessed is the Physician who descended and
cut painlessly
And healed the sores with a mild medicine.
His child was the medicine that takes pity on
sinners.
Blessed is the One who dwelled in the womb,

And in it he built a palace in which to live,
a temple in which to be,
A garment in which to be radiant and armor
by which to conquer.
Blessed is the One whom our mouth is not
sufficient to thank,
Whose gift is too great for those gifted with
speech;
Nor are the senses sufficient to give thanks
for his grace;
For however much we thank him, it is too
little,
And because it is of no use for us to be silent
and unnerved,
Let our weaknesses return to God a song of
thanksgiving.
HYMNS ON THE NATIVITY 3.18-21.[19]

THE WORD DWELLS AMONG US TO SAVE US.
HILARY OF POITIERS: This is the cause of our
life, that we have Christ dwelling in our fleshly
nature, in virtue of his flesh, and we shall live
through him in the same way as he lives through
the Father. We live through him by nature,
according to the flesh, that is, having acquired
the nature of his flesh. Then surely he has the
Father in himself according to the Spirit, since
he lives through the Father. The mystery of the
real and natural unity is to be proclaimed in
terms of the honor granted to us by the Son,
and the Son's dwelling in us through his flesh,
while we are united to him bodily and inseparably. ON THE TRINITY 8.16.[20]

THE SON OF GOD ENERGIZES HUMANITY.
GREGORY OF NYSSA: For he who exists eternally did not submit to a bodily birth because
he wanted to live, but in order to recall us from
death to life. Then since what was needed was
the ascent of the whole of our nature from
death to renewal of life, he stretched out a hand,
as it were, to the prostrate body, and in bending down to our dead corpse he came so near

---

[18]ESH 85. [19]ESH 87-88. [20]LCF 58.

to death as to come in contact with our state of mortality and by his own body to bestow on human nature a beginning of the resurrection, by raising up through his power the whole of humanity along with himself. For that humanity that received the Godhead[21] and through the resurrection was raised up with the Godhead came from no other source than from the mass of human nature. Catechetical Lectures 32.[22]

The Watchman Awakens the Human Race. Ephrem the Syrian: The Watcher[23] rose up from within the grave, for he was sleeping while awake, and he came and found the peoples asleep.[24] He shouted for joy and cried out and awakened them. The sleeping people thanked the Watcher who made them watchers on earth.[25] Hymns on the Nativity 6.24.[26]

The Self-Giving Divine Mercy

The Word of God Comes to Free the World. Athanasius: God is first the creator of people and then becomes their Father by virtue of his Word that dwells in them. With respect to the Word this is reversed; God is by nature his Father and later becomes his creator and maker when the Word assumes a flesh that is created and made, and thus becomes man. . . . Since he assumed created nature and became like us in respect of his body, it is reasonable for him to be called our "brother" and "the firstborn." For though it was after us that he became man (for us and our brother by likeness of body), he is still called, and is, the firstborn in this respect, that when all people were perishing according to Adam's transgression, his flesh was the first of all to be saved and set free, since it had become the body of the Word; and we henceforth are saved just as his body was saved, by becoming "incorporate"[27] with it. . . . He is the Only-Begotten because of his begetting from the Father; the "firstborn" because of his coming down to creation and his mak-

ing of many brothers. Against the Arians 2.61-62.[28]

The Incarnation Enriches the World. Ephrem the Syrian:

Thanks be to that gracious One, the cause of all our virtues.
Blessed is he who did not reproach, for he was the gracious One.
Blessed is he who did not avert his gaze, for he is also the just One.
Blessed is he who was silent and reproached: he restored life by both.
Powerful is his silence, and reproachful.
Gentle is his strength even though he accuses,
For he reproached the false one, but he kissed the thief.
Glory to the Farmer, the hidden One of our thought.
His seed fell on our earth and enriched our intellect.
Its harvest was a hundredfold for the storehouse of our souls.
Let us worship the One who sat down and rested,
Who walked within the way, and he was the Way on the way
And the Gate of entry for those who enter the kingdom.
Blessed is the Shepherd who became the sheep for our absolution.
Blessed is the Vineshoot that became the cup of our salvation.
Blessed also is the Cluster, the source of the medicine of life.

---

[21]Literally, the "God-receptive man." [22]LCF 146-47. [23]The Syriac word means angelic power. Here Ephrem uses it to refer to the risen Christ as the Lord of angels who is watchman (waker-up) of the soul. The play is on the Watchman who was awake while he was asleep (in the tomb, but simultaneously harrowing hades). [24]The Gentiles who were guarding the tomb. [25]The resurrection is that power that effects the transformation of humanity from mortal flesh into creatures endowed with immortal spiritual life. [26]ESH 114. [27]Here Athanasius refers to the Pauline principle of becoming "one body with Christ" (Rom 12:5). [28]ECF 393.

Blessed also is the Ploughman
Who himself became the grain of wheat that
    was sown and the sheaf that was reaped.
He is the master Builder who became a tower
    for our refuge.
He is the one who himself constructed the
    senses of our minds
So that we might sing on our lyre what the
    mouth of the bird cannot sing in its melo-
    dies.
HYMNS ON THE NATIVITY 3.12-16.[29]

THE INCARNATION MAKES US CHILDREN OF GOD. JOHN CHRYSOSTOM: "And the Word was made flesh," he says, "and dwelled among us."[30] After saying that those who received him "were born of God and became children of God,"[31] he states the basic cause underlying this ineffable honor, which is the fact that the Word became flesh, and the Lord assumed the form of the slave.[32] The one who is a natural Son of God became a Son of man, in order to make children of God out of the children of men. The lofty is mingled with the lowly but suffers no damage to its own glory, while the lowly rises out of the depths of its lowliness. This is what happened with Christ. He in no way diminished his own nature through this descent, but he raised us, who were sitting forever in dishonor and darkness, up to indescribable glory. In somewhat the same way a king who speaks with care and concern to a very poor person in no way shames himself, but he makes the poor person illustrious and admired by all. In a case of transitory human glory, therefore, association with an inferior does no damage to a superior; how much truer is this, then, when it is a question of that pure and blessed essence that has nothing transitory about it (either by means of loss or gain) but possesses all good things unchangeably and in a fixed form forever? So when you hear that "the Word became flesh," do not be upset or disturbed. The divine essence did not change into flesh (it is sacrilegious even to think this); no, it remained what it was and assumed the form of the servant. HOMILIES ON THE GOSPEL OF JOHN 11.11.[33]

---

[29]ESH 86. [30]Jn 1:14. [31]Jn 1:12-13. [32]Jn 1:14; Phil 2:7. [33]MFC 2:130.

AND FOR OUR SALVATION

καὶ εἰς ἕνα κύριον Ἰησοῦν Χριστόν,	Et in unum Dominum Jesum Christum,	We believe in one Lord, Jesus Christ,
τὸν υἱὸν τοῦ Θεοῦ τὸν μονογενῆ,	Filium Dei unigenitum,	the only Son of God,
τὸν ἐκ τοῦ πατρὸς γεννηθέντα	et ex Patre natum	eternally
πρὸ πάντων τῶν αἰώνων,	ante omnia saecula	begotten of the Father,
φῶς ἐκ φωτός,	[Deum de Deo], Lumen de Lumine,	[God from God], Light from Light,
Θεὸν ἀληθινὸν ἐκ θεοῦ ἀληθινοῦ,	Deum verum de Deo vero,	true God from true God,
γεννηθέντα, οὐ ποιηθέντα,	genitum, non factum,	begotten, not made,
ὁμοούσιον τῷ πατρί·	consubstantialem Patri;	of one Being with the Father.
δι᾽ οὗ τὰ πάντα εγένετο·	per quem omnia facta sunt;	Through him all things were made.
τὸν δι᾽ ἡμᾶς τοὺς ἀνθρώπους	qui propter nos homines	For us
καὶ διὰ τὴν ἡμετέραν σωτηρίαν	**et propter nostram salutem**	**and for our salvation**
κατελθόντα ἐκ τῶν οὐρανῶν	descendit de coelis,	he came down from heaven:
καὶ σαρκωθέντα ἐκ πνεύματος ἁγίου	et incarnatus est de Spiritu Sancto	by the power of the Holy Spirit
καὶ Μαρίας τῆς παρθένου	ex Maria virgine,	he became incarnate from the Virgin Mary,
καὶ ἐνανθρωπήσαντα,	et homo factus est;	and was made man.

HISTORICAL CONTEXT: Here as in other places in the creed, we find parallel phrases juxtaposed. The first of the pair, "for our sake," is mirrored with "and for our salvation." The reason for these parallels was a perceived need for increasing specification because of more particular contexts of controversy as the fourth century unfolded. The motive of the incarnation as an act of concern from the part of God toward the human race was a creedal element of the ancient *regula fidei* (rule of faith) that was designed to offset Gnostic belief in a divine power that stood away from this world. In the Gnostic system the supreme deity was interested only in liberating souls from a material world that had been created by an evil and alien power. The rule of faith had taught, to the contrary, that the supreme God is in fact the Creator of the visible as well as the invisible cosmos, and the sending of the Son of God to earth was "for our sake," motivated by love for God's own creation.

The second clause, "and for our salvation," came about because the Arian crisis had necessitated a deeper clarification of what that motive of God's advent might entail. What did salvation mean, and how was it effected by the descent of the Son of God? Arian theology tended to see the Son of God as one of the chief angelic powers of God, who had come to serve a pedagogic mission: to give examples, and right teachings to a race that had gone astray. This was a one-sided development of one of the many themes that had been found in the works of Origen in the third century. In the response of the Nicene fathers to the Arian movement we see a continual focus on the status of the incarnate Word as true God come among humankind. The advent of the deity in the flesh to the human race is not merely seen to be a pedagogic action, although there is much reflection on how the teachings of Jesus were important, and consequently there is a reiterated affirmation that salvation is not effected merely by exemplarist means. The incarnate Word is seen to bring a life-giving power back to the human race, which had lost the integral energy of life and immortality that had originally been given to it by the very Logos who made humankind. The Word returns to his own, in order to immortalize and deify a fallen humanity. "Deification by grace" became a leading way the fourth-century Fathers understood the salvific energy of the incarnation, a kind of synopsis of what our salvation entailed. Along the way it became a leading argument for the deity of the Son—as only what possessed true deity could offer life and salvation as its gift.

Overview: The incarnation of the Word refashions humankind as the image of God, a glory that it has wandered away from, to its bitter detriment (Irenaeus). The motive of the incarnation was to give humankind the gift of the life-giving Spirit of God and lead it back to the Father's glory (Irenaeus). For this reason the Word was willing to endure all things for the sake of his human creation, and in this election of suffering he sets disciples an example of faithful endurance (Epistle of Barnabas, Polycarp, Irenaeus, Gregory of Nazianzus). The descent of the Word of God among us was motivated by his desire to heal and save (Athanasius, Basil, Gregory of Nyssa). Everything he did was out of concern for our benefit (Hilary) or betterment (Augustine) or our sanctification (Gregory of Nazianzus). As an act of salvific power, the incarnation dispenses life and immortality to a dying race that had collectively lost its *energeia* of being as it had become alienated from God, its source of being (Irenaeus, Theodore, Gregory of Nyssa). The freely accepted indignities the incarnate Word submits to are for our ennoblement (Cyril of Alexandria) and our consolation (Theodore). He who was rich came down in order to pay off our debts (Leo, Basil). His presence abolished sin (Irenaeus). But its chief and most glorious effect was the reestablishment of the possibility of communion with God. The Word's incarnation was designed to effect no less than the deification of his faithful disciples, that is, their restoration to union and glory with God given to them as a redemptive and sanctifying grace (Irenaeus, Origen, Athanasius, Cyril of Alexandria, Augustine). This is the restoration of the priestly status once enjoyed by our race in this world (Gregory of Nyssa).

What Was Required to Save Fallen Humanity

The Incarnation Reestablishes the Image of God. Irenaeus: The Word existed in the beginning with God, and through him all things were made. He was always present with the human race, and in the last times, according to the time appointed by the Father, he has been united with his own handiwork and made man, capable of suffering. Thus we can set aside the objection, "If Christ was born at a certain time, it follows that he did not exist before that." For we have shown that the Son of God did not then begin to be: he existed always with the Father. But he was incarnate and made man, and then he recapitulated[1] in himself the long line of the human race, procuring for us a comprehensive salvation, that we might recover in Christ Jesus what in Adam we had lost, namely, the state of being "in the image and likeness of God." Against Heresies 3.18.1.[2]

The Word Restores Humanity. Irenaeus: God the Word restored Man[3] in himself, his ancient handiwork, that he might bring death to sin, strip death of its power, and give life to Man. Against Heresies 3.18.7.[4]

---

[1]Or, fulfilled. [2]*ECF* 112-13. [3]Irenaeus is clearly using "man" here to stand in for humankind, but it is an instance where it is best to leave the old semantic form of the English particular, insofar as he graphically sees this theology of recapitulation and substitution (the Word becomes man, humanity becomes deified) working not through abstractions but through the specific and discrete Pauline principle that all the human race fell in one man (individual), Adam, and all the elect have been restored in one man (individual), the second Adam, Jesus the incarnate Logos. [4]*ECF* 113.

THE WORD PLANS SALVATION IN THE SPIRIT. IRENAEUS: There is one God, who by his Word and Wisdom made and ordered all things. . . . His Word is our Lord Jesus Christ, who in these last times became man among humankind, that he might unite the end with the beginning, that is, humankind with God. Therefore the prophets received from this same Word their prophetic gift. They proclaimed his advent in the flesh, by which was effected the mingling and uniting of God and humankind according to the Father's pleasure. For the Word of God foretold from the beginning that God would be seen by humans and would live with them on earth and converse with them. It foretold that he would be present with his creatures to bring salvation to them and be seen by them. It also foretold that he would free us "from the hands of those who hate us,"[5] that is, from the whole spirit of transgression, and would make us "serve him all our days in holiness and righteousness."[6] It foretold that humanity, taking to itself the Spirit of God, should pass to the glory of the Father. AGAINST HERESIES 4.20.4.[7]

THE INCARNATION GIVES HUMANITY A NEW BIRTH. IRENAEUS: How can they be saved unless he was God who wrought their salvation on the earth? And how shall humanity pass to God unless God has passed into humanity? How shall humans be freed from the generation of death, except they pass into a new birth, wonderfully and unexpectedly given by God, for a token of salvation, a birth from a virgin, receiving a rebirth through faith? How can human beings receive adoption by God if they remain as they are by human birth in this world? AGAINST HERESIES 4.33.4.[8]

THE WORD DESTROYS DEATH. EPISTLE OF BARNABAS: And another thing, my brethren: if the Lord submitted to suffering for our souls (he, the Lord of the universe, to whom at the foundation of the world God had said, "Let us make humankind according to our image and likeness") then how did it happen that he submitted to suffering at the hands of people? Let me tell you. The prophets, who had received the gift from him, looked forward to him in their prophecies; and since it was ordained that he should manifest himself in the flesh, he voluntarily submitted to suffering that he might destroy death and establish the truth of the resurrection from the dead. EPISTLE OF BARNABAS 5.5-6.[9]

THE WORD ENDURES ALL THINGS FOR OUR SAKE. POLYCARP OF SMYRNA: Unceasingly, then, let us cling to our hope and the pledge of our justification, that is, Christ Jesus, who in his own body took the weight of our sins up to the cross; who did no wrong, nor "was treachery found on his lips."[10] On the contrary, for our sakes, that we might live in him, he endured everything. Therefore let us become imitators of his patient endurance and glorify him whenever we suffer for the sake of his name. This is the example he has set us in his own person, and this is what we have learned to believe. TO THE PHILIPPIANS 8.1-2.[11]

THE WORD DESCENDS TO EARTH TO HEAL AND SAVE. ATHANASIUS: Our guilt was the cause of the descent of the Word, and our transgression called forth his loving kindness, so that he came to us, and the Lord was displayed among human beings. For we were the occasion of his embodiment, and for our salvation he went so far in his love for humankind as to be born and to be displayed in a human body. ON THE INCARNATION 4.[12]

THE INCARNATE WORD DISPENSES IMMORTALITY. THEODORE OF MOPSUESTIA: It was necessary, therefore, that our Lord should take a soul, so that the soul should first be saved

---

[5]Lk 1:71. [6]Wis 9:2; Lk 1:75. [7]ECF 105**. [8]ECF 107*. [9]ACW 6:43. [10]Is 53:9. [11]ACW 6:79-80. [12]ECF 378.

from sin and, by God's grace, should achieve immortality. ON THE NICENE CREED 5.14.[13]

THE MIRACLE OF GOD'S PRESENCE IN US.

GREGORY OF NYSSA: The birth of Godhead in our nature should not reasonably present itself as a strange novelty to those whose notions are not too limited. For who, surveying the whole scheme of things, is so childish as not to believe that there is divinity in everything, clothed in it, embracing it, residing in it? For everything that is depends on "him who is," nor can there be anything that has not its being in him who is. Then, if all things are in the divinity and the divinity is in all things, why are people embarrassed at the divine plan displayed in the revelation that tells us of the birth of God in humanity, since we believe that God is not outside humankind even now? For even though the miracle of God's presence in us is not the same as that of his incarnation, still we equally acknowledge his existence in us, even now just as earlier in history. Now he is mingled with us as sustaining nature in existence, whereas when he first came he was mingled with our nature in order that our nature, by this mixing with the divine, should itself become divine. It was rescued from death and put out of reach of the tyranny of the enemy. Christ's return from death becomes for the mortal race the beginning of the return to immortal life. THE GREAT CATECHISM 25.[14]

THE LORD SUFFERS TO GIVE US HIS NOBILITY.

CYRIL OF ALEXANDRIA: The Lord of the universe, the only-begotten God, submitted himself to deprivation for our sakes, so that he might generously confer on us the privilege of brotherhood with him, and the beauty, all to be desired, of his own inherent nobility. But Nestorius[15] deprives us of all this glory, in saying that it was simply a man who was born to be our brother, and to explain to us what he considers to be a credible argument for this position he adds, "Observe what immediately follows: 'That he might prove to be a merciful and faithful high priest before God; for since he has himself experienced the test of suffering he is able to help those who undergo the test.'"[16] He who experiences suffering is the merciful high priest: The temple is capable of suffering, not God who gives life to that which suffers. Anyone who chooses to hold this opinion[17] and does not shrink from uttering it is making a division, again into two *hypostases*, in fact into two persons, the one being the Word from God the Father; the other being the one whom he lately introduced as the "God-bearing man."[18] I cannot believe that anyone will doubt this conclusion, assuring the distinction and separation between "he who experiences suffering" and "he who gives life."[19] AGAINST NESTORIUS 3.2.[20]

THE WORD STOOPS DOWN TO GRANT US ADVANTAGE.

HILARY OF POITIERS: The law of the physical world necessitates the advance of our nature toward increase: therefore it is reasonable to look for development to a higher order of nature. Increase is according to nature; decrease is against nature. So it was appropriate for God to be other than what he continued to be, while not ceasing to be what he had always been: for God to be born in human nature and yet not cease to be God; to contract himself even to conception, to the cradle, to infancy, all without departing from the power of God. This mystery[21] is not for his own sake but for ours. The assumption of our humanity was not an advancement for God, but the willing acceptance

---

[13]*LCF* 166. [14]*LCF* 134**. [15]Cyril's contemporary, the fifth-century archbishop of Constantinople, whom he accused of teaching that Jesus was a man associated with the deity rather than the unmediated presence of the deity in flesh. [16]Heb 2:17. [17]He accuses Nestorius of having held that view. [18]Nestorius liked to refer to Jesus under this title (*theophoros*). [19]Cyril's point, contrary to how he read Nestorius's theology, was that true faith required the church to confess that the selfsame one who suffered on the cross was the one who gave life to the world: that is, the incarnation produced one Lord Jesus Christ, both divine and human in his complex reality, but only one single person, and that person none other than the divine Word of God. [20]*LCF* 255-56. [21]Sacrament.

of his humiliation is our advantage. He does not lose the status of God, while he acquires divinity for humankind. On the Trinity 9.4.[22]

God Changes Humanity for the Better. Augustine: There is no need to fear that God should seem to suffer constraint in the tiny body of a child, for God's greatness is not in size but in moral power. . . . That moral power, without changing for the worse, took to itself the rational soul, and through that the human body, and the whole man, to change it for the better; in condescension taking from it the name of humanity, in generosity bestowing on it the name of divinity. Letter 137.8.[23]

Majesty Assumed Weakness. Leo the Great: Thus the properties of each nature and substance were preserved entire and came together to form one person. Humility was assumed by majesty, weakness by strength, mortality by eternity; and to pay the debt that we had incurred, an inviolable nature was united to a nature that can suffer. Letter 28.3 (The Tome of Leo).[24]

The Economy of Salvation: The Deification of God's Elect

The Incarnate Word Abolishes Sin. Irenaeus: But as he, our Lord, is our only true master, so he is truly the good and suffering Son of God, the Word of God the Father made the Son of man. For he strove and conquered. He was, as man, contending on behalf of the Father and through obedience canceling the disobedience. He bound the strong one and set free the weak, and he gave salvation to his handiwork by abolishing sin. For he is our most holy Lord, the merciful lover of the human race.[25] Against Heresies 3.18.6.[26]

The Glory of God Is a Living Human Being. Irenaeus: Since he "who effects all operations in all"[27] is God, his true nature and immensity cannot be discovered or described by his creatures. But he is by no means unknown to them. For through his Word all his creatures learn that there is one God, the Father, who controls all things and gives existence to all. As the Gospel says, "No one has seen God, except that the only-begotten Son, who is in the Father's bosom, has himself described him."[28] Thus the Son makes the Father known from the beginning. For he has been with the Father from the beginning, and he has shown to humankind the visions of the prophets, the different kinds of spiritual gifts, and his own ministry and the glorification of the Father in due sequence and order, at the fitting time for humanity's profit. For when there is due sequence there is consistency, and where there is consistency, there is the choice of the opportune time, and the choice of the opportune time brings benefit for humanity. But for this reason the Word was made the minister of the Father's grace to our race, for humanity's benefit. For humankind he wrought his redemptive work, displaying God to humankind and humankind to God. He safeguarded the invisibility of the Father, lest humans should ever become contemptuous of God, and that humanity should always have some goal to which it might advance. At the same time, he displayed God in visible form to humankind through his many acts of mediation, lest our race should be utterly remote from God and so cease to be. For the glory of God is a living human, and the life of a human is the vision of God.[29] For if the manifestation of God in creation gives life to all who live on earth, much more does the revelation of the Father through the Word bestow life on those who see God. Against Heresies 4.20.6.[30]

God Came to Save the Distressed. Irenaeus: "Christ," says Paul, "is the end of the

---

[22]LCF 50. [23]LCF 216-17. [24]LCF 278. [25]The *Philanthropos*. [26]ECF 107. [27]1 Cor 12:6. [28]Jn 1:18. [29]One of the most famous of all patristic aphorisms, synopsizing the life-giving dynamic of God's salvific economy. [30]ECF 103-4*.

Law, to obtain justification for every believer."[31] How could Christ be the end of the Law unless he were also its beginning? For he who brought the end wrought the beginning also. It is he himself who says to Moses, "I have surely seen the affliction of my people in Egypt, and I have come down to rescue them."[32] From the beginning he was accustomed, as the Word of God, to descend and ascend for the salvation of those who were in distress. AGAINST HERESIES 4.12.4.[33]

THE INCARNATION DEIFIES THE HUMAN RACE. IRENAEUS: Our Lord Jesus Christ, the Word of God, of his boundless love, became what we are that he might make us what he himself is. AGAINST HERESIES 5.preface.[34]

THE LORD GIVES THE SPIRIT TO ALL HUMANKIND. IRENAEUS: The Lord leads into the paradise of life those who obey his teaching, "consummating in himself all things, things in heaven and things on earth."[35] "Things in heaven" means spiritual things; "things on earth" refers to his dealings with humankind. He "consummated all things in himself" by joining humanity to Spirit and placing Spirit in humanity. He himself became the source of Spirit, and he gives Spirit to be the source of human life. For it is through Spirit that we see and hear and talk. He effected the consummation,[36] and declared war on our enemy and crushed him who in the beginning had led us captive in Adam. . . . The victory over the enemy would not have been rightly won had not his conqueror been born as man from a woman. For it was through a woman that the devil held sway over humankind from the beginning, when he set himself to be humankind's adversary. Therefore the Lord confesses himself to be the Son of man, restoring in himself that original man from whom is derived that part of creation that is born of woman. As it was through a man that our race was overcome and went down to death, so through a victorious man we may rise

up to life. As through a man death won the prize of victory over us, so through a man we may win the prize of victory over death. Nor would the Lord have made an end in his own person of that original enmity between man and the serpent . . . had he come from another father. AGAINST HERESIES 5.20.2–21.2.[37]

ALL RATIONAL BEINGS PARTAKE IN THE WORD. ORIGEN: That the operation of the Father and the Son is concerned as well with sinners as with saints is clear from this fact: that all rational creatures are partakers in the Word (for in the Greek "word" means "reason") and thus possess seeds, as it were, of wisdom and righteousness implanted in them. Christ is "Wisdom" and "Righteousness." All partake of him who truly is, who said through Moses "I am he who is."[38] . . . Further, it is said in the Gospel, "If I had not come and spoken to them, they would not be guilty, but now they have no excuse for their sins."[39] . . . This means that they have no excuse from the time when the divine reason or discourse has begun to show them in their heart the distinction between right and wrong. . . . Again, the Gospel teaches that humankind as a whole is not without a share in God, when the Savior says, . . . "The kingdom of God is within you." ON FIRST PRINCIPLES 1.3.6.[40]

THE WORD ACCEPTED WEAKNESS TO ENRICH US. ATHANASIUS: The Word was made man in order that we might be made divine.[41] He displayed himself through a body that we might receive knowledge of the invisible Father. He endured insults at the hands of people that we might inherit immortality. In himself he suffered no injury, being impassible and immortal and very Word of God. But in his impassibility he was guarding and saving

---

[31]Rom 10:4. [32]Ex 3:7. [33]*ECF* 102-3. [34]*ECF* 106. Athanasius would later popularize this axiom (*On the Incarnation* 54). [35]Eph 1:10. [36]Restoration of the human race. [37]*ECF* 112*. [38]Ex 3:14. [39]Jn 15:22. [40]*ECF* 332. [41]Athanasius is alluding to the famous phrase first enunciated by Irenaeus *Against Heresies* 5.preface.

suffering people, for whose sake he endured this treatment. On the Incarnation 54.[42]

The Word Is Incarnate in Order to Deify Us. Athanasius: He assumed a created human body, that, having renewed it as its creator, he might deify it in himself and thus bring us all into the kingdom of heaven through our likeness to him. . . . We should not have been freed from sin and the curse had not the flesh which the Word assumed been by nature human (for we would have nothing in common with what was alien to us). So too humanity would not have been deified, if the Word who became flesh had not been by nature derived from the Father and his true and proper Word. For it was for this reason that the conjunction was of this kind, that he might join him who by nature was human to him who naturally belonged to the Godhead, that his salvation and deification might be sure. . . . There would have been no profit to us humans if either the Word had not been truly and by nature the Son of God or the flesh that he assumed had not been real flesh. Against the Arians 2.70.[43]

The Word Assumes Flesh to Render It Divine. Athanasius: The flesh is ignorant, but the Word, as Word, knows everything, even before it comes to be. For when the Word was made man he did not cease to be God, nor because he is God does he avoid what is human. Far from it; rather, being God, he has taken the flesh to himself, and, in flesh, deified the flesh. In the flesh he asked questions; in the flesh he raised the dead. He knew where Lazarus lay, but he still asked. . . . The all-holy Word of God bore our ignorance so that he might bestow on us the knowledge of his Father. Against the Arians 3.38.[44]

The Incarnation Breaks the Power of Death. Athanasius: If the works of the Godhead had not taken place by means of the body, humankind would not have been made

divine. If the properties of the flesh had not been ascribed to the Word, humans would not have been thoroughly freed from them. But as it is the Word became man and took as his own the properties of the flesh. Thus, because of the Word which has come in the body, these attributes[45] no longer adhere to the body but have been destroyed by the Word. Henceforth humans no longer remain sinful and dead according to their own[46] attributes, but they rise in accordance with the Word's power and persist immortal and incorruptible. Whence also as the flesh is said to have been begotten from Mary, the mother of God, he himself is said to have been begotten, he who bestows birth on all others so that they come into being. This is in order that he may transfer our birth to himself, that we may no longer return as earth to earth, but, as being joined with the Word from heaven, may be carried up with him into heaven. Against the Arians 3.33.[47]

The Power of the Word Shines in Humility. Basil of Caesarea: It is also on your account that he "does not know the hour and the day"[48] of judgment, although nothing is outside the knowledge of the true Wisdom, for "all things came into being through him."[49] Even among people no one is ever ignorant of what he had made. But this is part of his dispensation, because of your weakness, so that sinners should not be plunged into despair by the narrow limits of the appointed time, thinking that no space or repentance is left them. Similarly, it is so that those who are fighting a long campaign against the opposing force should not leave their post because the time is protracted. Letter 8.6.[50]

The Incarnate Lord Pays the Debt of Sin. Basil of Caesarea: If the Lord did not

---

[42]ECF 404. [43]ECF 404*. [44]ECF 399-400. [45]He refers to the endemic characteristics (*idiomata*) of humanity: death and corruptibility. [46]That is, natural. [47]ECF 399. [48]Mt 24:36. [49]1 Cor 8:6. [50]LCF 68.

come to dwell in our flesh, then the ransom did not pay the fine due to death on our behalf, nor did he destroy through himself the reign of death. For if the Lord did not assume that over which death reigned, death would not have been stopped from effecting his purpose, nor would the suffering of the God-bearing flesh have become our gain: he would not have killed sin in the flesh. We, who were dead in Adam,[51] would not have been restored in Christ . . . that which was alienated from God by the serpent would not have been brought back by him. LETTER 261.2.[52]

THE SUFFERINGS ARE FOR OUR SALVATION.

GREGORY OF NAZIANZUS: For who compelled him to be born at all, or to mount the cross?[53] As I have said, he represents, in himself, our condition. It was we who were formerly forsaken and neglected, but we have now been brought near and saved by the sufferings of the impassible one. Similarly, when he utters the verses that follow in that psalm, he is taking to himself our folly and our wrongdoing, for the twenty-first psalm clearly refers to Christ. ORATION 30.5.[54]

THE WORD'S SACRIFICE FOR HUMANITY.

GREGORY OF NAZIANZUS: Is it not clear that the Father accepts the sacrifice? This is not because he demanded or needed it but because this was part of the divine plan, since humankind had to be sanctified by the humanity of God; so that he might rescue us by overcoming the tyrant by force and bring us back to himself through the mediation of the Son, who carried out this divine plan, to the honor of the Father, to whom he clearly delivers up all things. ORATION 45.22. [55]

THE INCARNATION MAKES US PRIESTS.

GREGORY OF NYSSA: But the spiritual Lawgiver, our Lord Jesus Christ, strips the Law of its material veils and lays bare the types and allegories. First of all, he does not give commu-

nion with God only to one whom he separates from everyone else,[56] but he bestows this honor equally on all, offering the grace of the priesthood as common to those who desire it. Second, he does not manufacture the priestly beauty from alien adornments produced from dyes and curious devices of weaving,[57] but he puts on him his own native adornments, decking him with the graces of virtue rather than with an embroidered purple robe. ON THE LORD'S PRAYER 3.[58]

JESUS LIBERATES HIS CHURCH.

GREGORY OF NYSSA: Do you realize to what height the Lord raises his hearers through the words of the prayer, by which he somehow transforms human nature into what is divine? For he lays down that those who approach God should themselves become gods. Why, he says, do you go to God crouching with fear like a slave because your conscience pricks you? Why do you shut out holy audacity, which is inherent in the freedom of the soul because it has been joined to its very essence from the beginning? ON THE LORD'S PRAYER 5.[59]

THE INCARNATION MAKES US THE FAMILY OF GOD.

GREGORY OF NYSSA: Our life had been alienated from God, and its return to the high and the heavenly place was beyond its own unaided contrivance. For this reason, as the apostle says, "he who had no acquaintance with sin is made to be sin" and frees us from the curse by making our curse his own; and taking up the enmity that had come between us and God, "he slew (in the words of the apostle) the enmity in his own person." Sin, indeed, was the enmity. Thus, by becoming

---

[51]1 Cor 15:22. [52]*LCF* 70-71. [53]The context of his argument here is to refute those who argued that Christ's passibility in his earthly life was proof positive that he was not the powerful Logos. Gregory is alluding to the psalm of crucifixion (21:1 [LXX]): "My God, why have you forsaken me," and arguing that this should not be taken as evidence that Jesus was a mere human in despair in the face of death. [54]*LCF* 104. [55]*LCF* 112. [56]A reference to the ethnic exclusivity of old Israel. [57]The Levitical instructions for priestly vesture. [58]ACW 18:45. [59]ACW 18:72-73.

what we were, through his own person, he again united humanity to God. For through purity he brought into the closest kinship with the Father of our nature that "new person which is created after the likeness of God," in whom "the whole fullness of the Godhead dwelt in bodily form."[60] And along with himself he drew to the same state of grace all the nature that shares in his human body and is akin to him. AGAINST EUNOMIUS 12.1.[61]

THE WORD ENDURES ALL THINGS FOR OUR SAKE. GREGORY OF NYSSA: But like those who see a weak person being swept away by a torrent, and though they know that they may also be caught by the mud in the stream and suffer the battering of the stones carried down by the water, yet out of sympathy for the one in peril they do not shirk plunging in, so also our kind Savior willingly accepted insults and humiliations to save the one who was perishing as a result of deception. He descended into earthly life, since he knew beforehand his glorious ascension. He allowed his human part to die, since he foreknew also the rising. For he did not rashly take a dangerous risk like an ordinary person and stake the outcome on the uncertainty of the future, but as God he disposed what lay ahead toward a stated and known end. DISCOURSE ON THE HOLY PASCHA.[62]

SACRAMENTAL UNION WITH THE LORD. HILARY OF POITIERS: Christ himself gives evidence of the nature of our life in him through the sacrament of the flesh and blood imparted to us, when he says, . . . "Since I live, you also will live; since I am in my Father, and you are in me, and I am in you."[63] If he means a unity merely of will, why did he describe a kind of order of ascent[64] in the establishment of that unity? His purpose surely was that we should believe that he was in the Father by nature, as being divine; whereas we are in him in virtue of his birth in the flesh, and he is in us through the mystery of the sacraments. Thus we

should have a doctrine of a unity consummated through the Mediator, since, while we abide in him, he would abide in the Father, and, thus abiding, should abide in us; and thus we should advance to unity with the Father. He is in the Father naturally, because of his generation: so we also should be in him naturally, while he naturally abides in us. ON THE TRINITY 8.15.[65]

THE INCARNATION RESTORED THE HEATHENS TO GOD. AMBROSE OF MILAN: The heathen have come, and in very truth have come into your inheritance, for they who came as heathen have become Christians. Those who came to invade your inheritance have been made coheirs with God. I have those as protectors whom I considered to be adversaries. That is fulfilled which the prophet sang of the Lord Jesus that "his dwelling is in peace," and "There he broke the horns of the bows, the shield, the sword and the battle."[66] For whose gift is this, whose work is this but yours, Lord Jesus? LETTER 20.21.[67]

THE LORD'S ECONOMY RECONCILES US. AUGUSTINE: When sins had made a wide rift between humanity and God, it was necessary that we should be reconciled to God and even brought to the resurrection to eternal life by means of a mediator who alone was without sin in his birth, life and execution, so that humankind's pride should be shown up and cured by the humility of God. Humanity is thus shown how far it had departed from God, since it was through the incarnation of God that it was recalled and through the God-man that an example of obedience was offered to the insolence of humankind. And so a fountain of grace was opened, not for any antecedent merit, but by the taking of "the form of a servant"[68] by the Only-Begotten. Proof of the bodily resur-

---

[60]Col 2:9. [61]LCF 142-43. [62]PMS 9:7. [63]Jn 14:20. [64]Namely, that there was a clear sense of taxonomy and distinction in the personal references Jesus used in that promise. [65]LCF 57-58. [66]Ps 76:3. [67]CCC 130. [68]Phil 2:7.

rection promised to the redeemed was given by anticipation in the person of the Redeemer himself. The devil was overcome by means of that very nature that, he rejoiced to think, he had entrapped. Yet humankind should not boast, lest pride should arise again. And there are other consequences of this mighty and mysterious work of the mediator that can be seen and described by those who benefit from it, or can be seen, though they cannot be described. ENCHIRIDION 108.[69]

GOD'S PROMISE GIVES US HOPE. THEODORET OF CYR: When I consider the divine law that calls those who are united in marriage "one flesh,"[70] I have no idea how to console the member left behind by the separation of death, for I am aware of the magnitude of the grief. But I do find many approaches to consolation when I think about the course of nature, about that decree that the Creator passed with the words "you are earth, and to earth you will return."[71] This is what happens daily everywhere on land and sea: either husbands arrive first at the end of their lives, or wives are the first to suffer this. But in addition to these reflections I also think of the hopes bestowed on us by our God and Savior, for here is why the mystery of God's plan[72] was accomplished: that we might learn that death had come to an end and not grieve too much when we were left alone through the death of those we love but might await that longed for hope of the resurrection. LETTER 18.11, TO NEOPTOLEMUS.[73]

---

[69]*LCF* 225. [70]Gen 2:24; Mt 19:5-6; Mk 10:8. [71]Gen 3:19. [72]The economy (*oikonomia*) of the incarnation. [73]MFC 2:202*.

HE CAME DOWN

καὶ εἰς ἕνα κύριον Ἰησοῦν Χριστόν,	Et in unum Dominum Jesum Christum,	We believe in one Lord, Jesus Christ,
τὸν υἱὸν τοῦ Θεοῦ τὸν μονογενῆ,	Filium Dei unigenitum,	the only Son of God,
τὸν ἐκ τοῦ πατρὸς γεννηθέντα	et ex Patre natum	eternally
πρὸ πάντων τῶν αἰώνων,	ante omnia saecula	begotten of the Father,
φῶς ἐκ φωτός,	[Deum de Deo], Lumen de Lumine,	[God from God], Light from Light,
Θεὸν ἀληθινὸν ἐκ θεοῦ ἀληθινοῦ,	Deum verum de Deo vero,	true God from true God,
γεννηθέντα, οὐ ποιηθέντα,	genitum, non factum,	begotten, not made,
ὁμοούσιον τῷ πατρί·	consubstantialem Patri;	of one Being with the Father.
δι᾽ οὗ τὰ πάντα ἐγένετο·	per quem omnia facta sunt;	Through him all things were made.
τὸν δι᾽ ἡμᾶς τοὺς ἀνθρώπους	qui propter nos homines	For us
καὶ διὰ τὴν ἡμετέραν σωτηρίαν	et propter nostram salutem	and for our salvation
κατελθόντα ἐκ τῶν οὐρανῶν	**descendit** de coelis,	**he came down** from heaven:
καὶ σαρκωθέντα ἐκ πνεύματος ἁγίου	et incarnatus est de Spiritu Sancto	by the power of the Holy Spirit
καὶ Μαρίας τῆς παρθένου	ex Maria virgine,	he became incarnate from the Virgin Mary,
καὶ ἐνανθρωπήσαντα,	et homo factus est;	and was made man.

HISTORICAL CONTEXT: The creedal phrase "came down (*katelthonta*) from heaven" is directly based on Jesus' words in the Gospel of John, describing himself as the living bread "that came down from heaven."[1] Ancient Christian witness to the incarnation as an act of the saving God is organized around this great verb that is found throughout the scriptural record but especially organizes the thought of the Johannine Gospel as a great drama of salvation worked out in the twin axes of epiphanies of the Word's "coming down" (*katabasis*) and "ascending on high" (*anabasis*): his exaltation and return to transcendent glory. In the Greek translation of the Old Testament, the term *katabasis* could signify a rich range of meanings. A *katabasis* could be that of the mother stooping down to her child (an image used in the psalms and the prophets to describe the compassion of the God of Israel) or the vigorous and swift descent to aid a friend against the attacks of a foe.[2] Perhaps the most dynamic meaning

of all was to connote the awesome descent of God to reveal his energy and action among humankind. "The coming down" was thus a cipher for the great theophanic epiphanies of God in the Old Testament, notably at Sinai and in the pillar of fire that God used to symbolize his presence leading the Israelites through the desert.[3] For such reasons the idea of "coming down to his people to save and illuminate" was inherent in this weighty biblical phrase, and we find it used in the early church as a keynote description of the act of the Word's incarnation: the quintessential example, for the Christians, of God's self-revelation and his compassionate "stooping down" to humankind.

Modern commentators have often spoken of two types of scheme being applicable in the images the church uses of Jesus: Christology from above or Christology from below. The early Fathers, however, are quite clear among themselves, and more or less unanimous, that there is only a movement of salvific energy from above to our side, from God to humankind, never a movement the other way around, such as the ascent of a blessed person to the throne of God. The initiative is entirely that of the divine Savior. This is perhaps one of the most striking differences between the Christology of the ancient church and that of recent times. The "coming down" of the Word of God into embodiment is described with great reverence among the Fathers as an act of profound compassion on the part of God, an act of humility and endurance, motivated by the desire to save and comfort the creation.

OVERVIEW: God's humility is humankind's glory (TERTULLIAN). God became man in order to teach humankind to be gods (CLEMENT OF ALEXANDRIA, ATHANASIUS). The Word stooped down to us out of compassion and love (ORIGEN, BASIL, GREGORY OF NYSSA). He emptied himself voluntarily for our sake (CYRIL OF ALEXANDRIA). But even though he comes down in great humility he remains God, since he came to save and deliver (ORIGEN, CYRIL OF ALEXANDRIA, LEO). He comes in humility, and yet he comes as fire (GREGORY OF NYSSA). The awesome epiphanies of the Old Testament give way to a new order of paradoxical humility (EPHREM). Such a mystery is understood fully only by the angels and by the elect (EPHREM, PSEUDO-DIONYSIUS). The One who comes to humanity is the servant of God (CLEMENT OF ROME, DIDACHE, ORIGEN, ATHANASIUS). The Servant is sinless (GREGORY THE GREAT), and in his servant ministry he shows profound greatness (ORIGEN). This ministry encapsulates all his incarnate economy (GREGORY OF NAZIANZUS). As a poor servant he stands in solidarity with all the poor and humble (CLEMENT OF ROME). As a servant he is ready and suffers obediently (EPISTLE OF BARNABAS, TERTULLIAN, ATHANASIUS). Even in his lowliness and humility, this manifestation of his saving power is profoundly divine (GREGORY OF NAZIANZUS).

The Voluntary Constraint of the Divine Power

GOD'S HUMILITY IS HUMANKIND'S GLORY. TERTULLIAN: All that you demand as worthy of God will be attributed to the Father who is invisible, unapproachable, serene, in fact what I may call the God of the philosophers. All that you cavil at as unworthy will be ascribed to the Son, who is seen, heard, approached; the agent and servant of the Father, who combines in himself man and God; God in his works of power, man in his weaknesses, so that he may confer on humanity as much as he withdraws from divinity. In fact, in this way of thinking, all that you see as my God's disgrace is really the mystery of human salvation. God lived with humanity, as man, that humanity might be taught to live the divine life. God lived on humanity's level that humanity might be able to live on God's level. God was found weak that humanity might become most great. If you disdain a God like this, I doubt if you can wholeheartedly believe in a God who was crucified. But how perverse is your attitude toward both the modes of the Creator. AGAINST MARCION 2.27.[4]

GOD INCARNATE TEACHES HUMANS TO BE DIVINE. CLEMENT OF ALEXANDRIA: If you do not believe the prophets . . . the Lord himself will speak to you: "who, being in the form of God, did not regard his equality with God as a prize to be grasped, but abased himself."[5] This is the God of compassion, yearning to save humankind. The Word himself at this point speaks to you plainly, putting unbelief to shame, and I mean the Word of God, who became man just that you may learn from a man how it may be that Man should become God. EXHORTATION TO THE GREEKS 1.8.(4).[6]

---

[1]Jn 6:41, 51, 58. [2]Num 14:45. [3]Ex 19:20; Num 12:5; Ps 18:9; Is 64:3. [4]ECF 168**. [5]Phil 2:6-7. [6]ECF 244*.

The Word Stoops Down to Earth.

ORIGEN: One might answer this charge[7] first concerning the nature of the divine Word who is God, and then concerning the soul of Jesus. In the first place, we may say that as in nursing mothers the quality of food changes to milk, suitable to the nature of the child . . . so in dealing with humanity God changes the power of the Word, whose nature it is to nourish the human soul, in accordance with the merit of the individual. And to one he comes as "the rational pure milk"[8] (in the scriptural phrase) . . . to another he is imparted as "solid food." There is no question of the Word's being false to his own nature in becoming nourishment for each person in accordance with his or her capacity to receive it. . . . But if one takes the change to have reference to the soul of Jesus, in entering the body, then we shall ask, What is meant by "change"? As regards change of essential being, we do not admit it, either in respect of his soul or even concerning any other rational soul. If it be meant that his soul is subject to limitations from the body with which it was mingled, or arising from the place to which it came, then we would ask, Does any incongruity result for the Word in bringing down a Savior for the human race, because of his great love for humankind? For none of those, who were before him proclaimed as healers, had such power as the soul of Jesus displayed in its works, when it descended to the afflictions of human beings on behalf of our race. AGAINST CELSUS 4.18.[9]

The Word's Kenosis Was Voluntary.

ORIGEN: Jesus, before he became a grown man, while still a little child, made progress,[10] since he "abased himself";[11] for no one makes progress if he is already perfect, as progress implies the need of progress . . . but having "abased himself," he then took back the things of which he had stripped himself, since he had done this as a voluntary act.[12] HOMILIS ON JEREMIAH 1.7.[13]

He Comes to Earth but Is Unchanged.

ORIGEN: For this divine descent he had no need of change . . . for he remains unchanged in his essential being while he descends to take part in human affairs by the providence and dispensation of God. AGAINST CELSUS 4.14.[14]

The Word Takes a Body in Order to Deify the Race.

ATHANASIUS. The Scripture says "gave to him,"[15] but this does not refer to the Word himself; for as we have said, even before he became man he was worshiped by the angels and by the whole creation in respect of his unique heritage. It was because of us, and for us, that this also is written of him. For as Christ died and was exalted as man, so, as man, he is said to receive what, as God, he always had, in order that this great gift might extend to us. The Word was not degraded by receiving a body, so that he should ever need to seek to receive God's gift. Rather, he deified what he put on; and, more than that, he bestowed this gift on the human race. AGAINST THE ARIANS 1.42.[16]

The Word's Love Motivates the Incarnation.

BASIL OF CAESAREA: "My Father is greater than I."[17] This text is much employed by those ungrateful wretches, the devil's brood.[18] But I am confident that even in this saying the consubstantiality[19] of the Son

---

[7]Celsus, a second-century pagan apologist, had argued that the Christian doctrine of the incarnation (a divine epiphany through the medium of Jesus of Nazareth) had logically to be a matter of deceit from start to finish: either that of a god pretending to be a human or that of a human pretending to be a god. If it was not a deceit, he said, then it was an illogicality on the grounds that a change had entered into the divinity, which contradicts the unchangeability inherent in divine nature. Origen answers his charges a century later in *Against Celsus*. [8]Heb 5:12-13; 1 Cor 3:2. [9]ECF 294-95. [10]Origen's immediate context here is to comment on the significance of Jer 1:6, "I do not know how to speak, for I am too young," and saying that it is a text to be applied to the incarnation of Christ. [11]He is alluding to the concept of the kenosis (self-emptying; see Phil 2:5-11). [12]Origen then goes on to say that therefore the text of Is 7:15-16 is fulfilled in him. [13]ECF 303. [14]ECF 294. [15]"Gave to him a name above all names" (Phil 2:9). [16]ECF 384*. [17]Jn 14:28. [18]He refers to the Arian party. [19]That Father and Son are *Homoousios*.

with the Father is demonstrated. For I know that comparison can only properly be made in respect of things of the same nature. We speak of an angel as greater than an angel, a person more righteous than a person, a bird swifter than a bird. If these comparisons are made between things of the same species, and if the Father is said to be greater than the Son, it follows that the Son is consubstantial with the Father. But there is another meaning contained in the saying. Is there anything extraordinary in his admission that his Father is greater? He is the Word and has been "made flesh,"[20] and he was seen as inferior to the angels in glory and inferior to people in beauty. "You have made him a little lower than the angels."[21] And, "We saw him, and he had neither grace nor beauty; he was lacking in beauty in comparison with all the rest of humankind."[22] All this he endured because of his great compassion toward his handiwork, that he might rescue the lost sheep and bring it back safe to the flock[23] and restore safe and sound to his own land the man who went down from Jerusalem to Jericho and so fell into the hands of robbers.[24] LETTER 8.5.[25]

LOVE DESCENDS TO US OUT OF HIS PITY.
GREGORY OF NYSSA: If, then, love for humanity is a special characteristic of the divine nature, here is the reason you are searching for; here is the cause of the presence of God among humans. Our diseased nature needed a healer. Humankind in its fall needed someone to set us upright. We who had lost the gift of life stood in need of a life-giver, and we who had dropped away from fellowship with good wanted one who would lead us back to good. We who were shut up in darkness longed for the presence of the light. The captive sought for a ransomer, the fettered prisoner for someone to take his part, and he who was held in the bondage of slavery longed for a deliverer. Were these, then, trifling or unworthy wants to importune the Deity to come down and take a survey of the nature of humankind, when humankind was so

miserably and pitiably conditioned? THE GREAT CATECHISM 15.[26]

THE WORD BECAME FLESH BUT REMAINED GOD. CYRIL OF ALEXANDRIA: Following in every respect the confessions of the holy Fathers,[27] which they have drawn up under the guidance of the Holy Spirit who spoke in them,[28] and keeping close to the meaning that they had in view and journeying, so to speak, along the king's highway,[29] we affirm that the very only-begotten Word of God, begotten of the very substance of the Father, true God of true God, Light that is from Light, by whom all things were made, both in heaven and on earth, came down for our salvation and emptied himself out of his condescension, and became incarnate and was made man. This means, having taken flesh of the holy Virgin and made it his own from the womb, he consented to be born as we are and came forth as a human being from a woman. He did not cast away what he was, but even in the assumption of flesh and blood, he remained what he was, namely, God in nature and truth. THIRD LETTER TO NESTORIUS (LETTER 17).[30]

THE SON CAME DOWN BUT NEVER LEFT HIS FATHER. LEO THE GREAT: The Son of God, therefore, coming down from his seat in heaven and yet not withdrawing from his Father's glory, born after a new order by a new mode of birth,

---

[20]Jn 1:14. [21]Heb 2:7, 9. [22]Is 53:2-3. [23]Jer 50:6; Lk 15:4. [24]Lk 10:30-31. [25]*LCF* 68. [26]NPNF 2 5:487*. [27]Here he is referring to the fathers of the Council of Nicaea (325). [28]Cyril is one of the first Greek fathers so explicitly to advance the theory that patristic theology bears some of the character of the inspired writings of sacred Scripture, on the same principle that as the Lord once spoke through the prophets, so in latter days he also speaks through his elect and inspired saints, those theologians who were the great saints and fathers (the word also means bishops and spiritual teachers) of the people. The idea still carries weight in the Orthodox and Catholic traditions of theology. [29]A rhetorical phrase that signified the royal way (the broad and central track through an argument) or what we might even call the common-sense unanimity among great teachers (avoiding the extremes of opinion). [30]CCC 281-82**.

enters this lower world. In a new order, that is, because invisible in what belongs to himself he became visible in what belongs to us, and he, the incomprehensible, willed to be comprehended; abiding before time, he began to exist in time; the Lord of the universe, drawing a shadow over the immensity of his majesty, took the form of a servant; the impassible God did not abhor to become man, subject to suffering, and, immortal as he is, to become subject to the laws of death; but he was also born by a new kind of birth, inasmuch as inviolate virginity, which knew not the desire of the flesh, now furnished the substance of flesh. LETTER 28.4 (THE TOME OF LEO).[31]

INCARNATION ALTERNATES MAJESTY AND HUMILITY. LEO THE GREAT: From his mother the Lord took nature, not sin. Jesus Christ was born from a virgin's womb by a miraculous birth, and yet his nature is not on that account unlike to ours, for he that is true God is also true man. There is no unreality in this unity since the humility of the manhood and the majesty of the deity are alternated. For just as the God is not changed by his compassion, so the man is not swallowed up by the dignity of the Godhead. LETTER 28.4 (THE TOME OF LEO).[32]

The Hiddenness of Deity in the Humanity

THE WORD ADAPTS TO HIS CREATURES' NEEDS. ATHANASIUS: Why did he say "not even the Son knows"[33] when in fact he knew? I think every believer knows the answer: that he spoke, as elsewhere, as man, because of the flesh. This does not show a defect in the Word but rather defect of human nature, of which ignorance is a characteristic. Since he was made man, he is not ashamed to profess ignorance because of the ignorance of flesh, to show that though knowing as God he is ignorant according to the flesh. AGAINST THE ARIANS 3.43.[34]

THE DIVINITY RECEIVES THE NATURE OF FLESH. HILARY OF POITIERS: The Son of God was born of a Virgin and the Holy Spirit for the sake of humankind. . . . He was made man of a virgin so that he might receive into himself the nature of flesh, that the body of humankind as a whole might be sanctified by association with this mixture.[35] He, through whom humankind was created, did not need to be made man. It was we who needed that God should be made flesh and dwell in us, that is, should dwell within all flesh, in its entirety, by taking our flesh to himself. His humility is our ennoblement; his shame is our honor. He who is God coexisted with us in flesh, and thus we have been restored from the flesh to the divine nature. ON THE TRINITY 2.24-25.[36]

A CHILD AT THE BREAST YET RULING THE UNIVERSE. CYRIL OF ALEXANDRIA: Neither do we say that the flesh was converted into the divine nature, nor surely that the ineffable nature of God the Word was debased and perverted into the nature of flesh. For the nature of God is unchangeable and unalterable, ever continuing altogether the same, according to the Scriptures. We, however, say that the Son of God, while visible to the eyes, and a babe, and in swaddling clothes and still at the breast of his virgin Mother, nevertheless filled all creation as God and was seated with his Father. For the divinity is without quantity and without magnitude and without limit. THIRD LETTER TO NESTORIUS (LETTER 17).[37]

THE ANGELS RECOGNIZED WHO THE CHILD WAS. EPHREM THE SYRIAN: That chief of the angels greeted you as the pledge of holiness. The earth became for him a new heaven in which the Watchers[38] came down and praised. The sons of the height gathered around your

---

[31]CCC 318. [32]*LCF* 279-80. [33]Mk 13:32. [34]*ECF* 400. [35]Hilary's language of mixture would soon come to be regarded as hopelessly vague and was ultimately rejected by the Council of Chalcedon in 451. [36]*LCF* 53*. [37]CCC 282*. [38]The angels.

dwelling because of the King's Son who dwelled in you.[39] Your earthly habitation became like heaven above by their vigil. HYMNS ON THE NATIVITY 25.17.[40]

THE OLD REVELATION GIVES WAY TO A NEW IMAGE.

EPHREM THE SYRIAN: The scattered symbols you have gathered from the Torah toward your beauty,[41] and you set forth the prototypes in your gospel as well as powers and signs from nature. You mixed pigments for your portrait. You were observed by yourself, and you portray yourself, O Painter who also portrayed his Father in himself! The two portray one another. Prophets, kings and priests, all of them created, have portrayed you, though they were unlike you. Created servants are not at all sufficient, for you alone are sufficient to portray yourself. Your portrait has been fully drawn. You perfected it by your advent. The drawings were swallowed up by the strength of the pigments, resplendent in all colors. Faded is the drawing of the temporal lamb. Resplendent is the glory of the true Lamb. Very weak too is the drawing of the staff . . . the cross of light . . . and the fixed serpent: in the wilderness it portrayed the crucified body. The transitory symbols have been completed and swallowed up by the truth that does not pass away.[42] . . . By the shining forth of your advent the shadows have been illuminated. The types have come to an end, but the allusions persist. The flash of the symbols has been swallowed up by your rays. Your symbols have passed away, but your prophets have not passed away. HYMNS ON VIRGINITY 28.2-5.[43]

HIS DEITY AND HIS HUMANITY ARE INSCRUTABLE.

PSEUDO-DIONYSIUS: Even the plainest article of divinity, namely, the incarnation and birth of Jesus in human form, cannot be expressed by any language or known by any mind, not even by the first of the most exalted angels. That he took human substance is a mysterious truth that we have received; but we know not how from the Virgin's seed[44] he was formed in another manner than is natural, nor how (his dry feet supporting the solid weight of his material body) he walked on the unstable substance of the water; nor do we understand any of the other things that belong to the supernatural nature of Jesus. THE DIVINE NAMES 2.9.[45]

The Form of God and the Form of a Servant

JESUS THE SERVANT WHO SAVES.

CLEMENT OF ROME: We ask you, Master,[46] to be our helper and protector. Save those among us who are in distress; have mercy on the humble; raise up the fallen; show yourself to those in need; heal the godless; turn back those of your people who wander; feed the hungry, release our prisoners; raise up the weak; comfort the discouraged. Let all the nations know that you are the only God and that Jesus Christ is your servant and that we are your people and the sheep of your pasture. 1 CLEMENT 59.4.[47]

THE HOLY VINE OF DAVID.

DIDACHE: Regarding the Eucharist, give thanks as follows. First, concerning the cup: We give you thanks, our Father, for the holy Vine of David your servant, which you have made known to us through Jesus, your servant. To you be the glory for evermore. Next, concerning the broken bread: We give you thanks, our Father, for the life and knowledge that you have made known to us

---

[39]The poem is here addressed to Mary. [40]ESH 204. [41]The word has arranged all the biblical types in Scripture as a manifestation of his glory as finally revealed in the incarnation. [42]Ephrem argues that the coming of the Word in person, in the flesh, brings the prototype, the ultimate reality to which all the symbols of biblical prophecy once referred. Once the original comes, the vivacity of the truth shines forth better than in old depictions of it. [43]ESH 386-87. [44]He is being deliberately paradoxical rather than biologically naïve: how could such a conception be possible or be described? [45]ODN 75-76*. [46]The text has the character and style (many biblical passages being conflated together) of a very early instance of the great eucharistic prayer (*Anaphora*) of the Roman church. [47]AF 95-97.

through Jesus, your servant. To you be glory for evermore. As this broken bread was scattered over the hills and then, when gathered, became one mass, so may your church be gathered from the ends of the earth into your kingdom. For yours is the glory and the power through Jesus Christ for evermore. DIDACHE 9.1-4.[48]

THE WISDOM OF GOD IN THE FORM OF A SERVANT. ORIGEN: We have said that all souls who lived in this world needed many helpers or rulers or assistants.[49] So in these last times, when the end of the world was already imminent and the whole human race was approaching final perdition, and when not only those who were ruled but also those to whom the responsibility of ruling had been entrusted had all grown weak; people at this time no longer needed such help as this nor defenders of the same nature as themselves, but they implored the aid of the very Author and Creator of their being, that he might restore to humanity the discipline of obedience and restore to the ruling powers the discipline of ruling, for this discipline had been broken and infringed. Hence the only-begotten Son of God, who was the Word and Wisdom of God, though he was "with the Father in the glory, which he had before the world was,"[50] "abased himself, and taking the form of a servant, was made obedient unto death"[51] that he might teach obedience to those who could not achieve salvation save through obedience. And he also restored the laws of ruling and reigning that had been broken, by "subjecting all enemies beneath his feet"[52] . . . not only was he made obedient to the Father "even to the death of the cross," but even in the consummation of the age, when he gathers up all in himself, whom he subjects to the Father . . . with them and in them he himself is also said to be subjected to the Father. ON FIRST PRINCIPLES 3.5.6.[53]

THE IMAGE OF GOD, A SERVANT FOR OUR SAKE. ATHANASIUS: When it says "God highly exalted him,"[54] the words "highly exalted" do not signify the exaltation of the substance of the Word; that was and is always equal with God. The exaltation is of the manhood. These words are said after the incarnation of the Word, to make it clear that the terms "humbled" and "exalted" refer to the human nature. . . . The Word, being the image of the Father and immortal, "took the form of a servant," and as man he endured death for our sake in his own flesh, that thus he might offer himself to the Father on our behalf. Therefore also as man he is said be highly exalted because of us and on our behalf, that as by his death we all died in Christ, so also in Christ himself we may all be exalted, being raised from the dead and ascending into heaven "where Jesus the forerunner has entered for us."[55] And if it is now for our sake that Christ has entered into heaven, though he was before and always is the Lord and the maker of the heavens, it is therefore for our sake that Scripture speaks of his being exalted. Just as he who himself sanctified all, equally says that he sanctifies himself to the Father for our sakes; it is not that the Word can "become" holy, rather that he himself should sanctify all of us in himself. AGAINST THE ARIANS 1.41.[56]

FIRE STOOPS DOWN BUT ALSO ASCENDS. GREGORY OF NYSSA: Fire has by nature an upward tendency, but by divine power it is brought down to earth, and so Elijah was himself raised on high[57] when he was enveloped in the heavenly flame that then hastened to resume its natural upward motion. In the same way the power of the most High, which is something immaterial and formless, received the "form of a servant" in the subsistence[58] it received through the Virgin, and then it brought this to its own sublimity, transmuting that form into its own

---

[48]ACW 6:20*. [49]He signifies angelic guardian spirits. [50]Jn 17:5. [51]Phil 2:8. [52]Heb 10:13; Eph 1:22; Heb 2:8. [53]ECF 292-93. [54]Phil 2:9. [55]Heb 6:20. [56]ECF 383-84. [57]The context of the remarks is a discussion of Elijah's ascent into heaven on the fiery chariot. [58]Hypostasis.

divine and imperishable nature.[59] AGAINST
APOLLINARIS 25.[60]

THE SERVANT EMBRACED BY THE MASTER.
GREGORY OF NYSSA: The flesh is passable in
nature; the Word is active. The flesh is not
capable of creating the universe; the Godhead's
power is not capable of suffering. . . . It is not
the human nature that raises Lazarus; it is not
the impassible power that weeps for him. . . . It
is clear that the blows of the passion belong to
the servant in whom the Master was, but the
honors belong to the Master who was enveloped
by the servant; so that because of the conjunction and connection the attributes of each
nature become common to both, and the Master
takes on himself the servant's stripes while
the servant is glorified by the Master's honor.
Hence the cross is said to be the cross of "the
Lord of glory,"[61] and "Every tongue confesses
that Jesus Christ is Lord."[62] AGAINST EUNO-
MIUS 5.5.[63]

THE FORM OF GOD AND THE FORM OF A
SERVANT. THEODORE OF MOPSUESTIA: He is
not merely God, nor is he merely man, but in
truth he is both by nature, God and man. He is
God the Word, the one who assumed; and he is
the man who was assumed.[64] He who is "in the
form of God" assumed "the form of a servant,"
and the form of a servant is not the form of
God. In the form of God, he is one who is God
by nature and one who assumed the form of a
servant, while the form of a servant is one who
is man by nature and who was assumed for our
salvation. He who assumed is not the same as
he who was assumed. The one who assumed is
God, while the one who was assumed is man.
The one who assumed is by nature the same as
God the Father, for he is God with God. . . .
But he who was assumed is by nature the same
as David and Abraham, whose son he is and
from whom he is descended. Hence he is both
the Lord of David and his son. ON THE NICENE
CREED 8.1.[65]

How the Son Took the Form of a Servant

A SERVANT SHOWED US GREATNESS. ORI-
GEN: Let us employ an illustration so that we
may more fully understand in what way the
Savior is the representation of the being of God.
The illustration does not fully or adequately
express the meaning of the phrase[66] we are
discussing; but it may be regarded as adopted
to make just this point: that the Son, "though
being in the form of God abased himself" because he intended, through the self-abasement,
to display to us the fullness of Godhead. Let
us suppose a statue of such a size as would fill
the whole world, of such immensity that no
one could contemplate it. Let us then suppose
that another statue was made, identical with
the first in respect of the shape of the limbs,
the features, the whole outward appearance and
the material, like it in all respects apart from
the immense size. This would be made for this
purpose: that those who could not contemplate
and behold the enormous statue might look at
the small copy and claim that they had seen the
original, insofar as the copy, being a complete
likeness, preserved all the lines of the limbs
and the features, in fact the whole appearance
and the actual material of the other. ON FIRST
PRINCIPLES 1.2.8.[67]

SERVANTHOOD SIGNIFIES SALVATION. GREG-
ORY OF NAZIANZUS: But in respect of his "form
of a servant," he comes down to join his fellow
servants and assumes a form that is not his

---

[59]That is, in the incarnation, the divine power (the Word) stooped
down to earth, set aflame the human nature for its deification (salvation) and then resumed its state of glory at the right hand of the
Father. [60]LCF 136**. [61]1 Cor 2:8; Jas 2:1. [62]Phil 2:11. [63]LCF
138. [64]It is clear enough that the Syrian theologian Theodore
uses the concept of the "man who was assumed" to signify what
the other Greek writers habitually meant by the "human nature,"
but in the next generation this whole language of "assumed man"
came into major crisis, and after the Council of Ephesus in 431 it
became ever afterwards associated with the heresy of Nestorius
(an implication of multiple personality in Jesus) and was largely
dropped thereafter. [65]LCF 167. [66]"The form of God" (Phil
2:5-11). [67]ECF 295-96*.

own, taking on himself me and what belongs to me, so that in himself he may consume the evil, just as fire consumes wax or the sun consumes the mists of earth, and that I may share in what belongs to him, by reason of this commixture.[68] Therefore he does honor to obedience in action and has experience of obedience as a result of his suffering. For the disposition of obedience was not enough, any more than it is for us, unless we proceed to put it into practice; for disposition is demonstrated by action. . . . Thus Christ can know our experience at firsthand and take our infirmity into account, along with what we have to endure. . . . For if because of the concealing screen[69] the light that shone in this life's darkness was persecuted by the darkness (the darkness, I mean, of the evil one the tempter), then what persecution will befall the darkness of people in their weakness? ORATION 30.6.[70]

IN CHRIST, THE FORM OF A SERVANT IS SINLESS. LEO THE GREAT: Thus there was born true God in the entire and perfect nature of true man, complete in his own properties, complete in ours. By "ours" I mean those that the Creator formed in us at the beginning, which he assumed in order to restore. For in the Savior there was no trace of the properties that the deceiver brought in and that humankind, being deceived, allowed to enter. He did not become partaker of our sins because he entered into fellowship with human infirmities. He assumed the "form of a servant" without the stain of sin, making the human properties greater but not detracting from the divine. For that emptying of himself, whereby the invisible rendered himself visible, and the Creator and Lord of all willed to be a mortal, was a condescension of compassion, not a failure of power. Accordingly, he who made humankind, while he remained in the form of God, was himself made man in the form of a servant. Each nature preserves its own characteristics without diminution, so that the form of a servant does not detract from

the form of God. LETTER 28.3 (THE TOME OF LEO).[71]

OUR TRUE MASTER IS A SERVANT IN TYPE ONLY. HADRIAN I: For although in prophetic type he was called a servant because of the condition of the servant's form that he received from the Virgin, as the Scripture says: "Have you considered my servant Job, that there is no one like him on the earth?"[72] And even so, with Saint Gregory[73] we understand that this is meant historically as applied to the holy Job but allegorically as applied to Christ. The fact that Scripture described Christ, typically,[74] as a servant in the person of Job is surely no reason why we should give him the name of servant, is it? LETTER TO THE BISHOPS OF SPAIN AND GALICIA.[75]

The Humility of the Son

CHRIST STANDS WITH THE HUMBLE. CLEMENT OF ROME: For Christ is with those who are humble, not with those who exalt themselves over his flock. The majestic scepter of God, our Lord Christ Jesus, did not come with the pomp of arrogance or pride (though he could have done so) but in all humility, just as the Holy Spirit spoke concerning him. For he says, "Lord, who believed our report? And to whom was the arm of the Lord revealed? In his presence we announced that he was like a child, like a root in thirsty ground. He had no attractiveness or glory. We saw him, and he had no attractiveness or beauty; instead his attractiveness was despised, inferior to that of other men. He was a man of stripes and of sorrow, knowing

---

[68]Of deity and humanity. [69]The veil of the flesh that masked the divinity in Jesus from the eyes of the evil one. [70]*LCF* 104-5. [71]*LCF* 279. [72]See Job 1:8. [73]Gregory the Great *Moralia on Job*. [74]That is, in the type, or sacred symbol, of a scriptural passage. [75]*TCT* 189*. Pope Hadrian (772-795) was writing a strong letter to the episcopal synod of Spain, which had complained to him that it needed help in refuting the Adoptionist movement in their territory—the doctrine that Christ was a simple human being lifted up into relationship with the divinity by grace.

how to endure weakness, and his face is turned away; he was dishonored and not blessed." This is the one "who bears our sins and suffers pain for our sakes, and we regarded him as subject to grief and stripes and affliction." And yet he was "wounded because of our sins and was afflicted because of our transgressions."[76] 1 Clement 16.1-5.[77]

Christ Is a Model of Humility. Clement of Rome: And again he himself says, "But I am a worm and not a man, a reproach among men and an object of contempt to the people."[78] "All those who saw me mocked me, they spoke with their lips; they shook their heads, saying, He hoped in the Lord, let him deliver him, let him save him, because he takes pleasure in him."[79] You see, dear friends, the kind of pattern that has been given to us. For if the Lord so humbled himself, what should we do, who through him have come under the yoke of his grace? 1 Clement 16.15-17.[80]

The Suffering Servant. Epistle of Barnabas: Surely, then, the Son of God came in the flesh to fill to the brim the measure of the sins of those who had persecuted his prophets to death. This, therefore, is the reason why he submitted to suffering, for God speaks of the chastisement of his flesh as something due to them: "When they have smitten the shepherd, then the sheep of his flock will perish."[81] But this suffering was due to his choice. It was ordained that he should suffer on a tree, since the inspired writer attributes to him the following words: "Save me from the sword," and, "Pierce my flesh with nails, because bands of evildoers have risen against me."[82] And again he says, "Behold, I present my back for scourgings and my cheek for blows; my face I set as a solid rock."[83] Epistle of Barnabas 5.11-14.[84]

Christ's Kenosis, for a Mysterious Purpose. Hilary of Poitiers: To take the form of a servant and to remain in the form

of God are not the same thing, and he who remained in the form of God could not have taken the form of a servant except by his self-emptying, since the combination of both forms is inconsistent. But he who emptied himself is the same as he who took the form of a servant. If he ceased to exist, he could not have taken, since to take entails the existence of the taker. Thus the self-emptying of the form is not the abolition of the nature, since he who emptied himself did not cease to exist, and he who took continued to be. The identity of emptier and taker involves a mystery,[85] but not a ceasing to be.[86] . . . Christ was one and the same when he changed his outward fashion and again when he reassumed it. On the Trinity 9.14.[87]

Christ's Humility Is Godlike in Its Depth. Gregory of Nazianzus: He who gives riches becomes poor, for he assumes the poverty of my flesh, that I may assume the richness of his Godhead. He that is full empties himself, for he empties himself of his glory for a short while, that I may have a share in his fullness. What is the riches of his goodness? What is this mystery that is around me? I had a share in the image; I did not keep it. He partakes of my flesh that he may both save the image and make the flesh immortal. He communicates a second communion far more marvelous than the first, inasmuch as then he imparted the better nature, whereas now he himself partakes of the worse. This is more godlike than the former action, this is loftier in the eyes of all men of understanding. Oration 38.13.[88]

The Son's Obedience to Death

The Son Entrusts His Life to His Father. Tertullian: You find him crying out in his suffering, "My God, my God, why have you

[76]Is 53:1-5 (LXX). [77]*AF* 45-47*. [78]Ps 22:6 (Ps 21 [LXX]). [79]Ps 22:7-8; Lk 23:35. [80]*AF* 47-49. [81]Mt 26:31. [82]See Ps 22:6-8 (Ps 21:7-9 [LXX]). [83]Is 50:6. [84]ACW 6:43-44. [85]*Sacramentum.* [86]*Interitus.* [87]*LCF* 50-51. [88]NPNF 2 7:349*.

forsaken me?"[89] Then, either the Son was suffering, forsaken by the Father, and the Father did not suffer; or, if it was the Father who was suffering, to what God was he crying?[90] But this was the cry of flesh and soul (that is, of the man), not of the Word and the Spirit (that is, not of God); and it was uttered for the very purpose of showing the impassibility of God who thus forsook his Son in delivering his humanity to death. This was the apostle's meaning when he wrote, "If the Father did not spare his Son";[91] and before him Isaiah declared, "The Lord has delivered him up for our sins."[92] He forsook him in not sparing him; he forsook him in delivering him up. Yet the Father did not forsake the Son, of course, for the Son entrusted his spirit into the Father's hands. In fact, he thus entrusted it, and straightway died, for while the spirit remains in the flesh it is utterly impossible for the flesh to die. Thus to be forsaken by the Father was death to the Son. The Son therefore both dies at the Father's hand and is raised up by the Father according to the Scriptures. AGAINST PRAXEAS 30.[93]

HE SUFFERS AND YET RISES ABOVE SUFFERING. ATHANASIUS: And it was this body that, after it had risen from the dead, Thomas handled[94] and saw in it the marks of the nails that the Word himself endured when he saw them fixed into his own body and did not prevent them even though he could have done so,

but he appropriated to himself what belonged to the body as belonging to himself, the incorporeal Word. So, when the body was struck by the guard, he said, "Why did you strike me?"[95] as himself the one who suffered; and even though the Word was by nature intangible, still he said, "I gave my back to the scourges and my cheeks to the blows, and I did not turn my face away from shameful spitting."[96] For the Word was present with the human body, and what it suffered he referred to himself so that we might be made able to partake of the Godhead of the Word. It was a marvel that he was the one suffering, yet not suffering: suffering insofar as the body that was his very own suffered, yet not suffering insofar as the Word, being God by nature, is impassible. The incorporeal One himself was present in the passable body, and the body had in itself the impassible Word, who all the time was abolishing the infirmities of the body itself. This he was doing, and this is how it came about, so that he might take what was ours and offer it up in sacrifice so as to abolish it and in return clothe us with what was his. This is why the apostle said, "This corruptibility must put on incorruption." LETTER TO EPICTETUS 6.[97]

---

[89]Mt 27:46; see also Ps 22:1. [90]Tertullian was addressing a group who postulated that Father and Son were the same entity under different revelatory guises. [91]Rom 8:32. [92]Is 53:5; 1 Jn 4:10. [93]ECF 171-72. [94]Jn 20:26-27. [95]Jn 18:23. [96]Is 50:6. [97]CACC 384.

FROM HEAVEN

καὶ εἰς ἕνα κύριον Ἰησοῦν Χριστόν,	Et in unum Dominum Jesum Christum,	We believe in one Lord, Jesus Christ,
τὸν υἱὸν τοῦ Θεοῦ τὸν μονογενῆ,	Filium Dei unigenitum,	the only Son of God,
τὸν ἐκ τοῦ πατρὸς γεννηθέντα	et ex Patre natum	eternally
πρὸ πάντων τῶν αἰώνων,	ante omnia saecula	begotten of the Father,
φῶς ἐκ φωτός,	[Deum de Deo], Lumen de Lumine,	[God from God], Light from Light,
Θεὸν ἀληθινὸν ἐκ θεοῦ ἀληθινοῦ,	Deum verum de Deo vero,	true God from true God,
γεννηθέντα, οὐ ποιηθέντα,	genitum, non factum,	begotten, not made,
ὁμοούσιον τῷ πατρί·	consubstantialem Patri;	of one Being with the Father.
δι' οὗ τὰ πάντα εγένετο·	per quem omnia facta sunt;	Through him all things were made.
τὸν δι' ἡμᾶς τοὺς ἀνθρώπους	qui propter nos homines	For us
καὶ διὰ τὴν ἡμετέραν σωτηρίαν	et propter nostram salutem	and for our salvation
κατελθόντα **ἐκ τῶν οὐρανῶν**	descendit **de coelis,**	he came down **from heaven:**
καὶ σαρκωθέντα ἐκ πνεύματος ἁγίου	et incarnatus est de Spiritu Sancto	by the power of the Holy Spirit
καὶ Μαρίας τῆς παρθένου	ex Maria virgine,	he became incarnate from the Virgin Mary,
καὶ ἐνανθρωπήσαντα,	et homo factus est;	and was made man.

HISTORICAL CONTEXT: The gospel lies behind the ensuing clause of the creed when it says: "No one has gone up to heaven except the one who came down from heaven; the Son of man who is in heaven."[1] Christian reflection tended to begin from this point and move downwards. The heavenly Son of man descends to the earth and is manifested as the suffering Son of man on this earth. It is remarkable from the earliest known iterations of the creed how the same subject reference is used throughout all the christological statements. The heavenly Son is described as one and the same subject as the earthly savior; no distinction between the two states is made in relation to the one person. In the earliest centuries of the church, that personal unity was often taken for granted. The context of argument supplied by the Gnostics had made it imperative for the catholic pre-Nicene theologians to insist that the Son of God was a mediator and savior from the very throne of God. It was no alien God that had made the material world or who had appeared within it as a savior, but, on the contrary, it was the Logos-maker who came down to that very creation he had once fashioned.

As the fourth century dawned, however, confusion began to rise about the subjectival relation of the heavenly Son of God to Jesus of Nazareth. It had partly been caused by some speculations of Origen, roughly sketched out as they were in those early years of the third century, that tended to speak of the Logos-Sophia uniting with the preexistent Soul Jesus, one of the original spiritual creation that so united itself in love to the divine Word that it offered itself as the soul-medium of the immaterial Logos's personal presence on earth. Origen's theory of the intermediating Soul Jesus was meant by him as a mode of the personal unity of the incarnate Lord. However, if pressed by hard logic, the theory could suggest to critics that the Logos and Jesus were two

[1]Jn 3:13 (Jerusalem Bible).

distinct persons. By the fourth century, Arian theorists were already arguing a distinction between the heavenly and earthly Sons of God, and taking the issue further to suggest that the Logos itself was not "divine of the divine" but a "creature from the Uncreated." The Nicene fathers, therefore, used this creedal clause to reaffirm the full weight of the ancient rule of faith's intentionality in using a single subject in all the christological clauses: that the heavenly Son of God was none other than Jesus of Nazareth and that all the deeds and acts of the earthly savior were deeds and acts of the Word. Throughout the fourth century, and indeed for long after, the ramifications of that central statement had to be elaborated and explained with greater precision and sensitivity; nevertheless, the confession that the heavenly Son and the earthly Messiah were one and the same person was the major contribution of the Nicene Creed, and to it the fifth-century theologians, such as Cyril of Alexandria, keep returning, to insist that no christological nuance should ever lose sight of that belief.

OVERVIEW: The lowliness of the heavenly Lord is a model for all his church (APOSTOLIC CONSTITUTIONS). When the Lord came down from heaven and appeared on earth in all his humility, it vastly confused the proud spirit of Satan and caused his downfall (EPHREM). The heavenly Lord put on a vesture of humility and taught humility as his key doctrine (ISAAC). The descent to earth shows how the human powers are absorbed into the deity and have divine power as their context (IRENAEUS). The Word directly and powerfully energizes all that Jesus does (CLEMENT OF ALEXANDRIA). The Word of God and no other clothed himself in a human life (ISAAC). In the person and deeds of the incarnate Lord a profound unity of the divine and human is witnessed at every turn (ORIGEN, ATHANASIUS, GREGORY OF NYSSA). His humanity and his humble condition veiled the divine glory that was his (TERTULLIAN), but

the Lord took to himself, and made his own, all that was part of our condition (PSEUDO-DIONYSIUS). For our sake the great God entered into a life within time (ORIGEN). His descent from heaven was motivated by his desire to save humankind (IRENAEUS, CLEMENT OF ALEXANDRIA). This coming down from heaven was in fact a lifting of the earth back to its heavenly destiny (CLEMENT OF ALEXANDRIA).

The Lowliness of the Son of God

IMITATE THE HUMILITY OF THE LORD. APOSTOLIC CONSTITUTIONS: We, therefore, who have a Master, our Lord Jesus Christ, why do we not follow his doctrine since he renounced repose, pleasure, glory, riches, pride, the power of revenge, his mother and brethren, and moreover his own life, on account of his piety toward his Father and his love to us the race of mankind; and he suffered not only persecution and stripes, reproach and mockery but also crucifixion that he might save the penitent, both Jews and Gentiles. If, therefore, he for our sakes renounced his repose, was not ashamed of the cross and did not esteem death inglorious, why do not we imitate his sufferings and renounce on his account even our own life, with that patience that he gives us? CONSTITUTIONS OF THE HOLY APOSTLES 5.5.[2]

JESUS' HUMILITY CONFUSED SATAN. EPHREM THE SYRIAN: In the wilderness Satan tempted you, and now his feasts and festivals in the wilderness have disappeared. On the mountain he tempted you, Lord, with worship, and mountains are no longer the places of his worship. Since he set you on the top of the temple, you have overthrown the top of his temples. The hunter was fooled; in the trap set for you he was caught unawares. By the stone with which he tempted you were broken the stones that he carved for emptiness. Since he dared to say to you, "Throw yourself down," he fell down and

---

[2]ANCL 17:119 (part 2).

perished because of you. The one falling down cast down the one who had come to cast down the One from above. Satan led the Lord up on high unaware that the lowly One who thus went up would cast him down from the height. Hymns on Virginity 13.10-11.[3]

Humility Is the Raiment of the Word.
Isaac of Nineveh: Wishing to open my mouth, O brethren, and speak on the exalted theme of humility, I am filled with fear, even as a man who understands that he is about to discourse concerning God with the art of his own words. For humility is the raiment of the Godhead. The Word who became man clothed himself in it, and therewith he spoke to us in our body. Every person who has been clothed with it has truly been made like to him who came down from his own exaltedness, and hid the splendor of his majesty and concealed his glory with humility, lest creation should be utterly consumed by the contemplation of him. Creation could not look on him unless he took a part of it to himself and thus conversed with it, and neither could it hear the words of his mouth face to face. The people of Israel were not even able to hear his voice when he spoke with them from the cloud. How, then, should creation be able to bear the vision of him openly? The Israelites were so afflicted that they said to Moses, "Let God speak with you, and you shall hear his words for us; but do not let God speak with us, in case we die."[4] So terrible is the sight of God that even the mediator [Moses] said, "I fear exceedingly and tremble."[5] The splendor of his glory appeared on Mount Sinai, and the mountain smoked and trembled in fear of the revelation that was in it, so that even the beasts that approached the lower parts of it died. Ascetical Homilies 77.[6]

God Saved the World Through Humility. Isaac of Nineveh: If zeal had been appropriate for putting humanity right, why did God the Word clothe himself in the body, using gentleness and humility in order to bring the world back to his Father? And why was he stretched out on the cross for the sake of sinners, handing over his sacred body to suffering on behalf of the world? I myself say that God did all this for no other reason than to make known to the world the love that he has; his aim being that we, as a result of our greater love arising from an awareness of this, might be captivated by his love when he provided the occasion of this manifestation of the kingdom of heaven's mighty power, which consists in love, by means of the death of his Son. Gnostic Chapters 4.78.[7]

The Lord's Humility Saves Us. Isaac of Nineveh: O Christ who is "covered with light as though with garment,"[8] who for my sake stood naked in front of Pilate, clothe me with that might that you caused to overshadow the saints, whereby they conquered this world of struggle. May your divinity, Lord, take pleasure in me and lead me above the world to be with you. O Christ, on you the many-eyed cherubim are unable to look because of the glory of your countenance, yet out of your love you accepted spittle on your face. Remove the shame from my face, and grant me to have an unashamed face before you at the time of prayer. The Second Part 2.5.22-23.[9]

The Obscuring of the Divine in the Flesh

The Word's Humanity Was Absorbed in Glory. Irenaeus: As he was man that he might be tempted, so he was the Word that he might be glorified. The Word was quiescent, that he might be capable of temptation, dishonor, crucifixion and death; while the manhood was swallowed up in the Godhead in his victory, his endurance . . . his resurrection and ascension. Against Heresies 3.19.3.[10]

---

[3]ESH 319. [4]Ex 20:19. [5]Heb 12:21. [6]*AHSIS* 381*. [7]CS 175:52. [8]Ps 104:2. [9]CS 175:59. [10]ECF 106.

THE LORD'S LABORS WERE ENERGIZED BY THE WORD. CLEMENT OF ALEXANDRIA: With unsurpassable speed and unexampled good will the divine power, having shone on the world, has filled everything with the saving seed. Such a work in so short a time the Lord would not have achieved without the divine power assisting. He was despised for his appearance but is worshiped for his work. He is the purifying, saving, delectable Word, the divine Word, who is truly God most manifest, made equal to the Ruler of all; because he was the Son, and "the Word was with God."[11] EXHORTATION TO THE GREEKS 10 (110).[12]

THE LORD WAS GOD HIDDEN IN THE FLESH. TERTULLIAN: Was not God really crucified? Did he not really die after real crucifixion? Did he not really rise again, after real death? If not, then Paul's determination was mistaken, "to know nothing among you save Jesus crucified";[13] mistaken too his insistence on his burial, his emphasis on his resurrection. Then our faith also is mistaken, and our hope in Christ a mere illusion. . . . Spare us the one and only hope of the whole globe, for you are destroying the indispensable glory of the faith. All that is unworthy of God is for my benefit. I am saved if I am not ashamed of my Lord. For he says, "If anyone is ashamed of me, I shall be ashamed of him."[14] Nowhere else do I find grounds for shame that may prove me, through "despising the shame,"[15] to be nobly shameless and happily foolish. The Son of God was born: shameful, therefore there is no shame. The Son of God died: absurd, and therefore utterly credible. He was buried and rose again: impossible, and therefore a fact. . . . Thus the quality of the two modes of being displayed the humanity and the divinity: born as man, unborn as God; in one respect carnal, in the other spiritual; in one respect weak, in the other exceedingly strong; in one respect dying, in the other living. The proper qualities of the two conditions, the divine and the human, are attested by the equal reality of both natures:

with the same faith the Spirit and the flesh are distinguished; the works of power attest the Spirit of God; the sufferings attest the flesh of man. . . . If the flesh with its sufferings was a figment, then the Spirit with its mighty works was unreal. Why do you cut Christ in half with a lie? He was wholly truth. Believe me, he preferred to be born than to be in part a lie. ON THE FLESH OF CHRIST 5.[16]

THE WORD TOOK TO ITSELF ALL THAT WAS HUMAN. PSEUDO-DIONYSIUS: Again, it is by a differentiated act of God's benevolence that the superessential[17] Word should wholly and completely take human substance of human flesh and do and suffer all those things that, in a special and particular manner, belong to the action of his divine humanity.[18] In these acts the Father and the Spirit have no share, except of course that they all share in the loving generosity of the divine counsels and in all that transcendent divine working of unutterable mysteries that were performed in human nature by him who as God and as the Word of God is immutable. So do we strive to differentiate the divine attributes, according as these attributes are undifferentiated or differentiated.[19] THE DIVINE NAMES 2.6.[20]

THE DEITY CLOTHES ITSELF IN A HUMAN BEING. ISAAC OF NINEVEH: O wonder! The Creator clothed in a human being enters the house of tax collectors and prostitutes, and when they turn toward him, through his own action, he was urging them, providing them, by means of his teaching, with assurance and

---

[11]Jn 1:1. [12]ECF 237. [13]1 Cor 2:2. [14]Mt 10:33. [15]Heb 12:2. [16]ECF 172-73. [17]In Dionysius, a common term signifying that the divine being is above all materiality, form and conception and thus is beyond all language's subtlety in being able to describe it. [18]To describe the closeness of divine-human interpenetration in the activity of the one Christ, Dionysius prefers the adjective *Theandric* (God-manly). [19]By which he means the theological distinction of which works of God are common to all the divine persons of the Trinity and which are particular to one of the persons. [20]ODN 73.

reconciliation with him. And he sealed the word of truth with true testimonies, consisting in miracles and signs. Thus the entire universe, through the beauty of the sight of him, was drawn by his love to the single confession of God, the Lord of all, and so the knowledge of the one Creator was sown everywhere. THE SECOND PART 2.11.28.[21]

The Living Word

GOD WAS ALWAYS WITH HIS WORD. THEOPHILUS OF ANTIOCH: God had his immanent Word within his own bowels[22] and begot it along with his wisdom, uttering it before all things.[23] God used this Word to assist in what God made, and through it God made all things.[24] This Word is called beginning, because it begins and rules over all things made through it. This Word, therefore, was Spirit of God,[25] the Beginning,[26] the Wisdom and Power of the most High,[27] and it came down into the prophets and spoke through them about the creation of the world and about everything else. For the prophets did not exist when the world came into being; what did exist were God's wisdom, which is in God, and God's holy Word, which is always with God.[28] God's Word, through whom God made all things,[29] is God's power and wisdom.[30] This Word, then, assumed the character of the Father and Lord of all, was present in the garden[31] in God's character and conversed with Adam. For divine Scripture itself teaches us that Adam said he heard the voice.[32] And what else is the voice but the Word of God, which is also God's Son? This is to be understood, not as the poets and writers of myth, who speak of the sons of gods born through sexual intercourse, but rather as truth describes the Word, which is immanent power in God's heart. For before anything came into being, God had this as a counselor,[33] since it was God's mind and intelligence. Whenever God wished to make what God had decided to make, God begot the Word and brought it forth

into being, firstborn of all creation;[34] God did not get rid of the Word but rather begot God's Word and converses with it forever. We are taught, therefore, by holy Scripture and by inspired people, as one of them, John, says, "In the beginning was the Word, and the Word was with God;"[35] he shows that at the start God was alone and the Word was in God. Then he says, "And the Word was God; all things were made through it, and without it was made nothing." Since the Word, therefore, is God and born from God, whenever the Father of all wills to do so, he sends the Word to some place, and the Word is present and is heard and seen there, for it is sent by God and is situated in a place. To AUTOLYCUS 1-2.[36]

The Eternal God Entering Time

THE ETERNAL EMBRACES THE TIME-BOUND. ORIGEN: Though the God of the whole universe descends in his own power with Jesus to live the life of people, and the Word that "was in the beginning with God and was himself God"[37] comes to us; yet he does not leave his home or desert his state. The result is not that one place is emptied of him while another is full, which did not before contain him. The power and divinity of God takes his dwelling as he wills, and where he finds a place for himself: God does not change his place. . . . When we speak of his leaving one and filling another, we shall not be speaking of locality but asserting that the soul of the worthless and utterly degenerate is deserted by God, while the soul of one who wishes to live according to virtue, either advancing toward this or already living a virtuous life, is filled with the divine spirit or partakes of it. Therefore in respect of Christ's descent, or the sojourn of God

---

[21]CS 175:55-56. [22]A common ancient rhetorical figure for "in the heart" or immanently. [23]Alluding to Ps 45:2 (Ps 44:2 [LXX]). [24]Jn 1:3. [25]Or, divine spirit. [26]Col 1:18. [27]1 Cor 1:24. [28]Prov 8:27; Jn 1:1-2. [29]Jn 1:3. [30]1 Cor.1:24. [31]Garden of Eden. [32]Gen 3:10. [33]Wis 8:9. [34]Col 1:15. [35]Jn 1:1. [36]MFC 2:54-55. [37]Jn 1:1.

with people, there is no need of his leaving his greater state. AGAINST CELSUS 4.5.[38]

JESUS IS ONE WITH THE WORD. ORIGEN: If you are able to conceive of the Word as having been restored, after he had become flesh and all that he became for the benefit of mortal people, becoming, that is, for them what each of them needed to become; having been thus restored, I say, that he might become what he was "in the beginning with God," existing as God the Word in his own glory. Then you will see him sitting on the throne of his glory, the very same Son of man who was known as the man Jesus; for he is one with the Word in a far different sense from that in which "those who cling to the Lord are of one spirit with him."[39] COMMENTARY ON THE GOSPEL OF MATTHEW 15.24.[40]

EVERYTHING IN JESUS' LIFE IS OF THE WORD. ATHANASIUS: The Scripture speaks of the exaltation of the Word "from the lower parts of the earth,"[41] since the death is also ascribed to him. Both events are spoken of as his, since it was his body, and not another's, that was exalted from the dead and taken up into heaven. Again, since the body was his body, and since the Word was not external to it, it is natural that on the exaltation of his body he, as man, should be said to be exalted, on account of the body. If then he did not become man, let this not be said of him. But if "the Word was made flesh,"[42] then resurrection and exaltation must be ascribed to him, in respect of his manhood, that the death ascribed to him may be a redemption for the sins of humans and an annihilation of death and that the resurrection and exaltation may because of him be kept secure for us. He who is the Son of God himself became the Son of man. As Word, he gives from the Father; for all that the Father does and gives he too does and supplies through him. As the Son of man he himself is said, humanly, to receive what proceeds from himself. For he received it according to the exaltation of human nature. This exaltation was its deification, an

exaltation that the Word himself always had in respect of the Godhead and perfection that was his own as inherited from his Father. AGAINST THE ARIANS 1.45.[43]

JESUS IS THE SAVING WORD. GREGORY OF NYSSA: The Christian faith, which in accordance with the command of our Lord has been preached to all nations by his disciples, is neither of people or by people but by our Lord Jesus Christ himself, who being the Word, the Life, the Light, the Truth, and God, and Wisdom, and all else that he is by nature, for this cause above all was made in the likeness of humanity and shared our nature, becoming like us in all things, yet without sin. He was like us in all things, in that he took on him manhood in its entirety with soul and body, so that our salvation was accomplished by means of both. AGAINST EUNOMIUS 2.1.[44]

God's Descent from Heaven to Fallen Humanity

THE WORD DESCENDS TO SAVE HUMANKIND. IRENAEUS: The name of God or Lord is given only to him who is God and Lord of all, who said to Moses, "My name is I am. And you shall say to the Israelites, 'he who is' has sent me to you."[45] The name of God and Lord is given also to his Son, Jesus Christ our Lord, who makes humans into the children of God if they believe in his name. And the Son says to Moses, "I have come down to rescue this people."[46] For it is the Son who descended and ascended for the salvation of people. Thus, through the Son who is in the Father and has the Father in himself, "he who is" has been revealed. The Father bears witness to the Son; the Son proclaims the Father. So Isaiah says,[47] "I am witness, says the Lord God, and so is

---

[38]ECF 293-94. [39]1 Cor 6:17. [40]ECF 297*. [41]Eph 4:9; see also Ps 63:9. [42]Jn 1:14. [43]ECF 384-85. [44]NPNF 2 5:101. Some modern scholars refer to this treatise as the "Refutation of Eunomius's Apology." [45]Ex 3:14. [46]Ex 3:8. [47]Is 43:10.

the child[48] whom I have chosen, that you may know and believe and understand that I am." AGAINST HERESIES 3.6.2.[49]

THE LORD RAISES HUMANITY ON HIGH.
CLEMENT OF ALEXANDRIA: Man [humanity] was free, in his innocence, and then found himself bound by his sins. The Lord, on his part, wished to free him from his fetters, and, himself being bound in the flesh (and here is a divine mystery!) grappled with the serpent and enslaved the tyrant, death; and, wonder of wonders, though man was straying through pleasure and though he was held captive by corruption, the Lord displayed him set at liberty by his outstretched arms. O wondrous mystery! The Lord was laid to rest, and man was raised up. Man was cast out of paradise; and now he receives a reward greater than that of obedience, the reward of heaven. EXHORTATION TO THE GREEKS 11 (111).[50]

THE WORD COMES DOWN TO US FROM LOVE.
CLEMENT OF ALEXANDRIA: God is himself love, and because of his love he pursued us. In the case of the eternal generation of the Son, the ineffable nature of God is manifested as that of a Father, and yet his sympathy for us all is like that of a mother. It was from love that the Father pursued us, and the great proof of this is the very Son whom he begot from himself and that love which was the fruit produced from his love. This love was the reason he came down and assumed human nature. This was why he willingly endured the sufferings of humanity, that by being reduced to the level of our weakness he might raise us to the level of his power. And just before he poured out his offering, when he gave himself as a ransom, he left us a new testament, saying, "I give you my love."[51] What is the nature and extent of this love? He laid down his life for each one of us, that life which was worth the entire universe. What he requires in return is that we should do the same for each other. WHO IS THE RICH MAN THAT IS SAVED? 37.[52]

---

[48]Or, Servant. [49]*ECF* 104. [50]*ECF* 242. [51]Combination of Jn 13:1, 34; 14:27; 17:26. [52]*ECF* 240**

BY THE POWER OF THE HOLY SPIRIT

καὶ εἰς ἕνα κύριον Ἰησοῦν Χριστὸν,	Et in unum Dominum Jesum Christum,	We believe in one Lord, Jesus Christ,
τὸν υἱὸν τοῦ Θεοῦ τὸν μονογενῆ,	Filium Dei unigenitum,	the only Son of God,
τὸν ἐκ τοῦ πατρὸς γεννηθέντα	et ex Patre natum	eternally
πρὸ πάντων τῶν αἰώνων,	ante omnia saecula	begotten of the Father,
φῶς ἐκ φωτός,	[Deum de Deo], Lumen de Lumine,	[God from God], Light from Light,
Θεὸν ἀληθινὸν ἐκ θεοῦ ἀληθινοῦ,	Deum verum de Deo vero,	true God from true God,
γεννηθέντα, οὐ ποιηθέντα,	genitum, non factum,	begotten, not made,
ὁμοούσιον τῷ πατρὶ·	consubstantialem Patri;	of one Being with the Father.
δι᾽ οὗ τὰ πάντα ἐγένετο·	per quem omnia facta sunt;	Through him all things were made.
τὸν δι᾽ ἡμᾶς τοὺς ἀνθρώπους	qui propter nos homines	For us
καὶ διὰ τὴν ἡμετέραν σωτηρίαν	et propter nostram salutem	and for our salvation
κατελθόντα ἐκ τῶν οὐρανῶν	descendit de coelis,	he came down from heaven:
καὶ σαρκωθέντα **ἐκ πνεύματος ἁγίου**	et incarnatus est **de Spiritu Sancto**	**by the power of the Holy Spirit**
καὶ Μαρίας τῆς παρθένου	ex Maria virgine,	he became incarnate from the Virgin Mary,
καὶ ἐνανθρωπήσαντα,	et homo factus est;	and was made man.

HISTORICAL CONTEXT: Just as "flesh" signified the sin and fragility of humanity in the biblical literature, so did "Spirit" signify the power and energy of God. The attribution of a distinct hypostatic identity of the Holy Spirit, as not simply a cipher for divine power and presence but a specific and focused person of the Trinity, was a theology that was clarified only after the great christological crisis. In fact, it can be said that in the history of Christian thought, the personal subsistence of the Holy Spirit as a distinct member of the Trinity is something that grows out of the reflection on the significance of the divine person of Jesus. It might be truer to say that the two trajectories grow up alongside one another.

The greatest theologians who formulated the Early Church's doctrine of the deity of Jesus were always the very ones who were also its chief interpreters of the glory of the Holy Spirit. Nowhere is this more evident than in Athanasius, Basil of Caesarea, Gregory of Nazianzus, Cyril of Alexandria, Maximus the Confessor and John of Damascus. These were the greatest protagonists of patristic Pneumatology and were, as well, the leading pillars of Nicene Christology.

The creed here refers the dynamic of the act of incarnation to the agency of the Holy Spirit and the Virgin Mary. The Spirit thus initiates the flesh in a way that flies in the face of all Gnostic suppositions that tended to suggest that the Spirit was hostile to or opposite to the flesh. Behind the creedal phrase lies the Lukan text of what the angel Gabriel explained to the Virgin about her overshadowing by the divine power, an image that recalled the great drama of Genesis 1:2 and thereby suggested the incarnation was the Spirit's renewing of the creation, where it is said, "And thus the child shall be holy."[1] In almost all patristic literature, the Holy Spirit is associated with the divine energy of sanctification. In the course of the Monarchian disputes of the second

---

[1] Lk 1:35.

and third centuries (Paul of Samosata was an example) and then again in the fourth-century Arian crisis, some theologians had approached Jesus' godly power and his status as a godly witness in terms of his election by the divine Spirit. If the Lord was holy, for this school, it was seen to be a result of his special inspiration by the Spirit. The Nicene patristic witness is clear and cogent in response to this. The Lord is himself the giver of the Spirit and so cannot be understood as simply one more of the line of ancient prophets. The Holy Spirit indeed anointed him with grace, but that is to be understood as the anointing of his humble humanity, in which he was a model vessel of the Spirit, though all that the Lord did was in the unity of the Trinity. Jesus' possession of the divine Spirit is the quintessential sign that he is the Father's own Word, in the unity of the Trinity where all possess one another in love and energy. The incarnate Lord's gift of the Spirit to the world, through the power *(dynamis)* of the incarnation, is described by Cyril of Alexandria as no less than the regeneration of the human race.

OVERVIEW: Jesus did not have the Spirit in the way the ancient prophets possessed it; rather, he knew all things that were to pass and spoke out of his own knowledge (PSEUDO-CLEMENT OF ROME). Throughout his ministry, the Holy Spirit longed to exalt him (EPHREM). At the river Jordan, the Spirit came down to dwell on him, something that was a sign for the prophet John, whom the Lord and Spirit thereby sanctified (EPHREM). The Spirit by which Jesus performed miracles was not alien to him or a gift but rather was his own Spirit (CYRIL OF ALEXANDRIA). The Spirit is always one with the Son in the perfection of the divine unity (ATHANASIUS). In all the acts of Jesus the Trinity works as one, although only the Son of God assumed the flesh (SYNOD OF TOLEDO). The Spirit is especially seen in the anointing it gave to the humanity of Jesus, a gift that signified Jesus' role and status as the divine giver of the Spirit to the

world (ATHANASIUS). The Spirit's glory is also seen manifested in the power of the resurrection of Christ (THEODORE). Christ's gift of the Spirit to the world is the veritable beginning of a new humanity (CYRIL OF ALEXANDRIA).

The Spirit Enables the Mission of the Son

UNLIKE ALL OTHER PROPHETS. PSEUDO-CLEMENT: But our Master did not prophesy after this fashion but, as I have already said, being a prophet by an inborn and ever-flowing Spirit and knowing all things at all times, he confidently set forth, plainly as I said before, sufferings, places, appointed times, manners and limits. PSEUDO-CLEMENTINE HOMILIES 3.15.[2]

THE SPIRIT'S CLOSENESS TO JESUS. EPHREM THE SYRIAN: The Spirit in the temple longed to exalt him, and when he was crucified, it tore the veil and departed. HYMNS ON THE NATIVITY 25.16.[3]

THE SPIRIT DWELLS ON HIM. EPHREM THE SYRIAN: O Levitical lamp sent before the sun![4] O Servant who was ordered to baptize his Lord but who waited for the Holy Spirit to descend to dwell on the great One who had become small. Let this persuade us that John, who baptized him, was exalted, and the servant who bathed him was pardoned; sanctified was the river that received him. HYMNS ON VIRGINITY 32.5.[5]

THE SPIRIT IN THE RESURRECTION. THEODORE OF MOPSUESTIA: The apostle also said, "The letter kills, but the Spirit gives life,"[6] and showed us that he will make us immortal. And again in another passage, "The first Adam was made a living soul, and the second Adam a quickening Spirit."[7] He shows by his words

---

[2]ANCL 17:63 (part 1). [3]ESH 204. [4]The poet refers to John the Baptist. [5]ESH 404-5. [6]2 Cor 3:6. [7]1 Cor 15:45.

that Christ our Lord was changed in his body, at the resurrection from the dead, to immortality by the power of the Holy Spirit. He likewise said in another passage, "He was declared to be the Son of God with power and by the Spirit of holiness and rose up from the dead, Jesus Christ our Lord."[8] And, "If the Spirit of him that raised up Jesus Christ from the dead dwells in you, he that raised up our Lord Jesus Christ from the dead shall also give life to your dead bodies because of his Spirit that dwells in you."[9] Our Lord also said, when teaching us concerning his body, "It is the Spirit that gives life, the flesh profits nothing,"[10] in order to show that he also had immortality from the Holy Spirit and to demonstrate this point to others. Such an act belongs indeed to the nature that is eternal and the cause of everything, because to him who is able to create something from nothing belongs the act of life, that is to say, to make us immortal so that we should always live. Even among created beings those who have an immortal nature are considered higher in rank, and it is, therefore, clear and evident that he who is able to perform this act is also able to perform other acts. God shows that it is the prerogative of the divine nature to do this in saying, "Know now that I am he, and there is no God beside me: I kill, and I make alive; I wound, and I heal."[11] He shows that it is his exclusive prerogative to raise from the dead and to free from their pain those who are wounded. On the Nicene Creed 10.[12]

The Trinity in the Works of the Lord.
Synod of Toledo (675): We likewise believe that Father, Son and Holy Spirit have one substance; yet we do not say that the Virgin Mary gave birth to this one undivided Trinity but only to the Son, who alone assumed our nature into union with his own person. Further, it should be believed that the whole Trinity effected the incarnation of this Son of God, because the works of the Trinity cannot be divided. Still, it was the Son alone who took a servant's form[13] to his one person; not in the unity of the divine nature but

into that which is proper to the Son, not what is common to the three persons. This form was joined to him in a personal union, that is, in such a way that the Son of God and the Son of man are the one Christ. Furthermore, the same Christ in these two natures consists of three substantial principles: of the Word, which must belong exclusively to God's essence; of a body; and of a soul, which latter belong to his true humanity. Eleventh Council of Toledo, Creedal Statement.[14]

The Spirit Inspires the Mission of the Son.
Synod of Toledo (675): Again, with regard to the question whether the Son could be both equal to and less than the Holy Spirit, just as he is believed to be in one way equal to the Father and in another to be less than the Father, we answer as follows: According to the form of God he is equal to the Father and the Holy Spirit; according to the servant's form he is less than either Father or Holy Spirit, because neither the Holy Spirit nor God the Father, but the person of the Son alone, assumed the human nature according to which he is believed to be less than the former two persons. Further, it is believed that this Son is distinct in his person, but without any separation, from God the Father and the Holy Spirit; but the human nature was taken from humankind. Moreover, the person is associated with humanity, but the divine nature, or substance, is with the Father and the Holy Spirit. Besides, the Son is not sent by Father only, but it must be believed that he is also sent by the Holy Spirit, because he himself says through the prophet, "And now the Lord has sent me, and his Spirit."[15] He can also be understood as sent by himself, inasmuch as the action of the whole Trinity is known to be indivisible. This Son, who was called the Only-Begotten before time, has become the firstborn within in time: the Only-Begotten because of

---

[8]Rom 1:4. [9]Rom 8:11. [10]Jn 6:63. [11]Deut 32:39. [12]MFC 3:159-60. [13]Phil 2:7. [14]TCT 185. [15]Is 48:16.

his divine nature; the firstborn because of the human nature that he assumed. ELEVENTH COUNCIL OF TOLEDO, CREEDAL STATEMENT.[16]

THE SPIRIT IS ONE WITH THE SON. ATHANASIUS: These people[17] refuse to suppose the Son of God a creature; how can they endure even to hear the Spirit of the Son so spoken of? If they refuse to class the Son with created things, because of the unity of the Word with the Father . . . how can they dare to call the Spirit a created thing, when the Spirit has the same unity with the Son as the Son has with the Father? They safeguard the unity of God by not dividing the Son from the Father; how is it that they fail to understand that by thus dividing the Spirit from the Word, they no longer safeguard the one Godhead in Trinity; for they tear it apart and mix with it an alien and different element . . . by making the Spirit to be of a different essence. What kind of divine life is this, compounded of Creator and created? LETTER TO SERAPION 1.2.[18]

THE LORD IS ANOINTED WITH THE SPIRIT. ATHANASIUS: "Your throne, O God, is forever . . . God anointed you . . . above those who share in you."[19] Kings of Israel became kings on being anointed; the Savior, on the contrary, though he was God, and always reigned with his Father's sovereignty and though he was himself the supplier of the Holy Spirit, is nevertheless said on this occasion to be "anointed"; that here again, as he is said to be anointed, as man, with the Spirit, so he might provide for us humans, besides exaltation and resurrection, the indwelling and personal possession of the Spirit. AGAINST THE ARIANS 1.46.[20]

THE LORD'S HUMANITY IS SANCTIFIED BY THE DIVINE SPIRIT. ATHANASIUS: Before he became man he, as the Word, supplied the Spirit to the saints, as being his own; so when he was made man he sanctified all by the Spirit and says to his disciples, "Receive the Holy Spirit."[21] . . . It is not the Word, as Word, that is advanced, for he has all things, eternally, but we humans, who have in him and through him the source of our receiving these things. For when he is said to be anointed as man, it is we who are anointed in him. When he is baptized, it is we who are baptized in him.[22] AGAINST THE ARIANS 1.48.[23]

The Son Is Sustained by the Spirit

THE LORD RECEIVES AND GIVES THE SPIRIT. CYRIL OF ALEXANDRIA: Next, he says as well, that the Spirit also came down from heaven on him. Do they pretend that the Holy Spirit came down on the Word of God while still abstract and incorporeal and represents him who bestows the Spirit as made partaker of his own Spirit? Or rather is this their meaning, that having received the Spirit in his human nature, he in his divine nature baptizes in the Holy Spirit? For he is himself singly and alone and verily the Son of God the Father, as the blessed Baptist, being taught of God, bore witness, saying, "And I saw and bore witness that this is the Son of God!" HOMILIES ON THE GOSPEL OF LUKE 10.[24]

CHRIST THE FIRSTFRUITS OF THE NEW NATURE. CYRIL OF ALEXANDRIA: Along with other goods, he promises to give the Holy Spirit once again, since without him humanity could not be restored to a firm and stable possession of the other goods. He sets the coming of Christ as the time for the Holy Spirit to descend on us. He promises this, "In those days I will pour out my Spirit manifestly and clearly on all flesh."[25] The time for this generosity and liberality brought the Only-Begotten to earth in

---

[16]*TCT* 186-87. [17]He is referring to a group known as the Tropici. They refused to allow that the Son of God was a creature but felt that there was not sufficient biblical warrant to conclude other than that the Spirit was a creature. [18]*ECF* 405. [19]Ps 44:6 (Ps 45:6-7 [LXX]). [20]*ECF* 385*. [21]Jn 20:22. [22]See Jn 17:22. [23]*ECF* 385-86. [24]*CGSL* 76. [25]Joel 2:28.

flesh, as a man born of woman according to the holy Scripture.[26] God the Father again gave the Holy Spirit; Christ received the Spirit first, as the firstfruits of the renewed nature. John the Baptist witnessed this: "I saw the Spirit descend from heaven and rest on him."[27] How was it that he received? We must explain what we have said. Did he receive what he did not have? In no way! The Spirit belongs to the Son. He is not sent into him from outside, as God bestows the Spirit on us. The Spirit is naturally in him just as he is in the Father. The Spirit proceeds through him to the saints as the Father bestows him on each one in the appropriate way. We say that the Son received the Spirit insofar as he had become human, and it was appropriate for him to receive him as a human. . . . The Only-Begotten did not receive the Holy Spirit for himself; the Spirit is his, is in him and is given through him, as we have already said. As human, he had the whole of human nature in himself, in order to renew all of humanity and restore it to its original state. . . . The Only-Begotten became human like us so that the good things that were returned and the grace of the Spirit might first be grounded in him and thereby firmly preserved for the whole nature. It was as though the only-begotten Word of God extended the stability that is proper to his own nature to us, to the human nature that had in Adam been condemned to be changeable and prone to both error and perversion. In the same way, therefore, that the fall of the first human resulted in a loss for all humanity, so the whole race has acquired the benefit of the divine gifts in him who knows no change. COMMENTARY ON THE GOSPEL OF JOHN 5.2.[28]

The Son's Gift of the Spirit to the World

THE SPIRIT POURS FORTH FROM CHRIST.

CYRIL OF ALEXANDRIA: And when he says of the Spirit, "He shall glorify me,"[29] if we understand the words rightly, we shall not say that the one Christ and Son received glory from the Holy Spirit, as being in need of glory from another, for the Holy Spirit is not superior to him and above him. But since, for the manifestation of his Godhead, he made use of the Holy Spirit for the working of miracles, he says that he was glorified by him, just as anyone of us might say, of his strength, for instance, or his skill in any matter, "they shall glorify me." For though the Holy Spirit has a personal existence[30] of his own and is conceived of by himself, in that he is the Spirit and not the Son, yet he is not therefore alien from the Son. For he is called the Spirit of Truth, and Christ is the Truth, and he is poured forth from him just as he is also from God the Father. THIRD LETTER TO NESTORIUS (LETTER 17).[31]

THE SPIRIT IS THE LORD'S OWN. CYRIL OF ALEXANDRIA: If anyone says that the one Lord Jesus Christ was glorified by the Spirit, as though the power that he exercised was another's, received through the Spirit and not his own, and that he received from the Spirit the power of countervailing unclean spirits and of working divine miracles on people, and does not rather say that it was his own Spirit by whom he wrought divine miracles, let him be anathema. THIRD LETTER TO NESTORIUS (LETTER 17).[32]

THE SON GIVES THE SPIRIT TO THE WORTHY. CYRIL OF ALEXANDRIA: The Word, therefore, that became man is, as it appears, God, and the fruit of the Father's substance. But it may be that those will object to this who divide the one Christ into two sons; those I mean who, as Scripture says, are animal, and dividers[33] and having not the Spirit to confess that he who baptizes in the Holy Spirit is the Word of God, and not he who is of the seed of David. What answer shall we make, then, to this? Yes!

---

[27]Jn 1:32. [28]MFC 3:162, interpreting Jn 7:39. [29]Jn 16:14. [30]*Hypostasis.* [31]CCC 285. [32]CCC 287. [33]A reference to Ps 22:12-13 and an ironic allusion to Nestorius, whom Cyril accused of dividing (rending) Christ into two.

We too affirm, without fear of contradiction, that the Word being God as of his own fullness bestows the Holy Spirit on such as are worthy; but this he still wrought, even when he was made man, as being the one Son with the flesh united to him in an ineffable and incomprehensible manner. For so the blessed Baptist, after first saying, "I am not worthy to stoop down and loose the thong of his shoes,"[34] immediately added, "He shall baptize you in the Holy Spirit and in fire"; plainly while having feet for shoes. For no one whose mind was awake would say that the Word, while still incorporeal and not as yet made like unto us, had feet and shoes, but only when he had become a man. Inasmuch, however, as he did not then cease to be God, even so he performed works worthy of the Godhead by giving the Spirit to those who believed in him. For he, in one and the same person, was at the same time both God and man. HOMILIES ON THE GOSPEL OF LUKE 10.[35]

WE HAVE THE SPIRIT OF THE SON IN OUR HEARTS.

CYRIL OF ALEXANDRIA: For the Holy Spirit indeed proceeds from God the Father but also belongs to the Son. It is even often called the Spirit of Christ, though proceeding from God the Father. And to this Paul will testify, saying, at one time, "They that are in the flesh cannot please God. But you are not in the flesh, but in the spirit, if so be the Spirit of God dwells in you. But if anyone does not have the Spirit of Christ, he is none of his."[36] And again, "But because you are children, God has sent the Spirit of his Son into your hearts, crying Father, our Father."[37] The Holy Spirit, therefore, indeed proceeds, as I said, from God the Father, but his only-begotten Word, as being both by nature and truly Son, and resplendent with the Father's dignities, ministers the Spirit to the creation and bestows the Spirit on those that are worthy. For in truth he said, "All things that the Father has are mine."[38] HOMILIES ON THE GOSPEL OF LUKE 11.[39]

THE GIFT OF THE SPIRIT IS THE SECOND

BIRTH OF HUMANITY.

CYRIL OF ALEXANDRIA: And the Evangelist says that the heavens were opened, as having long been closed. For Christ said, "Henceforward you shall see the heavens opened and the angels of God ascending and descending on the Son of man."[40] For both the flock above and that below being now made one, and one chief Shepherd appointed for all, the heavens were opened, and humankind on earth was brought near to the holy angels. And the Spirit also again came down as at a second commencement of our race and on Christ first, who received it not so much for his own sake as for ours, for by him and in him are we enriched with all things. It is in accord with the economy of grace that he endures with us the things that pertain to human nature, for how else would we have seen him emptied, when in his divine nature he is the fullness? How did he become poor as we are, if he did not conform himself to our poverty? And how did he empty himself, if he refused to endure the limitations of human meagerness? HOMILIES ON THE GOSPEL OF LUKE 11.[41]

THE LORD BAPTIZES IN THE SPIRIT.

CYRIL OF ALEXANDRIA: And after this, he again brings forward a second proof, saying, "I indeed baptize you in water, but he shall baptize you in the Holy Spirit and in fire."[42] And this too is of great importance for the proof and demonstration that Jesus is God and Lord. For it is the sole and peculiar property of the Substance that transcends all[43] to be able to bestow on humans the indwelling of the Holy Spirit and make those that draw near to it partakers of the divine nature. But this exists in Christ, not as a thing received or by communication from another, but as his own and as belonging to his substance, for he baptizes in the Holy Spirit. HOMILIES ON THE GOSPEL OF LUKE 10.[44]

---

[34]Mk 1:7. [35]CGSL 75-76*. [36]Rom 8:8. [37]Gal 4:6. [38]Jn 16:15. [39]CGSL 79. [40]Jn 1:51. [41]CGSL 81**. [42]Mt 3:11. [43]Namely, divinity. [44]CGSL 75.

THE GIFT OF THE SPIRIT AFTER CHRIST'S GLORIFICATION. CYRIL OF ALEXANDRIA: He has also given them the godlike power of remitting the sins of whomsoever they will and of retaining those of all others. But that among people there was no spirit of adoption before the resurrection of Christ from the dead and his ascent to heaven, the most wise Evangelist John makes plain where he says, "For the Spirit was not as yet, because Jesus was not yet glorified."[45] Yet certainly, how can the Spirit be unequal in eternity to God the Father and the Son? When did he not exist, who is before all? For he is equal in substance to the Father and the Son. But inasmuch as Christ, he says, was not yet glorified (that is to say, had not yet risen from the dead and ascended to heaven), the spirit of adoption did not as yet exist for humankind. But when the only-begotten Word of God ascended up into heaven, he sent down for us in his place the Comforter, who is in us by him. And this he taught us, saying, "It is expedient for you that I go away; for if I do not go away, the Comforter will not come to you; but when I have departed, I will send him to you."[46] HOMILIES ON THE GOSPEL OF LUKE 38.[47]

WHY HE REJOICES IN THE SPIRIT. CYRIL OF ALEXANDRIA: Whoever loves instruction must not approach the words of God carelessly and without earnestness but, on the contrary, with eagerness, since it is written, "He who takes care will find abundance."[48] Let us examine the Scriptures, therefore, and especially what is meant by the expression "he rejoiced in the Holy Spirit."[49] The Holy Spirit proceeds from God the Father as from the fountain but is not foreign to the Son. Every property of the Father belongs to the Word, who by nature was truly begotten from him. Christ saw that many had been won over by the operation of the Spirit, whom he bestowed on those that were worthy and whom he had also commanded to be ministers of the divine message. He saw that wonderful signs were accomplished by their hands and that the salvation of the world by this had now begun (I mean by faith). Accordingly he rejoiced in the Holy Spirit, and that means he rejoiced in the works and miracles wrought by means of the Holy Spirit. For he had appointed the twelve disciples, whom he also called apostles, and after them seventy others, whom he sent as his forerunners to go before him into every village and city of Judea, preaching himself and the things concerning him. And he sent them, nobly adorned with apostolic dignities and distinguished by the operation of the grace of the Holy Spirit. He gave them power over unclean spirits, in order to cast them out. Having performed many miracles, therefore, they returned saying to him, "Lord, even the devils are subject to us in your name."[50] HOMILIES ON THE GOSPEL OF LUKE 65.[51]

CHRIST INVOKES THE PENTECOSTAL SPIRIT. ROMANOS THE MELODIST: As soon as they had completed their supplications,[52] they signed them, having sealed them with faith and sent them on high. Their Teacher read them and said, Of your own free will, O Paraclete, under no order, but as you wish, descend. For the disciples, whom I gathered for you and the Father, await you, the ones whom I instructed when I said, "Make disciples of the nations," proclaiming the Father, honoring the Son and praising the all-Holy Spirit. KONTAKION ON PENTECOST 6.[53]

---

[45]Jn 7:39. [46]Jn 16:7. [47]CGSL 164*. [48]Prov 14:23. [49]Lk 10:21. [50]Lk 10:17. [51]CGSL 277. [52]The poet refers to the prayers of the mother of God and the apostles gathered together in the upper room, praying immediately before Pentecost. [53]SLS 211.

HE BECAME INCARNATE

καὶ εἰς ἕνα κύριον Ἰησοῦν Χριστὸν,	*Et in unum Dominum Jesum Christum,*	*We believe in one Lord, Jesus Christ,*
τὸν υἱὸν τοῦ Θεοῦ τὸν μονογενῆ,	*Filium Dei unigenitum,*	*the only Son of God,*
τὸν ἐκ τοῦ πατρὸς γεννηθέντα	*et ex Patre natum*	*eternally*
πρὸ πάντων τῶν αἰώνων,	*ante omnia saecula*	*begotten of the Father,*
φῶς ἐκ φωτός,	*[Deum de Deo], Lumen de Lumine,*	*[God from God], Light from Light,*
Θεὸν ἀληθινὸν ἐκ θεοῦ ἀληθινοῦ,	*Deum verum de Deo vero,*	*true God from true God,*
γεννηθέντα, οὐ ποιηθέντα,	*genitum, non factum,*	*begotten, not made,*
ὁμοούσιον τῷ πατρί·	*consubstantialem Patri;*	*of one Being with the Father.*
δι᾽ οὗ τὰ πάντα ἐγένετο·	*per quem omnia facta sunt;*	*Through him all things were made.*
τὸν δι᾽ ἡμᾶς τοὺς ἀνθρώπους	*qui propter nos homines*	*For us*
καὶ διὰ τὴν ἡμετέραν σωτηρίαν	*et propter nostram salutem*	*and for our salvation*
κατελθόντα ἐκ τῶν οὐρανῶν	*descendit de coelis,*	*he came down from heaven:*
καὶ σαρκωθέντα ἐκ πνεύματος ἁγίου	***et incarnatus est*** *de Spiritu Sancto*	*by the power of the Holy Spirit*
καὶ Μαρίας τῆς παρθένου	*ex Maria virgine,*	***he became incarnate*** *from the Virgin Mary,*
καὶ ἐνανθρωπήσαντα,	*et homo factus est;*	*and was made man.*

HISTORICAL CONTEXT: The creedal clause had here before it the great biblical archetype of John 1:14: "The Word was made flesh and dwelled among us." A short while later the creed will make another pairing to assert that this means also "was made man." "Enfleshment" as spoken of in the Johannine prologue was given a slightly different set of associations in later Christian Greek literature. Here, in the creed, the Fathers speak of the Logos "putting on flesh" using the verb *sarkousthai*. The Greek verb can even mean "to grow fleshy." It is not exactly the same as the Johannine image "became flesh" (*sarx egeneto*), but it is close to it. In the pre-Nicene centuries, the Fathers were struck by the widespread biblical use of the term "flesh" to stand for humanity in all its fragility, and indeed its sinfulness. Paul had greatly extended reflection on the flesh in this sense and given the word a high significance in atonement theology, for the flesh was not only weak but also rebellious.

Almost all the best patristic theologians wished to affirm that the enfleshment of the Word was a powerful act of salvation and the healing of sin, as well as death, which was seen as the direct result of sin. Models of the incarnation were as yet not envisaged, but once again the Arian crisis of the fourth century made the need for them acute. Pagan myths abounded in stories of the gods coming down from above and turning into flesh, in the sense of having a temporary masquerade as earthly beings, either human or animal. Christian thinkers soon became at pains to distance Christology from the mythological modes of ancient discourse. But throughout the fourth century they were often pressed to articulate a more refined sense of what they meant by the Logos's enfleshment, or incarnation.[1]

Theories of early Nicenes, such as Apollinaris of Laodicea, that incarnation did not necessarily entail a complete humanization of the Word were divisive within the Nicene

---

[1] From the Latin term *incarnatio*, a "coming into flesh."

party as a whole as it tried to stand against Arianism and led to a stiffened resolve of the later Nicenes to insist that the Word's incarnation meant that he became a real man within the vicissitudes of history, though without losing his divine condition. The reluctance of the earlier Nicenes to admit the incarnate Lord possessed a human soul gradually gave way as the deeper implications were recognized. Although the creed was not explicit on the matter, the confession that Jesus was ensouled became central to the patristic defense of the true sacramentality of the incarnation.

OVERVIEW: The cross is the deepest point of the humility that the incarnation represents, but it is not the shame of Christians; instead, it is their glory and boast (CYRIL OF JERUSALEM). The mockery of the pagans should never distract us from our faith in the incarnation (CYRIL OF ALEXANDRIA). Many people stumble over Jesus as the incarnation of God, not understanding the doctrine of the two natures he represents (ISAAC). God became a man, and that simple fact means that it was God who saved us (IRENAEUS). In the incarnate Lord, the soul is the bond between the divinity and the flesh. It is a bond of such force that this is how we can speak of Jesus as God (ORIGEN). In times past God could be said to have dwelled in his saints, but never before had God done what is seen in the incarnation, that is, took a body to himself (ATHANASIUS, AUGUSTINE). The same one who as Word was universally present to the cosmos has now in the incarnation come in flesh to us (GREGORY OF NYSSA). Even if it sounds blasphemous and shocking, we still assert that the divine Word died in his human nature (TERTULLIAN). His incarnation was real and not symbolic (BASIL). It was the Word and no other who was made flesh (CYRIL OF ALEXANDRIA). The Word in this mystery of incarnation assumed all the human condition, not just parts of it, and particularly assumes a human soul in order to heal and save every part of what makes

up humanity (GREGORY OF NAZIANZUS).

The Scandal of the Gospel

THE CROSS IS NOT SHAMEFUL FOR BELIEVERS. CYRIL OF JERUSALEM: Let us never be ashamed of the cross of Christ. Others may want to hide it, but you[2] should openly mark it on your forehead,[3] so that the devils may behold the royal sign and flee trembling far away. Make this sign of the cross at eating and drinking, at sitting, at lying down, at rising up, at speaking, at walking, in short, over everything you do. For he who was crucified here below is now in heaven above. If after his crucifixion and burial he had remained in the tomb, we should indeed have had cause to be ashamed of the cross, but the very one who was crucified on Golgotha here [in Jerusalem] has ascended into heaven from the Mount of Olives, which is to the east of us. After having gone down from here[4] into hades, and come up again to us, he once more ascended away from us into heaven. His Father addressed him, saying, "Sit on my right hand, until I make your enemies your footstool."[5] CATECHETICAL LECTURES 4.14.[6]

DO NOT BE LED ASTRAY BY FOOLISH MOCKERS. CYRIL OF ALEXANDRIA: For the blessed Isaiah says, "Behold, a virgin shall conceive and bear a son; and they shall call his name Emmanuel, which, being interpreted, is, God with us."[7] But the Word was with us as God when he took our likeness and despised not the low estate of humankind, in order that he might save all beneath the heaven. And it is written again, "And you, Bethlehem, the house of Ephrata, are small to be among the thousands of Judah; out of you shall come the one who shall be the head

---

[2] The newly baptized, to whom Cyril is addressing this homily.
[3] As in parts of Christian Africa today, where the cross is tattooed on the brow. In Cyril's day it was a provocative challenge to new catechumens, as the age of persecution had so recently ended.
[4] He is delivering the sermon in the Church of the Holy Sepulcher.
[5] Ps 110:1. [6] NPNF 2 7:22**. [7] Is 7:14.

of Israel."[8] For Bethlehem was indeed small, and in comparison with the general populousness of the Jews, its inhabitants were very few; yet from it came Christ, as having been born in it of the holy Virgin, not as someone subject to the shadows of the Law but rather as ruler over both the Law and the Prophets. And so, we do not follow either the ignorance or the foolish novelties of gabblers, so that we do not join them as they fall into reprobate mentalities. Rather, we align ourselves with the pure teachings of the holy apostles and Evangelists, who show everywhere that Christ the Savior of all is at once both the Son and the Lord of David, in the manner we have already described. HOMILIES ON THE GOSPEL OF LUKE 137.[9]

UNDERSTAND THE TRADITION WITH WISDOM. ISAAC OF NINEVEH: Sometimes, things pertaining to the Lord's divinity, which are not compatible with human nature, are said with respect to his all-holy body. And similarly, lowly things are said concerning his divinity which actually pertain to his humanity. Many who do not understand the intent of the divine words have stumbled here with a stumbling from which there is no recovery.[10] ASCETICAL HOMILIES 3.[11]

The Word in the Flesh

THE EPITOME OF SALVATION. IRENAEUS: God became man, and it was the Lord himself who saved us. AGAINST HERESIES 3.21.1.[12]

THE WORD IS BONDED TO HIS OWN FLESH. ORIGEN: Therefore with this soul acting as a connecting link between God and flesh (for it was not possible for the nature of God to be mingled with flesh without a mediator), there was born the God-man, that substance being the connecting link that could assume a body without denying its own nature. . . . The Son of God by whom all things were created is called Jesus Christ, the Son of man. For

the Son of God is said to have died in respect of that nature that was certainly capable of death; and he is called the Son of man who is proclaimed about to come "in the glory of God the Father with the holy angels."[13] And for this cause through the whole of Scripture the divine nature is spoken of in human terms, and at the same time the human nature is accorded the distinctive epithets proper to the divine. For the saying, "The two shall be in one flesh, and they are now not two but one flesh only,"[14] is more applicable here than in any other reference. ON FIRST PRINCIPLES 2.6.3.[15]

GOD TOOK A BODY TO HIMSELF. ATHANASIUS: The Word was always God and sanctified those saints whom he visited in history and set all things in order in accordance with the Father's will. But later he himself became man, for our sakes, and, as the apostle says, the Godhead "dwelled" in the flesh "in bodily fashion."[16] This is as much as to say, "Though he was God, he had a body for his own, and using it as an instrument he has become man for our sakes." So it is that the properties of the flesh are said to be his, since he was in that flesh: hunger, thirst, pain, weariness, and the like, to which the flesh is liable. The works belonging to the Word (raising the dead, restoring sight to the blind, curing the woman's hemorrhage) he himself did through his own body. The Word "bore the weakness" of the flesh as his own, for the flesh was his flesh. The flesh assisted the works of the Godhead, for the Godhead was in the flesh, and the body was God's own. AGAINST THE ARIANS 3.31.[17]

THE WORD DIED IN THE HUMAN NATURE. TERTULLIAN: This notion is blasphemy.[18] Let

---

[8]Mt 1:23; Mic 5:2. [9]*CGSL* 546*. [10]He means christological heresy. [11]*AHSIS* 18**. [12]*ECF* 106. [13]Mk 8:38. [14]Mt 19:5-6. [15]*ECF* 299. [16]Col 2:9. [17]*ECF* 397-98. [18]That the monarchian theologians, who had said the Father and the Son were one and the same person, thereby implied that it was none other than the Father who had suffered on the cross.

it not be spoken. Let it be enough to say that Christ the Son of God died, because this is what it says in Scripture. When the apostle proclaims that Christ died, he feels the heavy responsibility of the assertion and adds, "according to the Scriptures," so as to soften the harshness of the pronouncement and to avoid presenting an obstacle to the hearer. But in Jesus two natures are established, a divine and a human one. It is surely agreed that the divine nature is immortal and the human nature mortal. So, it is clear that when the apostle says that "Christ died," he is speaking in respect that he is flesh and man and Son of man, not in that he is Spirit and Word and Son of God. He says that Christ, the anointed one, died, and so makes it clear that what died was that which had been anointed, namely, his flesh. . . . Therefore the Father did not suffer with the Son. Indeed, they are afraid of direct blasphemy against the Father and hope to alleviate by conceding that the Father and the Son are two persons, if, as they say, "the Son suffers while the Father suffers with him." Even here they are stupid. For to "suffer with" is to suffer. If the Father cannot suffer, he cannot "suffer with." . . . It is as impossible for the Father to "suffer with" as it is for the Son to suffer in respect of his divinity. But in what way did the Son suffer, if the Father did not suffer with him? The answer is, the Father is distinct from the Son in his humanity, not from the Son in his divinity. AGAINST PRAXEAS 29.[19]

THE INCARNATION WAS REAL, NOT SYMBOLIC.
BASIL OF CAESAREA: It is the nature of flesh to suffer division, diminution, dissolution; of animal flesh to experience weariness, pain, hunger and thirst, and to be overcome by sleep. It is the nature of a soul making use of a body to feel grief, care, anxiety, and the like. Some of these experiences are natural and inevitable for any living being, while others arise from perverse choice, brought on by a life without discipline or without training in virtue. So, it is clear that

the Lord accepted such natural experiences so as to establish that his incarnation was real and not a mere semblance. But those experiences that arise from wickedness and that defile the purity of our life, he rejected as incompatible with his unsullied Godhead. Therefore he is said to have been "born in the likeness of flesh of sin."[20] This does not mean, as these people suppose,[21] that he was "in the likeness of flesh" but was rather in "the likeness of the flesh of sin." In other words, he assumed our own flesh with all its natural experiences, but "he committed no sin."[22] Just as the death that is in the flesh (since it has been transmitted to us through Adam) was swallowed up by the Godhead, so the sinfulness was annulled by the righteousness that is in Christ Jesus. In the resurrection we receive back our flesh, which is no longer subject to death or liable to sin. LETTER 261.3.[23]

THE LORD SAVES THE WHOLE HUMAN BEING.
GREGORY OF NAZIANZUS: These people[24] must not deceive others or be themselves deceived into supposing that "the man of the Lord"[25] (to use their title for him who more truly is Lord and God) was without a human intellect.[26] For we do not separate the man from the Godhead; we teach that he is one and the same. Formerly he was not man, but only God the Son, before all ages, unconnected with a body or anything corporeal. But in time he became man also, assuming manhood for our salvation; passable in the flesh, impassible in the Godhead; limited in the body, unconfined in the spirit; on the earth and at the same time in heaven; belonging to the visible world, and also to the intelligible order of being; comprehensible and also incomprehen-

---

[19]ECF 169**. [20]Rom 8:3. [21]Apollinarian theologians who argued that Jesus' humanity was not the same as ours. [22]1 Pet 2:22. [23]LCF 69-70**. [24]The followers of Apollinaris. [25]*Kyriakon anthrōpon*. [26]Apollinaris had argued that the human *nous* (the spiritual intellect, and also the soul, or *psychē*) were superfluous in the incarnate Lord, since the *nous* of the divine Logos stood in for both. Athanasius and the later Nicene fathers replied that this would make the incarnate humanity different from that of the rest of the human race.

sible; so that man as a whole, since he had fallen into sin, might be fashioned afresh by one who was wholly man and at the same time God. LETTER 101.4, TO CLEDONIUS.[27]

GOD CAME AS FLESH AMONG US. GREGORY OF NYSSA: That Deity should be born in our nature ought not reasonably to present any strangeness to the minds of those who do not take too narrow a view of things. For who, when he takes a survey of the universe, is so simple as not to believe that there is Deity in everything, penetrating it, embracing it and seated in it? For all things depend on him who is, nor can there be anything that has not its being in him who is. If, therefore, all things are in him and he is in all things, why are they scandalized at the plan of revelation when it teaches that God was born among humankind; that same God whom we are convinced is even now not outside humankind? THE GREAT CATECHISM 25.[28]

THE WORD WAS BORN OF THE VIRGIN. CYRIL OF ALEXANDRIA: In saying that the Word was incarnate, we are not asserting any change in the nature of the Word or the transformation of the Word into an entire man, composed of soul and body. We are saying that the Word, in a manner indescribable and inconceivable, personally[29] united to himself flesh animated with a reasonable soul, and thus became man and was called the Son of man. And this was not by a mere act of will or favor or by taking to himself a mere personal presentation.[30] The natures that were brought together to form a genuine unity were different; but it was one Christ, and one Son, that was produced out of these two natures. We do not mean that the difference of the natures is annihilated because of this union, but rather that the deity and the manhood, by their inexpressible and inexplicable concurrence into unity, have brought about for us the one Lord and Son, Jesus Christ. It is in this sense that he is said to have been born of a woman, in respect of the flesh, though he existed and was begotten from the Father before all ages. . . . It was not that an ordinary man was first born of the holy Virgin and that afterwards the Word descended on him. No, the Word was united with the flesh in the womb and thus is said to have undergone a birth in the flesh, inasmuch as he made his own the birth of his own flesh. In the same way we say that he suffered and rose again. We do not mean that God the Word suffered in his deity . . . for the deity, being incorporeal, is impassible. But the body that was made his own endured these sufferings. Therefore he is said to have endured them for our sake. The impassible was in the body that suffered. In the same way we speak of his death. . . . Thus it is one Christ and Lord that we acknowledge, and as one and the same that we worship him, not as a man "associated in our worship" with the Word. SECOND LETTER TO NESTORIUS (LETTER 4).[31]

THE WORD ASSUMES THE FLESH OF HUMANITY. CYRIL OF ALEXANDRIA: For Scripture does not say that the Word united to himself the person of man but that "he became flesh." But this expression the Word became flesh is nothing else than that he became partaker of flesh and blood, like us and made our body his own. He came forth a man of a woman, not casting aside his being as God and the fact of his having been begotten of God the Father. Even in the assumption of flesh he remained what he was. This is the doctrine that strict orthodoxy everywhere prescribes. It is this doctrine we shall find the holy Fathers held. SECOND LETTER TO NESTORIUS (LETTER 4).[32]

THE WORD TAKES A BODY AS HIS OWN. AUGUSTINE: Christ did not take human form for a time,[33] to show himself to man in this guise,

---

[27]LCF 107. [28]NPNF 2 5:494-95. [29]Hypostatically. [30]*Prosōpon*. [31]LCF 258-59. [32]CCC 278**. [33]He wishes to contrast the incarnation with the temporary manifestations of the divine in earlier scriptural accounts (the pillar of fire, the burning bush, and so on).

an outward appearance that should thereafter be discarded. He took the visible form of man into the unity of his person, the form of God remaining invisible. Not only was he born in that form of a human mother, but he also grew up in it. He ate and drank and slept and was put to death in that form. In that same human form he rose again and ascended into heaven. He now sits at the right hand of the Father in that same human form, in which he is to come to judge the living and the dead, in which he will, in his kingdom, "be made subordinate to God who made all things subordinate to him."[34] AGAINST MAXIMINUS 1.19.[35]

[34]1 Cor 15:28. [35]LCF 216.

FROM THE VIRGIN MARY

καὶ εἰς ἕνα κύριον Ἰησοῦν Χριστόν,	Et in unum Dominum Jesum Christum,	We believe in one Lord, Jesus Christ,
τὸν υἱὸν τοῦ Θεοῦ τὸν μονογενῆ,	Filium Dei unigenitum,	the only Son of God,
τὸν ἐκ τοῦ πατρὸς γεννηθέντα	et ex Patre natum	eternally
πρὸ πάντων τῶν αἰώνων,	ante omnia saecula	begotten of the Father,
φῶς ἐκ φωτός,	[Deum de Deo], Lumen de Lumine,	[God from God], Light from Light,
Θεὸν ἀληθινὸν ἐκ θεοῦ ἀληθινοῦ,	Deum verum de Deo vero,	true God from true God,
γεννηθέντα, οὐ ποιηθέντα,	genitum, non factum,	begotten, not made,
ὁμοούσιον τῷ πατρί·	consubstantialem Patri;	of one Being with the Father.
δι᾽ οὗ τὰ πάντα εγένετο·	per quem omnia facta sunt;	Through him all things were made.
τὸν δι᾽ ἡμᾶς τοὺς ἀνθρώπους	qui propter nos homines	For us
καὶ διὰ τὴν ἡμετέραν σωτηρίαν	et propter nostram salutem	and for our salvation
κατελθόντα ἐκ τῶν οὐρανῶν	descendit de coelis,	he came down from heaven:
καὶ σαρκωθέντα ἐκ πνεύματος ἁγίου	et incarnatus est de Spiritu Sancto	by the power of the Holy Spirit
καὶ Μαρίας τῆς παρθένου	**ex Maria virgine,**	he became incarnate **from the Virgin Mary,**
καὶ ἐνανθρωπήσαντα,	et homo factus est;	and was made man.

HISTORICAL CONTEXT: The creed's description of the making flesh of the Word "as from the Holy Spirit and Mary the virgin" is a remarkable juxtaposition. Ancient thought regarded the male parent as entirely responsible for the transmission of life. The female womb was seen as merely an incubator where the seminal male principle grew and developed, nourished by the supply of blood but no other creative principle. Some commentators have argued that this ancient biological model is being invoked at this juncture, but it seems rather to be the case that the close association of the two agencies of the life of Jesus is meant by the creed to be divinity and humanity rather than male agency and female passivity as in secular Hellenistic biology. The root of the creedal phrase is thus a retelling of the Lukan narrative of the birth of the Savior (Lk 1:26-38), which celebrates the dynamic acts of a God who intervenes at decisive moments in the story of the life of Israel, particularly to fulfill the covenant promise to the Davidic line to rule over the house of Jacob.

From the earliest times, Mary was an object of intense fascination and deep devotion to early Christians. She features relatively few times in the canonical Gospels, though each appearance is deeply symbolic, but the apocryphal writings, such as the Proto-Evangelium of James, demonstrate that she was a major focus of deep and ancient veneration. In the second century she was already addressed as *theotokos*, or mother of God, and featured in the prayers of the simple believers as a heavenly advocate. Her role as supreme apocalyptic intercessor, alongside John the Baptist, at the throne of Christ the judge, is attested throughout early Christian tradition and is a reminder that the whole panoply of the most ancient Christian practice is not always reflected explicitly in the canonical biblical texts. Devotion to Mary was important in Egypt, where the cult of the God-Mother Isis was progressively dislocated by the church's reattachment of popular devotion from the old gods and goddesses to the Savior and his mother. By the fifth century, the titles of Mary had come to feature centrally in the christological controversy, and Mary's status as ever-virgin, immaculate and mother of God became subjects of conciliar definition. In each instance the figure of Mary the mother of the Lord is used to insist on the human reality of Jesus. When the church teaches that the incarnate Lord was the son of Mary, it is always shorthand for a rejection of the endlessly recurrent temptations to gnostic and docetic views that shied away, through various centuries, from the implications of his full acceptance of human fragility and limitation. The theology of the new Eve reflects what the church believes of the new Adam that issued from her.

OVERVIEW: Adam originally came from virgin soil, thus created by God, and this is why the new Adam thought it fitting to come from the Virgin, as from a new beginning (ATHANASIUS). The incarnate Word issued from a noble mother, who was a vessel of the Spirit (GREGORY OF NAZIANZUS). Her blood nourished him, but he took the Virgin's purity to be the substance of the flesh he made for himself (GREGORY OF NYSSA). When the Scripture calls the Lord Bread from heaven, it primarily signifies that he was not born of flesh and blood but from the heavenly conception of the Spirit of God in the Virgin (HILARY). She who bore him was the ever-virgin (LEO). His birth from a virgin was unique and wonderful. It was a new kind of birth for the rebirth of the human race, but it ought not to be understood as ascribing the paternity of the Son to the Spirit (SYNOD OF TOLEDO). Being the mother of the Christ, she is thus the mother of God. Those who deny this theology are devoid of the knowledge of God (GREGORY OF NAZIANZUS, THEODORET). If Christ is God, then it is clear that his mother is the *theotokos*, and in this Mary stands as a demonstration of his twofold reality as human and divine (CYRIL OF ALEXANDRIA). Mary the virgin mother is clearly a paradox (LEO), but she is also a focus of many other revelatory paradoxes in the mystery of Christ (EPHREM, THEODORET). Her significance was hidden from the ruler of this age, and so in her humility she became the stratagem of his downfall (GREGORY OF NYSSA). Mary is the new Eve (IRENAEUS) who reverses the ancient fall of the first Eve (TERTULLIAN) and brings forth the new Adam (IRENAEUS). Being of David's line, she ensures Christ's true descent from the house of David, as Messiah (IGNATIUS), and proves to all the world that the incarnate Lord is truly flesh and blood (IGNATIUS, POLYCARP, LEO).

The Virgin Birth

THE NEW ADAM RISES FROM VIRGIN SOIL.
ATHANASIUS: Aaron was not born a high priest but a man, and in course of time, when God

willed, he became a high priest . . . putting on over his usual clothes the ephod, breastplate and robe . . . and thus clad he entered in to the holy place and offered the sacrifice for the people. . . . So the Lord, "in the beginning was the Word,"[1] but when the Father willed that ransoms should be given for all and grace bestowed on all, then indeed, just as Aaron put on his robe, so the Word took earthly flesh, having Mary for the mother of his body, so as to correspond to the virgin soil from which Adam was made, that as a high priest, himself having an offering, he might offer himself to the Father and cleanse us all from sins. . . . As Aaron remained the same and did not change by assuming the high priest's dress . . . so the Lord did not become another by taking the flesh but remained the same and was clothed in it. AGAINST THE ARIANS 2.7.8.[2]

HE COMES FROM A NOBLE MOTHER. GREGORY OF NAZIANZUS: Here is my teaching about the novel birth of Christ. There is no shame involved, since sin alone is shameful. To him no shame attaches, as the Word formed him. Nor was he mortal with a mortal's transience, but he came from flesh that the Spirit had previously made holy, that of a noble mother, unwedded, and as a self-formed mortal he came and underwent purification for my sake. For he undertook all obligations, paying to the Law a due return for his nurture; indeed, as I see it, it was a parting gift to the Law as it withdrew from the scene. But when he had been heralded by the brightly shining lamp of great light, the lamp that preceded him at his birth and preceded him in his teaching,[3] proclaiming Christ my God in the midst of the wilderness, then was he fully revealed and went as intermediary to those peoples who were afar and those who were near, being a cornerstone joining both. He bestowed on mortals the twofold cleansing of the everlasting Spirit who purged for me the former evil born of flesh and made pure my human blood. For mine is the blood Christ my Lord poured

out, a ransom for primal ills, a recompense for the world. PERSONAL POEMS 8.64-81, ON THE TESTAMENTS AND COMING OF CHRIST.[4]

THE VIRGIN'S PURITY IS HIS MATERIAL SUBSISTENCE. GREGORY OF NYSSA: Human nature takes its subsistence from the conjunction of an intellectual soul with a body. . . . In the case of humankind in general we think of some life-giving power coming on matter, as a result of which a person is formed, consisting of soul and body. In the case of the virgin birth, the power of the Highest was implanted immaterially in the undefiled body and took the Virgin's purity as the material for the flesh, employing it as the contribution of the virgin body toward the formation of one who was in truth a new man . . . created after the likeness of God, not in the fashion of humankind. The divine power spread through all this compound nature equally, so that neither part was without its share in the Godhead. In both parts (that is, in body and soul) the two elements (the divinity and the humanity) duly coalesced and corresponded. . . . The divine nature was implanted in both body and soul in corresponding measure and became united to both. AGAINST APOLLINARIS 54.[5]

BORN OF THE VIRGIN BY THE HOLY SPIRIT. HILARY OF POITIERS: The Lord himself, when expounding the mystery of his nativity, said, "I am the living bread, I who came down from heaven."[6] He calls himself bread, for he himself is the origin of his own body. So that it should not be thought the power and nature of the Word left him when he became flesh, he spoke again of his bread, so that by "the bread that comes down from heaven" it might be understood that his body does not derive from human conception, being shown to be heavenly. It is "his bread," and this proclaims the assumption of a body by the Word, for he added, "Unless you eat the flesh of the Son of man and drink

---

[1]Jn 1:1. [2]ECF 387. [3]John the Baptist. [4]PA 45, 47. [5]LCF 137.
[6]Jn 6:51.

his blood, you will not have life in you."[7] He is the Son of man, and he himself descended as the bread from heaven. Thus by his "bread that comes down from heaven" and by the "flesh and blood of the Son of man" is understood the assumption of flesh conceived by the Holy Spirit and born of a virgin. ON THE TRINITY 10.18.[8]

CONCEIVED FROM THE EVER-VIRGIN. LEO THE GREAT: For he was conceived of the Holy Spirit, in the womb of the virgin mother, who brought him forth without loss of virginity, even as she conceived him without loss of virginity. LETTER 28.2 (THE TOME OF LEO).[9]

BORN AS LIBERATOR FROM THE IMMACU-LATE ONE. SYNOD OF TOLEDO (675): Of these three persons we believe that the Son alone assumed a true human nature, a sinless nature, from the holy and immaculate Virgin Mary for the liberation of the human race. He was born from her in a new manner and with a new birth: in a new manner because, though invisible in his divinity, he appears visibly in his humanity, and with a new birth because an undefiled virgin who did not have intercourse with man was made fruitful by the Holy Spirit and thereby furnished the substance for his human flesh. This virgin birth can neither be fully understood, nor can another example of it be pointed out. Were it fully understood, it would not be miraculous; were there another example, it would cease to be unique. However, we must not think that because Mary conceived when the Holy Spirit overshadowed her, this Spirit is therefore the Father of the Son, for thus we would seem to assert that there are two fathers of the Son, an assertion that is surely wrong. ELEVENTH COUNCIL OF TOLEDO, CREEDAL STATEMENT.[10]

Mary the Mother of God (Theotokos)

THOSE WHO DENY THE THEOTOKOS ARE ALIEN FROM GOD. GREGORY OF NAZIANZUS:

Anyone who does not admit that holy Mary is the mother of God (*theotokos*) is out of touch with the Godhead. Equally remote from God is anyone who says that Christ passed through the Virgin as through a channel, without being formed in her in a manner at once divine and human; divine, because without the agency of a man, and human, because it followed the normal process of gestation. It would be an offense to say that the human being was first formed and then the divinity supervened. This would not be the birth of God, rather an avoidance of birth. LETTER 101.5, TO CLEDONIUS.[11]

TO DENY GOD'S MOTHER IS TO DENY JESUS IS GOD. CYRIL OF ALEXANDRIA: I am amazed that there are some who are extremely doubtful whether the holy Virgin should be called mother of God or not. For if our Lord Jesus Christ is God, then surely the holy Virgin who gave him birth must be God's mother. . . . But you may say, "Now tell me, was the Virgin the mother of the Godhead?" My reply is that the living and subsistent Word of God is begotten of the substance of God the Father, as all acknowledge, and has his existence without beginning in time, always coexisting with his Father, having his being in and with the Father, and thus presented to our minds. But in the last times of this age, when he became flesh, that is, and was united with flesh endowed with a rational soul, he is said also to have been begotten through a woman according to the flesh. This mystery of the incarnate Word has some similarity with human birth. For mothers of ordinary people, in obedience to the natural laws of generation, carry in the womb the flesh that gradually takes shape and develops through the secret operations of God until it reaches perfection and attains the form of a human being; and God endows this living creature with spirit, in a manner known only to himself, as the prophet says, "He forms a man's spirit within him." The

[7]Jn 6:53. [8]*LCF* 51. [9]*CCC* 316. [10]*TCT* 184. [11]*LCF* 107**.

condition of flesh is very different from that of spirit. But although those mothers are only the mothers of bodies belonging to this world, still they are said to give birth, not to a part of a person but to the whole person, consisting of soul and body. . . . If anyone maintained that anyone's mother was only "mother of flesh" and not "mother of soul," he would be talking nonsense. For what she has produced is one living being, a composite of two dissimilar elements, but a single human being, with each element retaining its own nature. LETTER 1, To the MONKS OF EGYPT.[12]

THE SIGNIFICANCE OF THEOTOKOS. CYRIL OF ALEXANDRIA: Inspired Scripture says that the Word from God the Father was incarnate, that is, was united to flesh without confusion, hypostatically.[13] The body was united with the Word. The body, born of a woman, was not alien from him. Just as the body of each one of us belongs to the individual person, so the body of the Only-Begotten belonged to him. . . .

If the Word had not been begotten, according to the flesh, in the same way as we are, if he had not shared in our condition in this way, he would not have freed human nature from the guilt we inherited from Adam or have driven away the corruption from our bodies. . . . But you affect to be afraid that some of us may suspect that the Word begotten from the Father had the beginning of his existence from earthly flesh. You utterly destroy the mystery of the economy in the flesh[14] when you say that we must not give to the holy Virgin the title "mother of God" (theotokos). . . . You would yourself approve the correct and holy faith of those who so believe, if you would bring yourself to consider and to acknowledge that Christ is truly God, that he is one and is the only Son of the God and Father, not divided into God and man. You should say, rather, that he is one and the same, the Word from the Father, and man from a woman, just as we are, while he always remains God. AGAINST NESTORIUS 1.1.[15]

BECAUSE OF THE THEOTOKOS THE CURSE WAS LIFTED. CYRIL OF ALEXANDRIA: But since the holy Virgin brought forth, after the flesh, God personally united to flesh, for this reason we say of her that she is mother of God (theotokos), not as though the nature of the Word had its beginning of existence from the flesh, for he "was in the beginning, and the Word was God, and the Word was with God,"[16] and he is the Maker of the worlds, coeternal with the Father and the Creator of the universe; but, as we said before, the Virgin is called theotokos because having personally united man's nature to himself, the Word accepted even to be born in the flesh, from her womb. Not that he needed of necessity or for his own nature to be born in time and in the last ages of the world; rather, that he might bless the very first element of our being and that, a woman having borne him united to flesh, from that point onward the curse that was lying on our whole race might be made to cease, that which sends to death our bodies which are of the earth. So also might the sentence, "In sorrow shall you bring forth children,"[17] be annulled by him, and the words of the prophet might be verified, "Death prevailed and swallowed up, and then again God wiped away every tear from every face."[18] THIRD LETTER TO NESTORIUS (LETTER 17).[19]

TO AFFIRM THEOTOKOS IS OF THE SUBSTANCE OF THE FAITH. CYRIL OF ALEXANDRIA: Now the statements that your Religiousness[20] must anathematize are subjoined to this letter of ours. First: If anyone does not confess Emmanuel to be very God and does not acknowledge the holy Virgin consequently to be the mother of God (theotokos), for she brought forth after the flesh the Word of God become flesh, let him be anathema. Second: If anyone does not confess that the Word that is of God

---

[12]LCF 252. [13]Personally. [14]The incarnation and all acts of humility associated with it. [15]LCF 255**. [16]Jn 1:1. [17]Gen 3:16. [18]Is 25:8. [19]CCC 286. [20]Nestorius.

the Father has been personally [21] united to flesh and is one Christ with his own flesh, the same one being both God and man alike, let him be anathema. THIRD LETTER TO NESTORIUS (LETTER 17).[22]

GOD WAS INCARNATE OF MARY THE THEOTOKOS. CYRIL OF ALEXANDRIA: In accordance with this sense of the unconfused union,[23] we confess the holy Virgin to be *theotokos*, because God the Word became incarnate, and was made man and from the very conception united to himself the temple[24] taken from her. And as to the expressions concerning the Lord in the Gospels and Epistles, we are aware that theologians understand some as common, as relating to one person, and others they distinguish as relating to two natures; explaining those that befit the divine nature according to the Godhead of Christ and those of a humble sort according to his manhood. LETTER 39, TO JOHN OF ANTIOCH (THE FORMULA OF REUNION).[25]

THE THEOTOKOS AFFIRMS JESUS WAS FULLY HUMAN. CYRIL OF ALEXANDRIA: For you ought, I say, to be aware that almost the whole of our contention for the faith has grown out of our affirmation that the holy Virgin is the mother of God (*theotokos*). But if we affirm that the holy body of Christ, the Savior of us all, was from heaven and was not born of her, how can she be conceived of as *theotokos*? For whom in the world did she bear, if it be not true that she bore Emmanuel according to the flesh? Let them be treated with scorn, then, who mouth this kind of nonsense[26] about us. LETTER 39, TO JOHN OF ANTIOCH (THE FORMULA OF REUNION).[27]

THE FAITHLESS RESIST THE THEOTOKOS TITLE. THEODORET OF CYR: Just as I believe, therefore, in one God the Father and in one Holy Spirit who proceeds from the Father, so I believe in one Lord Jesus Christ, the only-begotten Son of God, begotten from the Father

before all the ages, "radiance of the glory and image of the Father's reality,"[28] who for the salvation of human beings was made flesh, and became human and was born of the Virgin Mary according to the flesh. Paul also taught us this: "To whom belong the patriarchs, and from whom is born, according to the flesh, the Christ, God who is over all, blessed forever. Amen."[29] And he also said, "Concerning his Son, who was born of the seed of David according to the flesh, and was designated Son of God in power according to the spirit of holiness."[30] For this reason we also call the holy Virgin the mother of God (*theotokos*) and consider those who reject this title to be people with no faith. LETTER 83.19, TO DIOSCORUS OF ALEXANDRIA.[31]

HE IS FATHER AND SON TO HIS MOTHER. SYNOD OF TOLEDO (675): Christ contains in himself, therefore, a twofold substance, that of his own divinity and that of our humanity. However, inasmuch as he proceeded eternally from God the Father, he has been born, and nothing more; for inasmuch as he proceeded from the Father, he is not to be considered as creature or as predestined; but inasmuch as he was born of the Virgin Mary, we must believe that he is not only born but is also a creature and predestined. Yet in his case both the generations were wonderful: for he was born of the Father before time, without any mother; he was born of his mother in this latter age, without any father. As God he produced Mary; as man he was produced by Mary; he himself was both father and son to his mother Mary. As God he is equal to the Father; as man he is less than the Father. Similarly, it must be believed that he is both greater and less than himself, because in the form of God even the Son himself is greater

---

[21]Hypostatically. [22]CCC 286. [23]Of divinity and humanity in the one Christ. [24]Of his body. [25]CCC 291. [26]Claiming that Cyril had taught that the flesh of Christ was from heaven, thus accusing him of Apollinarism. [27]CCC 292. [28]Heb 1:3. [29]Rom 9:5. [30]Rom 1:3-4. [31]MFC 2:206.

than himself, because of the assumed human nature that is excelled by the divine; whereas in the servant's form, he is less than himself, that is, by reason of the human nature that is clearly less than the divine. Just as he is clearly less than either the Father or himself, because of the assumed human nature, so too he is coequal to the Father according to his divine nature; and he and the Father are greater than the human nature that the person of the Son alone assumed. Eleventh Council of Toledo, Creedal Statement.[32]

The Nativity of the Christ

The Hiddenness of the Virginity of Mary. Ignatius of Antioch: Now the virginity of Mary and her giving birth were hidden from the ruler of this age,[33] as was also the death of the Lord; three mysteries to be loudly proclaimed, yet which were accomplished in the silence of God. How, then, were they revealed to the ages? A star shone forth in heaven brighter than all the stars; its light was indescribable, and its strangeness caused amazement. All the rest of the constellations, together with the sun and moon, formed a chorus around the star, yet the star itself far outshone them all, and there was perplexity about the origin of this strange phenomenon that was so unlike the others. Consequently, all magic and every kind of spell were dissolved, the ignorance so characteristic of wickedness vanished, and the ancient kingdom[34] was abolished when God appeared in human form to bring the newness of eternal life and what had been prepared by God began to take effect. As a result, all things were thrown into ferment, because the abolition of death was being carried out. To the Ephesians 19.[35]

Wisdom Built Himself a House. Gregory of Nyssa: It was not in respect of his divinity, as he is in himself, that he was born of a woman. Existing before creation, he receives a birth in flesh but not his existence. The Holy Spirit pre-

pared the way for the entrance of the Son's own power. The Son did not need any physical material to make ready a special habitation, but, as is said of Wisdom, he "built himself a house"[36] and made into a man the dust from the Virgin, by means of which he was mingled with human nature. Against Apollinaris 9.[37]

The Mysteries of His Birth. Leo the Great: The birth of the flesh is a manifestation of human nature; the childbearing of a virgin is a token of divine power. The infancy of the babe is shown by its lowly cradle; the greatness of the most High is declared by the voices of angels. He whom Herod wickedly strives to kill is like a human infant; but he is the Lord of all whom the magi rejoice humbly to adore. Letter 28.4 (The Tome of Leo).[38]

The Paradoxes of His Nativity. Ephrem the Syrian: Come and hear, my friends, about the hidden Son who was revealed in his body, yet hidden was his power. For the power of the Son is a fluid power; the womb did not confine it as it did the body. For while the power dwelled in the womb, it was forming babes in the womb. His power embraced the one who embraced him,[39] for if his power were curtailed all would collapse. Indeed, the power that contained all creation, while he was in the womb, did not desert all. He formed his individuality, the image, in the womb, and he formed in all wombs all persons. Although he grew up among the poor, from the storehouse of plenty he provided for all. While again she who anointed him was anointing him, with his dew and his rain he anointed the universe. The magi offered myrrh and gold, although hidden in him was a treasure of wealth. The magi offered to him from what was his own: myrrh and frankincense that he had brought into existence and created. By power from him

---

[32]TCT 185-86. [33]Satan. [34]Of the ruler of the world. [35]AF 149. [36]Prov 9:1. [37]LCF 134. [38]CCC 319. [39]Mary.

Mary's womb became able to bear the One who bears all. From the great treasury of all creation Mary gave to him everything that she gave. She gave him milk from what he made exist. She gave him food from what he had created. He gave milk to Mary as God. In turn, he was given suck by her as human. Her arms carried him, for he lightened his weight, and her bosom embraced him, for he made himself small. Who would be able to measure his grandeur? He diminished his measurements corresponding to the garment.[40] She wove it and clothed him in it who had taken off his glory. She measured it anew and wove it for him who had now made himself small. The sea bore him, and it became calm and abated. How did the arms of Joseph bear him? The womb of Sheol[41] conceived him and burst open, and how did the womb of Mary sustain him? With his voice he split stones on graves; and how did Mary's bosom sustain him? You came to humiliation to save all: Glory to you from all who were saved by you! Who is able to speak about the hidden Son who came down and put on a body in the womb? HYMNS ON THE NATIVITY 4.172-93.[42]

THE SYMBOLS OF HIS BIRTH. THEODORET OF CYR: This, then, is how the Lord Christ was born: he sucks his mother's breast as we do; he is placed in a crib that served as a food trough for animals and thus censures human foolishness and displays his own love for humanity. For he provides nourishment as God, and in his humanity becomes the food of human beings who were suffering from the terrible disease of foolishness. But now that human nature has cast off foolishness and taken on reason, it is welcomed at the mystical table, which is symbolized by the crib. ON DIVINE PROVIDENCE 10.4.[43]

Mary the New Eve

THE UNTILLED SOIL FROM WHICH NEW ADAM ARISES. IRENAEUS: He restored in himself his ancient handiwork. As through one man's disobedience sin gained entrance and death obtained power as a result of sin, so through the obedience of one man righteousness was introduced, and he causes life to flourish in human beings, who before were dead. And as Adam was first made from untilled soil and received his being from virgin earth (since God had not yet sent rain and man had not yet cultivated the ground) and was fashioned by the hand of God, that is, by the Word of God, "by whom all things were made,"[44] so he who existed as the Word restored in himself Adam, by his birth from Mary who was still virgin, a birth befitting this restoration of Adam. AGAINST HERESIES 3.21.10.[45]

THE FAITHFUL OBEDIENCE OF THE NEW EVE. IRENAEUS: Eve, by her disobedience, brought death on herself and on all the human race: Mary, by her obedience, brought salvation. AGAINST HERESIES 3.22.4.[46]

MARY REVERSES THE FAULT OF EVE. TERTULLIAN: The devil had taken captive the image and likeness of God,[47] but God restored it by a parallel process. For the word that was the architect of death found its way into the ear of Eve while she was still virgin; correspondingly, the Word of God, which was the builder of life, had to be introduced into a virgin, so that what had gone to destruction through the female sex should by the same sex be restored to salvation. Eve believed the serpent; Mary believed Gabriel. The one sinned by believing; the other by believing effaced the sin. But did Eve conceive nothing in her womb from the devil's word? She certainly did. For the devil's word was the seed for her, so that thereafter she should give birth as an outcast and give birth in sorrow. And in fact she bore a devil who

---

[40]The garment of flesh, or the body. [41]Biblical symbol of death. [42]ESH 101-3*. [43]MFC 2:199. [44]Heb 2:10; Jn 1:3. [45]ECF 113. [46]ECF 101. [47]Humankind.

murdered his brother; while Mary gave birth to one who should in time bring salvation to Israel, his own brother after the flesh and his own murderer. Thus God sent down into the womb his Word, the good brother, that he might wipe out the memory of the wicked brother. It was necessary that Christ should come forth for humankind's salvation from that place into which humankind had entered when already condemned. ON THE FLESH OF CHRIST 17.[48]

The Holy Family

HOW JOSEPH WAS MARY'S HUSBAND. CYRIL OF JERUSALEM: Let us remember these things, brethren: let us use these weapons in our defense. Let us not endure those heretics who teach Christ's coming as a phantom.[49] Let us abhor those also who say that the Savior's birth was of husband and wife, who have dared to say that he was the child of Joseph and Mary because it is written, "And he took her as his wife."[50] For let us remember Jacob, who, before he received Rachel, said to Laban, "Give me my wife."[51] She was called the "wife" of Jacob even before the wedding. So it was with Mary. Because she had been betrothed, she too was called the wife of Joseph. Note how accurate is the Gospel: "And in the sixth month the angel Gabriel was sent from God to a city of Galilee, named Nazareth, to a virgin espoused to a man whose name was Joseph,"[52] and so forth. And again when the census took place and Joseph went up to enroll himself, what does the Scripture say? "And Joseph also went up from Galilee, to enroll himself with Mary who was espoused to him, who was already pregnant." Even though she was with child, it still does not say "with his wife" but rather with her who was "espoused to him." For God sent forth his Son, says Paul, not made of a man and a woman but made "of a woman,"[53] that is, of a virgin. For the virgin also is called a woman, as we demonstrated before. For he who makes souls virgin was himself born of a virgin. CATECHETICAL

LECTURES 12.31.[54]

MARY'S SONG OF JOSEPH. ROMANOS THE MELODIST: "I will tell you," Mary said to the magi, "why I keep Joseph in my house: to refute all those who slander me. He will tell what he has heard about my child. For in his sleep he saw a holy angel who told him how I had conceived. In the night a fiery vision told the creature of thorn about the things that grieved him. That is why Joseph is with me, to show that there is a little child, who is God before the ages." KONTAKION ON THE NATIVITY 11.[55]

The Christ Born of David's Line

CHRIST IS THE DESCENDENT OF DAVID. IGNATIUS OF ANTIOCH: Continue to gather together, each and every one of you, collectively and individually by name, in grace, in one faith and one Jesus Christ, who physically was a descendant of David, who is Son of man and Son of God, in order that you may obey the bishop and the presbytery with an undisturbed mind, breaking one bread, which is the medicine of immortality, the antidote we take in order not to die but to live forever in Jesus Christ. TO THE EPHESIANS 20.2.[56]

THE SON OF DAVID WAS TRULY MAN. IGNATIUS OF ANTIOCH: Be deaf, therefore, whenever anyone speaks to you apart from Jesus Christ, who was of the house of David, who was the son of Mary; who really was born, who both ate and drank; who really was persecuted under Pontius Pilate, who really was crucified and died while those in heaven and on earth and under the earth looked on; who, moreover, really was raised from the dead when his Father raised him up, who (his Father, that is) in the same way will likewise also raise us up in Christ Jesus

---

[48]ECF 174. [49]The Docetics, who taught that Christ was an immaterial spirit who only appeared to be flesh. [50]Mt 1:24. [51]Gen 29:21. [52]Lk 1:27. [53]Gal 4:4. [54]NPNF 2 7:80. [55]SLS 7. [56]AF 149-51.

who believe in him, apart from whom we have no true life. To the Trallians 9.1-2.[57]

Some Deny His Human Descent as Christ. Ignatius of Antioch: Now note well those who hold heretical opinions about the grace of Jesus Christ that came to us; note how contrary they are to the mind of God. They have no concern for love, none for the widow, none for the orphan, none for the oppressed, none for the prisoner or the one released, none for the hungry or thirsty. They abstain from the Eucharist and from prayer, because they refuse to acknowledge that the Eucharist is the flesh of our Savior Jesus Christ, who suffered for our sins and whom the Father by his goodness raised up. To the Smyrneans 6.2.[58]

Jesus Is the Christ Come in the Flesh. Polycarp of Smyrna: For everyone "who does not confess that Jesus Christ has come in the flesh is antichrist,"[59] and whoever does not acknowledge the testimony of the cross "is of the devil."[60] And whoever twists the sayings of the Lord to suit his own sinful desires and claims that there is neither resurrection nor judgment, well, that person is the firstborn of Satan. Therefore let us leave behind the worthless speculation of the crowd and their false teachings, and let us return to the word delivered to us from the beginning. To the Philippians 7.1-2.[61]

Truly Christ and Truly Human. Leo the Great: Nor should Eutyches, speaking with intent to deceive, have said that the Word became flesh in such a way that Christ, born of the Virgin's womb, had the form of man but had not the reality of his mother's body. Or can it be that he supposed that our Lord Jesus was not of our nature because the angel, when sent to the blessed Mary ever-virgin, declared, "The Holy Spirit shall come upon you, and the power of the most High shall overshadow you; therefore also that holy thing[62] that shall be born of you shall be called the Son of God,"[63] on the supposition that, because the conception of the Virgin was an act of God, therefore the flesh of the one conceived was not of the nature of her that conceived it? But that birth, so uniquely wonderful and so wonderfully unique, ought not so to be understood that the distinctive character of its kind was lost through the novelty of its origin. For the Holy Spirit gave fruitfulness to the Virgin, but the reality of the body was received from her own body. When "Wisdom was building herself a house,"[64] the "Word was made flesh and dwelled in us,"[65] that is, in that flesh that he took from humanity and that he quickened with the spirit of a rational life. Letter 28.2 (The Tome of Leo).[66]

[57]AF 165. [58]AF 189. [59]1 Jn 4:2-3. [60]1 Jn 3:8. [61]AF 213-15. [62]The Fathers generally note the literal use of the neuter in this scriptural verse when commenting on it. [63]Lk 1:35. [64]Prov 14:1. [65]Jn 1:14. [66]CCC 317.

AND WAS MADE MAN

καὶ εἰς ἕνα κύριον Ἰησοῦν Χριστόν,	Et in unum Dominum Jesum Christum,	We believe in one Lord, Jesus Christ,
τὸν υἱὸν τοῦ Θεοῦ τὸν μονογενῆ,	Filium Dei unigenitum,	the only Son of God,
τὸν ἐκ τοῦ πατρὸς γεννηθέντα	et ex Patre natum	eternally
πρὸ πάντων τῶν αἰώνων,	ante omnia saecula	begotten of the Father,
φῶς ἐκ φωτός,	[Deum de Deo], Lumen de Lumine,	[God from God], Light from Light,
Θεὸν ἀληθινὸν ἐκ θεοῦ ἀληθινοῦ,	Deum verum de Deo vero,	true God from true God,
γεννηθέντα, οὐ ποιηθέντα,	genitum, non factum,	begotten, not made,
ὁμοούσιον τῷ πατρὶ·	consubstantialem Patri;	of one Being with the Father.
δι᾽ οὗ τὰ πάντα ἐγένετο·	per quem omnia facta sunt;	Through him all things were made.
τὸν δι᾽ ἡμᾶς τοὺς ἀνθρώπους	qui propter nos homines	For us
καὶ διὰ τὴν ἡμετέραν σωτηρίαν	et propter nostram salutem	and for our salvation
κατελθόντα ἐκ τῶν οὐρανῶν	descendit de coelis,	he came down from heaven:
καὶ σαρκωθέντα ἐκ πνεύματος ἁγίου	et incarnatus est de Spiritu Sancto	by the power of the Holy Spirit
καὶ Μαρίας τῆς παρθένου	ex Maria virgine,	he became incarnate from the Virgin Mary,
καὶ ἐνανθρωπήσαντα,	**et homo factus est;**	**and was made man.**

HISTORICAL CONTEXT: The earlier Christian confession of the incarnation as the Word being made flesh (turning around Jn 1:14) that we find in the previous clauses of the creed was being heavily pressed by the middle of the third century. At first the church had set the doctrine of the incarnation of the divine Word against all forms of Gnostic supposition that flesh and spirit were antagonistic opposites, in a world where the truth demanded only the flight of the spirit from the wickedness of materiality. With its unwavering insistence on the historicity of Jesus' life and its perennially valid and unique reconciliation of the world to God, the early doctrine of the incarnation offered a kerygma of a sacramental view of the harmony of the spirit and the flesh in the person of Christ. Here was a radical vision, profoundly new in the context of the Hellenistic world, of God's humble acceptance of limitations, in order to transfigure a race that had become enslaved to death.

But the mythological context of thinking was still pervasive in the ancient Greek world, and several thinkers after the Gnostic era were led astray by it in different ways. One such way is apparent in the Arian controversy, where strict desire to separate deity from all contact with flesh and history is noticeable. God is in his highest heaven, as far as the Arians were concerned, and Christ was a created servant of God sent to earth. Flesh and spirit can never mingle without the concept of the divine being defiled. Opposing them, some theologians, especially Apollinaris of Laodicea, wanted to teach that Jesus was God and, being the source of all intellect and wisdom, did not need a human mind when he assumed a human body but supplied his own eternal mind to the body and directed the soulless flesh of Christ from his own power as Logos. This allowed Apollinaris to imagine a perfect inhabitation of the flesh by the Word, without the Word having to be limited in any way in his human life. The same desire to keep spirit and flesh separate in strict categories led to opposite denigrations of the reality of the incarnation. Arians denied its divine reality. Apollinarists denied its truly human authenticity.

In rising to the challenge of these two schools, the Nicene orthodox party took the brave step of embracing the paradoxes of a commitment to two difficult principles: that the Word of God, fully divine, was the one who was the single incarnate Lord, and that the Lord assumed a truly human life and lived it as his own life, in such a way that the suffering of his body could be said (shocking though it was to hear it) to be the sufferings of the impassible Word. It was understood that when one attributed suffering to the Word of God, one was always talking about the Word of God incarnate. Nevertheless, the radical commitment to the double notions of perfect Godhead and perfect manhood for the one incarnate Lord was a confession of faith that troubled the fourth and fifth centuries of the church in a deep way. It might even today be said to the central question of christological faith. The great Nicene teachers come back time and time again to the profound paradox that the incarnation represents. The Nicene fathers added "and was made man" to make sure that no one took refuge in mythological understandings of the Word assuming flesh (like a pagan Greek god masquerading at being human). For them, the incarnation was no less than the stooping down of the divine Lord to heal and comfort his own creation. Their eloquent and robust words retain all their power and force today.

OVERVIEW: The Word was made flesh and assumed a personal existence within history (GREGORY OF NAZIANZUS). The Word wove for himself a robe of flesh in the womb of the Virgin Mary (EPHREM). This means that he truly became a man (THEODORE, CYRIL OF ALEXANDRIA, AUGUSTINE) and did not simply inhabit a man (ATHANASIUS, AUGUSTINE). This stooping down into incarnation was no matter of shame for the Logos (GREGORY OF NYSSA,

AUGUSTINE). For a short time we saw him living in our weakness (GREGORY OF NYSSA), though he always remained what he was as God (CYRIL OF ALEXANDRIA). As a man the incarnate Lord was sinless and perfect (HILARY, AMBROSE). When he assumed the flesh, he thereby became the supreme mediator between divine spirit and the flesh (TERTULLIAN, CYRIL OF ALEXANDRIA, LEO). He had become small for our sake (EPHREM). In his incarnation he became the physician for the human race (EUSEBIUS, CYRIL OF JERUSALEM, GREGORY OF NYSSA). The incarnation was for our instruction and forgiveness (CLEMENT OF ALEXANDRIA, EUSEBIUS, CYRIL OF ALEXANDRIA), for our rescue (GREGORY OF NAZIANZUS) and for our exaltation (HILARY). By becoming flesh, the Word set a trap for death and broke its power over humanity (CYRIL OF JERUSALEM, CYRIL OF ALEXANDRIA, ROMANOS). He was firstborn of Mary, signifying that his humanity and life on earth were authentic (CYRIL OF JERUSALEM, ATHANASIUS). The incarnate Lord is the high priest of the human race (THEODORET) and the measure of the perfect human being (CYRIL OF ALEXANDRIA). He is the consummation of humanity, who offers up to God the entire race (GREGORY OF NAZIANZUS). His incarnation is a universal blessing on our race (AMBROSE, CHRYSOSTOM, AUGUSTINE). Because he was truly and fully a man (ORIGEN, AMBROSE, DAMASUS, COUNCIL OF CONSTANTINOPLE) he was endowed with a rational soul (HILARY, GREGORY OF NAZIANZUS, THEODORE).

In the person of Emmanuel (ATHANASIUS, EPHREM, ARNOBIUS, CYRIL OF ALEXANDRIA) two natures, of divinity and humanity, are brought into a unity (ATHANASIUS, APOLLINARIS, THEODORET) that is dynamically inseparable and profoundly organic, like a lily with its perfume or a soul with its own body (CYRIL OF ALEXANDRIA) or like heat within molten iron (ORIGEN). In this union of natures the one Christ is the sacrament of the reunion between God and humankind (HILARY). The way to confess this is to admit two natures but only one person (GREGORY OF NAZIANZUS, AMBROSE), but the two-ness must never lead us to think that the natures have not come together into an inseparable union (CYRIL OF ALEXANDRIA, CHRYSOSTOM). This is why the church offers only one single worship and adoration to the incarnate Lord as God in the flesh (CYRIL OF ALEXANDRIA, THEODORE, SECOND COUNCIL OF CONSTANTINOPLE).

When Scripture speaks of the Lord in diverse ways, it is referring to his two conditions (ORIGEN, AMBROSE, THEODORET), but a true disciple must understand that all Scripture refers always to one and the same Lord and Son under different figures (ATHANASIUS, CYRIL OF ALEXANDRIA, LEO, COUNCIL OF CHALCEDON). The closeness of the union is not a static or mechanical one, for the humanity of Christ is transfigured by it (ORIGEN, GREGORY OF NAZIANZUS, GREGORY OF NYSSA, CYRIL OF ALEXANDRIA). All the human acts of Jesus were thereby suffused by divine grace and power (CHRYSOSTOM, THEODORET, CYRIL OF ALEXANDRIA, LEO). In the incarnation the human will of Christ is perfectly conformed to the divine will in all things (ORIGEN, ATHANASIUS, GREGORY OF NAZIANZUS, GREGORY OF NYSSA). Thus, the confession of the ensouled Christ is important. He assumes the human will in order to heal it, for it was in the will that sin first abounded (GREGORY OF NAZIANZUS, THEODORE). It is necessary, then, to confess one person and two wills (THIRD COUNCIL OF CONSTANTINOPLE). The incarnate Lord may be known by many diverse titles (EPHREM), but his title as Son of man indicates his assumption of the flesh within history (GREGORY OF NYSSA, CYRIL OF ALEXANDRIA), though even so, we ought to note that it is the Son of man who sits on the heavenly throne as judge of the worlds (CYRIL OF ALEXANDRIA).

The Word Is Made Flesh

THE WORD ASSUMES A PERSONAL EXISTENCE. GREGORY OF NAZIANZUS: If anyone says that the Godhead operated in him by grace, as in a prophet, instead of being joined to the humanity in a permanent union, in respect of substance, such a man is himself devoid of such working of God within him; in fact he is filled with a contrary inspiration. LETTER 101.6, TO CLEDONIUS.[1]

THE LOGOS DOES NOT INHABIT A MAN, HE BECOMES ONE. ATHANASIUS: He became man, and did not come into a man. We must be clear about this, to avoid the notion that the Word dwelled in a man, hallowing him and displaying himself in him, as in earlier times the Word came to each of the saints. In that case there would have been no paradox, and those who saw him would not have been startled, as when they said, "Where does this man come from"[2] and, "You are a man. Why do you make yourself God?"[3] They were quite accustomed to this idea, as in the words "the Word of the Lord came"[4] to the various prophets. But in fact the Word of God, "through whom all things came into being,"[5] endured to become also Son of man and "humbled himself, taking the form of a servant";[6] and for this reason the cross of Christ is "a scandal to the Jews, but to us, Christ is God's power and God's wisdom."[7] For "the Word became flesh,"[8] as John says, and in Scripture "flesh" is commonly used for "man." AGAINST THE ARIANS 3.30.[9]

WE SEE THE WORD LIVING ON EARTH. GREGORY OF NYSSA: We do not ascribe our salvation to a mere man, nor do we admit that the incorruptible divine nature is liable to suffering and death. But we must certainly believe the inspired utterances that proclaim that the Word "which was in the beginning was God"[10]

---

[1]*LCF* 107-8. [2]Mt 21:10; Lk 5:21; 9:9; Jn 12:34. [3]Jn 10:33. [4]Gen 15:1; 1 Sam 15:10; 1 Kings 6:11. [5]Heb 2:10; 1 Cor 8:6. [6]Phil 2:7. [7]1 Cor 1:24. [8]Jn 1:14. [9]*ECF* 396. [10]Jn 1:2.

and that afterwards the "Word made flesh" was seen on the earth and lived in intercourse with people. And therefore we admit into our faith those ideas that accord with the inspired utterance. When we are told that he is light, power, righteousness, life and truth, that "through him the whole universe was made,"[11] we count all such statements as worthy of belief, and we refer them to the Word who is God. But when we hear of pain, sleep, need, distress, bonds, nails, the spear, the blood and the wounds and the burial and the tomb and other things of this kind, then, even though these are somewhat contrary to the epithets mentioned above, we nevertheless accept them as things to be believed and as true, in respect of the flesh, which we accept as part of our faith, together with the Word. It is impossible to consider the attributes proper to the flesh as existing in the "Word which was in the beginning." AGAINST EUNOMIUS 6.1.[12]

THE WORD ASSUMES THE WEAKNESS OF FLESH. GREGORY OF NYSSA: Apollinaris must not falsely represent our argument, saying that we assert that the only-begotten God was not always Christ. Christ existed always, not only in the time of the dispensation[13] but also afterwards. But the human nature did not exist before or after but only during the season of the dispensation. For the humanity did not exist before the birth from the Virgin, nor did the flesh remain, with its own properties, after the ascent to heaven.[14] "If once we knew Christ in the flesh, we do not still know him in this way."[15] For the flesh did not continue in being because God had been displayed in flesh. Human nature is subject to change, whereas the divine nature is unchangeable. Therefore the Godhead remains unmoved in face of every change, not being altered for the worse (for it does not admit of deterioration, nor is it susceptible of improvement), while the human nature in Christ undergoes a change for the better, from perishable to imperishable . . .

from short-lived to eternal, from corporeal to incorporeal, freed from the limits of a physical shape. AGAINST APOLLINARIS 53.[16]

GOD BECOMES REALLY HUMAN. AUGUSTINE: We are changeable, and we are changed for the better by becoming partakers of the Word. The Word is changeless and suffered no change for the worse when he became partaker of flesh by means of a rational soul. The Apollinarian heretics wrongly suppose that the man Christ either had no soul or had no rational soul. The Scripture, in saying "The Word became flesh,"[17] employs its customary idiom of using "flesh" for "man," in order to show the humility of Christ more emphatically, to avoid seeming to shun the title "flesh" as if it were something unworthy. The saying, "All flesh shall see the salvation of God"[18] is not to be taken as excluding "souls." "The Word became flesh" simply means "The Son of God became a Son of man." . . . Just as the accession of flesh to soul to constitute one man does not create a plurality of persons, so no plurality is effected by the accession of man to Word, so as to constitute one Christ. And the statement "the Word became flesh" is intended to make us understand the singularity of this person, not to lead us to imagine the conversion of the divinity into flesh. LETTER 140.12.[19]

The Assumption of the Flesh

JESUS THE MEDIATOR IS FLESH AND SPIRIT. TERTULLIAN: Therefore, learn with Nicodemus that "what is born in flesh" is flesh and what is born of the Spirit is spirit.[20] Flesh does not become spirit, or spirit flesh; they can clearly exist in one person. Jesus consisted of flesh and spirit; of flesh as man, of spirit as God. The angel at the time proclaimed him Son of God, in respect that he was Spirit, keeping for the

---

[11]Jn 1:3. [12]*LCF* 139. [13]That is, the economy of the incarnation in history. [14]In other words, the human nature is glorified in heaven. [15]2 Cor 5:16. [16]*LCF* 136. [17]Jn 1:14. [18]Lk 3:6. [19]*LCF* 217. [20]Jn 3:6.

flesh the title Son of man. Thus also the apostle confirms that he was composed of two realities, when he designated him the "mediator of God and people."[21] AGAINST PRAXEAS 27.[22]

THE LIMITS OF THE FLESH ARE NOT SHAMEFUL. TERTULLIAN: At any rate Christ loved humanity, humanity who is solidified in the womb, among all the uncleanness, who issues through the shameful parts, who is reared by means of all the indignities of infancy. For his sake Christ descended, for his sake he preached, for his sake "he humbled himself even unto death, the death of the cross."[23] Certainly he loved him whom he redeemed at so great a cost. . . . Therefore in loving humanity he loved the process of birth also, and his flesh. Nothing can be loved apart from that through which it has existence. Take away the process of birth, and then show me the person. Take away the flesh and then show me whom Christ redeemed. If these constitute those whom God redeemed, how can you represent them as humiliating to him,[24] seeing that he redeemed them? How can you represent them as unworthy of him, seeing that he would not have redeemed them, had he not loved them? He reforms our birth by a new birth from heaven. He restores our flesh from all that afflicts it. He cleanses it when leprous, gives it new light when blind, new strength when paralyzed, exorcizes it when possessed by demons and even raises it to life when dead. So what humiliation was there in being born in flesh? ON THE FLESH OF CHRIST 4.[25]

OUR HUMANITY WAS ASSUMED BY GOD. CYRIL OF ALEXANDRIA: This is why we gave way to them:[26] not to divide the one Son into two, God forbid, but only insofar as to confess that there occurred neither confusion nor mixing, but that the flesh was flesh assumed from a woman, whereas the Word was Word begotten from the Father, or rather that since the Word has become flesh, as John tells us, there is one Christ and Son and Lord. Try and get them all

to read carefully the letter of the blessed pope Athanasius.[27] Since in his day certain people were looking for an argument and saying that God the Word made a figurative body for himself out of his own nature, he argues throughout that the body was not consubstantial with the Word. And if it was not consubstantial then there must be two different natures out of which is understood the one and only Son. LETTER TO EULOGIUS.[28]

TRUE GOD BECOMES TRUE MAN. CYRIL OF ALEXANDRIA: We say that the unique Word of God, who was begotten of the very substance of the Father, who is true God of true God, the Light of Light, through whom all things came into being, both things in heaven and things in earth, coming down for the sake of our salvation and humbling himself even to emptying,[29] was made flesh and became man. That is, taking flesh of the holy Virgin and making it his own from the womb, he underwent a birth like ours and came forth a man of woman, not throwing off what he was, but even though he became man by the assumption of flesh and blood, yet still remaining what he was, that is, God indeed in nature and truth. We do not say that the flesh was changed into the nature of Godhead or that the ineffable nature of the Word of God was transformed into the nature of flesh, for he is unchangeable and unalterable, always remaining the same according to the Scriptures. THIRD LETTER TO NESTORIUS (LETTER 17).[30]

THE EMBODIED WORD WAS LIKE US BUT SINLESS. HILARY OF POITIERS: If, besides the mystery of weeping, thirst and hunger, the flesh (that is, the whole man) was assumed, then the

---

[21]1 Tim 2:5. [22]ECF 167-68. [23]Phil 2:8. [24]Tertullian is rhetorically addressing Marcion of Sinope, who had disparaged a fleshly existence of the Savior as something unbecoming. [25]ECF 172. [26]Explaining why he had signed the Formula of Reunion set to him by the Syrians, asserting the "two natures" abiding in Christ. [27]Athanasius's letter to Epictetus. [28]CACC 350. [29]Kenōsis (see Phil 2:5-11). [30]LCC 3:350.

flesh was subject to natural passions but not so subject as to be overwhelmed by the hurt of sufferings. . . . The ordinary behavior of the body was accepted to show the reality of his body. . . . When he took drink and food, he did not submit himself to bodily necessity but to customary bodily behavior. He had a body, but one appropriate to its origin; not owing its being to the faults of human conception, but existing in the form of our body by his divine power. He bore the form of a servant, but he was free from the sins and weaknesses of a human body, so that we might be in him through his birth from a virgin but that our weaknesses should not be in him in virtue of the divine power of his origin from himself. On the Trinity 10.24-25.[31]

There Is One Christ, Not Two Sons.

Theodoret of Cyr: I am not aware that I have ever so far taught a belief in two sons. For I was instructed to believe in one Only-Begotten, Jesus Christ our Lord, God the Word made man. But I understand the difference between flesh and Godhead, and in my opinion it is impiety to divide our one Lord Jesus Christ into two sons, just as also to take the opposite path and to speak of the Godhead of our Master, Christ, and his manhood, as one nature. Letter 109.[32]

The Human Face of God

The True Image of God. Eusebius of Caesarea: The material and senseless image, fashioned by base mechanic hands, of brass or iron, of gold or ivory, wood or stone, may be a fitting abode for evil spirits.[33] But that divine form, wrought by the power of heavenly wisdom, was possessed of life and spiritual being, a form animated by every excellence, the dwelling place of the Word of God, a holy temple of the holy God. Thus the indwelling Word conversed with and was known to human beings, as kindred with themselves; yet yielded not to passions such as theirs, nor owned, as the natural soul, subjection to the body. He did not part with

any of his intrinsic greatness. He did not change his proper Deity. For as the all-pervading radiance of the sun receives no stain from contact with dead and impure bodies, much less can the incorporeal power of the Word of God be injured in its essential purity or part with any of its greatness from spiritual contact with a human body. Oration on Constantine 14.3-4.[34]

The Word Came as Our Physician.

Eusebius of Caesarea: The Grecian myth tells us that Orpheus had power to charm ferocious beasts and tame their savage spirit by striking the chords of his instrument with a master hand. This story is celebrated by the Greeks, and generally believed, that an unconscious instrument could subdue the untamed brute and draw the trees from their places in obedience to its melodious power. But he who is the author of perfect harmony, the all-wise Word of God, desiring to apply every remedy to the manifold diseases of the souls of people, employed that human nature that is the workmanship of his own wisdom, as an instrument, by the melodious strains of which he soothed, not indeed the brute creation, but savages endued with reason, healing each furious temper, each fierce and angry passion of the soul, both in civilized and barbarous nations, by the remedial power of his divine doctrine. Like a physician of perfect skill, he met the diseases of their souls who sought for God in nature and in bodies, by a fitting and kindred remedy, and showed them God in human form. Oration on Constantine 14.5.[35]

The Immense God Makes Himself Small.

Ephrem the Syrian: If anyone seeks your hidden nature, behold, it is in heaven in the great womb of divinity. And if anyone seeks your revealed body, behold, it rests and looks out from the small womb of Mary. The mind

---

[31]*LCF* 53. [32]*LCF* 272-73. [33]He is referring to cult statues in the pagan temples. [34]NPNF 2 1:603. [35]NPNF 2 1:603.

wanders among your attributes, O rich One. Copious inner chambers are in your Godhead; contemptible appearances in your humanity. Who will measure you, great Sea who made himself small? We came to see you as God. Behold! You are a human being. We came to see you as a human being, and lo! the banner of your Godhead shines forth. Who can bear your transformations, O true One? HYMNS ON THE NATIVITY 13.7-9.[36]

THE HUMANITY OF GOD. EPHREM THE SYRIAN: The body taken from Mary rebuked that one who said that with another body the heavenly One dwelled in her.[37] Perfect is the body, but how did it grow with our bread? It has sweat and spit and tears and even blood. And if the ascended body is unsullied, still it resembles our body since it died. Renounce error and confess that their nature is one. HYMNS ON VIRGINITY 37.9.[38]

Why Did God Become Human?

THE NEW ADAM RESCUES HUMANITY. GREGORY OF NAZIANZUS: He who removes the curse[39] from me was called a curse on my account; he who takes away the sin of the world was called sin. And he becomes the new Adam to take the place of the old. In the same way he makes my insubordination his own, since he is the head of the whole body. So long as I am unsubjected and rebellious, by my refusal of God and because of my passions, Christ also is said to be unsubjected in respect of me. But when he has brought all things into subjection . . . then he himself has brought his subjection to fulfillment by bringing me over to a state of salvation. ORATION 30.5.[40]

THE INCARNATION EDUCATES US. CLEMENT OF ALEXANDRIA: The Lord, as God and man, gives us all kinds of profit and help. As God he forgives our sins; as man he educates us to be free from sin. CHRIST THE EDUCATOR 1.3.(7).[41]

HE BECOMES MAN TO RAISE HUMANITY. HILARY OF POITIERS: He is born as man, while remaining God: this is in contradiction of our natural understanding. That he should remain God, though born as man, does not contradict our natural hope. For the birth of a higher nature into a lower state gives us confidence that a lower nature can be born into a higher condition. ON THE TRINITY 9.4.[42]

THE INCARNATION ENTRAPS DEATH. CYRIL OF JERUSALEM: Thus we were saved by the very weapons with which the devil fought against us.[43] The Lord took from us a likeness to us, that he might save human nature. He took our likeness so that he might give greater grace to that which lacked; that sinful human nature might become partaker of God. "For where sin abounded, grace abounded overwhelmingly."[44] The Lord had to suffer for us, but if the devil had recognized him, he would not have dared to approach him. "For had they known, they would not have crucified the Lord of glory."[45] His body therefore became a bait for death, so that the dragon, hoping to swallow him, might vomit up also those whom he had swallowed. For death growing strong had swallowed us up, and yet "God has removed every tear from every face."[46] CATECHETICAL LECTURES 12.15.[47]

THE WORD ASSUMES HUMAN LIFE TO HEAL HUMANITY. CYRIL OF ALEXANDRIA: We maintain, therefore, that since human nature was suffering corruption because of Adam's transgression, and since our intellect was being tyrannized by the pleasures or rather the innate impulses of the flesh, then it was necessary that the Word of God should be incarnated for the

---

[36]ESH 138. [37]He is refuting Gnostic theories that the flesh of Christ was a phantasmal body. [38]ESH 426-27. [39]Gregory is reflecting on the significance of 1 Cor 15:25, which had been taken by the Arians as a proof text for the inferior status of the Son of God. [40]LCF 103. [41]ECF 246. [42]LCF 49. [43]He is commenting on Rom 7:23, which argues that the devil had used the flesh as a weapon against humanity. [44]Rom 5:20. [45]1 Cor 2:8. [46]Rev 7:17; see also Is 25:8. [47]LCF 36.

salvation of us who are on this earth. This was so he could make his own that human flesh that was subject to corruption and sick with its desires and destroy corruption within it, since he is Life and Lifegiver, bringing its innate sensual impulses to order. This was how the sin that lay within it was to be put to death, for we remember how the blessed Paul called our innate impulses the law of sin.[48] From the time that human flesh became the personal flesh of the Word it has ceased to be subject to corruption, and since he who dwelled within it and revealed it as his very own, knew no sin being God, as I have already said, it has also ceased to be sick with its desires. The only-begotten Word of God did not bring this about for his own benefit, for he is ever what he is, but evidently he did it for ours. And if we were subject to the evils following from Adam's transgression then Christ's benefit also must come to us, that is, incorruption and the putting to death of sin. This is why he became man. FIRST LETTER TO SUCCENSUS 9.[49]

THE LORD LIBERATES HUMANITY FROM DEATH. CYRIL OF ALEXANDRIA: The Scripture says that he was wearied from the journey, experienced sleepiness, anxiety, pain and all the blameless human passions[50] for this very reason, that we might believe that he did become man, even though he remained what he was, that is, God by nature. By contrast, to assure those who saw him that he was truly God, as well as being man, he worked divine signs, rebuking the sea,[51] raising the dead[52] and performing other wonderful works. He even endured the cross so that by suffering death in the flesh (though not in the nature of the Godhead) he might become the "firstborn from the dead."[53] He opened up the way for human nature to incorruption and despoiled hell, taking pity on the souls who were imprisoned there. FIRST LETTER TO SUCCENSUS 9.[54]

THE INCARNATION IS GOD'S WORK AS ME-

DIATOR. LEO THE GREAT: The distinctive character of each nature and substance remaining, therefore, unimpaired and coming together into one person, humility was assumed by majesty, weakness by power, mortality by eternity; and, in order to pay the debt of our condition, an inviolable nature was united to a nature capable of suffering, so that as a remedy suitable to our healing "one and the same mediator between God and people, the man Jesus Christ,"[55] was capable of death in the one nature and incapable of death in the other. Thus, in the whole and perfect nature of true manhood, true God was born, complete in what belonged to him and complete in what belonged to us. And by the words "what belonged to us" we mean what the Creator formed in us from the beginning and what he took on himself in order to restore; for that which the deceiver introduced, and people, being deceived, admitted, had no trace in the Savior. LETTER 28.3 (THE TOME OF LEO).[56]

The Fullness of God Dwelled Within Him

THE LORD MEDIATES WITH GOD. CYRIL OF ALEXANDRIA: He is called the "apostle and high priest"[57] of our confession, since he ministers to God the Father that confession of faith that we offer both to him and through him to God the Father (and certainly to the Holy Spirit also). We also confess that he is by nature the only-begotten Son of God, and we do not attribute the priesthood, both the name and thing, to another man beside him.[58] For he has become a "mediator between God and people, and the one who reconciles us to peace, since he has offered up himself as a smell of sweet savor to God the Father."[59] THIRD LETTER TO NESTORIUS (LETTER 17).[60]

---

[48]Rom 7:23. [49]CACC 356-57. [50]See Jn 4:6; Mt 8:24; 26:38. [51]Mt 8:26. [52]Jn 11:43. [53]Col 1:18. [54]CACC 357. [55]1 Tim 2:5. [56]CCC 317. [57]Heb 3:1. [58]Cyril thought that the Syrian tradition called the "man Jesus" the "priest mediator," as if he were somehow a different person from the divine Word made flesh. [59]1 Tim 2:5. [60]CCC 285**.

THE FINE WHITE LINEN OF THE MANGER.
EPHREM THE SYRIAN: In a manger the Lord of the universe reclined for the sake of the universe. Behold, O Bethlehem, David the king clothes himself in fine white linen. The Lord of David and Son of David hid his glory in swaddling clothes. His swaddling clothes gave a robe of glory to human beings. On this day our Lord exchanged radiance for shame, as the humble One. For Adam exchanged truth for evil, as a rebel. The gracious One took pity. His upright deeds conquered those of the perverse. HYMNS ON THE NATIVITY 5.3-5.[61]

DIVINITY WEAVES ITSELF A ROBE. EPHREM THE SYRIAN: But let us sing the birth of the firstborn, how divinity in the womb wove herself a garment. She put it on and emerged in birth; in death she stripped it off again. Once she stripped it off; twice she put it on. When the left hand snatched it, she wrested it from her, and she placed it on the right hand.[62] The power that governs all dwelled in a small womb. While dwelling there, he was holding the reins of the universe. His parent was ready for his will to be fulfilled. The heavens and all the creation were filled by him. The Sun entered the womb, and in the height and depth his rays were dwelling. He dwelled in the vast wombs of all creation. They were too small to contain the greatness of the firstborn. How indeed did that small womb of Mary suffice for him? It is a wonder if it sufficed for him. Of all the wombs that contained him, one womb truly sufficed: the womb of the great One[63] who begot him. HYMNS ON THE NATIVITY 21.5-7.[64]

HIS BIRTH SILENCES THE ANGELS. EPHREM THE SYRIAN: Between his birth and death he placed the world in the middle. By his birth and death he revived it. A thousand thousands stood; ten thousand ten thousands ran. Thousands and ten thousands were not able to investigate the One! All of them in silence, therefore, stood to serve him.[65] He has no consort except the child that is from him. Seeking him is in silence. When Watchers[66] went to investigate, they reached silence and were restrained. HYMNS ON THE NATIVITY 21.19-20.[67]

Born of a Woman That Humankind Might Be Born of God

BORN AS A REAL MAN FROM A VIRGIN MOTHER. CYRIL OF JERUSALEM: Believe also that he, the only-begotten Son of God, for our sins came down to earth from heaven, assuming a manhood subject to the same feelings as ours and being born of a holy Virgin and the Holy Spirit: and this not in appearance or in imagination but in reality. He did not pass through the Virgin as through a channel but truly took flesh and was truly fed with milk from her. He truly ate as we eat and drank as we drink. For if the incarnation was a figment, then our salvation was a figment. Christ was twofold; he was man, in what was visible; he was God, in what was invisible. He ate, as being really man like us (for he had the feelings of the flesh just as we have); but he fed the five thousand with five loaves, as being God. He died, as being really man, but as God he raised the body four days dead. CATECHETICAL LECTURES 4.9.[68]

THE INCARNATION IS NOT A PHANTASM.
ATHANASIUS: This[69] did not take place merely notionally as some have thought, God forbid! For when the Savior really and in truth became man, salvation was effected for the whole of humankind. If, as they say, the Word was only in the body notionally, and this notion is said to be a phantasm, then the so-called salvation and resurrection of humanity will also be found to have taken place merely in semblance, something the wicked Manicheans thought to be the case. But our salvation is no imaginary thing;

---

[61]ESH 106. [62]The humanity of the Lord was exalted to the right hand of the throne of glory after the ascension. [63]God the Father. [64]ESH 174-75. [65]God the Father. [66]Angelic powers. [67]ESH 177-78. [68]LCF 35-36. [69]The Word becoming a man.

nor is it the body only, but in reality the whole person, both body and soul, which has attained to salvation in the Word. So then, that which was derived from Mary was by nature human, according to the divine Scriptures, and the body of the Lord was real, and was real because it was the same as our own, for Mary was our sister, since we are all from Adam. LETTER TO EPICTETUS 7.[70]

FIRSTBORN OF MARY AND FIRSTBORN OF THE FATHER. EPHREM THE SYRIAN: Blessed is the Unlimited who was limited! Your majesty is hidden from us; your grace is revealed before us. I will be silent, my Lord, about your majesty, but I will speak about your grace. Your grace seized hold of you and inclined you toward our evil. Your grace made you a babe; your grace made you a human being. Your majesty contracted and stretched out. Blessed is the power that became small and became great! Glory to him who became earthly although heavenly by his nature! By his love he became firstborn to Mary although he is firstborn of divinity. He became in name the child of Joseph, although he is child of the heavenly One. He became by his will a human, although he is God by his nature. Glorious is your will and your nature! Blessed is your glory that put on our image! My Lord, your birth became mother of all creatures, since, again, she labored and gave birth to humanity which gave birth to you. Humanity gave birth to you physically; you begot her spiritually. Your birth became begetter of all. Blessed is he who became young and restored youth to all! Since human hope was shattered, hope was increased by your birth. The heavenly beings announced good hope to human beings. Satan, who cut off our hope, cut off his hope by his own hands when he saw that hope increased. Your birth became for the hopeless a spring gushing hope. Blessed is that hope that brought the gospel. HYMNS ON THE NATIVITY 23.2-6.[71]

The Necessity of the Incarnation

THE WORK OF THE INCARNATION. EPHREM THE SYRIAN: He put on the garments of youth, and helps emerged from them. He put on the water of baptism, and rays flashed out from it. He put on linen garments in death, and triumphs were shown by them. With his humiliations came his exaltations. Blessed is he who joins his glory to his suffering. All these are changes that the compassionate One shed and put on, when he contrived to put on Adam the glory that he himself had shed. He wrapped swaddling clothes with his leaves and put on garments instead of his skins. He was baptized for Adam's wrongdoing and embalmed for his death. He rose and raised him up in glory. Blessed is he who came down to put on a body and ascended. HYMNS ON THE NATIVITY 23.12-13.[72]

WHY DID GOD BECOME MAN? EUSEBIUS OF CAESAREA: And now let us explain the cause for which the incorporeal Word of God assumed this mortal body as a medium of intercourse with people. For how other than in human form could that divine and impalpable, that immaterial and invisible essence,[73] manifest itself to those who sought for God in created and earthly objects, unable or unwilling otherwise to discern the author and maker of all things? As a fitting means, therefore, of communication with humankind, he assumed a mortal body, as that with which they were themselves familiar; for like, it is proverbially said, loves its like. To those, then, whose affections were engaged by visible objects, who looked for gods in statues and lifeless images, who imagined the Deity to consist in material and corporeal substance, who even conferred on people the titles of divinity, the Word of God presented himself in this form. Hence he procured for himself this body as a thrice-hallowed temple, a sensible habitation of an intellectual power; a noble and most holy form, of far higher

---

[70]CACC 385. [71]ESH 188. [72]ESH 190. [73]Of the deity.

worth than any lifeless statue. ORATION ON CONSTANTINE 14.1-3.[74]

THE LORD AS KING AND PHYSICIAN. CYRIL OF JERUSALEM: Nurslings of purity and disciples of chastity, we raise our hymn to the virgin-born God with lips full of purity. Deemed worthy to partake of the flesh of the spiritual Lamb, let us take the head together with the feet,[75] the deity being understood as the head and the manhood taken as the feet. Hearers of the holy Gospels, let us listen to John the Divine. For he who said, "In the beginning was the Word, and the Word was with God, and the Word was God,"[76] went on to say, "And the Word was made flesh."[77] For neither is it holy to worship the mere man, nor religious to say that he is God only without the manhood. For if Christ is God, as indeed he is, but took not human nature on himself, we are strangers to salvation. Let us then worship him as God but believe that he also was made man. For neither is there any profit in calling him man without Godhead nor any salvation in refusing to confess the manhood together with the Godhead. Let us confess the presence of him who is both King and Physician. For Jesus the King, when about to become our physician, girded himself with the linen of humanity and healed that which was sick. CATECHETICAL LECTURES 12.1.[78]

THE INCARNATION EFFECTS RECONCILIATION. CYRIL OF ALEXANDRIA: Do not simply look on him who was laid in the manger as a mere babe, but in our poverty see him who as God is rich, and in the measure of our humanity him who excels the inhabitants of heaven. This is why he is glorified even by the holy angels. And how noble was the hymn: "Glory to God in the highest, and on earth peace and good will among people!"[79] For the angels and archangels, thrones and lordships, and high above them the seraphim, preserving their settled order, are at peace with God. Never in any way do they transgress his good pleasure, but they are firmly established in righteousness and holiness. But we, who are wretched beings, have set up our own lusts in opposition to the will of our Lord, and thus we had put ourselves into the position of being his enemies. But Christ has abolished all this. He is our peace, for he himself has united us to God the Father, "having taken away from the middle the cause of the enmity, which is sin,"[80] and so he justifies us by faith, and makes us holy and without blame and calls us near to him when we were once were afar off. Besides this, he has created the two people[81] into one new person, thereby making peace and reconciling both in one body to the Father. For it pleased God the Father to "form into one new whole all things in him, and to bind together things below and things above"[82] and to make those in heaven and those on earth into one flock. Christ, therefore, has been made for us both peace and goodwill, by whom and with whom to God the Father be glory and honor and might with the Holy Spirit, to the ages of ages. Amen. HOMILIES ON THE GOSPEL OF LUKE 2.[83]

THE MEANING OF SALVATION. CYRIL OF ALEXANDRIA: But how then, they object, was he baptized and received also the Spirit? To which we reply, he had no need of holy baptism, being wholly pure and spotless, and holy of the holy. Nor had he need of the Holy Spirit, for the Spirit that proceeds from God the Father is of him and equal to him in substance. We must now, therefore, at length hear what is the explanation of the economy.[84] God in his love to humankind provided for us a way of salvation and of life. For believing in the Father, Son and Holy Spirit and making this confession before many witnesses,[85] we wash away all the filth of sin, and are enriched by the communication of

---

[74]NPNF 2 1:603. [75]The paschal symbol of eating the head and feet of the entire lamb. [76]Jn 1:1. [77]Jn 1:14. [78]NPNF 2 7:72. [79]Lk 2:14. [80]Eph 2:14. [81]He refers to the union of Jew and Gentile in the church. [82]Eph 1:10. [83]CGSL 54**. [84]The economy of the incarnation. [85]At the sacrament of baptism.

the Holy Spirit, and "are made partakers of the divine nature"[86] and gain the grace of adoption. It was necessary, therefore, that the Word of the Father, when he humbled himself to emptiness and deigned to assume our likeness,[87] should become for our sakes the pattern and way of every good work. For it follows that "he who in everything is first"[88] must in this also set the example. HOMILIES ON THE GOSPEL OF LUKE 11.[89]

THE PURPOSE OF THE INCARNATION. RO-MANOS THE MELODIST: No king thinks it an indignity, when he wishes to worst his enemy, if he puts on a soldier's uniform. And so God, seeking to wound the one who wounded Adam, became incarnate from a virgin and becomes completely a snare for the all-wicked one. He who is before the ages takes our form, to whom without seed a virgin gives birth, and after childbirth remains still a virgin. KONTAKION ON THE MOTHER OF GOD 2.[90]

True Humanity Revealed in the Incarnate Son

HIGH PRIEST OF THE HUMAN RACE. THEO-DORET OF CYR: The church follows in the footsteps of the apostles and contemplates in the Lord Christ both perfect divinity and perfect humanity. He took a body, not because he needed one but to provide immortality to all bodies through his own. In the same way, he took the Soul, which rules the body, so that every soul might, through his, share in immutability. For even though souls are immortal, they are not immutable but constantly undergo many changes, experiencing pleasure, first from one object, then from another. We go wrong, therefore, when we undergo change, and we tend toward things that are less good. But after the resurrection bodies enjoy immortality and incorruptibility, while souls enjoy freedom from passion and immutability. . . . This is why the only-begotten Son of God took a body and soul, preserved them free of

all blame and offered them as a sacrifice for our human race. He was, therefore, designated our high priest, but he was called high priest, not as God but as a human being.[91] As a human being, he makes the offering, but as God, he receives the sacrifice, together with the Father and the Holy Spirit. If only the body of Adam had sinned, then only the body would have needed cure, but the body did not sin alone. The soul, in fact, sinned first, for thought first pictures the sin and then carries it out through the body. It was, therefore, absolutely right for the soul also to obtain a cure. We have learned that the divine nature is immortal, for the part that could suffer did so, while the part that could not suffer remained free of suffering. God the Word became human, not to make the nature that could not suffer capable of suffering, but to give freedom from suffering, through his suffering, to the nature that could suffer. LETTER 146.22-23, TO THE MONKS OF CONSTANTINOPLE.[92]

THE MEASURE OF THE PERFECT MAN. CYRIL OF ALEXANDRIA: To say that "the child grew and became strong in spirit,"[93] being filled with wisdom, and that "the grace of God was on him" must be taken as referring to his human nature. And closely examine, please, the profundity of the dispensation. The Word endured to be born in human fashion, although in his divine nature he has no beginning and is subject to no time. He who as God is all perfect submits to bodily growth. The incorporeal One has limbs that advance to the ripeness of manhood. He is filled with wisdom

---

[86]2 Pet 1:4. [87]Phil 2:5-11. [88]Rom 8:29. [89]*CGSL* 80. [90]SLS 17-18. [91]The attribution of the title "High Priest" to Jesus, was a matter of acute controversy between Alexandrian and Syrian theologians in this era (fourth to fifth centuries), especially a matter of conflict between Theodoret and Cyril of Alexandria. The Syrians saw it as a specially apt title to connote the human nature (manhood) of Christ, whereas Cyril regarded it as necessary to attribute all the titles to the one divine Word who was acting in a human body. [92]MFC 2:208. [93]Lk 2:40.

who is himself all wisdom. What do we say to this? Through these things we see one who was in the form of the Father, being made like to us. The rich is seen in poverty, the high in humiliation, and one who possesses all the fullness of God is described as "receiving." So thoroughly did God the Word empty himself. The things that are written of him as a man show the manner of the emptying. It was impossible for the Word begotten of God the Father to admit anything like this into his own nature, but when he became flesh, even a man like ourselves, then he is born according to the flesh of a woman and is said also to have been subject to the things that belong to the human condition. Though the Word, as God, could have made his flesh spring forth at once from the womb even in the condition of a grown man, this would have been in the style of a strange portent. Accordingly, he chose to give the habits and laws of human nature power even over his own flesh. Homily on the Gospel of Luke 5.[94]

The Gentle Deliverer. Cyril of Alexandria: Christ, therefore, rose up to deliver the inhabitants of the earth from their sins, and to seek the lost and save those who had perished. For this is his office and, if we may say, the fruit of his godlike gentleness. He will count worthy of this gentleness all those who have believed in him, by whom and with whom, to God the Father be praise and dominion, with the Holy Spirit, to the ages of ages. Amen. Homily on the Gospel of Luke 127.[95]

The Full Humanity of the Son

A True Man. Origen: The Lord when he took flesh was tempted by every temptation by which human beings are to be tempted. He was tempted for this purpose, that we might overcome through his victory.... From this[96] we may see that it is not the Son of God [i.e., in his divine nature] that speaks, but the human

nature that the Son of God deigned to assume; ... it is clear that it was not God but man who was tempted. Homily on the Gospel of Luke 29.[97]

The Intelligent and Ensouled Man.
Gregory of Nazianzus: Anyone who has placed his hope in a human being who lacked a human mind[98] is himself truly mindless and does not deserve a complete salvation. For "what was not assumed was not healed."[99] What is saved is that which has been united with God. If it was half of Adam that fell, then half might be assumed and saved. But if it was the whole of Adam that fell, it is united to the whole of him who was begotten and gains complete salvation. Then let them not envy us this complete salvation or equip the Savior only with bones and sinews, with the mere representation of a man. If his humanity lacked a human soul, that is what the Arians allege, so that they may attribute suffering to the divinity, on the grounds that that which gives the body life must share the body's experience. If his humanity had a soul, then it was either irrational or intellectual. If irrational, how would there be true humanity? For a person is not a beast without intellect. It would follow that there was an outward appearance, a facade of humanity, while the soul was the soul of a horse, or an ox, or one of the beasts without intellect. It will be that which is saved; and I have been cheated by the Truth, since I have been rejoicing, while a different being has received the honor. If it was an intellectual soul, then the humanity did not lack a human mind, and our opponents must stop behaving with this real mindlessness. Letter 101.7, To Cledonius.[100]

---

[94]*CGSL* 63**. [95]*CGSL* 507**. [96]Origen makes an extensive interpretation of various texts uttered by the Son of God, especially "Man shall not live by bread alone but by every word that falls from the mouth of God." [97]*ECF* 301. [98]A sardonic reference to the Apollinarist Christology, which he attacks throughout this letter. [99]Gregory here quotes the principle that Origen first enunciated. [100]*LCF* 108.

THE LORD HEALS THE MIND AND SOUL.
GREGORY OF NAZIANZUS: Let us see what,
for them, is his purpose in becoming man, or,
to use the phrase they prefer, of his becoming flesh. If the purpose is that God should be
confined, who is otherwise unconfined, and
that he should move about among people in
the flesh, as beneath a screen, then it is a clever
disguise, a subtle piece of play acting that they
represent. I need not say that it was in fact
possible for him to be in touch with people in
other ways, as in the burning bush, and when he
appeared in earlier times in human form. But
if his purpose was to remove the condemnation
of our sins by sanctifying like with like, then,
just as he needed to take on flesh because of the
condemnation of flesh and soul because of the
soul's condemnation, he must necessarily have
a mind for the same reason. The mind in Adam
did not merely stumble into sin; it was primarily
affected, as physicians say about illnesses. For
that which received the commandment failed to
keep it, and in thus failing it dared to commit
the transgression; and that which transgressed
stood in the greatest need of salvation; and
that which needed salvation was also assumed.
Therefore mind was assumed. LETTER 101.11,
To CLEDONIUS.[101]

CHRIST SANCTIFIES ALL HUMAN ACTION.
GREGORY OF NYSSA: But Christ, the repairer
of evildoing, assumes manhood in its fullness,
and saves humanity and becomes the type and
figure of us all, to sanctify the firstfruits of every action and leave to his servants no doubt in
their zeal for the tradition. Baptism, then, is a
purification from sins, a remission of trespasses,
a cause of renovation and regeneration. ON THE
BAPTISM OF CHRIST.[102]

THE SCANDAL OF HIS REAL HUMANITY.
GREGORY OF NYSSA: Apollinarius says, "The
Greeks and the Jews plainly refuse to believe
because they will not hear of a God who was
born of a woman." Why does he now, when

talking of his birth, pass over the flesh in
silence, although what was born of the flesh
was undoubtedly flesh, as the Lord says in one
place? No; he wants the flesh itself, which was
born, to be divinity and to make out that God
has not been displayed in flesh. And therefore
he says, "But God was endued with flesh before
the ages and subsequently was born by means
of a woman and underwent the experience of
death, as the necessary consequence of assuming human nature." By this assertion he does
not allow him true humanity, he makes him
submit to suffering as a man, but he does not
grant him participation in human nature. For
how can that be a man that is said to be not of
the earth[103]? For Scripture says that humanity
takes its origin from Adam and that he came
into being at the beginning from the earth.
That is why Luke, in drawing up the geneal-
ogy of him "who was regarded as the son of
Joseph,"[104] ends by saying, "the Son of Adam,"
tracing the origin of his descent step by step
through his ancestors. Therefore one who was
not born of the human race is assuredly not a
man but some other kind of being. AGAINST
APOLLINARIS 25.[105]

**SOUL AND MIND ARE PART OF THE INCAR-
NATE LIFE.** THEODORE OF MOPSUESTIA: The
disciples of Arius and Eunomius say that he
took a body but not a soul; the divine nature,
they say, supplied the place of a soul. They
abased the divine nature of the Only-Begotten
to such an extent that, declining from its natural grandeur, it performed the actions of the
soul, imprisoning itself in that body and performing the functions necessary for the body's
existence. Consequently, if the divinity took the
place of a soul, he would not have felt hunger or
thirst; he would not have been tired or had need
of food, for all these experiences come to the
body because of its weakness and because the

---

[101]LCF 108-9. [102]NPNF 2 5:519. [103]Apollinaris had confessed
the flesh of Christ as heavenly. [104]Lk 3:23. [105]LCF 135.

soul is incapable of satisfying its needs. It was necessary that the Son should assume not only a body but also an immortal and rational soul. It was not only the death of the body that he had to abolish, but also the death of the soul, which is sin. . . . It was necessary that sin, the cause of death, should be removed, and consequently death would be abolished with the removal of sin. It is evident that the tendency to sin has its origin in the will of the soul. ON THE NICENE CREED 5.9-11.[106]

MAN COMPOUNDED OF BODY AND SOUL. HILARY OF POITIERS: Jesus Christ is both Son of God and Son of man. . . . The Son of man is the same person as the Son of God; he who is in the form of God is the same as he who was born as complete man in the form of a servant. Just as, by the nature determined for us by God when man was first created, man is born as a creature of body and soul, so Jesus Christ, through his own divine power, was man and God, compounded of body and soul. He had in himself the whole reality of manhood and the whole reality of Godhead. ON THE TRINITY 10.19.[107]

HE ASSUMED MAN IN PERFECTION AND FULLNESS. AMBROSE OF MILAN: I, therefore, ask on what principle some people assume that a soul was not taken by the Lord Jesus. Is it because of a fear that Christ might slip through having human sensuality? It is certainly said that the lust of the flesh is in conflict with the law of the mind. But the author of this saying is far from supposing that Christ could have been brought into the bonds of sin by the law of the flesh. In fact, he himself believed that he could be helped by Christ, when he was in the turmoil of human frailty. He says, "Unhappy man that I am! Who will free me from the body of this death? Thanks be to God through Jesus Christ our Lord."[108] . . . When he took on him human flesh, it follows that he took the perfection and fullness of incarnation, for there was no imperfection in Christ. And so he took flesh

to bring flesh to life: he assumed a soul, but it was a perfect, rational and human soul that he assumed and took. For who can deny that he took a soul, when he himself says, "I lay down my soul for my sheep."[109] ON THE SACRAMENT OF THE LORD'S INCARNATION 64-66.[110]

THE LORD IS PERFECT MAN WITHOUT SIN. AMBROSE OF MILAN: God the Word did not take the place of the rational soul, capable of understanding, in the flesh that was his own. God the Word took on him a rational soul, capable of understanding; a human soul, of the same substance as ours. He took flesh like ours, of the same substance as our flesh. He was indeed a perfect man but without any stain of sin. ON THE SACRAMENT OF THE LORD'S INCARNATION 76.[111]

THE PERFECT HUMANITY OF THE LORD. COUNCIL OF CONSTANTINOPLE (381): We also preserve unperverted the doctrine of the incarnation of the Lord, receiving the dispensation of the flesh as neither without soul nor without mind nor incomplete but knowing that he existed as perfect God, the Word, before all ages, and became perfect man in the last days for our salvation. SYNODICAL LETTER.[112]

THE SAVIOR'S COMPLETE HUMANITY. DAMASUS OF ROME: This we are certainly surprised to find, that there are said to be some[113] among our own people who, in spite of their having a pious understanding of the Trinity, nevertheless, in respect of the mystery of our salvation, know neither the power of God nor the Scriptures and so fail to be of a right mind. They venture to say that our God and Savior Jesus Christ took from the Virgin Mary human nature incomplete, that is, without mind. Alas, how nearly they approach the Arians with a

---

[106]LCF 166. [107]LCF 51. [108]Rom 7:25. [109]Jn 10:15. [110]LCF 179. [111]LCF 180. [112]Synopsis of the Synodical Tome of the First Council of Constantinople (381) (LCC 3:344). [113]Damasus was attacking the supporters of Apollinaris in Rome.

mind like that! The latter speak of an incomplete divinity in the Son of God; the former falsely affirm an incomplete humanity in the Son of man. Now if human nature were taken incomplete, then the gift of God is incomplete and our salvation is incomplete, because human nature has not been saved in its entirety. And what then will become of that saying of the Lord, "The Son of man came to save that which had been lost"[114] in its entirety, that is, in soul and in body, in mind and in the whole substance of its nature? If, therefore, human nature had been lost in its entirety, it was necessary that that which had been lost should be saved. But if it was saved without mind, then the fact that that which had been lost was not saved in its entirety will be found contrary to the faith of the gospel, since, in another place, the Savior says, "Are you angry at me because I have made a man's body whole, in its entirety?"[115] Further, the essence of the first sin itself and of the entire perdition of humanity lies in humanity's mind, for if, at the first, man's mind to choose good and evil had not perished, he would not have died. How then are we to suppose that, at the last, that needed no salvation which is acknowledged to have been chief in sinning? We, who know that we have been saved whole and entire according to the profession of the catholic church, profess that complete God took complete man. Wherefore take heed that, by their understanding of sound doctrine, the very minds of those be saved who as yet do not believe that the mind has been saved. LETTER 2.[116]

HIS HUMANITY DOES NOT DEFILE THE DEITY. AUGUSTINE: Let us not listen to those who say that it was not a real manhood that the Son of God assumed, that he was not born of a woman but displayed to the beholders a false flesh and a feigned appearance of a human body. Those people do not know that the substance of God, which directs the whole creation, is utterly incapable of being contaminated: and yet they acknowledge that the

visible sun diffuses its rays through all manner of physical dirt and corruption but preserves their spotless purity. If, then, visible purity can be in contact with visible impurity and escape contamination, how much easier was it for the invisible and unchangeable Truth to avoid pollution when it freed humanity from all its infirmities by assuming the whole man: man's spirit, and, in consequence, man's soul, and, in consequence, man's body. ON THE AGONY OF CHRIST 20.[117]

Recapitulating Humanity

THE SON PRESENTS HUMANITY TO THE FATHER. GREGORY OF NAZIANZUS: The Son sets all things in subjection to the Father. The Father sets all things in subjection to the Son.[118] The Son acts; the Father approves. Thus, he who has made things subject presents to God that which has been subjected, making our condition his own. Such seems to me to be the meaning of the cry, "My God, my God, why have you forsaken me?" He himself was not forsaken, neither by the Father nor by his own divinity (as some suppose, as if the divine nature were afraid of the suffering and therefore removed itself from the sufferer). ORATION 30.5.[119]

THE SON CONSUMMATES THE HUMAN RACE. GREGORY OF NAZIANZUS: "God will be all in all"[120] in the time of restoration. This does not mean the Father, with the Son merely absorbed again into him, like a firebrand snatched out of a great fire and then returned to it (for I hope that the Sabellians will not employ this text to their own destruction). It means the whole

---

[114]Lk 19:10. [115]Jn 7:23. See, for example, Mt 9:22; 14:36; 15:28; Jn 5:6. [116]Fragment 2 of the Acts of the Synod of Rome (377) (CCC 87-88). [117]*LCF* 218. [118]Gregory is commenting on the scriptural phrase "All things will be subjected" (1 Cor 15:28) and arguing that it ought to be understood not as signifying the subordination of the Son but rather the mutuality of the Father's relation to the Son. [119]*LCF* 104*. [120]1 Cor 15:28.

Godhead and tells of the time when we shall no longer be a plurality as we are now because of our motions and passions, having in ourselves scarcely anything of God; but we shall be entirely godlike, capable of receiving all God and nothing but God. This is the consummation to which we are hastening.[121] ORATION 30.6.[122]

THE CREATOR LEADS OUR NATURE INTO BATTLE. THEODORET OF CYR: This divine love is so overwhelming that God declared that the only-begotten Son (the consubstantial one, born from God's womb before the daystar, with whom God worked in forming creation) was our healer and savior and granted us, through him, the gift of adoption. For the Creator saw that human beings had gone over willingly to the cruel tyrant, that they had fallen into the very pit of evil, that they were trampling boldly on the laws of nature and that visible creation, which spoke of and proclaimed the Creator, could not win over these people who had sunk into ultimate insensibility; seeing all this the Creator worked out our salvation with wisdom and justice. For the Creator did not wish to give us freedom through the use of force alone or to employ only mercy as a weapon against the one who enslaved human nature, lest the latter should call that mercy unjust; instead, the Creator devised a way that is filled with love for humanity and adorned with justice. The Creator united the conquered nature to himself and leads it into battle, preparing it to undo that defeat, to fight against the one who had wickedly conquered it long ago, to destroy the power of the one who had shamefully enslaved it and to recover its former freedom. The Lord Christ is born of a woman, therefore, just as we are, although this birth contains another element, namely, virginity. For it was a virgin who conceived and bore the Lord Christ. When you hear the word *Christ*, think of the only-begotten Son, the Word, begotten of the Father before the ages, clothed in human nature, but do not imagine that this plan of God which we

proclaim is contaminated in any way. For nothing can defile the pure nature of God. Let us, then, stand in awe before the one who did not entrust our care to angels but took on himself the task of treating and curing human beings. ON DIVINE PROVIDENCE 10.2-3.[123]

MARY'S SONG TO THE SAVIOR. EPHREM THE SYRIAN: I shall not be jealous, my Son,[124] that you are both with me and with everyone. Be God to the one who confesses you, and be Lord to the one who serves you and be brother to the one who loves you so that you might save all. While you dwelled in me, both in me and outside of me, your majesty dwelled. While I gave birth to you openly, your hidden power was not removed from me. You are within me, and you are outside of me, O Mystifier of his mother. When I see your outward image before my eyes, your hidden image is portrayed in my mind. In your revealed image I saw Adam, but in the hidden one I saw your Father who is united with you. HYMNS ON THE NATIVITY 16.1-3.[125]

THE INCARNATION BLESSES HUMANITY. AMBROSE OF MILAN: When he took on the flesh of a human being, it follows that he took on the perfection and plenitude of becoming flesh, for there is nothing imperfect in Christ. And so he took on flesh in order to raise it again; he assumed a soul, but he assumed and took on a perfect, human and rational soul. I say that he took on a soul, for the Word of God did not become live in its flesh by replacing our soul; the Word, rather, assumed both our flesh and our soul by assuming human nature perfectly. He assumed the soul, I say, in order to bless it with the sacrament of his becoming flesh; he took on my emotions and feelings in order to cure them. But why should he take on flesh without a soul, since it is certain that nonintelligent flesh and the irrational soul are neither guilty of sin nor

---

[121]Col 3:11. [122]*LCF* 105. [123]MFC 2:198-99. [124]The poet imagines the Virgin Mary speaking to her child. [125]ESH 149.

deserving of reward? He took on for us, therefore, that which was in greater danger. ON THE SACRAMENT OF THE LORD'S INCARNATION 6.[126]

HE MAKES CHILDREN OF NATURE INTO CHILDREN OF GRACE. AUGUSTINE: For the only Son of God by nature became a Son of man out of pity for us, so that we who were mortal by nature might, through him, become children of God by grace. While remaining unchangeable, he assumed from us our nature, so that he could assume us through it. While holding on to his divinity, he came to share in our weakness, so that we might change for the better, through our participation in his immortality and righteousness, by shedding what is sinful and mortal in us and preserving the good that he did through our nature, after that good had been filled with the highest good through the goodness of his nature. For just as we fell into such a terrible evil as this through the sin of one human, so, through the righteousness given by one human who was also God, shall we reach that good that is so exalted.[127] THE CITY OF GOD 7.3.[128]

Honoring Humanity

THE HUMANITY IS ANOINTED WITH THE SPIRIT. CYRIL OF JERUSALEM: Christ was not anointed by people with oil or material ointment, but when the Father appointed him as Savior of the whole world he anointed him with the Holy Spirit, as Peter says. . . .[129] Christ was anointed with the spiritual oil of gladness, the Holy Spirit who is called the oil of gladness because he is the cause of spiritual gladness. And so you are anointed with chrism, being made partakers and fellows of Christ. CATECHETICAL LECTURES 21.2.[130]

THE LORD'S LOVE FOR THE HUMAN RACE. HILARY OF POITIERS: The virgin, the birth, the body, and later on, the cross, the death and the lower world,[131] these are our salvation. For the sake of the human race the Son of God was born of the Virgin and the Holy Spirit; he even ministered to himself in this process, for his own power, the power of God, overshadowed her,[132] sowed the seeds of the body and started the process resulting in the flesh. He did this so that he could become human through the Virgin and take the nature of flesh to himself, so that, through the association produced by this mixture, the body of the whole human race might be sanctified through him. As a result, just as all were hidden in him through the bodily reality that he chose to be, so he could be communicated to all through the invisible reality that he possessed. The invisible image of God[133] did not, therefore, reject the shame involved in a human beginning, and he passed through the indignities to which our nature is subject, namely, conception, birth, crying and cradle. What can we possibly do, then, that would be a fitting return for such deep affection and esteem? The one, only-begotten God, sprung from God in an ineffable way, is placed in the womb of the holy Virgin and grows into the form of a small human body. The one who encompasses everything, and within whom and through whom all things exist,[134] is brought forth in accordance with the laws of human birth. The one at whose voice archangels and angels tremble (and heaven, earth, and all the elements of this world are dissolved[135]) is heard when a baby cries. ON THE TRINITY 2.24-25.[136]

HIS HUMANITY IS WORTHY OF THE THRONE. JOHN CHRYSOSTOM: What, then, is the dwelling place that the Word inhabited? Listen to the prophet who says, "I will raise up the dwelling place of David that had fallen."[137] Our nature had truly fallen, and had fallen with an incurable fall, and it needed only that powerful hand. For the only way to raise it up

---

[126]MFC 2:144. [127]Rom 5:15. [128]MFC 2:152. [129]Acts 10:38. [130]*LCF* 44. [131]The descent into Hades. [132]Lk 1:35. [133]Col 1:15. [134]1 Cor 8:6. [135]2 Pet 3:10-12. [136]MFC 2:136. [137]Amos 9:11.

was for the one who had shaped it in the beginning to stretch out a hand to it and shape it perfectly all over again through the rebirth of water and the Spirit. And here is the awesome and hidden mystery: the Word inhabits the dwelling forever, for it put on our flesh, never to lay it down again but to have it with it forever. If this were not so, the Word would not have judged it worthy of the royal throne, nor would the Word, while wearing it, have been worshiped by the whole army above, angels, archangels, thrones, principalities, dominions and powers. What word, what idea can express this great honor, so truly marvelous and awe-inspiring, that was bestowed on our human race? What angel or archangel could express it? No one anywhere, in heaven or on earth, could do it. For God's works are great, and God's kindnesses are so mighty and marvelous that an accurate description of them is beyond not only the human tongue but even an angel's power. We too, therefore, shall stop talking for a while and be silent. . . . It is, therefore, an act of sheer madness, and one deserving dreadful punishment, not to contribute what we can, after we have been given such great honor; this is especially so, since the profit from all this comes back to us again and since innumerable good things are available to us in them. For all of this let us give thanks to the God who loves humanity, not only through our words but much more through our actions, so that we might obtain the good of the future life. HOMILIES ON THE GOSPEL OF JOHN 11.15-16.[138]

The Union of the Two Natures

TWO NAMES CONJOINED IN EMMANUEL. EPHREM THE SYRIAN: Blessed are you, O church, in whom even Isaiah rejoices in his prophecy: "Behold, a virgin will conceive and bring forth a child"[139] whose name is a great mystery, whose explanation was revealed in the church. Two names were joined together and became one: "Emmanuel." El is with you always,

who joins you with his members. HYMNS ON THE NATIVITY 25.5.[140]

EMMANUEL, GOD WITH US IN OUR INFIRMITY. ARNOBIUS THE YOUNGER: Today we celebrate the feast of his nativity, that generation by which he deigned to come to us by means of Israel and to be made as Emmanuel, or "God with us" in the infirmity of the flesh, though never "with us" in the iniquity of our heart. He comes to us through what he assumed from us and liberates us by that means, insofar as he always remained in his own station. Indeed, the Lord visited his servants by means of mortal infirmity, so that he could set us free by his unchanging truth. This is the generation I refer to: the one that human fragility allows; not that generation of his which took place outside of time, which is altogether motherless, but the one that occurred within time, which is altogether fatherless. This is the Son of a virgin and spouse of a virgin,[141] the one who was born of an undefiled mother and delivered in incorruptible truth, whom now we praise and love and worship. For he it is who by his mercy has overthrown the craftiness of the devil and given us our triumph. CONFLICT WITH SERAPION 2.31.[142]

HOW EMMANUEL IS THE REDEEMER. CYRIL OF ALEXANDRIA: Only recently we saw the Emmanuel lying as a babe in the manger and wrapped in human fashion in swaddling bands but extolled as God in hymns by the host of the holy angels. For they proclaimed to the shepherds his birth, God the Father having granted to the inhabitants of heaven as a special privilege to be the first to preach him. And today too[143] we have seen him obedient to the laws of Moses, or rather we have seen him who as God is the Legislator subject to his own decrees. And the reason of this the most wise Paul

---

[138]MFC 2:132. [139]Is 7:14. [140]ESH 201. [141]The church. [142]Cetedoc 0239.2.31.2121-33; CCL 25A:169. [143]As the liturgy of the day has recounted the story of the circumcision of Christ.

teaches us, saying when we were babes we were enslaved under the elements of the world, "but when the fullness of the time came, God sent forth his Son, born of a woman, born under the law, to redeem them that were under the law."[144] HOMILIES ON THE GOSPEL OF LUKE 3.[145]

EMMANUEL IS THE DEITY MADE FLESH AMONG US. ATHANASIUS: As for those who imagine that the Word came to a certain man born of Mary in the way he came to each of the prophets, it is pointless examining this, for their wild notion carries its own refutation on its face. For if this was the way he came, why was this man born of a virgin rather than being born from a man and a woman, as all the other saints have been born? If this was the way the Word came, then why is the death of every saint not said to have taken place "for us," but only the death of this man? And if the Word dwelled with all the prophets, why is it said in regard to Mary's son alone that he dwelled "once only at the completion of the ages"?[146] If he came as he did in the saints of former times, why was it that all those others did not rise again after death? Why was it Mary's son alone that rose again on the third day? If the Word came just as he did in all the rest, why is it that Mary's son alone is called Emmanuel, insofar as she gave birth to a body filled with Godhead? For Emmanuel signifies "God with us." If this was how he came, why is he spoken of as eating, and drinking, and laboring and dying only in the case of Mary's son, and not in every saint who ate, and drank, and labored and died? All that his body suffered is spoken of as if he himself suffered it. In the case of all the others it is said simply that they were born and died, but of Mary's son only is it said that "the Word became flesh."[147] And so, it appears that to all the others the Word came in order that they should prophesy. But from Mary the Word took flesh and came forth as man, being in his nature and essence the Word of God but according to the flesh made man, as Paul said, from the seed of David and the flesh of Mary.[148] This is the one the Father made manifest when he said at the Jordan and on the mountain, "This is my beloved Son, in whom I am well pleased."[149] This is the one the Arians have denied but we recognize and worship, not dividing the Son and the Word but knowing that the Word himself is the Son, through whom all things were made and we were redeemed. LETTER TO EPICTETUS 11-12.[150]

EMMANUEL—THE LILY AND ITS PERFUME. CYRIL OF ALEXANDRIA: Our Lord Jesus Christ compares himself with a pearl, saying, "The kingdom of heaven is like a merchant looking for fine pearls."[151] . . . And I find him using another image to reveal himself to us when he says, "I am a flower of the plain, a lily of the valley."[152] For in his own nature he possesses the divine brightness of God the Father, while at the same time he gives out his own fragrance, a sweet spiritual perfume. In the case of the pearl and the lily the underlying physical body is perceived, while the brightness or fragrance is apprehended after its own manner; and these are apprehended as different from the things in which they subsist, yet they inhere in these inseparably, belonging to them and not alien from the bodies that possess them. I believe that we should think and judge in the same way about Emmanuel. Divinity and flesh are by nature diverse in kind, yet the Word's body was his own; the Word united to that body was not separated from it. This is the only way in which we should conceive of Emmanuel, "God with us." AGAINST NESTORIUS 2.(PREFACE).[153]

The Son as One Person

THE ONE INCARNATE LORD. ATHANASIUS: Being God, he became man, and then as God

---

[144]Gal 4:3. [145]*CGSL* 55. [146]Heb 9:26. [147]Jn 1:14. [148]Rom 1:3. [149]Mt 3:17; 17:5. [150]*CACC* 388. [151]Mt 13:45. [152]Song 2:1. [153]*LCF* 254-55.

he raised the dead, healed all by a word and changed the water into wine. These were not human acts. But as wearing a body he felt thirst and weariness and suffered pain. These experiences are not appropriate to deity. As God he said, "I in the Father, the Father in me"; as wearing a body he thus attacked the Jews, "Why do you seek to kill me, when I am a man who has told you the truth, which I heard from my Father?"[154] And yet these are not events occurring disconnectedly, distinguished according to their quality, so that one class may be ascribed to the body, apart from the divinity, the other to the divinity, apart from the body. They all occurred inseparably conjoined, and the Lord who marvelously performed those acts by his grace was one. He spat in human fashion, but his spittle had divine power, for by it he restored sight to the eyes of the man blind from birth. When he willed to make himself known as God, he used his human tongue to signify this, when he said, "I and the Father are a unity."[155] He cured by his mere will. Yet it was by extending his human hand that he raised Peter's mother-in-law when she had the fever and raised up from the dead the daughter of the synagogue ruler when she had already passed from life. LETTER TO SERAPION 4.14.[156]

THERE ARE NOT TWO SONS. THEODORET OF CYR: You can be sure that no one ever heard us proclaiming two sons. In fact, such teaching is, in my view, execrable blasphemy. For Jesus Christ is one Lord, through whom are all things. I acknowledge him as God before the ages and as man at the end of the days, and I offer one adoration as to the Only-Begotten. But I have been taught the distinction between flesh and Godhead, for the union is without confusion. . . . The sayings concerning the Lord that show a humility appropriate to the nature assumed we ascribe to him as such; those that befit the Godhead, and are evidence of that nature, we attribute to him as God. However, we make no separation into two persons, but

we teach that both types of sayings belong to the one Only-Begotten. Some of them belong to him as God, Maker and Lord of the universe, some to him as made man for us. LETTER 104.[157]

THE UNITY OF CHRIST. APOLLINARIS OF LAODICEA:[158] We confess . . . that he is the same Son of God, and God according to Spirit, but Son of man according to flesh, that the one Son is not two natures (persons), one to be worshiped and one without worship, but one incarnate nature[159] of God the Word, to be worshiped with his flesh in one worship. LETTER TO JOVIAN 1.[160]

ONE CHRIST, SON AND LORD. CYRIL OF ALEXANDRIA: We maintain, however, that this cannot be the case.[161] We have learned from the divine Scriptures and the holy Fathers to confess one Son and Christ and Lord. This is the Word of God the Father born from him in an ineffable and divine manner before the ages, and the same one is born from the holy Virgin according to the flesh, for our sake, in the last times of this age. Since she gave birth to God made flesh and made man, for this reason we also call her the mother of God. There is, therefore, one Son, one Lord Jesus Christ, both before the incarnation and after it. The Word of God the Father is not one distinct Son, with the one born of the holy Virgin being another and different son. No, it is our faith that the very one who was before the ages is the one who was born from a woman according to the flesh. It is not as if his Godhead took the beginnings of its existence or was called into being for the

---

[154]Jn 14:11; Jn 8:40. [155]Jn 10:30. [156]ECF 398-99. [157]LCF 272. [158]In the late fourth century this letter of Apollinaris was reattributed to Athanasius and was quoted as an Athanasian authority by Cyril of Alexandria, who had a copy of it in his archives, under Athanasius's name. It was Apollinaris's statement of faith to the new emperor, Jovian, after the death of Julian. [159]In this instance the one incarnate nature (*physis*) signifies what later thought would clarify as "person." [160]CCC 96. [161]That there are two persons manifested in the Christ, one divine and the other human.

first time through the holy Virgin, but rather, as I have said, the eternal Word is said to have been born from her according to the flesh. For his flesh was his very own in just the same way as each one of us has his own body. FIRST LETTER TO SUCCENSUS 4.[162]

CHRIST'S INTEGRAL UNITY. CYRIL OF ALEXANDRIA: Nestorius pretends to acknowledge that the Word, who was God, was incarnate, and made man, but he does not recognize the meaning of the incarnation, and he uses the term "two natures"[163] and separates them, dividing off the divinity and keeping the manhood apart, as being attached to the Godhead by "habitual conjunction," merely by equality of honor or authority. What he says is, "God is indivisible from the visible [i.e., the manhood]: therefore I am not separating the honor of that which is not divided; I divide the natures but unite the worship." Now the brethren of Antioch[164] have accepted the components in Christ that are presented to our minds, but simply and solely in the sphere of thought:[165] they have spoken of a difference of natures (for, as was said above, Godhead and manhood are not the same in natural quality), but they confess one Son and Christ and Lord, and they say that, since he is really one, there is in him one personality. In no way do they divide the things that have been united. They refuse the notion of a division in nature, a notion that the introducer[166] of these disastrous novelties has decided to entertain. LETTER 40, TO ACACIUS OF MELITENE.[167]

THE HYPOSTATIC UNION OF THE LORD. CYRIL OF ALEXANDRIA: There is therefore one Christ and Son and Lord, not as if man were conjoined with God by a union of dignity or authority. For equality of honor does not unite the nature, and Peter and John, for instance, are of equal honor with each other, as both apostles and holy disciples, but the two are not made into one. Nor do we think of the mode of conjunction as by association, for this is not enough for a natural union or as by an acquired relation, as we, "being joined to the Lord,"[168] as it is written, "are one spirit with him." Indeed, we reject the term "conjunction"[169] as not sufficiently indicating the union. . . . Nor is the Word the God or Lord of Christ, since God the Word and his flesh are united in one person, though as man he was under God and under the Law. THIRD LETTER TO NESTORIUS (LETTER 17).[170]

ALL GOSPEL ATTRIBUTES REFER TO ONE LORD. CYRIL OF ALEXANDRIA: We do not divide the terms used in the Gospels of the Savior as God or man between two hypostases, or persons, for the one and only Christ is not twofold, though he is thought of as out of two and as uniting different entities into the indivisible unity, as man is thought of as of body and soul, and yet not as twofold but one out of both. . . . For if it is necessary to believe that, being God by nature, he became flesh, that is, man ensouled with a rational soul, for what reason should some be embarrassed by some of his sayings that may be such as befit humanity? . . . All the terms used in the Gospels are to be referred to one person, the one incarnate hypostasis of the Word. There is one Lord Jesus Christ, according to the Scripture. THIRD LETTER TO NESTORIUS (LETTER 17).[171]

NO SEPARATION IN THE ONE CHRIST. CYRIL OF ALEXANDRIA: What I would say to my good

---

[162]CACC 353. [163]Cyril believed that Nestorius's insistence that two abiding realities (natures) marked the life of Christ was a mask for an underlying belief that he meant two persons. [164]The Syrian patriarchate deliberating the matter of Nestorius's orthodoxy after the Council of Ephesus (431). [165]That is, one can confess the notional difference of divinity and humanity in Jesus, but only if one accepts that in his concrete historical existence Jesus was the divine Word of God who ineffably united divinity and humanity in his single person. Cyril accepts that Syrian Christology does this, albeit with a different language stress from his own Alexandrian tradition, but is arguing here that Nestorius did not do this. [166]Nestorius. [167]LCF 260. [168]1 Cor 6:17. [169]The preferred term of Nestorius to connote the christological union (*synapheia*). [170]LCC 3:351. [171]LCC 3:352.

Nestorius is that although we speak of Christ as man and at the same time God, we are not making a division in so speaking. Rather, we knew this same Son and God and Word of the Father even before his incarnation. And, after that, we knew him as made man, in our condition and incarnate. Nestorius, in contending that he is not to be thought of as a mere man but as God and man, attributes the crown of thorns and the rest of his sufferings to the man, separately and exclusively, and acknowledges that he gives to him "joint adoration with the divinity." And he goes further in impiety in saying that he worships him not, as is right, as being truly God and Son but as having become "the advocate of the authority of the Word." The division that he makes is clear from his acknowledgment that worship is to be given with the divinity: for what is worshiped with, something else is surely quite distinct from that with which it is said to be worshiped. But we are accustomed to worship Emmanuel with one single worship, not separating from the Word the body that was personally united to him. Against Nestorius 2.10.[172]

The Christological Union Is Profound.

Cyril of Alexandria: If Nestorius's term "conjunction"[173] means the unity that we conceive, that is, a unity of person,[174] then he would be justified in claiming to teach that "there is no division in Christ, as Christ; there are not two Christs, two sons." . . . But if this is so, how is it that you, Nestorius, allege that the one and indivisible Christ is "twofold, not in status but in nature"? Because the Word of God the Father took flesh and came forth as man in our condition, he is not therefore to be called twofold; he who in his own proper nature is outside of flesh and blood is one being, in the flesh. If anyone kills an ordinary human being, he is not to be accused of two crimes, even if a man is to be considered as composed of soul and body, and the experiences of these two components are by nature different. We should think of

Christ in the same manner: he is not twofold; he is one single Lord and Son, the Word of God the Father, in the flesh. I myself acknowledge that there is a very great difference, indeed the greatest disparity, between divinity and humanity. These terms clearly denote things essentially diverse and utterly dissimilar. But when the mystery of Christ is presented to us, then the principle of unity does not ignore the difference, but it excludes division. It does not confuse or mingle the natures. The Word of God partook of flesh and blood, and the Son is conceived of as one and is so named. Against Nestorius 2.6.[175]

The Significance of the Concept of Union.

Cyril of Alexandria: Let them take account of this. When one speaks of a union, one does not signify the concurrence of a single factor but surely of two or more that are different from one another in nature. So, if we talk of a union, we confess it to be between flesh endowed with a rational soul and the Word; and those who speak of "two natures" understand it in this way. However, once we have confessed the union, the things that have been united are no longer separated from one another but are thereafter one Son; and One is his nature since the Word has been made flesh. Letter to Eulogius.[176]

The Hypostatic Union of the Word with the Flesh.

Second Council of Constantinople (553): For, thinking of the union in diverse ways, some, in accordance with the ungodliness of Apollinaris and Eutyches, assuming the disappearance of the components, affirm the union by confusion; while those who accept the ideas of Theodore and Nestorius, rejoicing in division, introduce the union of relation. But the holy church of God, rejecting the impiety of each heresy, confesses the union

---

[172]LCF 253-54. [173]Synapheia. [174]Hypostasis. [175]LCF 253. [176]CACC 350.

of God the Word with the flesh by composition, that is, by hypostasis. For the union by composition in the mystery of Christ not only preserves the components unconfused but also accepts no separation. ANATHEMA 4.[177]

ONE OF THE TRINITY IN THE FLESH. SECOND COUNCIL OF CONSTANTINOPLE (553): If anyone does not confess that our Lord Jesus Christ who was crucified in the flesh is true God and Lord of glory and one of the holy Trinity, let him be anathema. ANATHEMA 10.[178]

The Personal Unity Witnessed in the Son

UNITED LIKE HEAT IN MELTING IRON. ORIGEN: To provide a fuller explanation of the matter, it seems not inappropriate to use a simile, although in so hard and difficult a matter there are no adequate parallels to employ. . . . Iron is capable of cold and heat. If then some mass of iron is put into the fire, it receives heat in all its pores and veins and becomes wholly fire, if it never leaves the fire or is taken from it. Now shall we say that this mass, which is by nature iron, when placed in the fire and burning ceaselessly, is capable of cold? No, rather we say . . . that it has become wholly fire, since we discern nothing but fire in it. In the same way that soul that is always in the Word, in Wisdom, in God, as the iron is in the fire, is God in all that it does and feels and knows. ON FIRST PRINCIPLES 2.6.6.[179]

THE PROFOUND DEPTH OF THE UNION. ORIGEN: But if we say that the soul of Jesus is united with this great Son of God in the closest unity so that they are inseparable, this assertion need cause no surprise. For the sacred narratives know of other examples of things that are two in their own nature that are reckoned as one and are one. For example, it is said of a man and wife, "They are no longer two, but one flesh"[180] and again, "He who is joined to the Lord is one spirit."[181] And who is joined to

the Lord more than the soul of Jesus, who in equal manner is joined to the Lord, the absolute Reason, Wisdom, Truth, Righteousness? If this is so, there is no duality between the soul of Jesus and God the Word, the "firstborn of all creation." AGAINST CELSUS 6.47.[182]

THE SACRAMENT OF MEDIATION. HILARY OF POITIERS: Anyone who fails to see Christ Jesus as at once truly God and truly human is blind to his own life. To deny Christ Jesus, or God the Spirit or our own flesh, is equally perilous. "If anyone acknowledges me before people, I shall acknowledge him before my Father who is in heaven. But if anyone denies me before people, I shall deny him before my Father who is in heaven."[183] . . . Christ has been appointed as in himself the mediator, for the salvation of the church, and in that sacrament of mediation between God and mankind he is one being, yet he is both God and man. By the union of the two natures he is one entity comprising both natures; but in such a way that in either capacity he lacked nothing of the other, so that he did not cease to be God by being born as man or fail to be man by remaining God. This is the true faith of human blessedness, to proclaim God and man, to acknowledge Word and flesh; not to fail to recognize God because he is man or to fail to see the flesh because he is the Word. ON THE TRINITY 9.3.[184]

TRUE REVERENCE MEANS UNDERSTANDING THE UNION. CYRIL OF JERUSALEM: Religion does not allow us to worship the mere man, and it is not true reverence to speak of him as God only, separate from his manhood. For if Christ is God (as he truly is) but did not take manhood, then we are aliens from salvation. Let him, then, be worshiped as God, but let it be believed that he also became man. For it is to no avail to call him man without his divinity, and

---

[177]LCC 3:379-80. [178]LCC 3:381. [179]*ECF* 298. [180]Mt 19:6.
[181]1 Cor 6:17. [182]*ECF* 297-98. [183]Mt 10:32-33. [184]*LCF* 49.

we do not receive salvation if we fail to acknowledge his manhood together with his Godhead. CATECHETICAL LECTURES 12.1.[185]

TWO NATURES BUT ONLY ONE PERSON.
GREGORY OF NAZIANZUS: If anyone introduces two sons, one derived from God the Father, the other from his mother, not being one and the same, then such a person fails to attain "the adoption of children"[186] that is promised to those who rightly believe. There are indeed the two natures, the divine and the human (the human nature comprising soul and body) but not two sons or two gods; nor have we here two human beings, even though Paul speaks in this way of the inner and the outer element in human nature. To sum up the matter: there are two separate elements of which the Savior is composed (the invisible is not identical with the visible or the timeless with the temporal), but there are not two separate beings; emphatically not. Both elements are blended into one, the divinity taking on humanity, the humanity receiving divinity, or however one may phrase it. In short: I say there are two elements but not two beings. LETTER 101.5-6, TO CLEDONIUS.[187]

ONE PERSON SPEAKS THROUGH TWO NATURES. AMBROSE OF MILAN: Let there be an end of useless disputes about words, for the kingdom of God, as Scripture says, "does not consist in persuasive arguments"[188] but in clear demonstration of power. Let us observe the distinction between the divinity and the flesh. It is the one and the same Son of God who speaks in both, for both natures are present in one and the same subject. But though it is the same person who speaks, he does not always speak in the same way. In him you may see at one time the glory of God, at another the feelings of man. ON THE CHRISTIAN FAITH 2.77.[189]

ONE INCARNATE PHYSIS. CYRIL OF ALEXANDRIA: The flesh is flesh and not Godhead, even though it became the flesh of God. Similarly

the Word is God and not flesh even if he made the flesh his very own in the economy. Given that we understand this, we do no harm to that concurrence into union when we say that it took place out of two natures. After the union has occurred, however, we do not divide the natures from one another, nor do we sever the one and indivisible into two sons, but we say that there is one Son, and as the holy Fathers have stated, "one, incarnate nature[190] of the Word." FIRST LETTER TO SUCCENSUS 6.[191]

DIVERSE NATURES BROUGHT INTO UNITY.
CYRIL OF ALEXANDRIA: We too must adhere to these words and these doctrines, considering what is meant when it is said that the Word that is of God "was incarnate and was made man." For we do not affirm that the nature of the Word underwent a change and became flesh or that it was transformed into a complete human being consisting of soul and body. Rather, we affirm that the Word personally[192] united to himself flesh animated with living soul in an ineffable and inconceivable manner and thereby became man and was called Son of man. We affirm that this did not happen on the basis of mere will or favor or by the simple assumption to himself of a human person. While the natures that were brought together into this true unity were diverse, there was of both, one Christ and Son. It was not as though the diversity of the natures was done away by this union, but rather Godhead and Manhood completed for us the one Lord and Christ and Son by their unutterable and unspeakable concurrence into unity. SECOND LETTER TO NESTORIUS (LETTER 4).[193]

THE UNION IS LIKE THE SOUL IN A BODY.
CYRIL OF ALEXANDRIA: Surely it is beyond dispute that the Only-Begotten, being by nature

---

[185]LCF 36. [186]Rom 8:23; Gal 4:5. [187]LCF 107. [188]1 Cor 4:20. [189]LCF 178. [190]The key term here is *physis*. The phrase, therefore, means "one incarnated concrete reality of God the Word in the flesh." [191]CACC 355. [192]Hypostatically. [193]CCC 277**.

God, became man not by conjunction,[194] as Nestorius alleges, regarded as a merely external link or a moral connection, but by a genuine union, in a manner beyond explanation or understanding. Thus he is thought of as one single being; all that he says is consistent with himself and will prove to be entirely the utterance of one person.[195] For as soon as this union has taken place, there is a single nature presented to our minds, the incarnate nature of the Word himself. Something like this can of course be observed in our experience, for a single person is really a composite being, made up of unlike elements, namely, soul and body. Further, it must be observed that we assert that the body that was united to God the Word was animated by a rational soul. It is important to add that there is a great difference between the flesh, considered in its own nature, and the essential nature of the Word. But although the things so named are conceived as different and separated by their diversity of nature, Christ is still apprehended as one being, made up of the two elements. The divinity and the humanity come together in a real unity of mutual accord. AGAINST NESTORIUS 2.(PREFACE).[196]

ONE SON AND LORD TO BE WORSHIPED.
CYRIL OF ALEXANDRIA: Confessing then the personal[197] union of the Word with the flesh, we worship one Son and Lord, Jesus Christ. We do not put apart or separate man and God, as though they were connected with one another simply by a unity of dignity and authority (for this is vain babbling and nothing else). And we certainly do not call the Word of God Christ in one sense and the one who was born of a woman Christ in another sense. We know only one Christ, the Word which is of God the Father, who is now together with his own flesh. For then [when he took flesh] he was anointed with us as man, and even now to those who are worthy to receive it, he himself gives the Holy Spirit, and not by measure, as the blessed Evangelist John tells us.[198] THIRD

LETTER TO NESTORIUS (LETTER 17).[199]

NEVER DIVIDE THE ONE SON AND LORD.
CYRIL OF ALEXANDRIA: We must not therefore divide the one Lord Christ into two sons. Some who do this add an assertion of a "union of persons,"[200] but this assertion will not serve to restore their decline to a sound statement of the faith. Scripture does not say, "The Word united to himself the *prosōpon* of a man," but rather it says, "the Word was made flesh."[201] And that means precisely this, that he became partaker of flesh and blood, just as we do, and made our body his own. He issued as man from a woman, but he did not cast off his being God and his generation from God the Father. He assumed our flesh, but even in doing this he remained what he was. SECOND LETTER TO NESTORIUS (LETTER 4).[202]

NEVER DIVIDE PERSONALITIES IN JESUS.
CYRIL OF ALEXANDRIA: If anyone in the one Christ divides the personalities after the union, that is, the human and the divine, connecting them only by a connection of dignity or authority or rule and not rather by a union of natures, let him be anathema. If anyone distributes to two persons or subsistences the expressions used both in the Gospels and in the Epistles, or used of Christ by the saints or by him of himself; attributing some to a man conceived of separately, apart from the Word which is of God, and attributing others (the ones befitting God) exclusively to the Word which is of God the Father, let him be anathema. THIRD LETTER TO NESTORIUS (LETTER 17).[203]

ONE BEING, ONE PERSON IN CHRIST. CYRIL OF ALEXANDRIA: As to the manner of the incarnation of the Only-Begotten, then theoretically speaking (but only insofar as it appears to

---

[194]*Synapheia.* [195]*Prosōpon.* [196]*LCF* 254. [197]Hypostatic. [198]Jn 3:34. [199]CCC 282**. [200]*Prosōpa.* [201]Jn 1:14. [202]*LCF* 259. [203]CCC 287.

the eyes of the soul) we would admit that there are two natures united, but only one Christ and Son and Lord, the Word of God made man and made flesh. If you like, we can take as our example that very composition that makes us human beings. For we are composed of body and soul, and we perceive two natures; there is one nature of the body and a different nature of the soul, and yet there is one human being from both of them, in terms of the union. This composition from two natures does not turn the one person into two, but as I have said, there is one being by the composition of body and soul. FIRST LETTER TO SUCCENSUS 7.[204]

THE SAME ONE, GOD AND MAN. COUNCIL OF CHALCEDON (451): Following, therefore, the holy Fathers, we confess one and the same our Lord Jesus Christ, and we all teach harmoniously that he is the same perfect in Godhead, the same perfect in manhood, truly God and truly man, the same of a reasonable soul and body; consubstantial with the Father in Godhead, and the same consubstantial with us in manhood, like us in all things except sin; begotten before ages of the Father in Godhead, the same in the last days for us, and for our salvation, born of Mary the Virgin *theotokos* in manhood, one and the same Christ, Son, Lord, unique; acknowledged in two natures without confusion, without change, without division, without separation; the difference of the natures being by no means taken away because of the union but rather the distinctive character of each nature being preserved and combining in one person and hypostasis, not divided or separated into two persons but one and the same Son and Only-Begotten God, Word, Lord Jesus Christ; as the prophets of old and the Lord Jesus Christ himself taught us about him, and the symbol[205] of the Fathers has handed down to us. CREEDAL STATEMENT.[206]

The Interpenetration of the Divine and Human in One Person

THE NOTION OF INDISSOLUBLE CONJUNCTION. THEODORE OF MOPSUESTIA: We must hold fast to the knowledge of that indissoluble conjunction. Never for a single moment can that form of a servant be separated from the divine nature that has put it on. The distinction of natures does not annul the exact conjunction, nor does that exact conjunction destroy the distinction. The natures remain distinct in their existence, and their conjunction remains of necessity, because that which was assumed is associated with the assumer in honor and glory. ON THE NICENE CREED 8.13.[207]

TWO NATURES, NOT TWO SONS. THEODORE OF MOPSUESTIA: The fact that we speak of two natures does not mean that we are forced to speak of two Lords or two sons. This would be utter foolishness. When things are two in one respect and one in another respect, their conjunction, which makes them one, does not annul the distraction of natures, nor does that distinction prevent their unity. ON THE NICENE CREED 8.14.[208]

AN UNCONFUSED UNION. CYRIL OF ALEXANDRIA: But since certain people are trying to implicate us with the opinions of Apollinaris, saying, "If you maintain that the Word of God the Father incarnated and made man is one Son in a strict and compact union, perhaps you imagine or have come to think that some mixture or blending or confusion occurred between the Word and the body, even a transformation of the body into the nature of Godhead?" We are fully aware of such implications, and we refute such a slander when we say that the Word of God, in an incomprehensible manner, beyond description, united to himself a body animated with a rational soul and came forth as man from a woman, not becoming what we are by any transformation of nature but rather by a gra-

---

[204]CACC 355. [205]A reference to the Nicene Creed. [206]LCC 3:373. [207]LCF 167. [208]LCF 167.

cious economy. For he wished to become man without casting off his natural being as God, and even when he descended into our limitations and put on the form of the slave, even so he remained in the transcendent condition of the Godhead and in his natural state as Lord. FIRST LETTER TO SUCCENSUS 5.[209]

A TRUE UNION OF TWO NATURES. CYRIL OF ALEXANDRIA: We confess, therefore, our Lord Jesus Christ, the only-begotten Son of God, perfect God and perfect man, consisting of a rational soul and a body begotten of the Father before the ages as touching his Godhead, the same, in the last days, for us and for our salvation, born of the Virgin Mary, as touching his manhood; the same of one substance with the Father as touching his Godhead, and of one substance with us as touching his manhood. For of two natures a union has been made. For this cause we confess one Christ, one Son, one Lord. LETTER 39, TO JOHN OF ANTIOCH (THE FORMULA OF REUNION).[210]

ONE CHRIST HONORED WITH ONE WORSHIP. CYRIL OF ALEXANDRIA: We refuse also to say of Christ, "For the sake of him who assumes I worship him who is assumed; for the sake of him who is unseen I worship him who is seen."[211] One must shudder also to say, "He that is assumed shares the name of God with him who assumed." For he who speaks this way again makes two Christs, one God and one man. For he confessedly denies the union, according to which there is understood one Christ Jesus; not one jointly worshiped with another or jointly sharing the name of God with another, but one Christ Jesus, one only-begotten Son, honored with one worship with his own flesh. THIRD LETTER TO NESTORIUS (LETTER 17).[212]

THE WORD BUT PERSONALLY ASSUMED FLESH. CYRIL OF ALEXANDRIA: Neither do we say that the Word of God tabernacled in him who was begotten of the holy Virgin as in an ordinary man, lest Christ should be thought of as a God-bearing man.[213] For though the Word did tabernacle among us, and it is said that "in Christ dwelled all the fullness of the Godhead bodily,"[214] yet we so conceive of this that when he was made flesh, we do not define the indwelling in him in precisely the same manner as that in which one speaks of an indwelling in the saints; but being united by nature and not changed into flesh, he effected such an indwelling as the soul of man might be said to have in its own body. THIRD LETTER TO NESTORIUS (LETTER 17).[215]

THE UNCONFUSED AND TRUE UNION. SECOND COUNCIL OF CONSTANTINOPLE (553): If anyone who confesses that the union was effected out of two natures, deity and humanity, or speaks of one incarnate nature of God the Word does not so take these terms, as the holy Fathers taught, that out of the divine nature and the human, when the union by hypostasis took place, one Christ was formed, but out of these phrases tries to introduce one nature or substance of the Godhead and flesh of Christ, let him be anathema. For when saying that the unique Word was united by hypostasis, we do not mean that there was any mixture of the natures with each other, but rather we think of the Word as united with flesh, with each remaining what it is. Therefore Christ is one, both God and man; the same consubstantial with the Father in Godhead, and the same consubstantial with us in manhood. Equally, therefore, does the church of God reject and anathematize those who divide into parts or cut up and those who confuse the mystery of the divine dispensation of Christ. ANATHEMA 8.[216]

ONE WORSHIP OF THE INCARNATE LORD. SECOND COUNCIL OF CONSTANTINOPLE (553): If anyone says that Christ is to be worshiped in

---

[209]CACC 354. [210]CCC 291. [211]Citing phrases of Nestorius. [212]CCC 283. [213]Such as a saint is a God-bearer (*theophoros*), as distinguished from truly God. [214]Col 2:9. [215]LCC 3:350-51. [216]LCC 3:380-81.

two natures, from which two adorations are introduced, one proper to God the Word and one to the man, or if anyone in terms of destruction of the flesh, or of confusion of the Godhead and the manhood or strangely contriving one nature or substance of the components, so worships Christ but does not with one adoration worship God the Word incarnate with his own flesh, as the church of God has received from the beginning, let him be anathema. ANATHEMA 9.[217]

How the Fathers Resolved the Dilemma of the Persons

DOUBLE REFERENCE TO DIFFERENT STATES. ORIGEN: Some of the utterances of Jesus are those of "the firstborn of all creation"[218] who was in him, for example, "I am the way,"[219] and so on. Some were utterances of his perceptible human nature, for instance, "Now you seek to kill me, a man who has told you the truth that I heard from my Father."[220] So in this place [the agony in Gethsemane] he displays, in his human nature, both the weakness of human flesh and the willingness of spirit: weakness in the words "Father, if it is possible let this cup pass away from me,"[221] willingness of spirit in what follows: "But not as I will, as you will." AGAINST CELSUS 2.25.[222]

SCRIPTURE'S DIFFERENT STARTING POINTS. AMBROSE OF MILAN: When the Scripture has set out, as I said above, the twin substance in Christ, so that you may understand both the substance of divinity and the substance of flesh, it begins in this place ["A man is coming after me, who came into being before me"][223] with the flesh. For in holy Scripture there is no consistent rule; sometimes we begin with Christ's divinity and descend to the sacrament of his incarnation. Sometimes the starting point is the humility of the incarnation, and we rise up to the glory of the Godhead. . . . Here the writer begins with the Lord's incarnation, and he is to proceed to speak of his divinity, not in

such a way as to confuse the human and divine elements but to distinguish them. ON THE CHRISTIAN FAITH 3.65.[224]

DIVINE AND HUMAN—ONE PERSON. THEODORET OF CYR: We preach such a union of the Godhead and the manhood that we conceive of one indivisible person and recognize him to be at the same time God and man, visible and invisible, circumscribed and uncircumscribed. And all other qualities that signify divinity and humanity we ascribe to the one person. ERANISTES 3.[225]

HE RECEIVES YET GIVES THE SPIRIT. CYRIL OF ALEXANDRIA: He was anointed in human fashion like us, though he himself gives the Spirit to those who are worthy to receive it, and "not by measure," as the blessed Evangelist John says.[226] THIRD LETTER TO NESTORIUS (LETTER 17).[227]

THE PRINCIPLE OF UNCONFUSED UNION. CYRIL OF ALEXANDRIA: Therefore we acknowledge our Lord Jesus Christ, the only-begotten Son of God, perfect God and perfect man, consisting of rational soul and body. In respect of his divinity, he was begotten from the Father before the ages. In respect of his humanity, he was begotten also of the Virgin Mary, for us and for our salvation. He is also of one substance with the Father, in respect of his divinity, and he is of one substance with us in respect of his humanity. For a unity of two natures has come about. This is why we acknowledge one Christ, one Son, one Lord. In accordance with this principle of the union without confusion, we acknowledge the holy Virgin as mother of God (theotokos), because the Word was incarnate and made man, and from the very conception he united to himself the temple he took

---

[217]LCC 3:381. [218]Col 1:15. [219]Jn 14:6. [220]Jn 8:40. [221]Mt 26:39. [222]ECF 300. [223]Jn 1:30. [224]LCF 178-79. [225]The Beggarman (LCF 270). [226]Jn 3:34. [227]LCC 3:350*.

from her. As for the utterances about the Lord in the Gospels and apostolic writings, we know that the theologians regard some as common to both natures on the basis of one person, and others they distinguish, on the basis of two natures, referring the godlike utterances to the divinity of Christ and the lowly to his humanity. Letter 39, To John of Antioch (The Formula of Reunion).[228]

How to Attribute the Scriptures Properly. Cyril of Alexandria: In his sermons Nestorius pretends to say "one Son and Lord" but he refers the sonship and the lordship only to the Word of God, and when he comes to the economy again he speaks of the "man born of the woman" as a different lord conjoined to the Word by dignity or equality of honor. But to say that God the Word is called Christ for this reason, simply because he has a conjunction with the Christ, then if Christ has conjunction with Christ, as one to another, what difference is it from clearly stating that there are two Christs? The Orientals,[229] however have said nothing like this. They only tried to distinguish the term. They make the distinction in such as way as to say that there are some terms appropriate to the Godhead, some to the manhood, and some which are referred in common as being appropriate both to the Godhead and the manhood, except that they are attributed to one and the same person. This is not what Nestorius does, for he attributes some to God the Word on his own and others to the different son born of a woman. It is one thing to recognize a distinction in the terms but quite another matter to divide them between two persons, one beside another. Letter to Eulogius.[230]

The Styles of Scriptural Discourse. Cyril of Alexandria: And so, we unite the Word of God the Father to the holy flesh endowed with a rational soul, in an ineffable way that transcends understanding, without confusion, without change and without alteration,[231]

and we thereby confess one Son and Christ and Lord; the same one God and man, not someone alongside someone different, but one and the same who is and is known to be both things. For this reason he sometimes speaks economically as man, in human fashion, and at other times, as God, he makes statements with divine authority. First Letter to Succensus 6.[232]

The Principle of Christological Attribution. Leo the Great: Each nature performs its proper functions in communion with the other; the Word performs what pertains to the Word, the flesh what pertains to the flesh: the one is resplendent with miracles, the other submits to insults. The Word withdraws not from his equality with the Father's glory; the flesh does not desert the nature of our kind. Letter 28.4 (The Tome of Leo).[233]

Correct Christological Attribution. Leo the Great: As therefore, to pass over many examples, it does not belong to the same nature to weep for a dead friend with emotions of pity and to recall the same friend from the dead with a word of power when the stone was taken away that had covered the grave for four days; or to hang on the cross and, changing light into darkness, make all the elements to quake; or to be pierced with nails and open the gates of paradise to the malefactor's faith, so it does not belong to the same nature to say "I and my Father are one"[234] and to say "My Father is greater than I."[235] For although in the Lord Jesus Christ, God and man are one person, nevertheless the source of the shame that is common to both is one thing; the source of the glory that is common to both, another. For from our side

---

[228]*LCF* 259-60*. [229]He refers to the other Syrian theologians, especially John of Antioch and Theodoret of Cyr, who drafted the christological statements of 433 that Cyril had reviewed and acknowledged as orthodox. [230]*CACC* 350-51. [231]An important statement that would be inserted into a key point in the Chalcedonian symbol later in 451, for which this letter serves as a major source. [232]*CACC* 354. [233]*LCF* 280. [234]Jn 10:30. [235]Jn 14:28.

he possesses the humanity that is inferior to the Father, and from the Father he possesses the divinity that is equal to the Father. By reason, then, of this unity of person to be understood in both natures, the Son of man is said to have come down from heaven when the Son of God took flesh from the Virgin from whom he was born; and, again, the Son of God is said to have been crucified and buried, though he suffered these things not in the Godhead itself, wherein the Only-Begotten is coeternal and consubstantial with the Father, but in the weakness of human nature. Accordingly we all confess in the creed that the only-begotten Son of God was crucified and buried, according to that saying of the apostle, "For if they had known, they would never have crucified the Lord of glory."[236] LETTER 28.4-5 (THE TOME OF LEO).[237]

THE TWOFOLD CONFESSION OF FAITH. LEO THE GREAT: Now when our Lord and Savior himself was instructing the faith of his disciples by questioning them, he said, "Who do people say that I, the Son of man, am?"[238] And when they had recounted the diverse opinions of others, he said, "But you, who do you say that I am?" I (that is to say) who am the Son of man, and whom you behold in the form of a servant and in the reality of flesh, "who say you that I am?" Then blessed Peter, divinely inspired, and by his confession destined to profit all nations, exclaimed, "You are the Christ, Son of the living God." Not undeservedly was he proclaimed "blessed" by the Lord, and from the original rock drew the strength both of his power and his name confessing as he did that the selfsame person was both Son of God and Christ; seeing that the reception of one of these truths apart from the other profited not to salvation, and there was equal danger in believing the Lord Jesus Christ to be God only and not man also, or man only and not God. LETTER 28.5 (THE TOME OF LEO).[239]

SUMMARY OF CHRISTOLOGICAL FAITH.

COUNCIL OF CHALCEDON (451): For the synod is opposed to those who presume to rend asunder the mystery of the incarnation into a double sonship, and it deposes from the priesthood those who dare to say that the Godhead of the Only-Begotten is passable; and it withstands those who imagine a mixing or confusion of the two natures of Christ; and it drives away those who erroneously teach that the form of a servant that he took from us was of a heavenly or some other substance; and it anathematizes those who feign that the Lord had two natures before the union but that these were fashioned into one after the union. CREEDAL STATEMENT.[240]

The Two Natures

TWO NATURES DO NOT DIVIDE THE ONE SON. THEODORET OF CYR: We believe, as we were taught, in one Father, Son and Holy Spirit. For even though certain liars have said it, we have not been taught "two sons," nor were we baptized into two sons, nor do we believe in or teach anyone to believe in two sons. Just as we know one Father and one Holy Spirit, so we know one Son, our Lord Jesus Christ, the only-begotten Son of God, God the Word who became human. For we do not deny the particular properties of the natures, but just as we think that those people are wicked who divide the one Lord Jesus Christ into two sons, so we call enemies of the truth those people who attempt to blend the natures together. For we believe that the union took place without any blending, and we know that some properties belong to the humanity and others to the divinity. The human being, and I am referring to the human being in general, the rational, mortal, living being, has a soul and a body but is considered one living being; and the difference of the two natures does not divide the one

---

[236]1 Cor 2:8. [237]CCC 319-20. [238]Mt 16:13. [239]CCC 320. [240]CCC 336-37.

human being into two persons. In the one being we know the immortality of the soul and the mortality of the body, and we acknowledge that the soul is invisible while the body is visible, but that there is one living being, as I said, which is both rational and mortal. In the same way, we know that our Lord and God, I mean the Son of God, the Lord Christ, was one Son, even after becoming human. For the union admits of no division, just as it admits of no blending. And yet we know that the divinity has no beginning, while the humanity is more recent. For the latter springs from the seed of Abraham and David, since the holy Virgin is descended from them; but the divine nature was begotten from God the Father before the ages, outside of time, without any change and without any separation. If the distinction of the flesh and divinity were abolished, what weapons would we use in the battle against Arius and Eunomius? How could we crush their blasphemy against the Only-Begotten? For our part, we apply the lowly words as to a human being and the exalted and divine words as to God; and thus it is very easy for us to present the truth. LETTER 21.12, TO THE LAWYER EUSEBIUS.[241]

The Permeation of Human Nature with the Divine

CHRIST'S DIFFERENT MODES OF ACTION. ORIGEN: The Savior sometimes speaks concerning himself as a man, sometimes as concerning a more divine nature, a nature that is one with the uncreated nature of the Father. When he says, "Now you seek to kill me, a man who has spoken the truth to you,"[242] he says this knowing that what they sought to destroy was not God but man. But in saying, "I and the Father are one,"[243] "I am the truth and the life,"[244] and "I am the resurrection,"[245] he is not teaching them about the man whom the Jews sought to destroy. . . . "You know me and know where I am"[246] is said of himself as man, while "You know neither me nor my Father"[247] of his

Godhead. COMMENTARY ON THE GOSPEL OF JOHN 19.2.(1).[248]

THE HUMANITY OF CHRIST IS TRANSFIGURED. ORIGEN: He whom we confidently believe to be God and Son of God from the beginning is the absolute Reason [Logos], Wisdom and Truth. We affirm that his mortal body and the human soul in it, by virtue not merely of association but of unity and commixture with the Logos, has become possessed of the highest powers and, partaking in the divinity of the Logos, has become divine. . . . If such assertions are sound, is there anything irrational in the supposition that the quality of the mortal body of Jesus changed to a heavenly and divine quality through the providence of God who so willed it? AGAINST CELSUS 3.41.[249]

THE SUFFERING CHRIST IS THE LORD OF GLORY. AMBROSE OF MILAN: When we read that "the Lord of majesty was crucified,"[250] we must not imagine him crucified in respect of his majesty. It is because he is both God and man (God in virtue of his divinity, man in virtue of his taking flesh on himself) that Jesus Christ, the Lord of majesty, is said to be crucified. For, since he partook of both natures, the human and the divine, he underwent his suffering in the nature of man, so that without distinction he who suffered may be called "the Lord of glory," and he who descended from heaven may be called, in the scriptural phrase, "the Son of man." ON THE CHRISTIAN FAITH 2.58.[251]

THE CLOSENESS OF THE UNION. GREGORY OF NAZIANZUS: He made his appearance as God, with the assumption of human nature, a unity composed of two opposites, flesh and Spirit. The former he deified; the latter was already deified. O strange mixture! O marvelous blend-

---

[241]MFC 2:202-3. [242]Jn 8:40. [243]Jn 10:30. [244]Jn 14:6. [245]Jn 11:25. [246]Jn 7:28. [247]Jn 8:19. [248]ECF 300-301. [249]ECF 303-4. [250]1 Cor 2:8. [251]LCF 179.

ing! He who is, comes to be; the Uncreated is created, the Unconfinable is confined, through the mediation of the intellectual soul, that bridge between the divinity and the grossness of the flesh. ORATION 38.13.[252]

THE ASSUMED AND THE ASSUMER COMBINE. GREGORY OF NAZIANZUS: He was, and he becomes. He was above time; he became subject to time. He was invisible; he becomes visible. "He was in the beginning, and he was with God, and he was God."[253] "Was" is repeated three times, for emphasis. What he was, he laid aside; what he was not, he assumed. He did not become two, but he allowed himself to become a unity composed of two elements. For that which assumed and that which was assumed combine into a divine being. The two natures coalesce into a unity; and there are not two sons, for we must make no mistake about the commixture of the natures. ORATION 37.2.[254]

THE PARADOXES OF THE UNION. GREGORY OF NAZIANZUS: Was it something offensive that he showed mercy to you?[255] I find him the more admirable. For he stripped off none of his Godhead in bringing my salvation, a physician who descended to the world of evil-smelling passions. He was mortal, yet God, of the seed of David, but still the molder of Adam's form. He bore flesh, yet existed outside a body. He is son of a mother, yet she is a virgin. He was subject to limitation, yet [remained] beyond measure. A manger received him, while the magi were led by a star, as they came bringing gifts and bending their knees in worship. As a mortal man he came to the struggle, yet unconquered he prevailed over the tempter in the threefold conflict. Food was laid before him, yet he it was who fed thousands and turned water into wine. He was baptized, but himself cleansed sins and was proclaimed Son of the Eternal by the thundering voice of the Spirit. As a human being he took sleep, while as God he lulled the sea to sleep. He bent his knees in weariness, but

to the knees of the palsied he restored strength. He prayed, yet who was it who heard the supplications of the weak? He was both sacrifice and high priest, an offerer of sacrifice, yet God. He dedicated his blood to God and cleansed the whole world. Even when a cross raised him up, it was sin that was fixed by its nails. PERSONAL POEMS 2.59-77, ON THE SON.[256]

DIVINITY ADOPTS FRAGILE FLESH. GREGORY OF NYSSA: How will Apollinaris ascribe the feeding at the breast, the swaddling clothes . . . growth, weariness . . . burial, the tomb, the shrine? How are these congruous with God? For if his so-called God-in-flesh was always that which became visible as a result of his birth from Mary, and that which appeared was Godhead,[257] then the Godhead experiences all those things; the Godhead is suckled . . . is weary, sleeps, grieves. . . . The Godhead runs to the fig tree and does not know when the tree bears fruit; the Godhead does not know the day and the hour; the Godhead is beaten, bound, buffeted, receives the nails, bleeds, becomes a corpse, is buried and placed in a new tomb. . . . Who cried out that he was forsaken by God? If it was the one Godhead of the Father and the Son, who did the forsaking? . . . Surely he cannot avoid ascribing those utterances and experiences that display suffering and humility to the humanity; he cannot help admitting that the divine nature is unchangeable and impassible even when associated with human sufferings. AGAINST APOLLINARIS 24.[258]

THE INTIMACY OF DIVINE AND HUMAN. JOHN CHRYSOSTOM: Thus, in saying, "If possible, let this cup pass away from me" and, "Not

---

[252]LCF 106. [253]Jn 1:2. [254]LCF 106. [255]Gregory is ironically asking the Arians, who objected to ascribing human weakness to the divinity as something "offensive to religion," whether the mercy of salvation should be regarded as offensive. [256]PA 9*. [257]Apollinaris wished to ascribe everything in the incarnate life of Christ directly to the Word of God, without committing himself to accepting there was a human soul in Jesus. [258]LCF 135.

as I will, but as you will,"[259] he is merely demonstrating that he is really clothed with flesh which is afraid of death, for it is characteristic of the flesh to be afraid of death and to shrink from it in horror. And so sometimes he leaves the flesh deprived and stripped of his own activity, so that, by showing its weakness, he may help people to believe in the reality of his physical nature, while sometimes he hides this very weakness so that you may learn that he is not a mere man. . . . As God, he foreknows the future; as man, he trembles. On Those Who Attend the Gatherings 6.[260]

The Union Aligns the Two Natures.

GREGORY OF NYSSA: We assert that the body in which he accepted his suffering, being mingled with the divine nature, became through that intermixture identical with the nature that assumed it.[261] . . . We believe that whatever in our lowly nature was assumed in the fulfillment of his divine plan of love for humanity was also transformed to what is divine and immortal. As it says, "God made this Jesus, whom you crucified, Lord and Christ."[262] This passage of Scripture asserts that two things happened to one person: suffering at the hands of the Jews, honor from God. It is not meant that one person suffered and another was honored by exaltation. The apostle makes his meaning clearer by his following statement, "being exalted by the right hand of God."[263] Who was exalted? . . . God surely needs no exaltation, since he is the highest. Then he must mean that the humanity was exalted, and it was exalted by becoming Lord and Christ. And this happened after the passion. . . . The lowly nature of him who was crucified . . . in virtue of its commixture with the infinite and unlimited nature of the good remained no longer confined to the limits of its own properties but was raised up with the divine element by the right hand of God, and became Lord instead of servant, King and Christ instead of subject, Highest instead of lowly, God instead of man. AGAINST EUNOMIUS 5.5.[264]

The Fire Hidden in the Ember.

GREGORY OF NYSSA: The Godhead "empties" itself in order that it may come within the capacity of the human nature. The humanity is renewed by itself becoming divine through commixture with the divine. . . . It is like fire that often lies hidden below the surface of wood and is not observed by the senses of those who see, or even touch, the wood, and yet is manifest when eventually the wood kindles into flame. In the same way . . . he who is "the Lord of Glory"[265] thought nothing of that which most people would have regarded as shameful. He concealed the embers of his life beneath his bodily nature in fulfilling the divine plan by means of his death, and then he kindled it to flame again by the power of his own Godhead, warming into life that which had been brought to death and pouring that limited firstfruit of our nature into the infinity of his divine power. Thus he made it to be what he himself was, making the form of the servant to be Lord, the human son of Mary to be Christ and him who was crucified through weakness to be life and power. He made all that is reverently conceived as belonging to God the Word to be also in that which the Word assumed, so that those properties no longer seem to be in either nature by way of distinction and division. Rather, it seems that the perishable nature is re-created by commixture into the divine, since the divine prevails over it. In this way the human nature partakes of the power of the Godhead. It is comparable to saying that a drop of vinegar is mixed in the ocean and is thus turned into sea by that mixture, since the natural qualities of the liquid do not remain in the infinity of the prevailing element. . . . That which was crucified because of weakness has itself, through the prevailing power of him who dwelled within it, become what the

---

[259]Mt 26:39. [260]*LCF* 171. [261]An early Syrian type of Christology of commingling, which would later be censured by the Council of Chalcedon (451). Gregory here means that the humanity was transfigured by its assumption in the divinity. He especially refers to the status of the humanity in the glory of Christ after the ascension. [262]Acts 2:36. [263]Acts 2:33. [264]*LCF* 137. [265]1 Cor 2:8.

indweller is in very fact and title, namely, Christ and Lord. Against Eunomius 5.5.[266]

The Mixture of Grandeur and Humility. Gregory of Nyssa: God the Word highly exalted that which was lowly, and on him who had a human name he bestowed the "name above all names."[267] Thus came about that ineffable mixture and conjunction of human littleness and divine immensity, in virtue of which even those majestic divine names are rightly applied to the humanity and the Godhead conversely is addressed by human names. For it is the same person who has the "name above all names" who is also worshiped by all creation under his human name of Jesus. "At the name of Jesus every knee shall bow . . . and every tongue confess that Jesus is Lord."[268] Against Eunomius 6.4.[269]

Christ's Human Acts Were Suffused with Divinity. John Chrysostom: The Lord says, "I assumed manhood but never left it unmingled with the divine activity. I have acted now as man, now as God, thus showing my human nature and at the same time supporting faith in the incarnation: teaching that the humbler things are to be attributed to the manhood, the nobler to the Godhead, and by this unequal mixture of actions explaining the unequal union of the natures. By control over human experiences I showed that my sufferings were voluntary. As God, I restrained nature, and endured a forty-day fast; as man, I was hungry and weary. As God, I calmed the fury of the sea; as man, I was tested by the devil. As God, I cast out devils; as man, I am going to suffer on humanity's behalf." On the Four Days of Lazarus in the Tomb 1.[270]

The Lord's Body Is Charged with Divine Graces. Theodoret of Cyr: The incarnation of the Only-Begotten did not increase the number of the Trinity, so that it became a quaternity. The Trinity remained a Trinity

even after the incarnation. When we believe that the only-begotten Son of God became man, we do not deny the nature he assumed. We acknowledge, as I said, the assuming nature and the assumed. For the union does not confuse the distinctive properties of the natures. The air, which receives the light throughout its whole extent, does not lose its being as air, nor does it destroy the nature of the light. We see the light with our eyes; we recognize the air by our sense of touch. . . . It would be the extreme of folly to call the union of Godhead and manhood a confusion. . . . When heat is applied to gold, the gold partakes of the color and energy of the fire, but it does not lose its own nature. It remains gold, while behaving as fire. So our Lord's body is a body, but impassible, incorruptible, immortal. It is the Lord's body, divine and glorified with divine glory. It is not separated from the Godhead. It does not belong to someone else; it belongs to the only-begotten Son of God. Nor does it display to us another person, but the Only-Begotten himself, clothed in our nature. Letter 145.[271]

As a Small Child He Still Filled the Universe. Cyril of Alexandria: But when seen as a babe and wrapped in swaddling clothes, even when still in the bosom of the Virgin who bore him, he filled all creation as God and was enthroned with him who begot him. For the Divine cannot be numbered or measured and does not admit of circumscription. Third Letter to Nestorius (Letter 17).[272]

Christ's Body Is Luminous in Deity. Cyril of Alexandria: I have said, because it was God's own body it transcended all human things, yet the earthly body itself did not undergo a transformation into the nature of Godhead, for this is impossible, otherwise we would be accusing the Godhead of being created

---

[266]LCF 138-39*. [267]Phil 2:9; Eph 1:21. [268]Phil 2:11. [269]LCF 140. [270]LCF 171. [271]LCF 273. [272]LCC 3:350.

and of receiving into itself something that was not part of its own nature. It would be just as foolish an idea to talk of the body being transformed into the nature of Godhead as it would to say the Word was transformed into the nature of flesh. For just as the latter is impossible (for he is unchangeable and unalterable), so too is the former. It is not possible that any creature could be converted into the essence or nature of Godhead. The flesh is a created thing. We maintain, therefore, that Christ's body is divine insofar as it is the body of God, adorned with unspeakable glory, incorruptible, holy and life-giving; but none of the holy Fathers has ever thought or said that it was transformed into the nature of Godhead, and we have no intention of doing so either. FIRST LETTER TO SUCCENSUS 10.[273]

THE DIVINITY IS HIDDEN BY THE VEIL OF FLESH.

LEO THE GREAT: Even when he came to the baptism of John, his forerunner, the Father's voice thundered from heaven: "This is my beloved Son in whom I am well pleased."[274] This was to prevent him remaining unknown since his divinity was hidden by the veil of flesh. He whom the craft of the devil tempts as man is the same that the angels minister to as God. To hunger, to thirst, to be weary and to sleep, is obviously human, but to satisfy five thousand people with five loaves and to give the Samaritan woman that living water, a drink that will cause the drinker to thirst no more, is without question divine. The same is true about walking on the surface of the sea with feet that do not sink and calming the rising waves by rebuking the tempest. LETTER 28.4 (THE TOME OF LEO).[275]

The Intimacy of the Union

MIND IS BLENDED WITH MIND.

GREGORY OF NAZIANZUS: You, my good sir, as an Apollinarian, despise my mind[276] so that you may attach God to the flesh, on the ground that this is the only possible mode of attachment. You accuse me of anthropolatry, but you incur the charge of sarcolatry.[277] Your theory takes away the middle wall.[278] What, then, is my account of the matter, the account of a man of very small claim to learning or philosophy? I hold that mind is blended with mind, as being closer and more congenial.[279] So it is that Godhead and humanity are united through the mediation of mind standing between Godhead and the grossness of the flesh. LETTER 101.10, TO CLEDONIUS.[280]

AN INDISSOLUBLE AND INEFFABLE UNION.

THEODORE OF MOPSUESTIA: We learn from the sacred Books the distinction between the natures. . . . That which assumed was the divine nature, which does everything for us, whereas the other is the human nature, which was assumed on behalf of us all by him who is the cause of everything and is united to it in an ineffable union, forever indissoluble. ON THE NICENE CREED 8.10.[281]

FIRE PUTS ON A BODY.

EPHREM THE SYRIAN: The firstborn entered the womb, but the pure one[282] perceived not. He arose and emerged with birth pangs, and the fair one felt him; glorious and hidden his entry, despised and visible his emergence, since he is God at his entry but human at his emergence. What a wonder and confusion to hear: Fire entered the womb,[283] put on a body and emerged! HYMNS ON THE NATIVITY 21.21.[284]

THE HUMANITY IS TAKEN TO A NEW LEVEL.

GREGORY OF NYSSA: In our thought we dis-

---

[273]*CACC* 357. [274]Mt 3:17; 17:5. [275]*CCC* 319**. [276]The Apollinarists thought it was unfitting to ascribe a human mind to Christ. [277]The worship of flesh, a neologism coined by Gregory. [278]Referring to the golden mean of common sense. [279]That is, that the incarnate Logos also assumed a human mind along with the flesh. [280]*LCF* 108. [281]*LCF* 167. [282]The Virgin Mary. [283]In antiquity Mary is often called the burning bush (the unconsumed bush, as in the epiphany of God to Moses at Sinai), on this account that the fire of the divinity entered her but did not consume her. [284]ESH 178.

tinguish the working out of the divine plan by means of the flesh from the divine power considered by itself. . . . The flesh was not identical with the Godhead, until this too was transformed into the nature of divinity. So that it necessarily follows that one set of attributes is fitting for God the Word, another set to "the form of the servant." . . . He who was "highly exalted"[285] as a result of his suffering became Lord and Christ through his union with him who is in reality Lord and Christ. We say this, knowing, through what we have been taught, that the divine nature is always identical and consistent, while the flesh, in itself, is what reason and sense perception apprehend it to be. But when mingled with the divine, it no longer keeps within the limits of its own natural properties but is taken up to the level of the prevalent and transcendent. But our idea of the different properties of the flesh and the Godhead remains unconfused so long as we contemplate each of these by itself. For example, the Word existed before the ages, but the flesh came into being in these last times. AGAINST EUNOMIUS 5.5.[286]

THE TRANSFERENCE OF THE NAMES. GREGORY OF NYSSA: The human nature is glorified by his assumption of it; the divine nature humbles itself by this act of condescension but consigns the human element to suffering, while achieving, through its divine power, the resurrection of the element that suffered. Thus the experience of death is ascribed to him who has partaken of our passible nature because of the union of the man[287] with him, while the sublime appellations, congruous with divinity, descend on the man, so that he who was displayed on the cross is called "the Lord of glory,"[288] because of the mingling of his divine nature with the lowly element and the transference of the grace of those names from the divine to the human. AGAINST EUNOMIUS 6.2.[289]

UNION IS NOT CONFUSION. JOHN CHRYSOS-

TOM: From the words "he emptied himself"[290] you must not suppose a change or transfiguration or any kind of annihilation. While he remained what he was, he assumed what he was not: though he became flesh he remained God, in that he was the Word. In his flesh he was like a man, hence "in shape like a man." His nature did not alter; there was no confusion. . . . The phrases "he became" and "he assumed" are never used to govern "Godhead," but they are used to govern "manhood." The latter he "became" and "he assumed," but the former was always his. We must make no confusion or admit any separation. One God; one Christ, the Son of God. But when I say "one," I refer to a union, not a confusion: one nature is not transformed into the other but is united with it. HOMILY 7 ON PHILIPPIANS.[291]

THE INCOMPREHENSIBLE UNION. JOHN CHRYSOSTOM: By a union and conjunction God the Word and the flesh are a unity: there is no confusion or annihilation of substances but an ineffable and incomprehensible union. HOMILY 11 ON 2 JOHN.[292]

THE UNION IS LIKE A SOUL IN A BODY. CYRIL OF ALEXANDRIA: We do not say that the Word of God dwelled in him who was born of the holy Virgin as if in an ordinary man, for we must not regard Christ as a man who carried God within him. Although the Word dwelled in us and, as it is said, "all the fullness of the Godhead dwelled in Christ bodily,"[293] yet we should realize that when he became flesh the indwelling was not in the same manner as when he is said to dwell in the saints. In his case, having been united by a union of natures and not converted into flesh, he brought to pass such an indwelling as the soul of man may be said to have with its own body. There is, then, one

---

[285]See Phil 2:5-11. [286]LCF 137-38. [287]By which Gregory habitually means humanity. [288]Jas 2:1; 1 Cor 2:8. [289]LCF 140. [290]See Phil 2:5-11. [291]LCF 170-71. [292]LCF 170. [293]Col 2:9.

Christ, and Son and Lord. THIRD LETTER TO NESTORIUS (LETTER 17).[294]

THE LOGOS APPROPRIATES HIS INCARNATE SUFFERINGS. CYRIL OF ALEXANDRIA: But let your Holiness[295] act to stop the mouths of those who say that there was a mixture or confusion or blending of God the Word with the flesh, for it is likely that some are spreading the report also that I hold or say this. But so far am I from holding anything of the sort that I look on all who imagine that even a shadow of turning can befall the divine nature of the Word as being completely mad, and the same in relation to the thought that he is susceptible of change. For he remains what he always is and has undergone no alteration. Nor could he ever undergo alteration. Moreover, we all acknowledge that the Word of God is naturally impassible, even though, in his all-wise administration of the mystery, he is seen to attribute to himself the sufferings that afflicted his own flesh. This is why the all-wise Peter says, "Christ has suffered for us in the flesh"[296] and not in the nature of the ineffable Godhead. For in order that he may be believed to be the Savior of the World, he appropriates to himself, as I said, in view of his incarnation, the sufferings of his own flesh. LETTER 39, TO JOHN OF ANTIOCH (THE FORMULA OF REUNION).[297]

THE UNITY OF THE NATURES IN ONE LORD. LEO THE GREAT: Our Lord took from his mother nature, not sin. In our Lord Jesus Christ, born of a virgin's womb, the nature is not unlike ours just because his birth was wonderful. For he that is true God is true man. In this unity there is no element of unreality even if there are separate spheres. For just as God is not changed by the comparison exhibited, so the manhood is not absorbed by the dignity bestowed. Each form in communion with the other performs the function that is proper to it. Namely, the Word performs what belongs to the Word, and the flesh carries out what

belongs to the flesh. The one sparkles with miracles; the other succumbs to injuries. And as the Word does not cease to be on an equality with the Father's glory, so the flesh does not forgo the nature of our race. For (and it is a fact that must be repeated again and again), one and the same person is truly Son of God and truly Son of man. LETTER 28.4 (THE TOME OF LEO).[298]

Divine and Human Will in the Incarnate Son

THE HUMAN WILL CONFORMED TO THE DIVINE. GREGORY OF NAZIANZUS: The seventh of the Eunomian arguments from Scripture:[299] "I came down from heaven not to do my own will but the will of him who sent me."[300] If this saying did not issue from that which came down, we should have said that the expression took that form as coming from the human nature, not from the Savior regarded as such (for his will could not be in the least degree opposed to God, since it was wholly deified) but from him considered as man. For the human will did not completely conform to the divine will but struggled and wrestled against it, as it frequently does. This is the interpretation we have put on "Father, if possible, let this cup pass from, me. But let not my will, but yours, prevail."[301] It is not to be supposed that, regarded as Savior, he did not know whether it was possible or not or that his will resisted the will of God. But the utterance under discussion issued from him who assumed human nature (for it was the divine nature that came down) and not from the nature that was assumed. Therefore our reply will be that the saying does not imply

---

[294]CCC 282-83**. [295]Cyril is addressing the Syrian patriarch John of Antioch, asking him to stop his own theologians from accusing Cyril of teaching this doctrine of confusion. [296]1 Pet 4:1. [297]CCC 292-93**. [298]CCC 318-19. [299]The Arians offered this text as proof that the will of Christ and that of God were different, and thus that Christ was alien to the deity. [300]Jn 6:38. [301]Mt 26:39.

that the Son has a will of his own, apart from the Father's will, but that he has not. So the meaning of the words will be "Not to do my own will, for my will is not distinct from yours, but to perform the will that is common to you and me, for our will is one, as our Godhead is one." ORATION 30.12.[302]

THE LORD ASSUMES HUMAN WILL TO HEAL IT. THEODORE OF MOPSUESTIA: If, however, divine nature was sufficient for all these things, then human nature that was in need of the grace of salvation from God should not have been assumed, as according to the opinion of the heretics this same Godhead would have satisfied the requirements of human nature. In this case it would have been superfluous to assume a body at all, since the Godhead was able to perform all its acts. This, however, was not the will of God, who indeed wished to put on and raise the fallen humanity who is composed of a body and of an immortal and rational soul. And so, "as by one man sin entered the world, and death by sin, so also the free gift and the grace of God by the righteousness of one man might abound to many."[303] As death was by man, so also the resurrection from the dead will be by man, because "as we all die in Adam so in Christ shall all be made alive,"[304] as the blessed Paul testifies. Therefore it was necessary that he should assume not only the body but also the immortal and rational soul; and not only the death of the body had to cease but also that of the soul, which is sin. Since, according to the sentence of the blessed apostle, sin entered the world through man, and death entered through sin, it was necessary that sin, which was the cause of death, should have first been abolished, and then the abolition of death would have followed by itself. If sin were not abolished, we would have by necessity remained in mortality, and we would have sinned in our mutability; and when we sin, we are under punishment, and consequently the power of death will by necessity remain. It was, therefore, necessary that

sin should have first been abolished, as after its abolition there would be no entry for death. It is indeed clear that the strength of the sin has its origin in the will or the soul. In the case of Adam also it was his soul that first accepted the advice of error and not his body, because it was not his body that Satan persuaded to yield to him, to forsake God and to believe that his helper was a deceiver, in his desire for higher things. In following the advice of Satan, he transgressed the commandment of God and chose for himself those things that were contrary to the commandment of God. It was not his body that had to know these things but his soul. ON THE NICENE CREED 5.[305]

IN THE WILL, THE HEALING OF HUMANITY OCCURS. THEODORE OF MOPSUESTIA: It is with justice, therefore, that our Lord assumed the soul so that it should be first delivered from sin and be transferred to immutability by the grace of God through which it overcomes also the passions of the body. When sin is abolished from every place and has no more entry into the soul, which has become immutable, every kind of condemnation will rightly be abolished, and death also will perish. The body will thus remain immune from death because it has received participation in immortality. The blessed Paul confirms this in saying, "There is, therefore, now no condemnation to them who are in Christ Jesus, who walk not after the flesh, for the law of life in Christ Jesus has made you free from the law of sin and death."[306] ON THE NICENE CREED 5.[307]

Human Willing and the Divine Will

THE WILL OF JESUS CLINGS TO THE GOOD. ORIGEN: It cannot be doubted that his soul was of the same nature as other souls . . . but whereas all souls have the power of choosing

---

[302]LCF 109. [303]Rom 5:17. [304]1 Cor 15:22. [305]WS 5:56.
[306]Rom 8:2. [307]WS 5:58.

good and evil, the soul that belonged to Christ so chose to love righteousness that because of the boundlessness of this love it cleaved to righteousness without possibility of change or separation, so that . . . what was dependent on free choice became second nature. Thus we must believe that there was in Christ a human rational soul, but we must think of it as having no possibility of sin. ON FIRST PRINCIPLES 2.6.5.[308]

THE HARMONY OF THE TWO WILLS. ORIGEN: When he took on him the nature of human flesh, he fully accepted all the characteristic properties of humanity. So, it should be realized that he had a body of real flesh and not of mere appearance. This was why in this part of the Gospel[309] he prayed that the cup of suffering might pass from him. . . . It is noteworthy that the account of the agony is given in Matthew, Mark and Luke, who also tell of the temptation of Jesus by the devil. Yet John, while giving an account of the passion in the same way as the others, omits the prayer of Jesus that the cup might pass from him, as he also gives no account of the temptation. I think the reason for this is that the first three Evangelists are giving an account of Jesus rather in respect of his human than his divine nature, while John's interpretation has more regard to his divine nature. . . . So the first three relate the prayer of Jesus that the cup might pass from him, since to wish to avoid suffering is a human characteristic, arising from the infirmity of the flesh. John's purpose is to display Jesus as God the Word, and therefore, knowing that he is the Life and the Resurrection, he cannot admit that the impassible God shrank from the passion. COMMENTARY ON THE GOSPEL OF MATTHEW 92.[310]

THE UNITY OF CHRIST'S WILL WITH GOD. ORIGEN: Jesus says to them, "My food is that I may do the will of him who sent me and complete his work,"[311] fitting food for the Son of God, when he is a doer of the Father's will,

making the willing in himself just what it was in the Father, so that the will of God is in the will of the Son and the will of the Son is inseparable from the will of the Father, so that there are no longer two wills but one. And this unity of will is the reason for the saying of the Son, "I and my Father are one";[312] and because of this unity of will, he who has seen him has seen the Son and has also seen him who sent him.[313] COMMENTARY ON THE GOSPEL OF JOHN 13.36.[314]

CHRIST'S WILL ALWAYS CHOOSES GOD. ATHANASIUS: Here[315] he willed what he begged to be spared, for that was the reason for his coming as man. The willing was his . . . the timidity belonged to the flesh. . . . Because of the flesh he mingled his will with human weakness, that by abolishing this he might make man stouthearted in the face of death. AGAINST THE ARIANS 3.57.[316]

CHRIST ALWAYS EXALTS THE DIVINE WILL. GREGORY OF NYSSA: To feel dread when faced with suffering[317] belongs to human weakness . . . to endure the suffering in fulfillment of the divine plan belongs to the divine decision and the divine power. There is a distinction between the divine and the human will, and he who made our sufferings his own utters, as from his human nature, the words that suit the weakness of humanity, but he adds the second utterance because he wishes the exalted will, the will that is worthy of God, to prevail over the human, for humankind's salvation. In saying, "not my will," he indicated his manhood; in adding, "but yours," he displayed the conjunction of his Godhead with that of the Father; and in that Godhead, because of the communion of nature, there is no difference of will. AGAINST APOLLINARIS 32.[318]

---

[308]ECF 298-99. [309]He is discussing the exegesis of the agony in the garden. [310]ECF 301-2. [311]Jn 4:34. [312]Jn 10:30. [313]Jn 14:9. [314]ECF 335. [315]Athanasius is discussing the biblical narratives of the agony in the garden. [316]ECF 400*. [317]Commenting on Lk 22:42. [318]LCF 140-41.

Two Wills in Christ. Third Council of Constantinople (681): We also proclaim two natural willings or wills in him and two natural operations, without separation, without change, without partition, without confusion, according to the teaching of the holy Fathers, and two natural wills not contrary to each other, God forbid, as the impious heretics have said, but his human will following, and not resisting or opposing, but rather subject to his divine and all-powerful will. For it was proper for the will of the flesh to be moved naturally, yet to be subject to the divine will, according to the all-wise Athanasius. For as his flesh is called, and is, the flesh of God the Word, so also the natural will of his flesh is called, and is, God the Word's own will, as he himself says: "I came down from heaven, not to do my own will but the will of the Father who sent me,"[319] calling the will of the flesh his own, as also the flesh had become his own. For in the same manner that his all-holy and spotless ensouled flesh, though divinized, was not destroyed but remained in its own law and principle, so also his human will, divinized, was not destroyed but rather preserved, as Gregory the Theologian[320] says: "His will, as conceived of in his character as the Savior, is not contrary to God, being wholly divinized." Statement of Faith.[321]

The Communion of the Wills. Third Council of Constantinople (681): Preserving, therefore, in every way the unconfused and undivided, we set forth the whole confession in brief; believing our Lord Jesus Christ, our true God, to be one of the holy Trinity even after the taking of flesh, we declare that his two natures shine forth in his one hypostasis, in which he displayed both the wonders and the sufferings through the whole course of his dispensation,[322] not in phantasm but truly, the difference of nature being recognized in the same one hypostasis by the fact that each nature wills and works what is proper to it, in communion with the other. On this principle we glorify two natural wills and operations combining with each other for the salvation of the human race. Statement of Faith.[323]

The Status of the Humanity in the Union

Christ's Complete Humanity. Theodore of Mopsuestia: Our blessed Fathers said, "He was incarnate, and became man,"[324] in order that we should believe that he was a complete man who was assumed and in whom God the Word dwelled; that he was complete in all that belongs to human nature, composed of a mortal body and a rational soul, since it is "for man and for his salvation that he came down from heaven." . . . He put on himself a man like Adam, who after sinning received the sentence of death, so that by a like human being sin should be abolished from us and death annihilated. On the Nicene Creed 5.17.[325]

Christ's Integrity of Human Life. Augustine: As in the unity of a person a soul is united to a body to constitute a human being, so God is united to man, in unity of person, to constitute Christ. In the former case there is a mixture of soul and body, in the latter a mixture of God and man. But this should not be interpreted on the analogy of the mixture of two liquids, where neither preserves its identity. . . . When the Word of God was mixed with a soul possessing a body, he assumed soul and body together. Letter 137.11.[326]

Christ Is Fully Human. Synod of Toledo (675): In this miraculous conception "Wisdom built for itself a house"[327] in that "the Word was made flesh and dwelled among us."[328] However, the Word was not turned into flesh and changed in such a way that he ceased to be God because he willed to become man. But the

---

[319]Jn 6:38. [320]Gregory of Nazianzus. [321]LCC 3:383-84. [322]Incarnate life. [323]LCC 3:384. [324]In the Nicene Creed. [325]*LCF* 166. [326]*LCF* 217. [327]Prov 14:1.

Word was made flesh in such a way that in him there is not merely the Word of God and the human flesh, but there is also a rational human soul, and this entire being is called God because of the presence of God and man because of the presence of man. In this Son of God we believe that there are two natures, one of his deity, the other of his humanity, which the one person of Christ has so united in himself that there can never be any separation, either of the divinity from the humanity or of the humanity from the divinity. Hence it is that Christ is perfect God and perfect man, in the unity of one person. And when we say that there are two natures in the Son, we do not intend to put two persons in him, for thus there would seem to be a fourth element added to the Trinity, which is utterly false. For God the Word did not assume a human person but a human nature, and with the eternal person of his divinity he united the temporal substance of his humanity. ELEVENTH COUNCIL OF TOLEDO, CREEDAL STATEMENT.[329]

The Son of Man

"SON OF MAN" SIGNIFIES THE HUMILITY OF THE MANHOOD. CYRIL OF ALEXANDRIA: Jesus clearly set his glory before his opponents, saying, "But after this the Son of man shall sit on the right hand of the power of God."[330] When, he says, I was in form like unto you, though by nature and in truth the Son of God the Father, you made no account of me. And yet how was it not right that the excellent art of the dispensation in the flesh should not escape your notice, inasmuch as you are learned in the Law and nurtured in the writings of Moses? Indeed, the predictions of the holy prophets are not unknown to you. But since you have brought yourselves to so great want of knowledge, and being filled with utter ignorance, do not recognize my mystery, then I shall have to tell you directly that there is granted to you only a short and narrow season for your pride and wickedness against me, even until my precious cross.

For immediately after this I shall clothe myself in honor. I ascend to the glory that I had from the beginning. Even in the flesh I am made the partner of God the Father on his throne, and I possess sovereignty over all. HOMILIES ON THE GOSPEL OF LUKE 150.[331]

THE SON OF MAN SITS ON THE DIVINE THRONE. CYRIL OF ALEXANDRIA: And so, meeting your questions, he sought to show both that he is the Christ and that by nature and truly he is the Son of God the Father. For he said, "You shall see the Son of man sitting on the right hand of power."[332] And tell me, I pray, whose is it to sit with the Father, but his who by nature is the Son? For of all that is made nothing whatsoever may boast of sitting on the throne of Deity; for every created being is put under the feet of the divine and supreme nature, which rules over all and transcends every thing whatsoever that has been brought into being. God the Father alone is set on the throne high and lifted up, but he shares his seat with the Son, who is ever with him and sprang by nature from him. HOMILIES ON THE GOSPEL OF LUKE 151.[333]

THE TITLE SIGNIFIES THE INCARNATION. GREGORY OF NYSSA: At what point, then, does Eunomius assent to the truth? Is it not when he says that the Lord himself, "being the Son of the living God, not being ashamed of his birth from the Virgin, often named himself, in his own sayings, 'the Son of man'"? For this phrase we also allege for proof of the community of essence,[334] because the name of Son shows the community of nature to be equal in both cases. For, as he is called the Son of man by reason of the kindred of his flesh to her of whom he was born, so also he is conceived, surely, as the Son of God, by reason of the connection of his essence with that from which he has his existence,

---

[328]Jn 1:14. [329] *TCT* 185. [330]Lk 22:69. [331]*CGSL* 596**. [332]Mk 14:62. [333]*CGSL* 601-2. [334]That the Christ had the same human nature as humanity.

and this argument is the greatest weapon of the truth. For nothing so clearly points to him who is "the mediator between God and man"[335] (as the great apostle called him) as the name of Son, equally applicable to either nature, divine or human. For the same person is Son of God and was made, in the incarnation, Son of man, that by his communion with each, he might link together by himself what were divided by nature. Now if, in becoming Son of man, he were without participation in human nature, it would be logical to say that neither does he share in the divine essence, though he is Son of God. But if the whole compound nature of humanity was in him, for he was "in all points tempted like as we are, yet without sin,"[336] it is surely necessary to believe that every property of the transcendent essence is also in him, as the word *Son* claims for him both alike; the human in the man, but in God the divine. If, then, the appellations, as Eunomius says, indicate relationship, and the existence of relationship is observed in the things, not in the mere sound of the words[337] (and by things I mean the things conceived in themselves, if it be not overbold thus to speak of the Son and the Father), who would deny that the very champion of blasphemy[338] has by his own action been dragged into the advocacy of orthodoxy, overthrowing by his own means his own arguments. AGAINST EUNOMIUS 3.4.[339]

MARY'S SONG OF THE MANY-NAMED CHRIST. EPHREM THE SYRIAN: [Verse]: My mouth knows not how to address you, O Son of the living One. I tremble to dare to address you as son of Joseph, for you are not his seed. Yet I shrink from denying the name of him to whom I have been betrothed. [Refrain]: Praise to you, Son of the most High, who put on our body. [Verse]: Although you are the Son of the One, I shall call you henceforth Son of many, for myriads of names do not suffice for you, for you are Son of God and Son of man and Son of Joseph and Son of David and Lord of Mary. HYMNS ON THE NATIVITY 6.1-2.[340]

---

[335]1 Tim 2:5. [336]Heb 4:15. [337]Eunomius had argued that biblical words connoted metaphysical realities: thus, if Christ was Son of man, this proved he was a human being, not a deity. Gregory argued in return that if Eunomius is right in his hermeneutical theory, he has to be wrong in his own christological conclusions. In the wider context the Cappadocian fathers argued that the Eunomian hermeneutics were wrong: that scriptural texts were far more flexible and symbolic than simply connoting essences at every utterance. [338]The Arian Eunomius. [339]NPNF 2 5:145. [340]ESH 111.

CONCLUSION

Often patristic theology has been caricatured as some form of lapse from the higher standard of the biblical age that preceded it. The thought of the Fathers is supposed, by some, to represent dogmatizing at its worst: wrangles of venal bishops, summons to the secular arm to enforce orthodoxy when reasonable debate has failed and cartloads of obscure philosophy and semantics muddying the clear streams of the Scriptures. This is, perhaps, a widespread sentiment, though few, when asked, can ever confess to having read much of the Fathers. To remedy that defect was one of the reasons behind the inspiration of this present series. The Fathers have always had their opponents, and those opponents, throughout history, have not always had the good of the church as their heart's desire. By now, however, the reader of this volume will have seen what a vacuous cliché such a view of patristic decline represents. If any single fact emerges from this collection of sources on the early church's understanding of Jesus, it must surely be that the Christians of the first five centuries were so deeply rooted in the Scriptures that they could not conceive any theological formulation of the faith that was not, demonstrably and primarily, rooted in, based on and inspired by the evangelical account, as that was read through the illustrative lenses of the Law, the Prophets and the Psalms.

There is not a paragraph from the primary sources gathered in this book that is not evidently woven out of biblical exegesis. Admittedly it may not always be exegesis that convinces or moves us in the present, but then again, in the main, their interpretation of Scripture avoided the fanciful, was attentive to the text and constantly sought after a sober sense of scriptural truth, something that they felt to be more than semantic exactitude. What they sensed was the presence of the God of grace who inspired the Scriptures and who was manifested in dazzling light most fully and comprehensively in the person of the Savior. All in all they had a mystical approach to the Bible. Perhaps it is something that has been eroded too much in the church of the present age. It should be a matter of some wonder, for example, that the profound and illuminating commentaries on sacred Scripture by the Fathers have so determinedly been banished from the modern theological academy.

It is this character of christocentricity that marks all patristic theology. It is something that is obviously and abundantly represented in this present volume, which focuses on the creedal clauses devoted to the person of Jesus, the Christ and Savior. But this volume, although partial by nature, does not thereby falsify the picture, for all of early Christian thought is marked by this character of christocentricity. The devotion of the ancients to Jesus is profound and heartfelt. Their understanding of the Lord is also something that is remarkably dynamic. Although they often talk much in terms of abstracts (it was the rhetorical fashion of the day) such as death, life, humanity, redemption, and so on, their concern in all they argue about is always with the practical. They understand Jesus to be the Savior and Liberator. Their supreme christological principle, on which they assessed and scrutinized different types of theory about him, was that in Christ there is given to the faithful church the full revelation of the invisible Father. This revelation of God is personally delivered in and through Jesus, and they go on to affirm that this revelation (not a mere epiphany) is intrinsically healing, reconciling and life-giving. In order to protect this overall dynamic of the economy of salvation in Christ, they are determined to insist on all the paradoxes involved in Christology (the death of God, the mental limitations of the supreme wisdom and so on). It did not spring from any perverse delight in making the gospel message difficult or incredible but simply because they cannot ever bring themselves to lose sight of the heart of the Good News.

This is something so simple that it is almost incredible: incredible because it beggars imagination. God has stooped down in mercy to enter the life of his creatures and share their sorrows with them. He has lifted up the weak and the broken to himself, and he healed their pain by abolishing their alienation. Within this act of compassion he has set a veritable structure of deliverance and healing. The incarnation (the enfleshment of the divine Logos) is a veritable deification of humanity. The Fathers see it always as an energy of enlightenment and healing. By this term, deification, so beloved of the Greek theologians, is meant all that the Latin fathers would convey by redemptive grace. The incarnation of God is celebrated by all the patristic theologians as the deification of the human race. What had formerly been alienated from God and had fallen into the corruption of sin and death is now restored to a higher destiny and a closer communion. How succinctly the old Roman paschal antiphon put it: "O happy fault of Adam, which merited so great a redemption!"

How much the Fathers loved to play with the rhetorical paradoxes that followed from that simple statement that it was God, and no other, who became flesh. Their play is an attempt to come to terms with it: a movement from the majesty of God to humility so utterly at variance with all the expectations of the wise of this world. In a Hellenistic world where for centuries the faithful synagogue had been battling against the casual idolatries of polytheists, the early Christians were never for a moment unaware of the shock value of their claim that in the incarnation it was God, and no other, who had come among us to save and heal. They are willing to explain, time and again, that they too renounced the mythological scandals of the pagans, and they too affirmed the supreme monotheism of a single Godhead. Nevertheless, the Jesus story had moved them into a new comprehension of God and thereby into a new covenant founded on Jesus. Like the writers of the sacred Scriptures, they are driven on by the need to communicate that central message of the faith.

The claim that in Jesus the divine Word was made flesh—made human, that is—led them inexorably to have to revise almost everything else in the house of theology. Monotheism, understood in a trinitarian fashion, is no simple matter. Its articulation did not fall to earth conveniently. The agonizing growing pains of the early church show us all the ins and outs of how they were thinking. One principle, however, remained steadfast in all authentic Christian reflection: that it was God and no other who came to save us in the incarnation. For this reason all the multitudes of easy solutions to the christological paradox were rigorously and consistently rejected. The main temptations were to lapse back into a mythological way of understanding Christ. Monotheism would be safe, surely, if only we understood that "Jesus" or "Son" was simply another name for "Father." Tertullian and others were quick to castigate this, for the implication that underlay it so blatantly (that Jesus was a vessel of God but not God himself). If only the word *divine* when applied to Jesus could be massaged, the heretics thought, eased away from its scandalous particularity and comprehensiveness. If only Christians could use it loosely, like the polytheists, then surely things would go more smoothly? Such has always been the temptation with Christology that seeks to slip away from the rigor of the authentic Christian tradition. Whether one calls that slipping away Photinianism, Adoptionism, Gnosticism, Arianism, or any number of the modern variants of the same thing, the same sentiment is always at the core—a sense of scandal that God could ever stoop to share a human life so intimately. This is nothing other than the refusal to take God seriously. The revelation of the face of God came not in power or glory but in humility and grace. Who would have expected such humility in the Messiah? Who would have expected that of all the signs of his presence he could have left to the church, he would have chosen the bread and wine of the artisan? Truly "you are a hidden God," the Scripture says.[1] Just as truly he is strange in his revelation. The incarnate Word reverses the wisdom of the ways of this world, which clings to its illusions in preference to the truth and celebrates pomp and power rather than graciousness or compassion.

And, ultimately, it is this sign of contradiction that patristic Christology protects and calls out to us even today to respect. For if, in the incarnation, God so humbled himself to show a pattern of redemption that was built out of the very fabric of mercy, then the true revelation of God is shown in the aspect of humility and kindness and the selflessness manifested in Christ. All types of heresy throughout the ages have thought they were merely offering proper honor to God by distancing Christology from such a pivotal position, shying away from what they saw as the "scandal" of the defilement of deity in the flesh. But this scandal is the heart of the Good News of the humility of God: the shocking revelation that the incarnate ministry of Jesus fully represents the true mind of God. But the Fathers argued back that what the heretics were creating was nothing more than an image of God taken from their own imaginations. We may well be led to think of God as magnificent and majestic, and so on. But the primary attributes of the divine, as manifested in the face of Christ, are those of compassion, healing and graciousness. Those who understand the implications of this find not only the revelation of truth in Jesus but also a way and a code of living that will ultimately lead them to assimilate their lives to the pattern of his.

And, last, that is perhaps exactly what the Fathers were arguing too. For one of the last things we might look back on, as we take our leave of them for the moment, is the profound character of pastoral guidance that illumines all this deep theological argument. In this they set us a very high standard. Bloviation, the abstraction of hot air in immense measures, is not peculiar to theologians, one presumes. But theologians have been guilty of more of it than most other professions of late. There is, in these patristic citations, a recurring current of pastoral practicality. What they want to know is, how do these saving truths help the faithful to remain faithful? How is theology connected with the real life of the church and with the real prayer life and real temptations of those who continue to profess Jesus as their Lord? How does it all lead us into a new standard of life that itself represents compassion to others? This is authentic theology. It speaks to the heart as well as the mind. It is intellectually elevated and spiritually illuminating all at the same time.

It gives us a gold standard of what Christian reflection can be. The gleam of gold endures, even through the sometimes dreary shroud of translation, and the necessary dust of the ages lying between us and them. For these reasons it has been a labor of love to present this literature yet again. Collected together, and multiplied by five as we proceed through the other volumes devoted to the Nicene Creed in this series, we will find no less than a magnificent monument to the apostolic faith. This is the heart of what the writer of 1 Timothy spoke about: "The church of the living God, the pillar and bulwark of the truth."[2]

---

[1]Is 45:15. [2]1 Tim 3:15.

OUTLINE OF CONTENTS

LIST OF ANCIENT AUTHORS
AND TEXTS CITED

Ambrose
Letters
On the Christian Faith
On the Sacrament of the Lord's Incarnation

Apollinaris of Laodicea
Letter to Jovian

Apostolic Constitutions

Arnobius the Younger
Conflict with Serapion

Athanasius
Against the Arians
Letter to Epictetus
Letter to Serapion
On the Incarnation
On the Synods

Augustine
Against Maximinus
City of God
Enchiridion
Letters
On the Agony of Christ
The Trinity

Basil of Caesarea
Against Eunomius
Homilies
Letter to Apollinaris
Letters

Clement of Alexandria
Christ the Educator
Exhortation to the Greeks
Stromateis
Who Is the Rich Man That Is Saved?

Clement of Rome
1 Clement

Council of Chalcedon (451)
Conciliar Anathemas
Creedal Statements

Council of Constantinople (381)
Synodical Letter

Cyril of Alexandria
Against Nestorius
Commentary on the Gospel of John
First Letter to Succensus
Homilies on the Gospel of Luke
Letter to Acacius of Melitene
Letter to Eulogius
Letter to John of Antioch (The Formula
  of Reunion)
Letter to the Monks of Egypt
Second Letter to Nestorius
Third Letter to Nestorius

Cyril of Jerusalem
Catechetical Lectures

Damasus of Rome
Letters

Didache

Ephrem the Syrian
Hymns on the Nativity
Hymns on Virginity

Epistle of Barnabas

Eusebius of Caesarea
Letter on the Council of Nicaea

Oration on Constantine

First Creed of the Council of Antioch (341)

Gregory of Nazianzus
Letter to Cledonius
On the Son, Theological Oration 3(29)
Orations
Personal Poems

Gregory of Nyssa
Address on Religious Instruction
Against Apollinaris
Against Eunomius
Discourse on the Holy Pascha
The Great Catechism
On Not Three Gods
On the Faith
On the Holy Spirit (Against Macedonius)
On the Lord's Prayer

Hermas
Shepherd

Hilary of Poitiers
On the Councils
On the Trinity

Ignatius of Antioch
To the Ephesians
To the Magnesians
To the Philadelphians
To the Smyrneans
To the Trallians

Irenaeus
Against Heresies

Isaac of Nineveh
Ascetical Homilies
Gnostic Chapters
The Second Part

John Chrysostom
Homilies on 2 John

Homilies on Philippians
Homilies on the Gospel of John
On the Four Days of Lazarus in the Tomb
On Those Who Attend the Gatherings

Leo the Great
Letter 28 (The Tome of Leo)

Letter to Diognetus

Marcellus of Ancyra
Letter to Pope Julius

Origen
Against Celsus
Commentary on the Gospel of John
Commentary on the Gospel of Matthew
Homilies on Jeremiah
Homilies on the Gospel of Luke
On First Principles

Polycarp of Smyrna
To the Philippians

Pseudo-Clement of Rome
2 Clement
Pseudo-Clementine Homilies

Pseudo-Dionysius
The Divine Names

Romanos the Melodist
Kontakion on Pentecost
Kontakion on the Mother of God
Kontakion on the Nativity

Second Council of Constantinople (553)
Anathemas

Second Creed of the Council of Antioch (341)

Socrates Scholasticus
Ecclesiastical History

Author/Writings Index

Scripture Index